Democratization in South Africa

Democratization in South Africa

THE ELUSIVE SOCIAL CONTRACT

Timothy D. Sisk

PRINCETON UNIVERSITY PRESS

PRINCETON, NEW JERSEY

Copyright © 1995 by Princeton University Press
Published by Princeton University Press, 41 William Street,
Princeton, New Jersey 08540
In the United Kingdom: Princeton University Press, Oxford

Library of Congress Cataloging-in-Publication Data

Sisk, Timothy D., 1960–
Democratization in South Africa: the elusive social contract / by Timothy D. Sisk.
p.   cm.
Includes bibliographical references (p.   ) and index.
ISBN 0-691-03622-5 (cloth)
1. Democracy—South Africa.   2. South Africa—Politics and government—1989–.
3. Social contract.   I. Title.
JQ1911.S57   1994   321.8′0968—dc20   94-16987   CIP

This book has been composed in Sabon

Printed in the United States of America

10   9   8   7   6   5   4   3   2   1

For Loyal Gould

Contents

Figures and Tables

Preface

THIS BOOK is an empirical study with a normative message. As an empirical study, it demonstrates that the dramatic political changes in South Africa in the last several years challenge conventional-wisdom theories about conflicts in "deeply divided societies" and the potential for democratization in them. Indeed, the universe of multiethnic states is profoundly changing (and expanding) in the wake of the Cold War's end: those in conflicts old and new, no longer overwhelmed by the umbrella of superpower patronage and manipulation, are more or less left to their own devices to negotiate an end to their self-defeating struggles or to continue fighting. Conventional wisdom and conventional theories of comparative politics alike view conflicts in such societies as primarily the manifestation of irrational passions; thus, there is little hope for their resolution and even less hope for democracy. Although there is, in my view, a pathological element in ethnic strife, existing theories have increasingly little explanatory value, given the new diversity of deep, riveting, and brutal conflicts. Some are moving toward resolution, others are not. New theorizing is required to explain under what conditions the divisions of divided societies can be reconciled and conflict managed through negotiated political transitions, and under what conditions continued fighting is more likely.

Normatively, South Africa—a country with an anomalous and unusual conflict generated by the peculiar nature of apartheid—paradoxically emerges as a model for how others in societies riven by ethnic, racial, religious, and ideological strife can potentially reorient their conflicts from the battlefield to conflict-managing institutions of a shared state. What can the rest of the world learn from the experiences of this society as it emerges from the "crime against humanity" of apartheid and the negotiation between a racially exclusive regime and a long-oppressed racial majority? South Africa's experience reveals the value of negotiation as a way of escaping long-standing conflict.

By exploring South Africa's experience with transition toward a post-apartheid democracy, I seek to illuminate the prospects and problems for national reconciliation in other divided societies in the face of deep and enduring divisions and continued violence. As old conflicts are resolved in the course of transition, new conflicts emerge. I firmly believe that an analysis of South Africa's transition can provide lessons for those in other divided societies seeking to escape the brutality of war in both what they should emulate and avoid. This book covers the period from roughly

1989 to November 1993, a very turbulent era in which the success of transition was by no means assured, even if it was likely.

My interest in the dramatic and historical transition toward a post-apartheid democracy in South Africa began with my mentor and friend, Dr. Loyal Gould, Director of the Heinz Koeppler Institute at Baylor University in Waco, Texas. This book is dedicated to him. As I was completing a Master of International Journalism degree under Dr. Gould's tutelage in late 1983, he persuaded me to abandon impending plans to serve as a staff assistant in the West German Bundestag (Europe is in decay, he argued) and go instead to South Africa; a short month later I found myself in the sweltering heat and loneliness of Bloemfontein in the Orange Free State, doubting whether the advice was as sound as it had seemed back home. A decade later, none of those doubts lingers.

Little did I know when I returned to the United States in mid-1984 that months later the townships would erupt in the four-year popular upsurge that would ultimately lead to apartheid's demise. My subsequent focus on "postapartheid" South Africa in a doctoral program seemed to many immature in the late 1980s as a stalemate evolved between an entrenched regime and dedicated revolutionaries. My persistent belief that reconciliation was possible in South Africa has in the long run borne fruit.

Portions of chapter 3 previously appeared in *Negotiation Journal,* for which permission for reproduction has been granted by Plenum Publishing Corporation.

The many friends, colleagues, and acquaintances who directly or indirectly helped me are too numerous to name, and I hope only that they will know who they are and accept my gratitude prima facie. I would like, however, to specifically acknowledge the invaluable help of some scholars who have guided me throughout my work on this project, both in its first form as a dissertation and in this substantially revised book: Cynthia McClintock, my steady, competent, and reliable dissertation director; Susan Wiley, who introduced me to the choice literature and taught me methodology; David Little, Senior Scholar at the United States Institute of Peace, who was particularly helpful with the formulations on fairness found in chapter 7; and Herbert Howe, Director of the African Studies Program at Georgetown University. Many thanks to Steve Stedman, Harvey Feigenbaum, and Bill Lewis, who commented on an earlier version of the manuscript. My thanks also go to Jacqueline Schwartz, who cheerfully produced a number of the illustrations with professional precision.

Further, I would like to acknowledge the hospitality, kindness, friendship, and assistance of professors Pierre du Toit and Hennie Kotzé at the University of Stellenbosch, where I was affiliated during dissertation field research in 1991, and the assistance of the many librarians and colleagues there and at other universities and institutions throughout South Africa. My thanks also goes to Senator J. William Fulbright, without whose fore-sight the Fulbright Scholar program would not exist and my field research would not have been possible. A special note of thanks is due David Screen of the Institute for a Democratic Alternative in South Africa, who assisted in developing my list of respondents.

I also thank Donald Rothchild for the labor of love he put into a young scholar's manuscript, reviewing it line-by-line and skillfully blending en-couragement and constructive criticism. I will try to emulate his devotion to scholarship. My appreciation goes to Pierre du Toit for his comments on the manuscript and for his encouragement and advice throughout the project. Steven Friedman of the Centre for Policy Studies in Johannesburg provided comments on an earlier draft of the manuscript, contributing invaluable insights and persuading me to refine my argument at many critical points. Of course, any remaining shortcomings are not attribut-able to any of these scholars or any of the many others who helped in the realization of this book.

Malcolm DeBevoise provided invaluable guidance and encouragement in bringing this project to fruition at Princeton University Press, and Cindy Crumine superbly edited the manuscript with meticulous preci-sion. Both made my experience with the Press a rewarding learning experience.

My parents, Chaplain Leroy and Nancy Sisk made innumerable sacri-fices to educate and nurture their children and they have my enduring appreciation and gratitude. So too, I thank my wife, Sarah Peasley, who contributed to this book through her many sacrifices, good counsel, per-sistent encouragement, and limitless patience throughout many years' and many more late nights' work.

Finally, I would like to acknowledge and thank the remarkably open and forthcoming interview respondents—and many other South Africans—who took the time and effort to talk frankly with a foreign researcher about their country, its turbulent past and present, and their visions of an ideal future. I will remember these remarkable individuals with great fondness for them and for their beloved country.

List of Abbreviations

ANC	African National Congress
APLA	Azanian People's Liberation Army
AV	Alternative voting
AWB	Afrikaner Weerstandsbeweging (Afrikaner resistance movement)
AZAPO	Azanian People's Organization
BC	Black Consciousness
CODESA	Convention for a Democratic South Africa
COSAG	Concerned South Africans Group
COSATU	Congress of South African Trade Unions
CP	Conservative party
DMI	Department of Military Intelligence
DP	Democratic party
FBIS	Foreign Broadcast Information Service
HNP	Herstigte Nasionale party
IDASA	Institute for a Democratic Alternative in South Africa
IFP	Inkatha Freedom party
NACTU	National Council of Trade Unions
NEC	National Executive Committee of the ANC
NEF	National Economic Forum
NP	National party
MK	Umkhonto we Sizwe (Spear of the nation)
MPNP	Multiparty Negotiating Process
PAC	Pan-Africanist Congress
PR	Proportional representation
PWV	Pretoria-Witwatersrand-Vereeniging
SACCOLA	South African Consultative Council on Labor Affairs
SACOB	South African Chamber of Business
SACP	South African Communist Party
SACTU	South African Congress of Trade Unions
SADF	South African Defense Force
SAP	South African Police
SAPA	South African Press Association
STV	Single transferable vote
TBVC	Transkei-Bophuthatswana-Venda-Ciskei
TEC	Transitional Executive Council
UDF	United Democratic Front

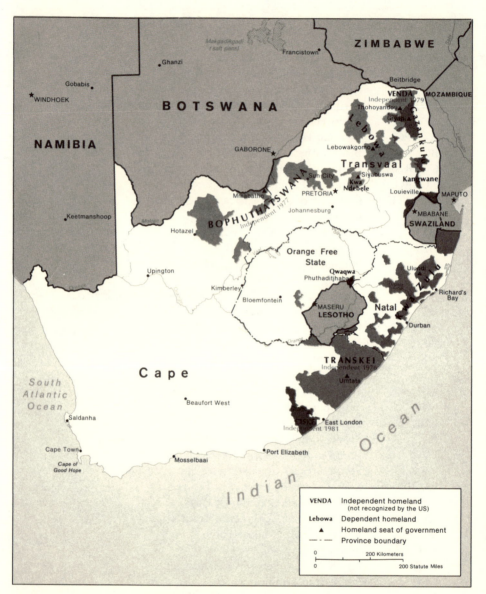

South Africa, Including Black Homelands

Democratization in South Africa

Introduction

> Throughout history, when a state has taken an exclusive and
> intolerant idea such as religion or ethnicity as its cornerstone,
> this idea has more often than not been the mainspring of vio-
> lence and war. In days gone by, religion had to be displaced as
> the basis of the state before frightful religious wars came to an
> end. And there will be little hope of putting an end to
> wars . . . until, in some similar fashion the "nation" in ethnic
> terms ceases to be the basis of a state.
> —Former Canadian Prime Minister Pierre Trudeau[1]

As THE Cold War fades into history, a different set of challenges to world peace arises. The fear of a mutually annihilating nuclear exchange be-tween the superpowers is transcended by a new specter of human self-destruction, one in which seemingly dormant forces of political identity—ethnicity, nationalism, communalism, and racism—resurge to fuel myriad conflicts within states. The disintegration of old empires and the redefinition of the rules of politics within them is potentially a source of destructive strife among peoples.

Some communally diverse states, such as the former Soviet Union and Yugoslavia, have simply disintegrated through secession or partition. In their wake, they have left constituent parts that are plagued by centrifugal tendencies. But given the continued bias of the international community toward existing international boundaries, secession or partition is likely to be very costly in human lives and suffering and, in most instances, unlikely to be sustainable or successful. The more likely outcome is the constant threat of civil war or, often, unbridled anarchy. Accordingly, the politics of deeply divided societies and the potential for conflict and coop-eration in them moves to the fore as the most critical area of investigation to understand whether or not such wars can be avoided or ended. Deter-mining how conflicts driven by identity politics are reoriented from the battlefield to the conflict-regulating institutions of an inclusive demo-cratic state is the critical challenge of our era.

An essential feature of transformation and transition in today's civil wars and internal strife is that, unlike in many previous instances, no single party to the conflict is likely to emerge as the sole victor.[2] Con-

[1] *Los Angeles Times*, 21 June 1990.

[2] Stedman (1991:6–7) has shown that most civil wars (77 percent), between 1900 and 1989 ended in either elimination, capitulation, negotiated surrender, or unstable negotiation.

versely, no party will likely lose the fight outright. With few exceptions, most states in transforming divided societies have not collapsed or succumbed to military coups or other forms of internal displacement; likewise, violent revolutionary struggles—particularly in the last decade—have been largely unsuccessful (except in Ethiopia and Afghanistan). Thus, one of the common threads that runs through the transitions in today's divided societies is the reality that change is more likely to come through negotiation. This usually means a protracted process in which the conflict is *transformed* from open struggle to a more confused and complex situation in which the violence on the ground endures, or threatens to re-emerge, even as negotiators gather around a table. The new role of United Nations intervention in divided societies, and in some exceptional instances (e.g., Cambodia) as an actual guarantor of the transition, is an additional feature of today's world that bolsters the search for negotiated settlements. Thus, the reorientation of conflict from bullets to ballots is a long, arduous, and often violence-ridden road.

This is a study of one of the most deeply divided societies of the twentieth century, South Africa. For several decades, it was a conflict well known for its intractable nature as a cohesive minority community dominated the majority population using the invidious weapon of institutionalized racial discrimination—*apartheid*. South Africa is especially interesting now because this very deeply divided society is indeed moving toward the creation of an inclusive democracy. South Africa is equally compelling because of the complexities that characterize the transition; which is at once about the decolonization of the last white minority regime in Africa (albeit from a form of internal colonialism) and the similarly difficult process of the replacement of authoritarian rule with democratic institutions in a society with deep and continuing conflict driven by identity politics. These processes take place under the strain of prolonged economic crisis, widespread inequalities between blacks and whites in status, wealth, and income, and staggering poverty among the black majority. The core premise of this book is that an analysis of the transition in South Africa and the transformation of the conflict in this divided society can generate new avenues of theory for understanding identity conflict dynamics and their amelioration in a world of potentially increasing strife.

South Africa is a test case of the possibility of negotiated settlements in societies deeply divided by racial, ethnic, religious, or other form of ascriptively based conflict. What led to the demise of apartheid as the guiding ideology and political program of the white minority in South Africa? Why did the National party (NP) government, which implemented apartheid, and the African National Congress (ANC), the leading anti-apartheid organization, choose to negotiate, and why did these negotiations broaden to include a wider range of centrist political actors? What are the prospects that a negotiated settlement will ultimately produce democratic political institutions? Most important, what kind of democratic institutions might be established, and can they be sustained?

There has been an implicit assumption by scholars of comparative politics who specialize in divided societies that such political conflict can be potentially ameliorated if only such societies would adopt certain types of democratic institutions, that is, through "political engineering" (Sartori 1968). I argue against that assumption. In the long search for a democratic solution to South Africa's conflict, Steven Friedman, director of the Johannesburg-based Centre for Policy Studies, summarizes the problem with political engineering: "There is a view of both sides, but especially right of center, that you can ensure the outcome by applying the appropriate constitution. . . . I can see no evidence of that. What emerges [in South Africa] will reflect the balance of power between the parties. Constitutions can't create realities that don't already exist."[3] Similarly, Frederick van zyl Slabbert, president of the Institute for a Democratic Alternative for South Africa, wrote in 1989, prior to the onset of negotiation or even the expectation that meaningful negotiation in South Africa would soon occur:

> There are many "constitutional experts" who have written South Africa into a democracy in their studies. South Africa has been inundated with "constitutional solutions": consociational democracy, federalism of various degrees, meritocracies, partition, etc. Nor does it serve much useful purpose to logically transplant some European constitution on to the South African situation and argue away the empirical contradictions with questionable "if only" clauses. Constitutional preferences have to be related to real political forces and only then can one begin to anticipate the elements of a likely or probable democratic constitution for South Africa.[4]

Yet the focus on constitution and constitutional design is understandable; the conflict in South Africa has been over the state—who controls it, and toward what end. Since its inception, the South African state has been the sole preserve of a dominant white oligarchy. Zola Skweyiya, chairman of the ANC Constitutional Committee, which long sought to achieve revolution in South Africa, has written, "The oppressed people of South Africa and their liberation movement were never consulted nor were their views solicited. . . . Through their concerted actions the anti-apartheid democratic forces challenged the very legitimacy of the apart-

[3] Interview with the author, 15 May 1991.

[4] Frederick van zyl Slabbert, "Is Democracy Negotiable?" (Paper presented to a conference on the conflicts in South Africa, Northern Ireland, and Israel and the attempts to find negotiated settlements, Bonn, 8–13 September 1989).

heid state and deliberately focused their attention on political questions and fundamentally the issue of the apartheid state" (1989:4). Ultimately, this struggle was successful: common citizenship, political equality, and a new constitution became absolute imperatives as even the white minority government accepted the basic premise that South Africa's majority black population would fully participate in a common polity.

This book investigates South Africa's transition from the perspective of institutional choice. As Ostrom (1991) argues, politics is guided by prevailing political institutions, or rule structures, and politicians and political actors employ "the logic of appropriateness"—that is, they operate *within* the rules based on what they perceive as appropriate behavior to advance their aims. However, when the rules of politics are in flux, for example, in times of transition, political actors employ "the logic of consequence." That is, they choose among alternative institutions based on the perceived consequences of those institutions for their expected interests into the future. Thus, the central theoretical question this study addresses is: On what basis do political actors choose among alternative institutions, and what are the prospects that, in the course of their strategic interaction, these choices will ultimately converge on a political system that is mutually acceptable? Answering this question can reveal whether conflict in a deeply divided society such as South Africa's can be mitigated through the creation of new, possibly democratic, political institutions or whether it cannot. And it can reveal even how a new political system might look, that is, whether democratic institutions may evolve and what type they may be.

The institutional choice approach explains why and how political actors, within their own milieu, seek to construct a democracy to escape a situation of violent conflict. Thus, as Friedman and van zyl Slabbert perceptively note, South Africa's postapartheid democratic institutions will be necessarily rooted in the historical context, ideological constraints, and balances of power that exist in that society. Constitutions formalize and codify political institutions but cannot create a newfound consensus in deeply divided societies; they reflect preexisting relationships. Political institutions emerge as an outcome of a process of redefining the rules of the political game, the end result of which is a formal, legal constitution. If *democratic* political institutions evolve as a contingent outcome of conflict, as Przeworski (1988) suggests, will the negotiations to escape the conflict generated by apartheid produce a democratic outcome?

In South Africa, remarkable convergence occurred among a set of centrist political actors on the parameters of a postapartheid democratic state. Through the haze of continued violence, setbacks in negotiation, threats from reactionaries and revolutionaries alike, and continued competition among the many political forces, the convergence is often obscured. Surprisingly, much of the convergence occurred even prior to formal constitutional negotiation, in the preliminary negotiation phase. Once the white minority and black majority realized they share a common destiny—that secession or partition is not a feasible alternative and that the slide into anarchy must be avoided—there was emerging agreement about what constituted a *fair* set of common political institutions. The middle ground, though razor thin, began to widen. Given this convergence, it is then possible, as van zyl Slabbert suggests, to foresee the specific elements of a postapartheid democracy. One can anticipate a new South African social contract, and understand why it is elusive.

A Least Likely Case

South Africa is an ideal case with which to investigate these broader concerns because it is one that can best test a wide range of hypotheses about the possibilities and limits of democratization under conditions not thought conducive to democracy—deep cleavages along ascriptive lines, a dearth of tolerance, low levels of economic development, high socioeconomic inequality, and so on. To be sure, other conflicts—for example, the thirty-one years of civil war in Ethiopia—have been more severe. Millions died in that conflict (over one million in 1984–85 alone) from the famine and starvation spawned by it; millions more were constantly at risk. Nevertheless, within South Africa and internationally, the conflict has been long perceived as more doggedly intractable and irresolvable than perhaps any other conflict.

Who would have said, at the height of a spiral of revolution and repression in 1986, that within a decade South Africa would be establishing widely negotiated institutions to create a new inclusive, pluralistic democracy? The stakes were then perceived as incredibly high, the depth of racial divisions too deep, the minority/majority disparity as numerically irreconcilable, and the struggle over the abolition of apartheid as necessarily a zero-sum game. Even with the dramatic changes in South Africa in the last several years, it is easy to make the argument for pessimism about South Africa's future and the prospects for democratic settlement, as some knowledgeable analysts have done (Ottaway 1993). This perception of South Africa is simply no longer accurate. Having formerly been regarded as a *least likely* case for democratization, South Africa is now firmly on that route. This fundamental fact makes it an important and perhaps critical case for analysis.[5]

Few societies have been more deeply divided than South Africa, for two

---

[5] See McClintock (1989) on the value of testing broader hypotheses in "least likely" cases.

important reasons. First, South Africa is the only society in which every member has been legally registered by race and ethnicity. Apartheid organized the state and society around rigidly imposed identities. Systematic de jure racial classification, and the exclusion of black South Africans from political, social, and economic power based on that classification, lies at the heart of the South African conflict. Comprehensive race classification was a unique practice of the apartheid state from the time the National party won an election in 1948 on the platform of codified racial segregation. Compulsory race classification in South Africa—and the necessarily subordinate status assigned to African, "Coloured," and Indian South Africans based on that differentiation and discrimination—spawned a violent reaction to eliminate it.[6]

The classification of persons by race was also the basis for the limitation of the franchise: black South Africans have been restricted from truly representative institutions, despite the fact that nationwide elections have taken place for whites regularly since 1910.[7] The limited extension of the franchise to Coloured and Asian citizens in 1984 notwithstanding (no more than 25 percent of these groups participated in what were argued to be "apartheid" elections), political power remained in the hands of whites; officially designated black South Africans remain effectively disenfranchised until the first nonracial election.

Race classification was manifested in South Africa by systematically categorizing every South African citizen according to officially defined racial and ethnic groups. During the heyday of apartheid, one's place on the population register—as established by the Population Registration Act—determined where one could live, work, learn, marry, romance, or even swim at the beach. This act, adopted by the whites-only House of Assembly by the narrow margin of 63-58 in mid-1950, was the cornerstone of apartheid. Although it was not the first apartheid law enacted by the National party government—the South Africa Citizenship Act, Mixed Marriages Act, and the Immorality Act preceded it—its repeal in June 1991 as the last apartheid law (as the government then claimed) demonstrates the extent to which it is at the heart of apartheid. The difficulty of prescribing identity was immense. As Carter writes: "The definitions of the Act illustrate the degree to which customary associations and community acceptance are decisive rather than color as such. A white person is one who is 'obviously white in appearance,' or by 'general repute and

---

[6] The terms refer to the four officially designated racial categories in South Africa: African, Coloured (mixed ancestry), Indian (or Asian), and white. The use of the term *black* in common parlance denotes all three other-than-white population groups; the term *nonwhite* is rightly considered derogatory by many South Africans and is not used in this work.

[7] White women were granted the franchise in 1929. Prior to 1913, blacks could vote if they met strict property and educational criteria; very few did.

acceptance.' But a person who is Coloured by general repute is ranked as such even if he is white in appearance" (1958:81).

Opponents of race classification in 1950 predicted the act was a grave mistake that would thrust South Africa into a violent conflict of its own making. A member of the United party remarked during parliamentary debate: "The epoch of the witch hunt is upon us. . . . In the end, in order to avoid infinite trouble and vexation, it will be far more convenient to have some distinguishing mark tattooed on your forehead like some oriental caste" (Carter 1958:82). Tragically, the results were as predicted. For example, in the final full year of the act's implementation, 1990, some 463 people were reclassified racially, demonstrating—if it indeed needed demonstration—that apartheid policies were simply unworkable, questions of morality aside.[8] By the opening of parliament on February 1991, President F. W. de Klerk announced that race classification would be repealed and that "the South African statute books will be devoid, within months, of the remnants of racially discriminatory legislation which have become known as the cornerstones of apartheid."[9]

Imposed racial identity was also intricately woven into the constitutional foundation of the state. Even in the reformist constitution adopted in 1984, race classification remained the fundamental principle on which the polity was built. Article 52 of that constitution directly references the Population Registration Act, specifying that the three chambers of parliament established (it is commonly known as the tricameral system) represent the white, so-called Coloured, and Asian population groups. Separate elections on separate voters rolls were employed to elect representatives for these communities. Blacks were wholly excluded from the system; in the scheme of "grand apartheid," they were to exercise their voting rights in the national states, or homelands, irrespective of whether they lived in those states or in greater South Africa. By designating the nationality of each and every South African and divvying up territory based on these classifications, apartheid also forcefully imposed ethnic identity. By 1992, South Africa's population of some 39 million consisted of nearly 30 million Africans (77 percent), 5.1 million whites (13 percent), 3.4 million Coloured (9 percent), and 1 million Indians (2.5 percent) (Cooper et al. 1993:254).

The 1991 repeal of race classification notwithstanding, the fusion of race into the constitution meant that only a wholesale redesign of the institutional structures of the South African state would end legal apartheid. Beyond the state, however, racial discrimination has been institu-

---

[8] As reported in the *Weekly Mail* (Johannesburg), 19–25 April 1991.

[9] The speech is reprinted in the *Argus* (Johannesburg), 1 February 1991. The repeal is more fully discussed at the beginning of chapter 2.

tionalized in the entire political and social structure of South Africa. The end of apartheid entails nothing less than a wholly new constitution for South Africa, a new set of political institutions. Above all, the conflict in South Africa has been a conflict over the racially exclusive control of the state.

A second reason why South Africa has been considered especially intractable is its place as one of the most unequal societies in the world: a relatively small and wealthy minority has dominated a large but impoverished majority. The overlap of racial and class divisions has made the conflict particularly invidious: an ascriptive feature is combined with extreme relative deprivation. Exacerbating the conflict was the use of the state by the white minority to further both racial exclusion and socioeconomic inequality. Disenfranchisement on the basis of race, and distributive policies that directly and indirectly bolstered the material interests of whites, was the core feature of South African politics throughout the twentieth century, and in previous centuries as well (Thompson 1990:111).

With marked correlation, membership in the political community brought with it an economic bounty. Access to political power has allowed whites to use the state to gain economic ascendancy. Job reservation in factories and mines, the employment of whites in the civil service, and distorted wage and price policies all played a role at various times. The conflict of apartheid is equally one generated by class differentiation, reinforced by racially exclusive legal structures and administration.[10] The interlocking politics of race and class cannot be ignored in any analysis of the South African conflict.

The magnitude of inequality in the distribution of income in South Africa has arguably been the highest in the world: various scholars have substantiated this point (Lewis 1990:40; McGrath 1990:94–96; McGrath 1985; Wilson and Ramphele 1989:18). International Monetary Fund economists, for example, calculate the Gini coefficient (a measure of income inequality that ranges between 0 with perfect equality and 1 with complete inequality) at 0.48 for 1987, one of the highest rates in the world for a country where such measures are available (Lachman

---

[10] Domination on the basis of race and class structures in South Africa has long been central to the analysis of the South Africa conflict, and many volumes have been written. Among the best and most rigorous are, in particular, Greenberg 1980; Simons and Simons 1961; Alexander 1979: esp. 11–30; O'Meara 1983; and Marks and Trapido 1987. The debate centers around the issue of whether South Africa is characterized by "racist capitalism" or "capitalist racism." Can capitalism in South Africa exist without racism, and vice versa? For a concise summary of the debate, however, see Adam's essay "Racist Capitalism versus Capitalist Nonracialism in South Africa" (1984). I argue later that the forces of capitalist modernization have eroded the pure, "Verwoerdian" vision of apartheid and the racism that it implied.

TABLE 1.1
Racial Distribution of Income in South Africa, 1985[a]

	Income Class						Percentage of Total Personal Income
	$0–2,999 (%)	$3,000– 4,999 (%)	$5,000– 7,999 (%)	$8,000– 10,499 (%)	$10,500– 15,999 (%)	$16,000+ (%)	
African	38	2	18	8	5	5	24.9
Asian	5	8	14	13	18	42	3.0
Coloured	26	22	19	7	12	14	7.2
White	2	1	2	2	10	83	64.9

Source: Adapted from McGrath 1990:95. Percentage of total personal income data from Dostal 1990:610.

[a]Excluding African households in white-controlled nonmetropolitan areas (i.e., white towns and white farms).

and Bercuson 1992). The inequality is even starker when one considers the distribution of the income along racial lines. Table 1.1 shows the highly skewed race distribution of income in South African by income class and percentage of total personal income. The table shows that whites dominate the upper end of the income scale (83 percent had annual incomes of R16,000+ ($5,333) in 1985, compared to only 5 percent of blacks), and that there is a virtual floor on white poverty.[11] Only 7 percent of whites have income below R8,000 ($2,667) per annum, which is just at the poverty line. The data point not only to extreme levels of inequality between racial groups, but to relatively equal distribution within races. Why is this so? The pattern finds its origins in the role that the state played in buoying white incomes in South Africa.

> The objectives of South African governments since the 1920s, especially since the National Party came to power, have been to eliminate the class of poor whites. The civilized labor policy and all of its successors put a floor under white incomes at the expense of blacks. The result is that the bottom end of the income distribution has all but been eliminated for white South Africans. It is often the large concentration of people at the bottom that provides extreme inequality according to Gini coefficients or any other measure. (Lewis (1990:41)

While the inequalities among racial groups—the structure of class divisions based on race, especially the differences between white and African groups—are important in assessing the degree of conflict in South Africa

[11] Throughout this work the U.S. dollar/rand exchange rate used is $1 U.S. = R 3.0 (December 1992).

over material interests, it is also important to consider the levels of absolute poverty that blacks in South Africa face. According to Wilson and Ramphele (1989:18), some 60.5 percent of blacks are living below the subsistence level of income in South Africa, and in the homelands, the rate of poverty among blacks is 81 percent. Sixteen million South Africans live below the poverty line. Currently, according to the World Bank, nearly half (48 percent) of the country's black males are unemployed.

Exactly how did apartheid impoverish black South Africans? Wilson and Ramphele identify six key aspects of what is termed "apartheid's assault on the poor": the shift from incorporation of blacks into the economy to dispossession; anti-black urbanization policies (pass laws); forced removals and relocations; inferior "Bantu" education; crushing of black political organizations; and destabilization of the black community life (1989:205–30). Thus the report concludes that "uprooting poverty" in South Africa will involve not only transformation of the economy, but "a fundamental redistribution of political power" (1989:5).

High levels of income inequality in South Africa occur in an environment of prolonged recession.[12] For nearly the entire decade of the 1980s, unemployment has risen steadily and average per capita private sector investment has dropped sharply. Formal sector employment grew at a meager 0.7 percent, whereas the economically active portion of the population grew at a pace of 2.6 percent annually. The elements of South Africa's economic crisis are intertwined: a negative risk profile and weak investor confidence due to political uncertainty, sustained double-digit inflation, declining terms of trade, balance-of-payments constraints, shortages of external sources of capital and technology due to economic sanctions, capital flight, a commodity-dependent economy and a sluggish gold price, high personal and corporate income taxes, low levels of skilled labor, duplication of services as a result of apartheid policies, high external debt, and falling relative demand (Schlemmer 1991d:2).

Even when the de jure apartheid is ended, its legacy—especially the material imbalances—will remain. The contests over land, jobs, health, education, housing, nutrition, and other private and public goods are at

---

[12] There is some evidence that the wealth gap between black and white in South Africa is beginning to close. Until 1970, the gap in racial distribution of income widened in South Africa, and then narrowed somewhat between 1970 and 1985. But the sharp downturn in economic performance in the late 1980s hit blacks especially hard, and the gap began to widen again. Indeed, a recent study shows that the gain in black incomes from 1970 onward has not resulted in improved per capita prosperity for blacks, in part because of a burgeoning black population. Despite a 318 percent rise in real income over the last three decades, in per capita terms, blacks have seen little gain (University of South Africa Bureau of Market Research, as reported in the *Sunday Times* [Johannesburg], 3 March 1991).

the core of the conflict even as relationships based ⁣
classification erode (Kane-Berman 1990). To resolve
Africa must go to extraordinary lengths to forge a ⁣
and ameliorate inequality and widespread deprivatic
can conflict, the two cannot be disjoined.

SOUTH AFRICA IN TRANSITION

This book describes the process of political transition in South Africa. As
the old order suffered its demise, the realization set in among the major
actors that the benefits of a potential positive-sum outcome to the
conflict—the creation of a jointly determined set of institutions to govern
a future, common, and democratic society—were greater than the costs
of continued confrontation in an environment ungoverned by common
rules. Once this realization was made among a core set of elites, convergence on exactly what kinds of rules should replace authoritarianism
evolved as a result of the strategic interaction among the political parties
that committed themselves to a negotiated settlement. This evolution was
guided by institutional choice: actors' preferences converged, and are
moving toward, a set of democratic institutions that are perceived as *fair*
given each party's history, ideology, interests, and power, and the effects of
strategic interaction. Moderate parties' positions began to converge on
what can be best characterized as a broad-based, multifaceted social contract: a concord among diverse peoples, across class lines, between political leaders and followers, and among the elements of an emerging civil
society.

I argue that seven discrete steps characterize the rule-making process of
a transition toward democratic rule in South Africa. Uniting each step of
the democratization process is the collapse and redefinition of the rules
of the political game. As society transformed, the old rules, apartheid and
its various mutations over the years, have been discarded as a result of a
number of factors—both systemic and proximate—even by the National
party that conceived and imposed them. The central issue of what should
replace the old rules, both during the transition and into the postapartheid era, captured the attention of all major political actors. As has
been shown, the process is both complex and dynamic; the steps are discrete and causally related, but can at times overlap. At each step of the
way, the politics of institutional choice, of political actors assessing alternative sets of rules and choosing among them, is central to the process.

1. *The old rule structure broke down.* The first step in the transition
process is the erosion of the authority of the old rule structure. In South
Africa, I will contend in chapter 2, apartheid failed due to four basic

uctural factors. The regime's first-order institutional choice preference of grand apartheid gave way to the subsequent-order preference of reform apartheid.

2. *A mutually hurting stalemate developed,* whereby no party to the conflict had the capability to unilaterally impose a new set of rules. During the 1980s, the conflict between the regime and liberation movement was one of each side seeking to impose its own set of rules on the other (the state through reform, the struggle through revolution). Borrowing Zartman's terms, a "mutually hurting stalemate" developed that eventually led to the conflict becoming "ripe" for resolution in 1989 (Zartman 1989; Zartman 1991:14).

3. *The parties chose to end the stalemate through negotiation* on the formulation of a new set of rules. Moving beyond the stalemate through inclusive negotiations to jointly write the rules is a critical step in the process. In South Africa, this was achieved only as the result of a confluence of structural and precipitating factors that came together at the right historical moment.

4. *The parties first developed a preliminary process* through which to write the new set of rules. The evolution of the negotiation process in South Africa reveals how a set of nascent institutional structures was created in the interregnum to discuss "talks about talks." At each step in this preliminary negotiation process, the institutions chosen by the political actors themselves kept the process going through a difficult and turbulent period of uncertainty.

5. *The parties then began to negotiate rules to govern the transition,* that is, the interim rules to be in place while a new order is under negotiation. As the actors began to anticipate the creation of a new set of democratic institutions, choices are made over the appropriate institutions to negotiate and write the new rules of politics. Chapter 5 shows how the institutional choices for the transition are intricately linked to the choices over alternative regime models, and chapter 6 describes the convergence on a democratization pact.

6. *The parties must negotiate the new rules of the political game and their enforcement,* that is, the structure of the institutions of post-apartheid democracy state. They design a set of democratic institutions, manifested in the writing of a new constitution that is perceived to be more or less permanent.

7. Finally, *the implementation of the new rules must be negotiated,* that is, the new regime must be inaugurated. Legitimating the agreement reached on an alternative set of political rules culminates the process, and is critical to its successful implementation. This is true of both interim arrangements and the final constitution.

By late 1993, South Africa had successfully completed five of the seven steps of a transition toward democracy. Both of the remaining steps contain an infinite number of potential pitfalls. Nevertheless, the transition is driven forward by the same simple reality of interdependence that caused the old order premised on exclusion to die and compelled the parties to negotiate new inclusive institutions.

This book demonstrates how the conditions that make a transition to democracy in a deeply divided society like South Africa possible include a high degree of interdependence and an approximately symmetrical balance of power. The right mix of precipitating events can turn an intractable stalemate into a ripe moment for negotiation. Beginning negotiation can usher in an uncertain interregnum, which can be turbulent and potentially fatal. Agreements on interim sets of rules play a critical role in turning the uncertainty of transition from a liability into a potential asset. History, ideology, and leadership loom large in the process, both as detracting and contributing factors. If democratization in a divided society is possible as a result of political parties and their leaders pursuing their own interests, can it be sustained? That depends in large part on exactly what kind of democracy is created, and on how effectively leaders can communicate their understanding of the need for cooperation to their followers.

South Africa's experiences illustrate that the politics of divided societies *may* be reoriented from the anarchic arena of conflict to the conflict-regulating institutions of a democratic state. The final outcome will await the deliberations of a constitutional assembly and an interim period of power sharing. In the end, a social contract is elusive but attainable. If South Africa succeeds, it will demonstrate that a social contract *is* possible in divided societies, despite resilient, deep conflicts of interest. Two essential prerequisites must exist: a shared sense of common destiny and the realization that hegemonic aims are, in the final analysis, self-defeating. Most optimistically, with these perceptions comes the recognition that multiethnic polities, if they are to avoid the tendency to degenerate into fratricidal war, must eschew ethnicity as the basis of political interaction. To meet the challenges into the twenty-first century, South Africa needs a democratic social contract, both for postapartheid interracial reconciliation and for socioeconomic reconstruction and upliftment. A social contract may not emerge—the conflict remains deep and complex, trust and tolerance are scarce commodities, and civil society is weak (Shubane 1991)—but a new democracy to regulate ongoing conflicts is conceivable and attainable.

That does not mean, however, the South Africa will not remain a deeply conflictual society, especially along ascriptive lines but also along class cleavages. Indeed, as Diamond (1990) writes, class conflict—which South Africa will surely face—presents a paradox for a democratizing society. For the successful management of class conflict through the institutions of the state (or even through the nonofficial institutions of structured class dialogue through "social partnership," for example), class cleavages must be moderate. This is complementary to Przeworski's observation (1988) that democracy needs class conflict to be stable, yet that same conflict undermines democracy because it is inherently unstable. So South Africa will continue to be riveted by conflicts, and it would be naive to think otherwise. Nevertheless, can the transition yield a set of democratic institutions to cope with it? If a social contract to regulate ascriptive and class conflict does emerge, it will be an object lesson for the peace-seekers in myriad other conflict-wracked multiethnic societies. They can learn lessons about how, and how not, to create a viable and just state to serve a common destiny in the new era, an era in which it is seemingly easier for politicians to encourage rather than prevent a slide into anarchy.

CHAPTER 1

Democratization in Divided Societies

THE TRANSITION from white minority rule to postapartheid democracy in South Africa offers an especially insightful case through which to analyze the politics of divided societies and to assess the possibilities of coping with deep-rooted conflict by creating a new democratic political order. This institutional choice approach, employed in this study, seeks to bridge the gap between rational choice orientations, which focus on calculated individual and collective decision making, and institutional analysis, which reflects a concern for the rules, norms, and structures that regulate human interaction (Ostrom 1991). This approach as adapted here fruitfully explains—in the context of the dramatic social transformation that occurred to bring about apartheid's demise—the decisions by political elites to seek a negotiated settlement, the dynamic that drives the negotiation process forward, the formulation of preferences over alternative political institutions in negotiation, and the range of likely outcomes. By focusing on the actual preferences of the political actors in their own milieu, we can begin to make inferences about whether democratic institutions have any chance of evolving in a divided society.

BEST VERSUS LIKELY

Analyzing how democratic institutions may actually be voluntarily *chosen* by antagonistic actors in a divided society is distinct from the focus of previous scholarship on democracy in divided societies. Previous scholarship reflects an overriding concern with what are believed to be the inherently *best* forms of democratic political institutions in the presence of deep communal conflict. I contend that for a divided society like South Africa to move from violent confrontation to the peaceful management of conflict through the democratic state, the major social actors must *themselves* choose to negotiate a new political order. Therefore, analytical priority should be given to bargaining processes. Moreover, recent scholarship on democratization has shown that the process of transition has a strong effect on outcomes. Once negotiation begins, political forces with converging interests bind together to create new political institutions, both for the interregnum and for the institutional structures of a new democratic state.

Democratization negotiations form the basis for further movement toward inaugurating democracy and set precedents for the nature of the institutions that ultimately prevail. As Rothchild perceptively notes, "the boundaries of [intergroup] relationships are constantly shifting in order to reflect the configuration of group power" (1973:12); thus, the movement from confrontation to cooperation involves a renewed series of bargaining processes over time. Outcomes must be linked to a *bargaining process followed by ongoing bargaining*, well beyond the initial point of inaugurating a new democracy. I believe that most scholarship about democracy in divided societies centers too much on examining the best outcomes, as opposed to looking at the ways these outcomes evolve through bargaining processes.

To resolve this problem and to more accurately assess the prospects for a conflict-mitigating democratic system—the creation of intermediary brokerage institutions—in divided societies, it is important to analyze under what conditions political actors in divided societies choose a democratic solution to manage their conflict. The institutional choice approach, by explaining why political actors make the institutional choices they make for the transition *and* the new political order, can help resolve this problem plaguing current scholarship. This approach explains how choices evolve as the result of strategic interaction with other actors in the course of negotiation. Knowing why actors make the choices they make, students of political change can describe the process of negotiated transition, explain the positions various actors take in negotiations, and make some tentative predictions about outcomes. Specifically, we can assess whether the outcome may be democratic, and what kind of democracy it might be. Such an analysis may even provide clues as to whether such a democracy can be consolidated.

Before explaining how the institutional choice approach resolves some problems plaguing scholarship on divided societies, I think it is important to understand on what issues scholars have heretofore concentrated. There is a good deal of excellent scholarship about what are arguably the *best* institutions for building democracy in societies divided by deep communal conflict. Within this scholarship, there are two prevailing prescriptions. On the one hand, those who advocate "power-sharing" solutions stress the importance of elite accommodation. Elites are argued to best understand that unmitigated conflict is self-defeating, and they therefore bind together to seek intergroup cooperation. Broad elite-coalition governments are backed by concrete assurances to discrete communal segments—the minority veto—that their vital interests will be protected from the feared or real tyranny of others. The premier and persistent advocate of this "power-sharing" approach is Arend Lijphart (1977a).

On the other hand, Donald Horowitz (1985) offers a different approach—also stressing the importance of coalition government—

which emphasizes integrative mechanisms that seek to promote moderation by politicians by providing incentives for them to appeal to voters beyond their own, narrow communal segments. Horowitz believes the right set of political institutions, rather than vetoes for minorities, can give majority coalitions a reason to woo minority voters, thus moderating on divisive ethnic themes and building tolerant multiethnic political parties that transcend traditional enmities.

Because *power sharing* is too broad a term to accurately describe the former view, I, like others, refer to this prescription as consociational democracy, or *consociationalism*. I think the latter approach is accurately described as *centripetalism*, because the explicit aim is to engineer a centripetal spin to the political system—to pull the parties toward moderate, compromising policies and to discover and reinforce the center of a deeply divided political spectrum. Both Lijphart and Horowitz argue that democracy is indeed possible in deeply divided societies, and they also agree that democracies in divided societies should be more inclusive, with consensus and conciliation the overriding principles of politics (assumptions that I share with them). But they differ on exactly how that democracy should be structured—on how political institutions should be arrayed—and how that conciliatory decision making should be accomplished. They differ on how intercommunal coalitions should be formed.

Fortunately, both Lijphart and Horowitz have spelled out their general differences in recent works that outline detailed recommendations for postapartheid political institutions which reflect their underlying differences on the best democratic and conflict-reducing political institutions for divided societies (Lijphart 1985; Horowitz 1991). Further, they both agree that the South African case can test the relative strengths of their arguments.[1]

By focusing on what outcome is likely, as opposed to what is believed to be best, this study reorients the agenda of previous scholarship. It is indeed correct to be concerned with the peaceful and inclusive governance of divided societies in today's myriad multiethnic states, but the questions are wrongly posed. The crucial scholarly question is not what institutions are *inherently best* for mitigating conflict in divided societies. Institution building in a divided society does not occur in a vacuum. The appropriate question is: During an actual process of democratization, under what conditions do political actors themselves choose political insti-

---

[1] Horowitz goes so far as to say "The special problems of racially and ethnically divided societies require more than usual measure of democratic ingenuity. . . . South Africa thus provides the quintessential challenge to democratic conflict management" (1991:xiii). Lijphart suggests that his power-sharing recommendations for South Africa "will remain the only possible plan for a peaceful, democratic, and unified South Africa, even when the chances of its adoption and successful operation decline" (1985:133).

tutions and vest in them an inclusive and cooperative approach to resolving conflict? To answer this question, the proper focus of investigation and the approach in this study is: *In the course of a negotiated transition to democracy, why do the actors take the positions they take?* This applies not only to their preferences for the structure of a future democracy, but for their choices of ad hoc institutional arrangements that arise in the course of the transition itself. Thus, the institutional choice approach can provide important clues about the real potential for conflict-mitigating democracy in divided societies, and the prospect for transition toward that goal.

THE POLITICS OF DIVIDED SOCIETIES

In deeply divided societies there is a fundamental dissensus among social forces over whether the existing political institutions, through which such conflicts should be channeled, are a legitimate instrument for solving problems. Rather, the rules of politics are often the rules of war, which are in effect no common rules at all. Conflict is waged in the metagame, and the prize is exclusive control of the state. Yet for these societies—barring complete state dissolution or secession—there appears to be no way out. Communities rarely disappear, even if they are temporarily defeated. Eventually, there is simply no alternative but, as Huntington (1972) writes, to "go on living together."

Divided Societies, Rational Violence, and the State

Politics in divided societies is guided by the forces of identity. The causes of conflict and their permutations vary significantly with each case, but they almost inevitably include a complex and explosive combination of ethnic nationalism, racial discrimination, religious intolerance, deep class divisions and distributive injustice, competing ideologies, external intervention, and, often, competition over territory. In contemporary political science, conflicts in deeply divided societies are analyzed in terms of cleavages: On what variables is the society divided, and on what variables is it not? Cleavages can be primarily ascriptive or based on "traits," such as race, caste, or ethnicity; attitudinal, based on opinions, such as ideology, or behavioral, based on organizational membership or voting patterns (Rae and Taylor 1970:1–5). One of the facts that makes the politics of divided societies so complex is that these cleavages are usually not mutually exclusive; an individual may have multiple cleavage traits—for example, a religious conviction—that may be simultaneously considered ascriptive, attitudinal, and behavioral. For this reason Rothchild and Foley refer to class and ethnicity, for example, as often "fluid and overlapping" (1988:235).

It is important to distinguish between multiethnic societies and deeply divided societies. Many societies, including, for example, the United States, are multiethnic societies that do not experience the deep and bitter conflicts that are the subject of this book. The problem is not necessarily the existence of "primordial sentiments"—group affiliations based on race, language, religion, ethnicity, tribe, custom, or perceived blood ties.[2] Rather, when such forms of identity become *politically salient,* conflict is likely to occur. Using the earlier jargon of "plural societies," Rabushka and Shepsle provide in their pioneering study of divided societies a cogent definition of the types of societies with which I am primarily concerned. "A society is plural if it is culturally diverse *and* if its cultural segments are organized into cohesive political sections. . . . Politically organized cultural sections, communally based political parties, the partitioning of major social groups (e.g., labor unions) into culturally homogeneous subgroups, and political appeals emphasizing primordial sentiments, serve as unambiguous indicators of a plural society" (1972:21).

The global interest in communal politics has more recently flourished as ethnic conflict becomes an ever-more-important concern in terms of threats to peace and international security, particularly in the post–Cold War era. Attempts to explain communal mobilization are vast, and perspectives differ on whether such mobilization occurs as a result of political and socioeconomic versus psychological variables. Most social science perspectives agree on the presumably uniform need of the individual to emphasize collective identity in a social context. I do agree that there are clearly psychological variables involved in ethnic mobilization, centered around the importance of status identification in a social context, which Horowitz describes as the pursuit of "relative group worth" (1985:143). And ethnic violence such as the scurrilous practice of "ethnic cleansing" in the former Yugoslavia leaves no doubt that a pathological dimension—a furious and irrational hatred—exists as well.

Yet ethnic mobilization and coalescence also occur because of material conditions, including unequal economic development, perceptions of relative deprivation, differential rates of modernization in society, forms of internal colonialism, or systematic discrimination and oppression. Grievances can be either political, such as demands for participation and inclu-

---

[2] The term *primordial sentiments* is Geertz's, who argued (1963) that fealty to communal identities undermines the cohesiveness of states because these groups compete with the state for citizen loyalties; thus, the task of new states is to subordinate these loyalties to civil politics.

sion, or distributive, related to the allocation of public goods. Many times grievances are a combustible mixture of both. Important additional variables in communal mobilization are the degree of intragroup cohesiveness, resource capacity, and the ability of political entrepreneurs to translate resources into political power within a given environment. Moreover, because ethnic identities are multifaceted and fluid, they can be politically salient at some times but not others.

Perceptions of the opponent are an essential aspect of conflict. Rothchild emphasizes the importance of reciprocal perceptions in intergroup relationships (a focus on an adversary's intent), an approach I share. Three general categories of reciprocal perceptions exist, he argues: an *essentialist* perception, where intergroup relations are characterized by the mutual perception that other groups fundamentally threaten physical, cultural, or social survival—or vital interests—of a collectivity, rendering compromise as necessarily weakening; a *pragmatic* perception, in which conflicts of interest exist, but a genuine search for positive-sum gains characterizes intergroup relationships; and, finally, a *reciprocative* perspective, in which groups successfully "seek to transform the structure of relations to achieve mutual interests, primarily through the use of the state as a mediator" (1986:87–93).

Although the communal group is certainly not just an ordinary interest group, communal pursuits and nationalist demands, hatred aside, can be understood in terms of value-maximizing behavior, often based on an accurate appraisal of group self-interest. Ethnic groups are generally rational political actors within their own social milieu. Certainly one common cause of communal mobilization is continued domination or fear of domination of a group by others (often economic, but regularly combined with status discrimination). A political economy of ethnic group behavior centered around the exclusion of public goods exists. Thus, the application of a choice-based approach derived from economics to the politics of a divided society is a powerful explanatory tool, albeit with some important limitations.

Strict or "hard" theorists of rational choice, such as Rogowski (1985:87–108), see such groups primarily in terms of value-maximizing behavior. Other "softer" choice theorists, such as Banton (1980:475–99; 1983), are more sensitive to the historical development and the ascriptive nature of these identities; he writes that among many ethnic groups "beliefs about a common heritage are used to create identities" (1983:397).[3] There is, additionally, an abiding and insurmountable understanding of the realities of historical experience—people work within the confines of

[3] For other important works in this field, see Meadwell 1989 and 1991 and Levi and Hechter 1985.

what comes before—of grievances and demands for retribution. Historical position and the persistence of ideology and belief are therefore powerful variants in the politics of divided societies.[4]

A "softer" choice approach explains the phenomena of ethnic politics well because it acknowledges that collective memory and ideology do play an important role in the politics of divided societies. Choice frameworks are fruitful in explaining common characteristics of the politics of divided societies. Rabushka and Shepsle—in the first systematic application of a choice approach to ethnic politics—cogently underscore the rational basis for the extremist politics to flourish in divided societies and for moderation to be undermined in electoral competition.

> Ethnic preferences are intense and non-negotiable. . . . Politicians reinforce perceptions of incompatible communal values, sooner or later, through the widespread use of ethnic appeals; that *intra-group* politics soon becomes the *politics of outbidding;* that brokerage institutions, e.g. the political parties of pluralistic democracies, become inefficacious; that communal institutions of aggregation are rapidly converted into corporate representatives on communal values; and that competitive politics ultimately leads to winners and losers whose temporary status is made permanent through the *manipulation of the electoral machinery.* (1972:66)

Although the winner-take-all characteristic of politics in divided societies is well understood, less appreciated are the intracommunal struggles between radical "true believers" and moderate pragmatists. A phenomenon I term the *elite-mass nexus* is central to understanding how intergroup relationships can degenerate under conditions of electoral contestation. Political leaders know that ethnic-group preferences are intense and salient. Such leaders have incentives to generate communal demands as an effective and reliable means of constituency mobilization. Ethnic demands generate conflict and divisiveness because they are often formulated in terms of claims for specific communal representation (or often overrepresentation) that come at the expense of other groups— precipitating the perception of a zero-sum game. Attempts at intergroup moderation in divided societies go against the grain of intense and salient communal preferences, and are usually less successful than appeals to communal solidarity. These relationships between communal leaders and followers perpetuate the essentially *centrifugal thrust* that characterizes the political dynamic of divided societies, reinforcing essentialist perceptions of real or potential foes. Thus, as Rabushka and Shepsle percep-

---

[4] I adopt in this work the definition of ideology provided by Gould: "Ideology is a pattern of beliefs and concepts (both factual and normative) which purport to explain complex social phenomena with a view toward directing and simplifying social political choices facing individuals and groups" (1964:315).

tively argue, the politics of communal outbidding leads to the "bankruptcy of moderation" (1972:86). In such an environment, it follows, moderate multiethnic coalitions simply do not survive.

Forms of political organization in divided societies reflect underlying social cleavages. The assertion that in divided societies where electoral competition is possible, political parties form around communal segments is a well-established tenet in the scholarly literature. Parties espousing a moderate platform that cross-cuts cleavages are unable to successfully compete with communally based parties. Horowitz, reflecting this scholarly consensus, argues that "nothing is as responsible for the conflict-promoting character of ethnic party systems than this configuration of competition" (1985:342).[5]

The relationships among the state, political parties, and organizations of civil society are complex and varied, and I will describe these relationships in South Africa throughout the book. By civil society actors, I refer to those social organizations which are generally autonomous of the state and are organized to advance a specific set of interests; their relationship to the state is one of interaction. Chazan (1982:172–73) distinguishes between voluntary associations, organized around specific interests, and primary associations, organized around ascriptive interests. From a theoretical perspective, it is important to note only that in divided societies, the forces of civil society are primarily of the latter type, and are allied to the parties and movements that reflect dominant cleavages of conflict. Indeed, although virtually all societies contain a mix of voluntary associations and ascriptive organizations, a critical characteristic of a divided society is the dearth of organizations that transcend ascriptive cleavages—overarching, cross-cutting organizations are absent. It is for this reason that Smith (1965) refers to culturally differentiated communities with essentially incompatible value structures existing within a single state as the hallmark of a divided society.

This brief analysis of the nature of politics in divided societies leads to some summary conclusions about the nature of politics in them, properties that transcend a wide variety of cases.

- Politics is polarized (either bi- or multipolar), usually along communal and class (but also ideological) lines, as a result of intense and salient preferences. The thrust of politics in divided societies is centrifugal.
- Political party constituencies reflect communal bases; political parties, although perhaps just a veneer for underlying ascriptive ties and ethnic bases in civil society, are the primary actors under conditions of electoral competition.

[5] Horowitz further suggests that a nonethnic bipolar party system imparts a centripetal force to the polity, whereas a biploar ethnic party system imparts a centrifugal force (1985:342–49).

- Due to the intolerance of ascriptive or ideologically driven politics, alternation in winning and losing governing coalitions among political parties is unlikely.
- The consequences of being in a permanent minority situation are perceived as so severe as to threaten a party's vital interest; the severity of the consequences varies with the party's estimate of its own power (the greater the perception of power, the less severe the consequences, and vice versa). Thus, relatively small parties with few resources will resort to strategic communal outbidding.

Along with these common patterns of politics, woven into the conflicts in divided societies is an additional common thread: a presumption of *dissensus* over the present rules of the political game. The state is viewed as so illegitimate that a significant portion of the people, often a cohesive communal group, chooses violence to change it. Deep conflicts in divided societies are a quintessential problem of collective action: If there is mutual benefit to be gained from cooperative behavior in a shared destiny, why do combatants in divided societies go on fighting? States in divided societies often serve as instruments of a dominant communal group or groups, and this helps explain why aggrieved communities target the state with their demands. The state has historically been perceived by pluralists as a distributor of privileges and a differentiator among social groups. Recent attempts to "bring the state back in" as an *autonomous* actor focus on the development of state interests that transcend the interests of the social actors upon which they rely for support.[6]

In many divided societies, however, state power is often monopolized or controlled by a single community or coalition of communities, whose members benefit in political and economic terms from this domination. The state is not an autonomous brokerage institution, but the exclusive domain of a single communal group or coalition of groups (Migdal 1988). Rothchild writes, "The state represents a valued prize to be sought after, not only because of its recruitment and allocative activities, but also because of its ability to influence (if not set) the terms and costs of intergroup relations" (1986:66). Thus, the political system in divided societies has been seen *not* as an impartial and autonomous actor. As Brass argues, "Every state . . . tends to support particular groups, to distribute privileges unequally, and to differentiate among various categories in the population. . . . The state itself is the greatest prize and resource over which

---

[6] One of the most important debates in contemporary comparative politics has been the relative emphasis given to society and the state. The movement toward a "return to the state" as enjoying analytical priority has been the subject of considerable disagreement. This debate is summarized in a symposium of papers in *American Political Science Review* 82 (September 1988): 854–901.

groups engage in a continuing struggle in societies that have not developed stable relationships among the main institutions and centrally organized social forces" (1985:9,29). It is no surprise that the political demands of aggrieved communal groups often aim at reconstructing the state or, even, overthrowing it. Exclusion from the rewards of politics by communal groups, particularly those which comprise a disadvantaged portion of society, strike at the very legitimacy of political institutions. According to Horowitz, "One common element to ethnic conflict in the modern world . . . is the highly focused relation to the state. . . . Parties in conflict make demands on the state and, in several cases, demands for some reconstitution or recomposition of the state" (1990:452).

The implications for the "highly focused" relationship of communal groups to state institutions are clear: communal claims are often claims for institutional change. When aggrieved communities cannot sufficiently affect policy changes to achieve their aims, they seek a change in institutions or changes in the ground rules of the political game.[7] Some opt for secession or dissolution of the state, others for a proportional share in existing state power, and still others for a revolutionary redistribution of state resources.

Violent conflict arises as a response to the perception of an insurmountable conflict of interest between actors. These conditions exist, according to Goodin, "whenever the full realization of the goals of one actor is incompatible with the full realization of the goals of another" (1976:26–27). The calculus of such conflicts of interests can be most simply described in terms of a simple zero-sum game; one player's loss is another's gain.[8] Given the demands of aggrieved communities for institutional change and the resistance to change that wins by the existing rules, politics is often conceived in terms of a zero-sum game; that is, when one group wins in a political conflict, others necessarily lose. Despite the optimal outcome that social conflicts will be resolved peaceably through the agreed-upon rules of the political game, more immediate calculations lead communal groups toward violence. Actors perceive their goals to be better furthered through violent conflict than through compromise and cooperative action. Given an essentialist perception of an opponent, it appears more reasonable to fight than to talk.

[7] In a study of constitutional change in Western industrial states, Simeon and Banting (1985:1–28) summarized that in five of eight cases, regional, ethnic, and language conflicts have combined to provide major sources of demands for constitutional change.

[8] Conflicts of interest are strong according to the asymmetry of the gain/loss ratio for a given player. If Player I gains twice what Player II loses, there is a stronger conflict of interest than if Player I gains only one-half of what Player II loses. Not only is the gain/loss consideration important, but the stakes of the conflict are as well. If Player I or Player II has much to win or lose, the stakes of the game are high. Conflict is most likely to be intense when there is an asymmetrical gain/loss ratio for the players and the stakes for either of them are very high.

Such is the case in revolutionary situations: at least one significant political movement or organization has as its aim total overthrow and reconstitution of the state, whereas the custodians of the state possess the strongly conflicting goal of institutional preservation. Theorists in the rational choice tradition, such as Popkin (1979; 1988:9–62), explain revolutionary movements in terms of collective action problems. Treating revolutionary outcomes as "public goods," the central question they address is: Why would an individual rationally choose to participate in collective violence? Popkin, in his seminal work on revolution in Vietnam, focuses on the role of "political entrepreneurs" who build systems of sanctions and incentives to overcome free ridership (1988:9). Taylor makes an important bridge to the politics of identity, arguing that cooperation in revolutionary pursuits is "more likely to succeed in conditions where relations between people are those characteristic of community" (1988:67).

In divided societies, extreme conflicts of interest, whatever their initial causes, result in conflicts over the way binding collective decisions are made through the rule-making institutions of the state. The claims of those engaged in deep conflicts of interest in divided societies, whether they are total secession, grants of autonomy or devolution, power-sharing schemes, radical redistributive policies, unfettered majoritarianism, or defense of the status quo, are *claims for a preferred set of rules* for political behavior. These claims, under conditions of enduring conflict, are put forth in zero-sum terms. Accordingly, a "protracted social conflict" (Azar and Burton 1986:29–239) continues ad infinitum without any real prospect for resolution. Politics in divided societies is usually a trap of such self-perpetuating conflict, not unlike the traps so accurately described by modern game theory.[9]

From Rational Violence to Cooperation

Under what conditions can a conflicts be transformed from confrontation to cooperation? The Prisoners' Dilemma game shows that conflicts of interest can conceivably be reconciled for mutual gain. Given the simple assumptions of the Prisoners' Dilemma game, individuals pursuing an immediate strategy of conflict produce suboptimal outcomes; that is, even if they might cooperate for mutual benefit, they do not (Brams 1985).[10]

---

[9] Traps are defined as games in which the players' choices lead them to a collectively worse outcome than would have been the case had they made other choices. In game-theoretic terms, traps are games in which the players' seemingly rational strategies lead to Pareto-inferior outcomes.

[10] The assumptions of a Prisoners' Dilemma game are described in Riker and Ordeshook 1973:250–51. They summarize the two-person game dilemma in the following manner, referring to acts of production: "Neither [person] has a private incentive to produce, even though, if they do jointly produce, they both gain."

In a divided society, one force that can transform confrontation to co-operation is a shear sense of war-weariness on the part of parties to a conflict. One of the most important conceptional breakthroughs in recent understanding of conflict is the appreciation that the condition of "hurting stalemate" (Touval and Zartman 1985:129–34), combined with a catalyst of an initial act of trust and cooperation, can begin a process of reconciliation through negotiation in conflict situations. A hurting stalemate exists when the status quo is mutually damaging and neither side can impose its "solution" to the conflict upon others.

The importance of the hurting stalemate is that actors who previously viewed the conflict as zero sum may—through awareness that no party to the conflict can win outright—change their perception to view the conflict as non–zero sum. Critical to this change from essentialist to pragmatic or reciprocative perceptions is the changing cost-benefit calculations of political leaders and communities in conflict. Political actors must recognize that a continuation of violent conflict no longer serves their interests as well as the alternative cooperative strategy of negotiation. Lijphart refers to the "self-negating prophesy"; he writes with reference to elite coalescence in divided societies: "Elites cooperate in spite of the segmental differences dividing them because to do otherwise would mean to call forth the prophesied consequences of the plural character of the society" (1977a:100–103). The seeds of cooperation are found in the mutual interest of social segments in conflict to *avoid a worse outcome*. Schelling writes, "If war to the finish has become inevitable, there is nothing left but pure conflict; but if there is any possibility of avoiding a mutually damaging war, of conducting warfare in a way that minimizes damage, or of coercing an adversary by threatening war rather than waging it, the possibility of a mutual accommodation is as important and dramatic as the element of conflict" (1980:5).

In a divided society, the transformation from an essentialist to pragmatic or reciprocative perception of foes is in essence the realization of the mutually beneficial nature of a *shared or common destiny*. Issues that were formerly nonnegotiable because of potential harm to vital group interests can be reassessed as negotiable when this critical threshold is crossed. In divided societies, this means that actors recognize that conflict is worse than cooperation; negotiation is the answer (Brams 1990).

Clearly, the underlying conditions of a conflict—the extent of relative deprivation, state dominance by a single communal group, a history of oppression, the relative strength of communal identity, the role of external actors in the international community, and so on—are important variables in its severity and perpetuation. However, it follows that the process to modify or redirect conflict in divided societies toward conflict-regulating institutions of the state implies meeting to the extent possible actors' demands for institutional change. Once parties to a conflict seek to avoid confrontation by choosing negotiation, the institutional reconfiguration of the state plays a pivotal role in the search for more peaceful politics.

State institutions do influence the nature of communal political interaction in divided societies. Their impact may exacerbate conflict or may help resolve it. Horowitz writes: "Some portion of the difference between hot and cool ethnic conflict is a function of raw conflict conditions—the structure of cleavages, the history of group encounters, and so on—and some portion is attributable to measures deliberately taken to reduce conflict. . . . The outcomes of ethnic politics depend on the interplay of conflict-fostering conditions and conflict-reducing processes and institutions" (1990:451).

But what kind of political institutions, according to students of divided societies, *best* ameliorate deeply divisive conflict? Most modern scholars concur that democratic regimes—those which provide for the free expression of political ideas, allow for citizen participation, offer free and fair elections, and respect fundamental human rights—have on the whole provided the greatest opportunity to accommodate ethnic demands and have thus better managed conflict.[11] Unlike the state in a divided society in conflict, captured by a communal group, in a democracy the state plays a "mediatory role," regularizing patterns of interaction and brokering competing demands (Rothchild and Foley 1988:234).

DEMOCRACY IN DIVIDED SOCIETIES?

Despite claims that democratic institutions best regulate communal conflict, democracy was historically viewed as ill-suited to divided societies.[12] John Stuart Mill wrote in 1861 that a "united public opinion" is a prerequisite ([1861] 1958:230). Modern political culture theory concentrates

[11] Lijphart writes, "Not only have non-democratic regimes failed to be nation-builders; they have not even established good records of maintaining intersegmental order and peace in plural societies" (1977a:227). Rothchild (1989b) writes that "hegemonic exchange" and "polyarchical" regimes, both of which are more responsive regime types, hold more promise for conflict resolution than do "hegemonic" regimes, an issue to which I will later return. Finally, Sklar (1987:688) argues that even the imperatives of fast-paced socioeconomic development do not justify policies of dictatorship, nor is there an empirically verifiable positive correlation between authoritarian rule and economic prosperity, or "developmental dictatorship."

[12] It is important to clarify what is meant by *democracy*. I employ the definition of democracy (in terms of what Dahl [1971:1–17] has called *polyarchy*) as a political system that provides meaningful and extensive *contestation* among individuals and groups, particularly political parties; political *participation* in selecting leaders and policies; and protection of *political liberties* to ensure the integrity of contestation and participation.

on the beliefs and norms of participation and tolerance associated with Western societies—these are lacking in most divided societies. Modernization theory argues that critical to the success of any democracy are certain requisites—levels of economic development that also do not exist in the vast majority of divided societies, especially those in the developing world.

Yet other analysts, notably Rabushka and Shepsle (1972), are pessimistic about democracy because of the inherent centrifugal pull of politics in divided societies created by the incentive system in conflictual multiethnic societies. Their analysis rests on their theoretical construct of divided societies, described earlier, which posits the predominance of identity politics and ethnic political behavior, particularly the ever-present politics of outbidding. They conclude, "Is the resolution of intense but conflicting preferences in the plural society manageable in a democratic framework? We think not" (1972:217).

Pessimism and Optimism

There are grounds for pessimism. After all, conflict has traditionally been "managed" in divided societies through hegemonic domination of one group or coalition of groups over society. The approach is usually an exclusive one, in which minority (or, sometimes, majority) communities are not provided the opportunity to influence, either directly or indirectly, policy outputs. But the approach may also be revolutionary, attempting to remove the minority or majority factor from political life through wholesale assimilation or extermination and genocide. Other strategies that fall in the hegemonic approach include subjugation, isolation, avoidance, or displacement of ethnic groups (Rothchild 1991:208–11). One can think of countless tyrannies that have resorted to such measures, either singularly or in combination. In between authoritarian regimes that seek to subdue opposing identity groups and democratic ones that broker relationships through the ballot box are what Rothchild (1986) refers to as "hegemonial exchange" regimes. In this arrangement, relations between the state and ethnic groups in "scarcity prone" and "soft-state" conditions are managed through informal understandings and bargaining rules. Although the relationship is based on reciprocity in bargaining, the procedural outcome is not fully participatory democracy, but rather a pragmatic multiethnic coalition that restricts the depth of mass participation as elites govern.

Yet today, the notion of democratic government even in the most fragmented societies must be reconsidered, and for two important reasons. First is the emerging international norm that accountable government and "good governance," which democracy provides, are inalienable human rights and that future international relations will be judged according to the presence or absence of democratic political systems. Second, there have been considerable innovations in the practice of democracy—what Sklar terms "developmental democracy" (1987:691ff.)—that broaden our appreciation of the prospects for democracy in the developing world. Despite the thirty or more cases of successful democratic transitions in the late-twentieth century, very few—with the possible exception of Nicaragua, Czechoslovakia (which peacefully bifurcated), the Philippines, Namibia, and Zimbabwe—can be broadly considered deeply divided societies. Indeed, none of the most deeply divided societies—such as Nigeria, Lebanon, Sri Lanka, Ethiopia, Sudan, Cyprus, and Chad, to name a few—has undergone a transition to full democracy that can be claimed to be fully inclusive or stable. There is ample empirical evidence for pessimism about the prospects for democracy in divided societies.

How can anyone be an optimist about democracy in divided societies? No analyst argues that politics in deeply divided societies facilitates democracy, or that conditions for it are usually favorable. But optimists believe that there is simply no viable alternative to democratic political institutions as a durable system of conflict management. As I mentioned earlier, there are two prescriptions for democratic success in divided societies: the power-sharing, or consociational, model most associated with Lijphart (1985, 1977a, 1990b);[13] and the integrative, incentives-based approach of Horowitz (1985, 1990, 1991), which I term centripetalism. While these students of the politics of divided societies agree on many issues, such as the salience of communalism and ethnic conflict, they disagree sharply on the institutional structures that best ameliorate such conflict.

Before honing in on the points of disagreement, I want to outline two areas in which the approaches overlap. First, these scholars reject a majoritarian model of democracy—either simple majority rule or a less demanding plurality rule such as the Westminster system—for divided societies. The reasoning is clear and relatively simple. Although a superior decision-making rule from an abstract theoretical point of view (Rae

---

[13] The literature on consociational democracy is well developed. While the groundbreaking work is Lijphart's, particularly his *Democracy in Plural Societies* (1977a), many other scholars have contributed to the approach. First, consociationalism has its antecedents in the earlier work of Lijphart (1968), which termed the approach "the politics of accommodation." Another important work of Lijphart's outlining the approach is "Consociational Democracy" (1969). Landmark works in the school include Barry 1975; Daalder 1971; and Pappalardo 1981. Several scholars, led by Jürg Steiner, have sought to extend the consociationalist approach to a broader framework of decision making in coalitions. See especially Steiner's articles (1981a, 1981b). Other scholars, such as Lembruch (1979), have related consociational theory to the corporatist model, arguing that these approaches are complementary; 1979. Lijphart (1985) catalogs and rejoins a wide range of critics of his approach.

1969), majoritarian democracy is argued by both Lijphart (1985:16–26) and Horowitz (1985:649–50) to produce winner-take-all, zero-sum politics. In divided societies where alternation is unlikely because of essentialist perspectives, majoritarianism will produce a permanent majority in which a dominant group or groups prevails (Bogdanor 1987:195). Such a situation, most scholars agree, leads to conflict.

Second, there is broad agreement that secession or partition in divided societies is, as Lijphart writes, "a solution of last resort" (1985:34). Secession and partition can work only in societies where communal groups are homogeneously concentrated in territories. Dividing a state into sovereign territorial units in which significant minority populations exist compounds, not solves, the problems of divided societies. And even if such an option is feasible, it often is costly in terms of the lives lost in the usual struggle to realize secessionist goals. Horowitz, particularly, has a well-developed argument (1985:588–92) on the often-destructive consequences of secessionist options in divided societies. For Horowitz, partition is viable only as "a fallback position" (1991:132). Until recently, secessionist drives did not garner the recognition of sovereignty that must be forthcoming from the international community for the movement's success. In a classic and oft-quoted formulation, Huntington writes: "The 20th century bias against political divorce, that is, secession, is just about as strong as the 19th century bias against marital divorce" (1972, foreword).

Both consociationalists and Horowitz focus on coalescent or collusive political behavior rather than on adversarial politics—the government-versus-opposition pattern—in divided societies.[14] That is, however, where the agreement ends; the differences are nuanced, but discrete and significant. How that coalescent behavior is to be structured—what the rules of the political game are—is the critical point of departure.

Collusive Democracy: Consociationalism

Advocates of consociationalism essentially rely on *elite cooperation* to successfully regulate conflict; they suggest in their model that even if there are deep communal differences at the mass level, overarching integrative elite cooperation is necessary and sufficient to assuage conflict. Nordlinger goes so far as to argue that elites "alone can initiate, work out and implement conflict-regulating practices, therefore they alone can make direct and positive contributions to conflict-regulating outcomes" (1972:73). Elites, or identity group leaders, directly represent various societal segments and consolidate the polity by forging political ties at the

---

[14] The coalescent/adversarial distinction is Lijphart's (1977a:25).

center. This is the case in many of the consociational democracies—Belgium, the Netherlands, Switzerland, Malaysia, and others—that have been considered successful conflict regulators by these theorists. An important premise lies behind the argument that elite accommodation is the source of moderation in a divided society: political elites realize that confrontational political behavior will result in serious conflict and that the only way to avoid such conflict is to cooperate. This is what Lijphart calls a "rational and purposive response to the facts of pluralism and interdependence" (1985:130). Consociationalism relies on four guiding principles around which institutions are to be structured (Lijphart 1977a; 1990b:494–95).

Grand Coalitions. Power sharing in the executive in a grand coalition, or a variant thereof, is argued to ensure that the minority is not permanently excluded from political power.[15] In grand coalitions, political elites—representing the various segments of society—thrash out their differences in an effort to reach consensus. The common denominator, and most important feature, is that decision making takes place consensually at the top among elites representing underlying social segments (Lijphart 1977a:31–36).

Minority or Mutual Veto. The second feature of consociationalism is the mutual or minority veto, through which each segment is given "a guarantee that it will not be outvoted by the majority when its vital interests are at stake" (Lijphart 1977b:118). Through the mutual veto, the majority's ability to rule is qualified by "negative minority rule" (Lijphart 1977a:36). The minority veto—at the heart of the concrete assurances of consociationalism—provides an *ironclad guarantee* of political protection to each segment. While the minority veto gives minorities the right to prevent action by others on the most sensitive issues, such as language, cultural, or education rights, it also serves a more important overriding goal. Like the Calhounian "concurrent majority," it invests each segment with the power to protect itself (Lijphart 1977a:37).

Proportionality. In every sphere of political life, the principle of proportionality lies behind consociational institutions. Proportionality is introduced at every level of government decision making (central, regional, and local) to give minority groups power, participation, and influence commensurate with their overall size in society. The principle is mani-

---

[15] Grand coalitions can occur either in the cabinet of parliamentary systems, in "grand councils," or as a grand coalition of a president and senior executives in presidential systems (Lijphart 1977b:118).

fested in two ways. First, in the electoral system, proportional representation (PR) is used to faithfully translate the strength of each segment into representation in parliament; parties are awarded seats in parliament commensurate with the proportion of votes they garner in an election. Second, the allocation of resources by the state—including public spending and the appointment of civil servants—should be doled out according to the proportionality principle.

Segmental Group Autonomy. Either through territorial federalism or "corporate federalism" (nonterritorial autonomy), consociationalism provides internal autonomy for all those groups who wish to have it by delegating decision-making authority to the segments. Lijphart draws distinctions between those issues which concern the common interest and those which are primarily concerned with the interests of the segments: on the former, decisions are made by consensus; otherwise, decision-making power is delegated to the segments. The basic principle underlying communal autonomy is "rule by the minority over itself in the area of the minority's exclusive concern" (Lijphart 1977a:41). An important feature of the call for entrenched group rights on certain issues is the principle of "voluntary affiliation." Group identification would not be predefined or determined; instead, the segments of society would be able to define themselves through the proportional electoral system.

What is most consistent about Lijphart's advocacy of the power-sharing model is that it is asserted to be the *only* viable option for democracy in divided societies: Lijphart writes: "For many plural societies of the non-Western world, therefore, the realistic choice is not between the British normative model of democracy and the consociational model, but between consociational democracy and no democracy at all" (1977a:238).

Collusive Democracy: Centripetalism

Horowitz proposes five mechanisms, in contrast to consociationalism, to reduce communal conflict in divided societies: dispersions of power, often territorial, which "proliferate points of power so as to take the heat off of a single focal point"; devolution of power and reservation of offices on an ethnic basis in an effort to foster intraethnic competition at the local level; inducements for interethnic cooperation, such as electoral laws that effectively require multiethnic electoral coalitions; policies to encourage alternative social alignments, such as social class or territorial differences, which place political emphasis on cross-cutting cleavages; and reduction in disparities between groups, regarding, for example, income or wealth inequality (1985:597–600). On face value, it would seem that there is little appreciable difference between the prescriptions of Horowitz and the consociationalists.

Indeed, Horowitz's prescriptions for conflict-regulating institutions for divided societies (and for South Africa) overlap those of Lijphart to a large degree—both advocate federalism, for example. Yet they are distinguished in important ways. Horowitz is an indefatigable critic of the consociational model for two important reasons (1985:568–76). First, he argues, the consociational approach emphasizes the ability of segmental elites to contain underlying communal conflict (preventing the outbidding danger). As noted earlier, the incentive for elite moderation in consociationalism is rooted in elite realization of the costs of conflict. "There is no reason to think automatically," Horowitz writes, "that elites will use their leadership position to reduce rather than pursue conflict" (1991:141). Horowitz (1985, 1991, 1993), therefore, rightly focuses on the incentives and disincentives for moderation a political system generates. In his view consociationalism not only overestimates deference by communal groups to their leaders and underestimates the power and role of dissatisfaction with intergroup compromise, it may even provide elites with incentives to encourage conflict. If individual elite power in the consociational system is only as strong as the constituency the leader represents, politicians can stir up hostilities among their communities to strengthen their own hand. Tsebelis describes this problem as "elite-initiated conflict" (1990b).

Second, consociational institutions maintain, legitimize, and strengthen communal claims against the state. Too much autonomy (for example, through a mutual veto), as Duchacek (1973:9) has also argued, can lead to further claims beyond the intention of the original agreement. This can encourage centrifugal forces in the polity that may be impossible to contain. It can also lead to *immobilisme*.[16] Even though advocates of consociationalism stress that the mechanisms they advocate allow segments to define themselves, in many divided societies the rather well defined nature of the segments (i.e., along well-worn ethnic, religious, linguistic, or racial cleavages) suggests that intersegmental conflict will overwhelm cooperation. Providing structural guarantees for communities, for example, through a minority veto, can provide built-in incentives for maintaining the rigidity of the segments.[17]

To counter the alleged defects of consociationalism, Horowitz (1985:601–52) offers a different prescription for divided societies. Rather than effectively entrenching communal representation, he argues, political institutions should encourage integration across communal divides. For democratic government to be effective in a divided society, according

[16] This term refers to a crisis of indecision in government and is a common criticism of inaction that can result from the use of the mutual veto.

[17] The Lebanese National Pact of 1943 is often cited as an example of the propensity of such arrangements to reaffirm segmental divisions.

to Horowitz, moderates must be rewarded, extremists sanctioned. The aim is to induce a centripetal spin to the political system by providing electoral incentives for broad-based moderation by political leaders and disincentives for extremist outbidding. This differentiates Horowitz from the consociationalists in two important respects.

First, the key to any successful democratic political system in divided societies, for Horowitz, is to provide demonstrable incentives for politicians to appeal beyond their own communal segments for support. The only assumption is this: politicians will do whatever they need to do to get elected; they are rational electoral actors (Horowitz 1991:261). When politicians are rewarded electorally for moderation, they will moderate. Given this premise, the polity can be engineered essentially to encourage intercommunal cooperation as a prerequisite for electoral success. Horowitz contends that incentives are better than consociational constraints (like the mutual veto) because they offer reasons for politicians and divided groups to behave moderately, rather than obstacles aimed at preventing them from pursuing hegemonic aims.

The second difference is a concern with constituency-based moderation rather than a reliance on the belief that political leaders alone can foster moderation. The solution to solving the problems associated with the mass-elite nexus is to design the electoral system so that leaders must appeal to underlying moderate sentiments in the electorate and must shun the forces of extremism. Leaders, by appealing to the most moderate sentiments of the electorate, foster compromise between themselves *and* their constituents. Looking for the basis of consent at the constituency level allows politicians to make the kinds of compromises they must make at the center if the divided society to to be truly democratic and stable. The key to constituency-based moderation is the electoral system. To safeguard minority interests, according to Horowitz, the system should make the votes of minority members count. What institutions are argued to have these effects?

A Presidential System.   A presidency, argues Horowitz, if elected directly on the basis of a supermajority distributional formula or a subsequent-preference voting method, is a less exclusive institution than is parliamentarism. There is a long-standing debate between the consociationalists such as Lijphart (1977a) and Linz (1990:51–70), who argue that parliamentarism is more inclusive, and Horowitz (1990:73–79), a rather lone defender of presidentialism.[18] The problem with a

[18] Lijphart does argue (1977a:33) that types of presidentialism and consociationalism are compatible, although the type of decision-making structure he advocates (grand coalition, as above) is clearly different from the broad-based presidential model advocated by Horowitz.

parliamentary-chosen executive, according to Horowitz, is that which-ever party or coalition of parties has a bare majority in the legislature can choose an executive without regard to the preferences of the minor-ity; parliamentary-chosen executives can fall in the winner-take-all, government-versus-opposition pattern of politics, which serves to further divide an already divided society. A minimum winning coalition forms the government. Combined with a strict separation of powers with the legislature, a separately elected presidency can proliferate points of power at the center, allowing some parties to win sometimes and others to win at other times.

Presidentialism is argued to have two important advantages in divided societies. First, if Horowitz's advice on a broadly distributed electoral requirement is taken, an executive who has the broadest possible national appeal can be elected. A strong, statesmanlike, moderate president—forced to appeal to the least common denominator of electoral sentiments—can serve a unifying, nation-building role. Second, a strong executive would be able to push legislation through a divided parliament. If strong but benevolent leadership is required, to make tough economic decisions or redress historical injustices, for example, a strong president may be required.

Federalism. Federalism can serve four important purposes in a di-vided societies, according to Horowitz. First, it can combine with the electoral system to encourage the party proliferation that is conducive to intersegmental compromise and coalition building. Second, politics at the regional and local levels can serve as training grounds for politics at the center; political leaders can form intergroup ties at the constituency level before they contest issues at the center. Third, federalism disperses con-flict at the center by resolving some issues at subtier levels, and may pro-mote subgroup cleavages in communally homogeneous federal states. Fi-nally, it creates difficulties for any parties hoping to get a hegemonic grip on the entire country; capturing all of the provincial states would be a difficult task.

Subsequent Preference Voting. To Horowitz, divided societies do in-deed need some proportionality in representation, but not just the straight system of party-list proportional representation that Lijphart generally advocates; rather, a system of preference voting—and prefera-bly among such systems, alternative voting (AV)—is required. To high-light the virtues Horowitz sees in AV, for example, it must first be differen-tiated from other, well-known types of PR electoral system, namely the party list. The list system, Lijphart argues (1990a:2–13), allows parties to choose lists of candidates and voters to vote for the party, often in a single national constituency. The proportion of votes for the party is directly translated into the same proportion of seats in parliament; that is, party lists provide for the most direct vote/seat ratio possible. Assuming no party wins an outright majority, seats are pooled to form a governing parliamentary majority. AV, a majoritarian system with some proportionality effects, relies not on seat pooling (coalitions formed after an election), but on vote pooling (coalitions based on preelection agreements). Voters choose not only their first preference, but specify second or third preferences as well. In addition to AV, Horowitz likes the single transferable vote (STV), where candidates can make vote-pooling agreements. The major precondition for a successful vote-pooling framework is sufficient party proliferation, large heterogeneous constituencies, and conditions that make vote pooling profitable: that is, when moderation by political leaders causes them to gain more second- and third-preference votes than the first-preference votes, they lose by appearing soft on communal interests.[19]

Why is subsequent-preference voting superior for divided societies, in Horowitz's view? The logic is this: in order to win, politicians must seek to obtain the second- or third-preference votes of those who would not ordinarily vote for them (presumably because they do not represent the voter's community). In order to gain those alternative votes, leaders must behave moderately toward other communal groups. Outbidding will not occur on the extremes; rather, politicians will try to outbid each other to appear moderate—they will compete with one another to find the political center. Centripetal forces will override centrifugal ones. The critical difference between the consociationalist system and Horowitz's is thus the formation of electoral coalitions *by constituents* as they specify their second or third preferences beyond their own narrow group interests.

From Options to Outcomes

This scholarly debate, unfortunately, inadequately links institutional outcomes to democratization processes. Whether a democratic transition in a divided society leads to an outcome that is essentially consociational or one that is closer to centripetalism is an altogether different question from the questions most scholars ask, with important implications for the durability of a future democracy and its ability to contain the centrifugal thrusts of a divided societies. According to both Lijphart and Horowitz, getting the right institutions (i.e., the institutions they advocate) can spell the difference between conflict reduction and a successful consolidation

[19] The last condition is critical. If the constituencies are too divided—if there exists no sentiment for accommodation in the electorate—vote pooling cannot establish it.

of democracy, and failure. But as studies on democratic transitions increasingly show, getting the institutions right depends less on political "engineering" than on the nature of the transition process. The more appropriate approach is to associate options with outcomes.

If democratic rule arguably provides the best alternative for escaping conflict, how and when is it possible for parties to a conflict themselves to choose to move from an exclusive political system to an inclusive, ostensibly democratic alternative? The central questions in analyzing democratic transitions are: When do various transitions start; that is, how are they initiated? What kinds of actors participate, and what roles do they play? What are the types of change, for example, regime collapse, reform, revolution, negotiation? What is the range of democratic outcomes, and how sustainable are they? This new literature has led to a fundamental reevaluation of previous arguments that certain preconditions—a high level of economic development and value consensus reflecting a "civic culture," for example—are required before a democratic political system can be established. These factors are now argued (Karl 1990:5) to be *outcomes* of democracy, not preconditions or requisites.

Democratization can be initiated in different ways, as a synthesis of the most salient arguments from the recent literature shows. First, democracy can be imposed or guaranteed by an external actor. More often than not, the international community or a former colonial power makes that choice, or democracy is imposed by conquest—the institutional choices made by actors in a society are constrained and subject to the review and veto of the external power. Second, a transition can occur when a regime collapses or is violently overthrown. Paradoxically, the evidence points to a hypothesis that democracy is most difficult to consolidate from transitions of this type: disparate social institutions are unable to concur on alternative choices or effectively implement them. Restoration, given the lack of coherent alternatives, is often easier than reconstruction. This is not the case in the third type of transition, that of reform from above, which occurs when a regime in power constructs new institutional rules that democratize without jeopardizing its role in a future order. Institutional choices are made solely by the incumbent regime. Finally, democratic transitions occur when liberalizers come to power and negotiate with the opposition. Such transitions often result in democratization pacts: negotiated transitions that involve agreement over alternative institutions. In such transitions, it is often the case that a new, liberalizing regime comes to power and realizes that—for its own security—it must negotiate with the opposition.

The fourth path of transition is the type that is the central focus of this book. In transitions such as these, democratization occurs as a result of a negotiated settlement between the incumbent regime and opposition.

From the Spanish experience, such transitions are known *ruptura pactada:* a break from the authoritarian past, but one that is the result of a series of pacts (O'Donnell, Schmitter, and Whitehead 1986). Others have termed the Spanish democratization path "transition through transaction" (Share 1986). I suggest that because of the intense nature of conflict in divided societies, transitions to democracy are unlikely to occur unless they are transitions that are negotiated. The basis of pacts is agreement on mutual restraint and the protection of vital interests, exactly the type of concerns that drive the divisive politics of divided societies.

Transition by Pact Making

Many of the democratizations in the last two decades—including the southern European, Latin American, and Eastern European experiences—have been negotiated transitions based on pact making. In the course of democratization, political leaders make deals on the nature of the future political order. Such pacts are usually elite-based agreements, sometimes ratified in popular referendums, other times affirmed in founding elections. When political leaders negotiate pacts, they do so on the basis of their own changing interests, their expectations of how different institutions may work, and the strategic interaction of the bargaining process. Recent work by Geddes on the democratization process in Latin America, for example, affirms that democratization is "driven . . . by the political interests of the individuals who design and construct these institutions" (1990:5).

O'Donnell, Schmitter, and Whitehead, in their influential four-part volume *Transitions from Authoritarian Rule: Prospects for Democracy,* define pacts as

> explicit, but not always publicly explicated or justified, agreement among a select set of actors which seeks to define (or better, redefine) rules governing the exercise of power on the basis of mutual guarantees for the "vital interests" of those entering into it. . . . At the core of a pact lies a negotiated compromise under which actors agree to forgo or underutilize their capacity to harm each other by extending guarantees not to threaten each other's corporate autonomies or vital interests. (1986: pt. 4, pp. 37–39)

Pacts may be either transitional, limited to establishing a temporary set of rules of the game to govern the period of transition, or "foundational," establishing the new rules of governance. The essence of pact making, as Karl (1990) has argued, is comprehensiveness, inclusion, and rule making. Such pacts, if aimed at protecting "vital interests" (Dahl 1973) are inclusive of all significant political actors who have interests at stake, and also tie the military (often an autonomous political actor) to rules that include civilian political interests. Pacts are inherently undemocratic because they limit the range of issues available for contestation; thus, pacted democratization has been called ushering in "democracy by undemocratic means" (Hagopian 1990).

Democratization through pacts implies bargaining over the new democratic order. It also implies the formation of nascent political coalitions that will exercise shared power in the new order. This is particularly the case when the outgoing regime is not fully powerless, that is, when it will have a role to play in the future order. This implication is important for divided societies, where states are often associated with identity group interests and where negotiation and bargaining are essential for moving beyond the condition of discord. Whereas parties are dispensable, communities are not.

The notion of pact making as negotiation and bargaining, based on strategic interaction among actors, is an important breakthrough in the comparative study of democratic transitions. Decisions made by actors on whether to cooperate or not cooperate are based on the perceptions of the intent of other actors and the positions the actors take during the negotiation process, and their perception of the balance of power. In terms of game theory, the process is an iterative one in which moves are made based on the expectations and interpretation of the moves of others (Brams 1990). The role of bargaining and power relationships is critical in the process of pact making. Borrowing on the work of Bacharach and Lawler (1981), du Toit (1989b:210–230) shows the importance of strategic behavior, bargaining power, and the relationship of interdependence among actors in divided societies.[20] The essential features of the bargaining relationship involve: power (present and potential), which can be defined in terms of an actor's own estimate of resources that can be brought to bear on the process; tactics, which translate resources and potential power into actual power in the course of a negotiation; and, finally, the dependence relationship, which concerns the symmetry or asymmetry in the power relationships of the parties to negotiation.

One of the most important advances made in the comparative study of democratic transitions is the recognition of the linkages between the type of transition and the outcomes that flow from such a transition. Karl writes:

It is no longer adequate to examine regime transitions writ large, that is, from the general category of authoritarian rule to that of democracy. Such broadguaged efforts must be complemented by the identification of different types

[20] Du Toit cites Young's definition of strategic behavior, which is a good one: "Strategic behavior is the behavior of any individual of a group involving a choice of action contingent upon that individual's estimates of the actions (or choices) of others in the group, where the actions of each of the relevant others are based on a similar estimate of the behavior of group members other than himself" (1989a:5,6).

of democracy that emerge from the distinctive modes of regime transition as well as an analysis of their potential political, economic, and social consequences. . . . Theorists of comparative politics [have shifted] their attention to the strategic calculations, unfolding processes, and sequential patterns that are involved in moving from one type of political regime to another. (1990:1,5)

I contend that democratic transitions occur in a set of analytically distinct stages, with each stage fundamentally linked to the previous stage and to subsequent stages; the nature of the democracy that emerges at the end of the process has its roots in the process itself (Hagopian 1990; di Palma 1990). Although this may be self-evident in broader terms, comparativists can begin to hypothesize about how the pieces of the democratization puzzle fit together, as I suggested in the seven-step model of South Africa's transition in the Introduction.

During the course of transitions, political parties as the primary actors engage in a process of contingent choice over the rules of the new political game. Such choices are contingent in that they are bounded by the choices of all other actors and by the tentative rules of transitional pacts and the bargaining power and resources of the actors (Blalock 1989:27–50). They are also constrained or enabled by the preexisting social conditions under which actors find themselves. That is, choices among alternative political institutions in a democratization process are made within structural-historical constraints (Karl 1990). These factors substantially influence the range of options political actors perceive to be available.

Theorists' new appreciation of relating options to outcomes reveals that the path of transition—imposition, revolution, reform, or pact making—has a critical bearing on democratic outcomes and on the prospects for the consolidation of democracy. Analyzing cases of democratization in Latin America, Karl shows that the type of transition yielded certain types of outcomes, some less democratic than others:

> Democratization by imposition is likely to yield conservative democracies that can not or will not address equity issues; . . . pacted transitions are likely to produce corporatist or consociational democracies in which party competition is regulated to varying degrees determined in part by the nature of foundational bargains . . . ; [and] . . . revolutionary transitions tend to result in one-party dominant democracies, where competition is also regulated. (1990:15)

Karl's findings suggest that pacted transitions result in corporatist or consociational outcomes. Du Toit makes a similar argument with reference to consociationalism, but from a different orientation. He contends that consociationalism evolves out a specific type of power relationship in which there is a roughly symmetrical distribution of bargaining power in a society.

Almost complete convergence of bargaining power increases the likelihood that agreements will be reached and that these agreements will be compatible with the principle of equality. . . . The favorable conditions for consociational models are met when the bargaining relationship is characterized by convergent (equal) bargaining power. . . . Power sharing among societal groups can be justified because of the mutual dependence of these groups upon each other and because of their lack of alternative sources of scarce values. (1989b:422, 425, 427)

If pacted transitions lead to consociational outcomes, there would be little room for Horowitz's argument that parties can eschew minority vetoes for the kinds of integrative institutions he advocates. After all, the purpose of pacts is to *guarantee* the protection of segments' vital interests. But Horowitz (1991:251–82) does argue that his institutional prescription can *also* emerge from a process of democratization, one in which the power balance may be at relative parity. Such a democratization process need not be one based on the agreements for reciprocal protection of vital interests in consociational arrangements, or pacts. Horowitz (1991:261) contends that opposing forces see each other not only as enemies and hegemons, but in a positive-sum view of relations, as potential allies with nonhegemonic aims. Pact making is narrow deal making, according to Horowitz, which runs counter to the needs of flexible transitions in divided societies; guarantees for the protection of vital interests in pacts "provide illusory security, easily pierced" (1991:136). Pacts "have all the characteristic problems all contracts have: the preferences of the parties change over time, conditions also change; the returns to the parties from the deal are uneven; and the deadlines laid down inevitably arrive. . . . The problem with intergroup pacts, in a word, is that to endure they need to be flexible; but to be formed they must be permanent, since the ripe moment may never come again" (1991:149). Because the features of consociational democracy that may emerge from pacted transitions are based on the mutual protection of vital interests, including those of incumbent elites, they are an inauspicious start for democracy. Hagopian (1990) argues, for example, that in Brazil pacts "hindered democratization" by strengthening incumbent interests, perpetuating state clientelism, and inhibiting the full development of political parties as interest aggregators. Moreover, she suggests, "pacts that preclude socioeconomic reform undermine democracy, not by neglecting to enact redistributive policies, but by removing issues on which ordinary citizens may wish to express preferences from the arena of legitimate discussion" (1990:153).

Pact making in divided societies offers additional perils for a new, inclusive democracy.

There is a more promising but still very uncertain vision of durable democratization. What makes it promising is that it is also solidly anchored in party
interests. The central feature of such a vision is that incentives can change, and
change dramatically, as the process of democratization is under way. The decision by each actor to commit or not to commit itself to the process induces
reactions on the party of every other actor. Before long, a different spectrum,
with different alignments, is visible, and a new structure of opportunities and
constraints can present itself. . . . An insecure future prompt[s] risk-averse behavior that inadvertently exchange[s] hegemonic possibilities for immediate
gains of a qualitatively different sort. . . . Potential hegemons [are] enticed into
becoming cooperators and democrats in spite of themselves. (Horowitz
1991:271, 276)

Horowitz takes a first step toward relating the democratization to his
prescriptive model. Lijphart (1992) has also sought to relate the process
of transition to consociational outcomes, most recently focusing on Eastern Europe. Can a pact-based transition, such as South Africa's, yield
other-than-consociational outcomes? Addressing this question requires
an investigation of the actual preferences of political actors in transition at
myriad levels of analysis—individual political elites and their relations
with followers, political parties as cohesive units and the nature of intraparty cleavages, and societal elites and civil society organizations. A central thesis of this book is that South Africa's transition has been based on
pacts, and the democratization pact reached in 1993 was essentially consociational; but I will also suggest that pacted transitions can conceivably
lead to consociational *or* centripetal democratic outcomes.

The Politics and Political Economy of Institutional Choice

In the course of negotiated transitions to democracy, political leaders,
political parties, and their allied forces in civil society make choices over
preferred alternative institutions, or rule structures, for the future polity.
These choices are selected from a set of alternative decision rules; that is,
choices must be made to decide the rules to determine how subsequent
decisions will be taken in the political system. Understanding that the
creation of new political institutions involves choosing among alternative
sets of rules of the political game rightly puts the analysis of the politics of
democratic transition before any analysis of constitutional models and
options. South Africa's negotiated transition will yield a new postapartheid constitution. Yet the legal document will reflect a set of rules to
govern political behavior in the new polity, and these rules will be the
product of institutional choice.

Thus, my concern is with choices *among* rules as institutions as distinguished from choices *within* rules (Ostrom 1990; Vanberg and Buchanan 1989). The "new institutionalism" in comparative politics renews appreciation for the role institutions play in politics.[21] Institutions are forms of sanctions and incentives mutually agreed upon in order to reconcile self-interested choices with the social good; they resolve problems posed to actors who create rules to eliminate (or regulate) uncertainty (Sened 1991). Institutions arise because they are mutually beneficial to a decisive set of political actors as they seek to resolve problems. The new institutionalism posits that the rules of interaction play a critical role in forming outcomes that flow from a political system, and that institutions are *chosen* by social actors to escape a problem (Ostrom 1990).

How are institutions the result of human designs or choice? Institutions are the formal rules of recurring political or social games that include a set of players and a sequence of moves exercised in the context of information (Tsebelis 1990a:92ff.).[22] From this perspective, the most important feature of institutions is that within a given rule structure, individuals are *assumed* to act in a self-interested manner to achieve their ends in response to others' behavior *and* to the institutional structure—they apply the logic of appropriateness. Individuals exercise "choice" in the establishment of institutions because they may either continue to try to achieve their ends within the existing institutions or try to change the rules in extrainstitutional efforts (March and Olsen 1989:160, 162).

Thus, the institutional choice approach seeks to explain both how actors make choices within a given set of institutional settings and how institutions are created or evolve. Ostrom (1991) argues that the new focus on institutionalism is a "real breakthrough" in social science because it begins to build bridges between the deductive orientation of rational choice theory and the inductive orientation of empirical approaches. Choices are made, in her view, by rational individuals, but they are made in the context of structural-historical conditions that define the appropriate rules of behavior. The central institutional-choice challenge

[21] For an exemplary early treatment of this theme, see March and Olsen 1984. The critical difference between institutions and social norms is that institutions involve the construction of "man-made rules imposed by participants in a social event upon themselves and other participants in the event" (Sened 1991:398). For the application of political economy and institutional approaches to Africa, see Bates 1981, 1992.

[22] As March and Olsen suggest, such rules—the "routings, procedures, conventions, roles, strategies, organizational forms and technologies around which political activity is constructed" (1989:32)—can be either formal and known (constitutions, laws, ordinances, etc.) or they may be informal, such as norms or customs (North 1990). Institutions are "nested games" in that one set of institutional procedures is considered to be nested in another, and so on; for example, parliamentary politics has been viewed by Tsebelis (1990a) as a game nested within the larger game of electoral politics.

actors face is thus to judge rationally among alternative sets of rules based on the expecting working properties of those rules as they operate over a set of known future issues. Expectations of the performance of the rules and expectations of how an actor may act within the rules—for example, forming coalitions or alliances with other actors—are essential features of the dynamics of institutional choice.[23]

Adapting the formalism of choice theory to the practical realities of real-world choices is likely to be unsatisfactory to both the formal theorist seeking precision and the practical politician seeking simple answers to complex phenomena (Ostrom 1991).[24] The institutional choice approach applied here is less robust than a more formal rational choice model, and for good reason. Blalock writes:

> Debates over . . . "rationality" often do not come to grips with precisely what it is that defines this rationality. If one means by the term a complete listing of all possible alternative courses of action and a highly accurate set of subjective probabilities that correspond to relative frequencies, then rational behaviors will of course never be found in the real world. . . . What can be argued, however, is that most actors will attach crude probability estimates to some

---

[23] Coalition forming, or more accurately the expectation of coalition forming, is an integral aspect of institutional choice, as will be shown with specific reference to South African political actors. Riker and Ordeshook define coalitions broadly to include "a wide variety of joint action to exploit a complementarity of interest" (1973:120). Coalitions can be formal and codified in an agreement or less formal, with actors acting in concert without explicit communication.

[24] Indeed, the contours of such real-world choices are complex and difficult to discern; as such, they do not lend themselves to pristine mathematical modeling offered by most rational choice theorists. Tsebelis refers to this complexity as a "giant game" for which a game theoretic approach would be "heroic" and impossible (1990a:9). A rigorous, formal model of choice is distinguished by its assumptions (March and Lave 1975:137–43). Such a formal model posits that when choices are made, those who are making them have a complete list of alternatives; map the consequences of each possible outcome; attach a value to each outcome; specify the probability of each outcome; and choose among the alternatives given by maximizing expected value. In this model, actors prefer those alternatives which are expected to minimize cost and maximize benefit over the long run. There are readily identifiable limits to this model of rational institutional choice. Ostrom (1991) describes limits to rational choice theories, namely, their lack of utility for normative and empirical analysis, as well as their limitations related to the roles of history, culture, and institutions. While actors may have a complete list of alternatives, they may be unable to map the consequences of each outcome because they may have inadequate information about aspects of the complex situation (Brams 1985:4); are unable to predict future events; have inadequate knowledge to forecast expected consequences or alternative outcomes; or may lack a single utility function for the multitude of values imbedded in the choice. They may also lack critical information. Each of these limitations on the choice model is in essence a limitation on the actors' ability to exercise complete rationality. The author owes a great deal of this formulation of the basic institutional choice problem to the assistance of Alexander George.

set of alternative courses of action, as for example whether or not to engage in a conflict with a powerful opponent, how far to carry a bluff, how strong a commitment to make, or what the response will be to a peace overture. (1989:38)

Thus a "softer" explanation to real-world choices is the best that can be expected of empirical research (Bates 1988:387).

Institutional choice is a matter of configuring a set of rules to constitute a regime that structures the strategic behavior and relationships among social actors. As suggested earlier, political transitions involve changes in the institutional design of the polity (Mozaffar 1992; Brady and Mo 1992). To change institutions, a society will undergo transaction costs in a change of regime and transformation costs associated with the resources social actors expend in order to affect a change of regime (North 1990). Thus, consideration of political transition in these terms allows for an analysis of the *path dependence* of institutional change, which links the process of transition to the outcomes of a democratization process (North 1990). I am therefore concerned with both institutions for the transition, such as interim arrangements, and for longer-term institutional arrangements, such as those reflected in a final postapartheid constitution. Institutional choice questions are important because they involve for an actor *expectations* over the long term of the working properties of the rule structures established and of the agenda of items to be decided by rules in the midst of the uncertainty of democratic transitions. Strategies can thus be linked to expected outcomes. As Tsebelis writes, "Because the expected life of institutions is much higher than the expected life of policies, both the consequences of an institutional choice and the uncertainty surrounding it are much more important elements in the calculation" (1990a:98).

The central problem in democratizing divided societies is to arrive at a rule to maximize incentives for actors to stay in the political game— ensure that the system is as procedurally and distributively fair as possible. In order to maximize such incentives, the rule must include opportunities for alternation in winning political coalitions. Actors, in order to continue playing the game, must expect that at least on some issues, some of the time, they will win—the important principle of alternation. As Miller writes, "Political conflict inevitably produced losers as well as winners. A fundamentally important question (and *the* question of political stability) is how to induce losers to continue to play the political game, to continue to work within the system rather than overthrow it" (1983:742).

Further, one of the central propositions of the institutional choice approach is that the economic environment influences the choice of political rules and that political rules influence economic outcomes. Thus, causality runs in both directions (North 1990:48). The question of whether democracy produces more efficient economic outcomes or economic development is a long-standing debate that I do not wish to enter into detail, for it is not essential to my argument.[25] However, I am concerned with why a political actor would choose one set of democratic institutions over another, and for this purpose it is necessary to consider what I term *the political economy of institutional choice,* that is, the nexus between choices over political institutions and economic structures and perceived future outcomes. How does the economic environment affect choices over alternative political institutions? How do choices among alternative political institutions affect economic outcomes?

The two questions posed above are linked. March and Olsen explain the circular nature of the relationship: "Political institutions affect the distribution of resources, which in turn affects the power of political actors, and thereby affects political institutions. Wealth, social standing, reputation for power, knowledge of alternatives, and attention are not easily described as exogenous to the political process and political institutions" (1984:163). My central concern is to demonstrate that in the course of South Africa's democratization an important aspect of institutional choice among sets of political rules is the *expected economic outcomes* perceived to flow from such choices. Just as actors can attach crude probability estimates—analyses of perceived costs and benefits—to the anticipated political ramifications of a given set of rules, so too they assess the anticipated distributive outcomes that may flow. A critical issue with respect to a democratization process is that the interests of these civil society actors are likely to be reflected in the positions of the political parties to which they are allied. Thus, the political and economic considerations of these actors significantly influence, I will show, the institutional choice considerations of political parties as they negotiate the rules of the new regime.

In divided societies especially, a central concern is that institutional choice outcomes must be perceived by actors to produce the equitable, efficient distribution of public goods. The political economy of institutional choice is also important, because as I will argue in chapter 7, achieving a social contract in South Africa requires a demonstrable positive-sum solution with respect to both political and economic outcomes. This will be particularly true with regard to the extent new political institutions can help reduce inequality.[26] Thus, the economic compo-

[25] For a recent, cogent, thorough consideration of this debate, see Diamond 1992.

[26] North views the adoption of certain kinds of institutions as a critical variable in economic success. "The institutional framework plays a major role in the performance of an

nent of institutional choices will be important with regard to the range of potential outcomes to the democratization process. Just as the political actors on the South African scene are negotiating a new political future, they are seeking to create a new economic order, too.

Changing Preferences and Convergence

My purpose is not just to analyze South African political parties' static preferences for postapartheid institutions, but to see how these preferences changed over time in the course of transition. Indeed, I seek *to map the process of convergence.* Actors reformulate their preferences as they move from their most desired alternative regime structure, the *ideal,* to the regime structure they perceive as achievable given the preferences of others, the *possible.* Moving from the ideal to the possible is really a matter of reformulating preferences away from those which can be unilaterally imposed toward the preferences of others through compromise. Following the advent of negotiation, preferences are formulated as not what is ideal, but what is "best attainable."[27] This occurs when actors converge on a set of institutions that they all perceive *to serve converging interests* and *to be fair* given the conditions they face, a point I more briefly developed in the Introduction and to which I will return to at the end of the book.

Antecedent variables inform institutional choices; that is, they exist prior to the preference and constrain, or in some instances enable, the range of choices and potential courses of action. Blalock (1989:136–50), as I described earlier, sees these variables as "environmental constraints" that causally precede other variables that explain institutional choices. I argue there are three. First, I discussed above that *the historical evolution of a conflict* influences choice calculations. Second, I also argued that systems of belief—*ideology*—play a role. Vanberg and Buchanan, in distinguishing between "interest" and "theory" components in institutional choice, write that "how a person chooses among potential alternatives is not only a matter of 'what he wants' but also of 'what he believes,' and for some kinds of choices an actor's beliefs or theories may play a crucial

---

economy. . . . The market is a mixed bag of institutions; some increase efficiency and some decrease efficiency. Nevertheless, contrasting the institutional framework in such countries as the United States, England, France, Germany and Japan with Third World countries of those in the historical past in advanced industrial countries makes clear that this institutional framework is the key to the relative success of economies, both cross-sectionally as well as through time" (1990:69).

[27] As Brams and Doherty (1992) have shown formally, actors must have a preference set in which their ideal (first order) and possible (subsequent order) choices are favored above the status quo; otherwise the negotiations lead to impasse.

role. We suggest that the second element is particularly important for constitutional choices, that is, for choices among rules" (1989:51). A third variable (or, more accurately, set of variables) is the *exogenous environment:* the wide range of events and influences going on around the world and in the immediate region that affect the context in which transitions take place and institutional choices are formulated.

The *expectations* of political actors over the working properties of alternative rules and how they may fare under such rules is a critical variable in explaining institutional choices. The expectation, or perception, of a political party's majority or minority status relative to others is an important factor in perceiving one's fate in a polarized, conflict-ridden, divided society. Choosing among alternative political institutions in the midst of a period of political transition, when *uncertainty* is heightened, will involve a reasoned estimate of the party's size relative to others and the perceived degree of variability in that size. This is especially true with respect to a transition that will culminate in a founding election. As Downs (1957) aptly notes, parties formulate policies in order to win votes, rather than winning votes in order to formulate policies.

Expectations of the power that a political party can wield in the arena of political conflict is a matter of resources at the disposal of the party, and of how those resources are employed. Blalock writes about "power as potential" (1989:26), defined by three subsets of variables in a multiplicative function. First are resources, the degree to which they are mobilized, and the efficiency of the mobilization effort. Mobilization and efficiency are related in a process of strategic interaction in the tactics actors employ, which comprises bargaining power. Bargaining power, Bacharach and Lawler (1981:39) point out, is based on dependence relationships. Power as potential is based in the degree to which one actor is dependent on another (Blalock 1989:43). Both expectations of size *and* power inform choices. It is important to note that power is operationalized in terms of actors' perception of their own resources, not on empirical standards. It is also important to note that size expectations and power relative to others are operationalized to include both the size of the constituency a political party represents and the array of civil society forces upon which it relies, as well as the resources available to the party. Some resources are endogenous, for example, control of the state or military, links to capital or trade unions, and some are exogenous, such as material or moral support derived from the international community.

Political party choices in an ideal world are mitigated in the course of strategic interaction. The dependence relationship among the actors—their relative bargaining power—assumes a critical role. Particularly, the relative *symmetry or asymmetry in the bargaining power relationship* becomes a consideration, as does the arrival at a mutually beneficial bargaining arrangement when the level of power among actors reaches approximate parity (Bacharach and Lawler 1981:53). In other words, bargaining power relationships can be either balanced or unbalanced, favorably or not, and when there is a roughly equal power relationship, the conditions for a mutually beneficial exchange are most likely to be present.

Under the conditions of strategic interaction, coalition forming, or efforts to augment or pool bargaining power, also enters the equation. Whether or not a party can expect to coalesce with parties possessing congruent interests is an equally important variable in the formation of institutional choice preferences. *Expectations of coalition forming* are part of determining the extent to which a party can expect to be in the majority or the minority, assuming parliamentary competition (Riker 1962; Brams 1990:211–25).

The range of preferences of alternative regime types as dependent variables refers both to institutions to govern future regime types and to the paths of transition. For example, a majoritarian model of transition could be an elected constituent assembly with a simple majority decision rule; a consociational transition model would be a government operating by a consensus decision rule; a partition transition model would be a unilateral declaration of secession. I thus distinguish between *nascent institutions* in the course of democratization and the institutions of a new democracy. Nascent institutions are recognized by political actors as transitional arrangements created to institutionalize interaction throughout the transition. Nascent institutions are those through which the new, ostensibly long-standing rules will be chosen. These dependent variables can describe both sets of institutions, I will show, and are distinct and mutually exclusive. In divided societies, there are four broad sets of institutional choice preferences (variations within the basic choice will be illuminated in later chapters).

- Majoritarianism (unrestrained simple majority rule)
- Centripetalism (incentive-based mechanisms)
- Consociationalism (concrete assurances)
- Partition (mutually exclusive arrangements, including loose confederation)

It is important to distinguish between these *preferences* and outcomes. As Mozaffar writes, "rational agents do not select outcomes. They select strategies which they anticipate will lead to expected outcomes" (1992:27). Actors formulate preferences in the context of strategic interaction, with knowledge about the choices of other actors and their relationships with them. Przeworski observes that "outcomes of particular conflict are not known ex ante by any of the competing political forces, because the consequences of their actions depend on actions of others,

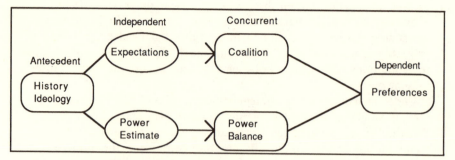

Fig. 1.1 An Institutional Choice Model

and these cannot be anticipated uniquely" (1991:12). Figure 1.1 summarizes the institutional choice variables in a model.

These variables of institutional choice can be linked a set of hypotheses about which kinds of political institutions political parties with different attributes would choose in a process of strategic interaction, that is, when their first-order preferences are mitigated by the preferences of others as a result of high levels of interdependence. In divided societies, the institutional choice approach would predict the following relationships (presented graphically in figure 1.2):

- Political parties with certain expectations of being in the majority in a favorably unbalanced power relationship choose *majoritarianism*.
- Political parties with certain expectations of being in the majority in a balanced power relationship choose *modified majoritarianism* (majoritarianism with features of centripetalism or consociationalism).
- Political parties with uncertain expectations of whether they will be in the minority or majority in a balanced power relationship choose *centripetalism*.
- Political parties with certain expectations of being in the minority in a balanced power relationship choose *modified consociationalism* (consociationalism with features of centripetalism or majoritarianism).
- Political parties with uncertain expectations of being part of either a minority or majority in an unfavorably unbalanced power relationship choose *consociationalism*.
- Political parties with certain expectations of being in the minority in an unfavorably unbalanced power relationship choose *partition*.

By way of conclusion, I offer four possible outcomes to a negotiation process in divided societies, two nondemocratic and two democratic. These outcomes imply that institutional change in a divided society may not result in democracy, which is not surprising, knowing the tendency of politics in divided societies to drift into extremism. Previous scholarship

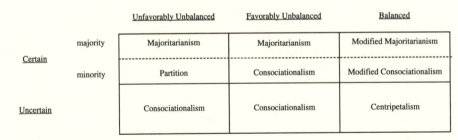

Fig. 1.2 Institutional Choice Hypotheses

on the politics of divided societies often dichotomizes outcomes in terms of hegemonic control versus power sharing. As Rothchild notes, however, "unless more precise conceptual tools are developed, social scientists will likely find it difficult to analyze state-ethnic relationships, or to make policy recommendations on facilitating constructive conflict by altering their terms of interaction" (1986:65). Thus, a more conceptually discrete set of outcomes is required:

- *Hegemonic control.* Hegemonic control occurs when one or more groups control the state to the exclusion of other groups and rule in a hegemonic fashion. The predominant characteristic of hegemonic control is the unilateral writing of the rules of the political game by a single political actor or a narrow coalition of actors. Following Lustick (1979), the control model essentially results in the subjugation of outgroups. I will argue that, at least with respect to South Africa's transition, the hegemonic control outcome would precipitate continued conflict, that is, civil war.[28]

- *Hegemonic exchange.* A more inclusive form of group interaction with the state, but one that is nonetheless hegemonic, is Rothchild's notion of hegemonic exchange, which "brings together some devices from control—in particular, the single- or no-party system and encapsulated decision-making—with some devices from consociation—mainly, the securing of state-ethnoregional and interethnic exchange and reciprocity by means of quiet behind-the-scenes negotiation and the application of the proportionality principle" (1986:72). The essential feature of such arrangements is that a coalition of centrist political actors defines the rules of political interaction jointly, but in order to defend their inclusive, moderate collusion, they must limit participation and contestation and, most likely, employ the coercive forces of the state against the forces of extremist ethnic outbidders. They bind together to avoid mutual damage. Hegemonic exchange regimes, however, do

---

[28] For a discussion of the consociationalism-control dichotomy, see Lustick 1979.

engage in "concertation," or "organized efforts at concerted decision-making where interested parties are explicitly included in a bargaining process and often in implementation as well" (Rothchild and Foley 1988:258).

- *Consociationalism.* The hallmark of a consociational outcome is broadly inclusive representation by segmental leaders, elite accommodation, and limits on majoritarianism. The rules of the political game are determined by a broadly inclusive group of political actors in concert, but this situation is made possible only by limiting participation to elites and narrowing the range of contestation to consensual politics. I will argue that consociationalism is tantamount to an elite pact, centering on the protection of vital interests through concrete assurances such as the minority veto.

- *Centripetalism.* A centripetal outcome is the adoption of a political system that eschews the concrete assurances of consociationalism in favor of an incentives-based approach to political moderation. Centripetalism affords greater constituency participation and interparty competition (alternation) than does consociationalism, thus approaching more closely the desiderata of a democracy with alternating majorities and minorities that cross-cut identity cleavages. I will argue, however, that the centripetal outcome need not be the specific institutions advocated by Horowitz, described earlier; rather, majoritarian institutions other than those he advocates can indeed provide a centripetal "spin" to the political system and create the effects he seeks to engender.

Transitions in divided societies may begin with elite pacts and power sharing (as I will argue with respect to South Africa), but a more deeply democratic outcome conceivably exists. A social contract in a democratizing multiethnic society can evolve when formerly antagonistic and deeply divided political leaders, parties, and organizations of civil society choose to escape self-defeating conflict and bind together to create a democratic polity that institutionalizes the principles of intergroup bargaining and cooperation. A social contract need not be democratic, and South Africa could develop a social contract that represents tacit agreement among key elites to keep participatory democracy to a minimum. Black labor and white business, along with the postapartheid state, could coalesce in a social contract that is short of democracy, neither allowing for full participation nor providing alternation in government. Even with this kind of social contract, similar to Rothchild's notion of hegemonic exchange, bargaining does not end with the social contract; indeed, a culture of ongoing negotiation is institutionalized.

The critical difference between a democratization that results in a consociational pact and one that produces a democratic social contract is that, with the latter, erstwhile foes eschew essentialist perceptions that lead to demands for mutual vetoes in the bargaining relationship and instead muster sufficient trust to submit to the uncertainties of winning and losing in the electoral game. In a democratic social contract, parties voluntarily reject mutual fear in favor of mutual gain. With a sense of shared destiny, consolidated by convergence through negotiation on what constitutes a fair set of institutions (both in political power and in distributive terms), a democratic social contract is conceivable in a divided society despite the seemingly inherent centrifugal forces that make intergroup accommodation so elusive.

CHAPTER 2

From Apartheid to Negotiation

THE CONVENTIONAL wisdom is that the transition to a postapartheid society began on 2 February 1990, the day State President F. W. de Klerk lifted the bans on the major anti-apartheid organizations, pledged to release Nelson Mandela and other political prisoners, and declared the door to negotiation open. While that event is an important milestone in the transition—and it took virtually every observer by surprise—it is important to look behind the decision to see it as the end product of a long and complex process of social and political transformation (Price 1991), and the culmination of the prenegotiation phase of South Africa's transition. What brought about apartheid's demise? Why did the parties choose to negotiate? How was South African politics transformed from polarization to consensus-seeking bargaining and negotiation?

My analysis highlights both the development of a mutually hurting stalemate as a necessary condition for the onset of formal negotiation and the important precipitating factors that fall under the general rubric of prenegotiation. The era of prenegotiation is fruitfully described as the phase in which "parties move from conflicting unilateral solutions for a mutual problem to a joint search for cooperative multilateral or joint solutions. . . . The activity lies not in conducting the combined search for a/*the* solution but in arriving at and in convincing the other party to arrive at the conclusion that *some* joint solution is possible" (Zartman 1989:4). Initial views of the conflict in South Africa as a zero-sum game gave way to the perception that a positive-sum outcome existed and was, in fact, attainable. I will show that negotiation became possible when the major parties perceived the balance of power as relatively symmetrical, an important fact for later assessing converging institutional choices for a postapartheid order.

APARTHEID'S DEMISE

On 17 June 1991, South Africa's white-dominated Tricameral Parliament passed legislation that brought the most important legal pillar of apartheid—the Population Registration Act, by which every South African was legally classified by race—crumbling down. De Klerk, in an address to an unusual joint sitting of the Tricameral Parliament, said: "The year 1991 will become known in history as the year in which South Africa finally removed statutory discrimination—apartheid—from its system. Now it belongs to history. The votes that have just taken place . . . have finally brought to an end an era in which the life of every South African was affected in the minutest detail by racially based legislation . . . which was born and nurtured under different circumstances in a departed era."[1] Ironically, the National party (NP) that invented apartheid would later discover an interest in its demise. What explains this outcome to the long and bitter history of apartheid?

The repeal of the Population Registration Act followed on President de Klerk's promises to South Africans and the international community earlier in 1991 that by the end of the parliamentary session, all apartheid laws would be wiped from the statute books. The apartheid albatross was perceived to be finally gone.[2] As for apartheid as ideology and political program, the regime had unequivocally turned its back on its erstwhile ideology and the political institutions created to realize it. Like all other actors on the South African scene, the ruling party formulated new institutional choices for a future political order.

What brought about apartheid's demise? O'Donnell and Schmitter write that the "typical sign that a transition has begun comes when these authoritarian incumbents, for whatever reason, begin to modify their own rules in the direction of providing more secure guarantees for individuals and groups" (1986:6). The repeal of South Africa's infamous Population Registration Act was a telltale sign that the demise of apartheid was indeed imminent and that the ruling party had begun to unilaterally change the core rules of the old political game. Much like authoritarian regimes elsewhere, the ruling party in South Africa had found that the costs of maintaining apartheid authoritarianism increasingly exceeded the benefits accruing from it.

The Paradox of Interdependence

The ultimate paradox of apartheid as an ideology and political system was the fundamental contradiction between a political policy of territorial segregation and racial disentanglement, or "separate development," and the integrationist needs of a modernizing and rapidly industrializing economy. While the political aims of territorial segregation sought to consign black South Africans to independent self-governing states, the economy demanded their labor in "white" urban areas.

The vision of total territorial separation of the races into autonomous political units, known by the early 1960s as "separate development,"

---

[1] *Hansard Parliamentary Debates*, 17 June 1991, col. 13057.

[2] It should be noted that the tricameral constitution is an apartheid law because representation in the three chambers of parliament is based on statutory race classification.

distinguishes the phenomenon of apartheid from other more simple forms of racial segregation.[3] It is what makes the South African case sui generis. From this perspective, the goal of political independence for whites in South Africa was both an ideology that justified South Africa's rigid social system, as well as a pragmatic way to manage the "race problem."

How was apartheid different? Whereas segregation in other countries envisioned a simple horizontal division, in which the civil rights of persons of color were perceived to be less than those of whites, apartheid was an ideology and policy that Giliomee asserts "envisaged a division between co-equal ethnic groups or nations" (1989:80). Afrikaner nationalism reached its nadir in 1948; victory in the first post–World War II election in South Africa brought a ripening of the ideology of apartheid. Under D. F. Malan, the NP won with a narrow five-seat majority, even though it enjoyed the support of only a minority of the white electorate (42 percent).[4] The NP won the election as an archetypical ethnic party; it outbid more moderate parties on divisive racial and ethnic themes, manipulated communal symbols for the purposes of group mobilization, inculcated fear and reinforced essentialist perceptions, and prevented any hope of a shared destiny with South Africans of other races.

During the early years of National party rule some of the more blatantly racist "pillars of apartheid" were enacted. It was only after H. F. Verwoerd became prime minister in the early 1960s that apartheid in its most pristine ideological form—the notion of separate development—evolved. Table 2.1 highlights the major apartheid laws and their enactment dates.

"Grand apartheid," or "separate development," envisioned nothing less than a grand experiment of social engineering aimed at dividing South Africa into pockets of racial and ethnic homogeneous regions, called national states "by using a full barrage of legislative, economic, and administrative strategies" (Berger and Godsell 1988:8–9). In the ensuing years, the NP pursued grand apartheid policies with little appreciation for their implications on the economy. Parliament created ten homelands, or "self-governing" states, and by 1981 four of them—Transkei, Bophuthatswana, Venda, and Ciskei—accepted nominal independence. A 1970 law stripped all black South Africans of citizenship rights in South Africa, making them foreigners in their own country.

---

[3] For a comparison of apartheid with other forms of racial segregation, see Greenberg 1980; Frederickson 1988; and Cell 1982. For a brief but interesting argument on the legal entrenchment of racial classification in other societies, notably Malaysia, see Horowitz 1991:27.

[4] This was the result of the vote-seat ratio disparity of the first-past-the-post electoral system.

TABLE 2.1
Major Apartheid Laws in South Africa (Act Number/Year of Enactment)

"Pillars" of Apartheid

Population Registration Act (30/1950)
Reservation of Separate Amenities Act (49/1953)
Group Areas Act (77/1957, as amended)
Industrial Conciliation Act (28/1956)
Extension of University Education Act (45/1959)
Prohibition of Improper Political Interference Act (51/1968)
Immorality Act (23/1957)
Prohibition of Mixed Marriages Act (30/1950)

Additional Related Legislation

Separate Representation of Voters' Act (46/1951 and 9/1956)
Promotion of Black Self-Government Act (46/1959)
Prohibition of Foreign Financing of Political Parties Act (51/1968)
Public Safety Act (3/1956)
Riotous Assemblies Act (17/1956, as amended)
Unlawful Organizations Act (34/1950)
Suppression of Communism Act (44/1950)
General Law Amendment Act (76/1962 and 37/1963)
Affected Organizations Act (31/1974)
Internal Security Amendment Act (79/1976)
Gatherings and Demonstrations Act (52/1973)

Legislation Promoting "Separate Development" in South Africa

Black Authorities Act (68/1951)
Promotion of Black Self-Government Act (46/1959)
National States Citizenship Act (26/1970)
Transkei Constitution Act (48/1963)
National States Constitution Act (21/1971)
Separate Representation of Voters Amendment Act (50/1968)
Status of Transkei Act (100/1976)
Status of Boputhatswana Act (86/1977)
Status of Venda Act (107/1979)
Status of Ciskei Act (110/1981)

Source: Kriek 1976:64–67. For an extensive catalog of apartheid laws, see also SAIRR 1978.

Despite too-little, too-late efforts in the mid-1970s to make the homeland system economically viable, the policies of separate development were an abject economic failure. By 1985, 13 percent of central government expenditures were dedicated to homeland development. Yet per capita production in the homelands, according to Lewis (1990:42–51), was less than 5 percent of the level in the rest of South Africa. The homelands, in addition to their failure to gain political legitimacy, were bankrupt. The dream of separate development stands in stark contrast to the reality of industrialization, urbanization, and economic interdependence in the apartheid era.

Shifting Sands in Afrikaner Nationalism

The policies of apartheid and separate development in South Africa were tools of Afrikaner nationalism aimed at protecting the ethnic group from the two forces that were perceived most threatening: the emerging black urban working class and the dominance of English capital. Conversely, a full range of state policies also sought to uplift the predominantly poor, mostly rural, less-educated farmers and workers and to place them into solidly middle-class, urban positions as civil servants, managers, businessmen, and skilled laborers.[5] Afrikaner ethnic nationalists used the distributed capacities of the state to improve the status of their community relative to all other groups. Esman (1987:408), relying on Giliomee's earlier analysis (1979:160–76), demonstrates the methods by which the National party used clientelism to improve the economic lot of its Afrikaner constituency. The NP implemented a mix of protectionism and direct subsidies: de facto job reservation, improved education and training, preferential trade and investment policies, and the most direct tool: extensive employment of Afrikaners in the civil service, the military, and, especially, state enterprises. The post-1948, state-driven capitalism was a successful vehicle for Afrikaner upliftment, and the group changed in important ways: the population became more urbanized and professional. Thus, there was a tremendous change in the National party constituency's interests. Apartheid, in some ways, became superfluous.

A critical split in Afrikanerdom occurred in 1982. Twenty-one NP members—led by Transvaal provincial leader Andries Treurnicht—cast votes of no confidence against Prime Minister P. W. Botha. The *broedertwis* (brotherly quarrel) between the factions was deep; it concerned the fundamental direction of white politics in South Africa (Giliomee 1992). Reformists recognized the shifting balance of power; those who clung to the old orthodoxy did not. Botha supported limited power sharing with South Africa's Coloured and Indian communities, whereas Treurnicht argued for reinvigorating Verwoerdian apartheid. The vote failed, and the dissidents, expelled from the party, re-formed as the Con-

---

[5] Esman argues that the transformation of the economic position of Afrikaners is, comparatively, the "most dramatic case on record" (1987:406).

servative party. Giliomee describes the years leading up to the 1982 split, especially 1976–82, as the "rollercoaster years" (1982:1), during which the ideological shift from apartheid orthodoxy to what historian Moodie (Giliomee 1982:10) has called the "ideology of survival" took place.[6] The National party, with an erstwhile monopoly on apartheid thinking, sought a new set of political rules for the political game.[7]

The Spiral of Discontent

While the economic, political, and ideological contradictions of apartheid became recognized by the perpetrators of apartheid, so too did the fact that the group toward whom the apartheid policy was aimed, the black majority, would resist.[8] The long struggle against apartheid in South Africa set the society on what was assumed to be an inevitable road toward revolution and civil war. Apartheid's victims sought to use all means to prevent its successful implementation and to achieve economic and political rights. The spiral of discontent in South Africa that eventually produced apartheid's demise followed a distinctive pattern: each successive period of resistance—1952, 1960, 1976–77, and 1984–88—was more intense and widespread, and the regime's efforts to contain revolution through repression were less and less effective.

Organized resistance to racial discrimination in South Africa is older than apartheid, and even older than the National party. Ironically, the African National Congress, Africa's oldest liberation organization, was founded in 1912 as the South African Native National Congress, some two years before the founding of the NP. By 1923, having changed its name to the African National Congress (ANC), the organization adopted a Bill of Rights, calling for constitutional equality.

When D. F. Malan and the NP won the 1948 election and began to implement the policies of apartheid, the ANC turned to a more confrontationist style of politics. As the pillars of apartheid were being erected—such as the Population Registration Act in 1950—the ANC responded with its first major program of resistance and began its transformation from a small elite to a mass-based organization. The cam-

[6] See also Adam 1978, 1983 and Baker 1987–88.

[7] The secretive Afrikaner Broederbond (brotherhood) played an important role in the formulation of the new strategy. Its 1989 document, titled "Political Values for the Survival of the Afrikaner," argued that the exclusion of blacks from political participation had become a "threat to the survival of the white man." For further information on the role of the Broederbond in formulating NP strategy at this critical turning point, see Giliomee 1992:22.

[8] Several excellent and fairly comprehensive studies on the struggle against apartheid have emerged since the onset of negotiation: see Marx 1992 and Lodge et al. 1991.

paign, begun on 26 June 1952, combined strikes and civil disobedience to confront implementation of apartheid laws such as separate amenities, segregated sections on trains, and curfew and pass laws. In 1955, the ANC joined forces with the white Congress of Democrats (which had sympathized with the Defiance Campaign), the South African Indian Congress, the Coloured People's Organization, and the South Africa Congress of Trade Unions (SACTU, formed in 1955) in a "Congress of the People." At Kliptown, a Coloured township near Johannesburg, the organizations met to debate the Freedom Charter, which was officially endorsed by the ANC in 1956. The charter embodied the ideals of "multiracialism" and a common South African nationhood beyond racial exclusivity, and embraced some ideals of traditional liberalism.[9] In response to the more accommodationist stance of the ANC, the Pan-Africanist Congress (PAC) was formed in 1959 by a breakaway group of "Africanists."

In 1960, at a PAC-organized demonstration against the hated pass laws, in the township of Sharpeville 69 people were killed (including eight women and ten children) and 180 wounded. As Lodge (1983:225) writes, "Sharpeville was a turning point in the struggle, when protest finally hardened into resistance, and when African politicians were forced to begin thinking in terms of a revolutionary strategy" (1983:225). Following the events at Sharpeville and the repressive action of the state in its wake, the ANC and the PAC both reassessed their commitment to nonviolent forms of protest action against apartheid. By mid-1961 both major African nationalist movements formed insurgency branches to step up the level of resistance against the continued introduction of apartheid, which intensified during the early years of Verwoerd's tenure. The ANC formed Umkhonto we Sizwe (MK, "spear of the nation") and the PAC formed Poqo (meaning "alone" in Xhosa).

Just prior to being banned in 1960, the ANC had begun to establish itself as an exile organization; over the course of the next three years, it set out to organize internationally and solicit support for its cause. By August 1962 many of the top leaders of the ANC were arrested at the Liliesleaf farm in Rivonia. The accused, including Nelson Mandela (already in prison on a lesser charge), were tried and found guilty of treason in June 1964, and imprisoned for life on Robben Island.

With conditions in exile trying, one of the few avenues of dissent open was student organizations, and in the late 1960s many African university students had become involved in various student movements, among them Black Consciousness organizations. By early 1973, however, the state moved to ban the most influential student leaders. Under the influ-

[9] The term *multiracialism* was subsequently replaced in the discourse by the term *nonracialism*.

ence of Black Consciousness, anger and frustration grew in the black communities in South Africa in the early 1970s. With a worsening economic situation and the resultant growing unemployment, strikes increased and political activity began to become resurgent. Forty-three percent of blacks were believed to live below the poverty line (Kane-Berman 1978:54). On 16 June 1976, some twenty thousand students, many under the influence of Black Consciousness philosophy, marched in Soweto (the largest black township in South Africa, just to the southwest of central Johannesburg) against a decree by the Department of Bantu Education that Afrikaans had to be used as one language of instruction in black secondary schools. Though the language issue was central, it was not the only grievance of the Soweto children. Indeed, as Kane-Berman (1978:25) argues, the revived militancy had been brewing for some eighteen months prior, and the demands included not just the problems of Bantu education, but the pass laws, political harassment, and the ever-present issue of franchise rights.

Though initially peaceful, the march in Soweto on 16 June turned into a melee, with police shooting indiscriminately at the marchers. A wave of unrest flared throughout the rest of 1976 and into much of 1977, including school strikes and boycotts, huge marches and demonstrations, sabotage of government offices, ongoing skirmishes with the police, and mass funerals. The state responded to events of 1976 with a widespread crackdown. Schoolchildren believed to be involved in the uprising were rounded up under the powers of section 6 of the Terrorism Act of 1967, which allowed police to hold persons incommunicado indefinitely, and many children—even those under the age of sixteen—were arrested under the wide powers provided to the police under this statute. Steven Biko, a Black Consciousness leader who had been arrested on 18 August 1977, died in detention twenty-six days later.

The events of 1984–88, when the spiral of discontent reached an apex, were decisive in the struggle against the system of apartheid. This era saw the most widespread and intense uprising in the cycle of revolt and repression. The development of black trade unionism and local autonomous community groups in the post-Soweto period was especially important for the wave of renewed resistance to apartheid and general township disturbances that would erupt in the mid-1980s. Beginning in 1973 black trade unionism began to reemerge. Statutory restrictions on black trade-union bargaining rights were lifted in 1979, in an effort to simply try to control the wave of union organization that could not be suppressed.[10] As

---

[10] Friedman (1987) traces the history of the union movement in South Africa, focusing particularly on the organization of "emerging" trade unions in the late 1970s, as opposed to the "parallel," or established, unions created by the state.

Friedman (1987:9) notes, what was being gained in the factories was now being demanded in the townships and political sphere.

In the townships, scores of local civic and ad hoc political organizations formed. The key event in the development of a broad front of locally grounded anti-apartheid organizations was the founding of the United Democratic Front (UDF)—a loose association of some six hundred community groups, trade unions, and churches—on 20 August 1983. The UDF coalesced around the principles of Charterism—populist nonracialism. In the same year, the National Forum Committee, consisting chiefly of the Azanian People's Organization (AZAPO, with a Black Consciousness orientation) and radical Western Cape groups, formed to counter the Charterist group.

Unlike the events of 1960, when black political protest preceded constitutional changes, in 1984, major uprisings followed them. On 3 September, violence in the Pretoria-Witwatersrand-Vereeniging (PWV) area, again led by youths, spread into general turmoil throughout the country, with the "epicenters" of violence in the Johannesburg townships and Eastern Cape. Two successive cycles of violence—in the PWV (September to November 1984) and in the Eastern Cape (February to May 1985)—erupted, and by 21 July 1985 the regime declared a limited state of emergency that affected a full quarter of the country's population. During the next year, filled with the turbulent events of growing insurrection, the state of emergency was extended to the entire country.

The cycle of revolt and resistance that erupted in the period 1984–88 was different from earlier patterns of resistance in several different ways. Friedman (1986) identifies six elements of a "sharp departure" from previous periods: for the first time in the struggle, violent resistance was aimed at those perceived to be collaborating with apartheid structures; the economic plight of blacks was substantially worse; foreign pressure had intensified; political activity shifted to the UDF-allied organizations, which included the enormously effective rent and business boycotts; the black trade union movement blossomed; and political organizations began to openly identify with the banned ANC and its imprisoned and exiled leadership. Once again, the rising tide of revolution in South Africa seemed as if an eruption of full-scale civil war was inevitable, if not already begun.

Table 2.2 shows the rising spiral of discontent in South Africa for the periods 1952, 1960, 1976–77, and 1984–88. The table illustrates how resistance to apartheid and the system geared to fight it were interlocked in an accelerating cycle of revolution and repression. How long before yet another round of violence and repression would begin? And if it began, how long would it last and how many lives would be lost? And the next time, would the state have the capacity to contain it? These questions

TABLE 2.2
The Spiral of Discontent: Rising Revolutionary Conflict
in South Africa, 1952, 1960, 1976–1977, 1984–1988

	Arrests	Related Deaths
Defiance Campaign (June 1952)	8,000	0
Sharpeville (1960)	18,000	67
Soweto (June 1976–Feb. 1977)	5,980	700[a] (575)[b]
1984–85 (Sept. 1984–July 1985)	14,000	740
1985–88 (July 1985–Dec. 1988)	31,000	3361

Sources: For data from 1952 and Sharpeville, Lodge 1983; for Soweto and for 1984–85, Howe 1985; and for 1984–88, IPSA 1989.
[a]South African Institute of Race Relations (SAIRR) estimate.
[b]Government-sponsored Cillie Commission reported figure.

were foremost in the minds of the National party leaders when they decided to finally dismantle apartheid.

The pursuit of apartheid entailed tremendous costs in international relationships for the South African regime, which in turn influenced the resources available to repress it. Apartheid in South Africa became one of the most pressing causes of the international community in the twentieth century. There is clear linkage between action in the international political arena and the ultimate end of apartheid in South Africa. Following in lockstep with the rising spiral of discontent in South Africa, the international community's attitude and approach to the struggle in South Africa changed dramatically after Sharpeville, especially at the United Nations (Stultz 1987).

Rejection of South Africa's policies grew steadily between Sharpeville and Soweto. In 1968 the first UN resolution was adopted that labeled apartheid "a crime against humanity" (2396 [XXIII]). In 1972, the United Nations refused to accept the South African delegation's credentials, and it lost its voting rights. The effects of punitive measures against apartheid in South Africa were manifested in two important ways. First, the international campaign effectively stifled the economy, particularly in the 1980s, such that the sheer macroeconomic costs of continued racial domination were raised to unacceptable levels. And second, sanctions and the resulting decline in economic performance had a profound effect on the perceptions and attitudes of white South Africans; whether or not the impact of sanctions on the bread-and-butter concerns of the dominant class was significant, the perception of economic harm was sufficient enough to lead to a softening in white political attitudes about the sustainability of apartheid.

The South African economy is a relatively open one, and its dependency on international trade and finance rests on the need for a market for its extractive industry products, for a source of capital for industrial modernization, and for a source of machinery and technology (Lewis 1990:86) Between 1960 and 1964, South Africa witnessed an enormous outflow of capital (Price 1987:105; Lewis 1990:64). When the townships erupted again in September 1984, the ramifications once more affected South Africa's international position. By September 1985, a year after the first widescale violence on the Rand, the anti-apartheid movement in the United States, which grew incredibly in size and influence in those years, successfully pressured U.S. institutional investors—pension funds, union and university trusts, and the like—to curtail and in many cases withdraw investments in firms dealing with South Africa. When President P. W. Botha, in August 1985, defiantly challenged the world to frustrate the policies of the South African regime, international creditor banks, following the lead of Chase Manhattan, called in their short-term loans, causing a foreign exchange crisis and a moratorium on interest repayment by the regime.

The costs of combating trade and financial sanctions, both informal and formal, combined with the costs of maintaining the security establishment at home (defense expenditures grew from 1 percent of the GDP in 1960 to 5 percent in 1980), mounted in the minds of decision makers in the South African government.[11] Even though in the long term, South Africa would have been able to fund itself, sanctions would have imposed tremendous costs on the economy, as Coker argues: "South Africa can finance up to 90% of investment from its own resources, but that the additional 10% of foreign capital makes all the difference between 2% or 5% growth a year" (1989:55–56). Most important, during the sanctions years, South Africa was cut off from the critical technology it needed for sustained economic development and paid heavy "political premiums" for commodities such as oil and munitions. As Price notes, the government faced a "fundamental security dilemma" (1987:108) in its efforts to protect the system of apartheid at home while maintaining access to markets, technology, and capital abroad. The dilemma could be resolved only by scrapping apartheid.

In a deeply divided state such as South Africa, a loss of ethnic cohesion—driven by changing interests and beliefs—undermines the ability of the ethnic regime to survive. This is especially true in terms of elite attitudes within the dominant group. Huntington (1981:11) writes:

---

[11] A number of major studies have focused on the costs of international trade and financial sanctions to the South African economy. See, as a sampling of more recent works, IRRC 1990; Bethlehem 1988; Lipton 1988; Love 1988; Southall 1988; and Becker 1988.

"revolutionary violence does not . . . have to be successful to be effective. It simply has to cause divisions among the dominant group over ways to deal with it." The imminent demise of apartheid in South Africa, brought on by the bankruptcy of a racial ideology, increasing domestic economic costs, growing internal unrest and its political, social, and economic costs, and an increasingly hostile international environment, finally led the ruling National party, which had invented and erected apartheid in 1948, in 1991 to turn its back on the very political institutions it worked so hard to build. The rules of the old political game became too costly compared to the benefits of creating a new political game that included the black majority.

POLARIZATION AND STALEMATE

Just as the ad hoc policies of segregation in the 1940s and early 1950s gave way to a more rigorous ideological formulation through the policies of separate development, in the late 1970s separate development gave way to an even more refined form of white domination, that of the "total onslaught." The justification of this ideological shift was simple: maintain the system of white domination and, to the extent possible, the aims of separate development (Ciskei and Venda were granted independence in 1979 and 1981, respectively) while adjusting the system to the realities of the post-Soweto pressures emanating from at home and abroad. Reform apartheid was an attempt to "share power without losing control" (van zyl Slabbert 1989).

Reform Apartheid

The origins of reform apartheid lie in the patterns of white politics prevailing when P. W. Botha became prime minister in September 1978; his election was a clear victory for the *verligte* faction within the National party, which advocated some liberalization. Botha brought the new pragmatic approach of total strategy. In this view, reform and security were intricately linked: reform was required to stave off mounting international and internal pressure—termed the "total onslaught"—and to maintain security, and security was necessary for reform. And the plan had a parochial political angle as well: to the verligte liberals Botha promised moves away from the strict ideological confines of apartheid, and to the *verkrampte* hard-liners he promised law and order and the basic bottom line: maintenance of white control.

The reform program launched by Botha in the early 1980s sought to provide participation to disenfranchised South Africans through co-optive structures within the overall control of the white-controlled central state. Coincidental with political reform was the move toward reforms in industrial relations and urbanization policies and an allowance for strictly limited participation of black South Africans in co-optive structures at the regional and local level. Reform apartheid was the first major shift from what was considered to be ideal to what was perceived to be possible.

At the center of the reform program was the "new dispensation": a set of unilaterally imposed political institutions that would—when combined with the eventual establishment of a still separate (until 1985, as yet undefined) structure for African representation—bring Coloureds and Indians into a central governmental and allow for reform institutions at the regional and local level to coincide with the security management structures already in place. The cornerstone of the reform program was a Tricameral Parliament to co-opt Coloureds and Indians into a "power-sharing" scheme while black disenfranchisement continued. Plans for a new system had been underway even in the Vorster years but came to the fore with the rise of Botha.[12] When they first faced the white electorate in 1981, Botha and the National party were returned to power with an only marginally reduced majority, having campaigned on a twelve-point plan that included power sharing with Coloured and Indian communities. In February 1983 Botha unveiled a new constitution, which was put before the electorate in a whites-only referendum held on 2 November 1983. Whites approved the new dispensation by a 66 percent majority. Botha had successfully sold the co-optation idea to his white constituency.

The new institutions set up a system that was at once very complicated and at the same time very simple.

- The parliamentary prime minister of the Westminster system was replaced by a de Gualle–style presidency with broad legislative and executive powers; the president was indirectly elected through the parliament.
- A three-chamber parliament was created with separate chambers for whites, Coloureds, and Indians based on the racial classifications of the Population Registration Act.
- A distinction between the "own" affairs of racially based population groups and "general" affairs of all population groups was created.
- The President's Council (which replaced the Senate in 1980) was to be given a legislative role in approving disputed bills. The President's Council was loaded in favor of the white majority through the 4:2:1 ratio.[13]

[12] In 1977, following the Soweto crisis, the Vorster government established a commission to investigate alternative constitutional options. These developments are described in Boulle 1984.

[13] The 4:2:1 ratio in the President's Council was the linchpin for retaining white control in the new system. Based on the relative population ratio of the white, Coloured, and Indian

White hegemony was assured through the 4:2:1 ratio, and Africans remained disenfranchised. The justification of separate development ideology—that Africans constitute ten separate nations—was used to argue that if chambers for Africans were to have been created, as constitutional development minister Chris Heunis said, "you would have to create a chamber for each of the ten black nations in South Africa and then one for each of the four independent states. . . . It is just not practical or possible."[14]

Although the tricameral plan was the centerpiece of reform, the state also sought to downplay the more odiously discriminatory aspects of apartheid by repealing those laws which highlighted the underlying inequalities associated with race classification. Table 2.3 lists the major reforms of the Botha era. The extent of these reforms indicates a recognition that simple apartheid as it had been known for nearly four decades was going to collapse. It was the regime's attempt to placate the critics of apartheid—to deracialize society to a certain extent—and to stave off the growing sanctions campaign abroad, just as it was trying to implement new institutions at home. Reform apartheid also aimed to create a black middle class to serve as a structural buffer between poverty-stricken blacks and more affluent whites. Nevertheless, as Baker argues, "a powerless but prosperous black middle class would be no guarantee of stability. . . . As long as political rights are defined by color, class interests will be frustrated and other more emotional forces will take over" (1988:48).

In the light of time, the tricameral system was clearly a failure, and it is viewed so even by those who erected it. Its fundamental flaw was the continued reliance of the system on the basic criterion of race and the exclusion of Africans. A former cabinet minister and NP secretary general, Stoffel van der Merwe, says: "The basic flaw is that it excluded black people. This was always seen that it was a temporary thing. . . . But that part of the argument was not accepted; therefore it gave rise to all these problems."[15] The institutional choice calculations that underlie reform

---

communities, the members of the President's Council are appointed on the ratio of four whites to two Coloureds to one Indian, with sixty members in all. If a bill—all legislation originates from the president—does not garner the support of one of the houses (after consideration by joint standing committees of all three houses), it can be referred to the President's Council for consideration. The President's Council can be requested to make either a recommendation or a decision; while a recommendation from the council is not binding on the houses, a decision is. The president can then sign the bill, enacting it into law, notwithstanding the objection of one or two of the Houses. The point is this: as long as the president enjoys the majority in the House of Assembly (white house), he will necessarily also enjoy a majority in the President's Council. If either the Coloured or Indian House refuses to pass his legislation, he can easily refer it to the President's Council, where the 4:2:1 ratio *guarantees* a majority and eventual enactment of the bill.

[14] *Cape Times*, 26 September 1983.

[15] Interview with the author, 25 June 1991.

TABLE 2.3
Major Reforms of the P. W. Botha Era, 1979–1989

- Scrapping of the Mixed Marriages and Immorality acts to make legal sexual and marriage relations across the color bar (1985)
- The acknowledgment of the rights of urban blacks to participate—in own affairs structures—in decision making through Black Local Authorities, multiracial Regional Services Councils, provincial executive bodies, and a joint executive authority for KwaZulu and Natal (1985)
- Changes in the Improper Political Interference Act, allowing for the formation of multiracial political parties (1986)
- Restoration of South African citizenship for those living and working outside the TBVC states (1986)
- The scrapping of influx control (Abolition of Influx Control Act) and the introduction of a uniform identity document (1986)
- The granting of ninety-nine-year leasehold rights for urban blacks in certain areas (1986)
- Making open university education available at certain universities (1986)
- Changes in the Group Areas Act that allowed for the opening of Central Business Districts to all traders (1987)
- The demarcation of certain residential areas as "gray areas" and (ex post facto) acknowledgment that certain neighborhoods could be legally integrated (1988)

apartheid were guided by a simple set of understandings: the belief by Botha and the leadership of the National party that the total strategy would work, that the ANC and the anti-apartheid struggle could be divided, co-opted, and neutralized. It was a classic zero-sum view of the conflict, one in which the government thought it could unilaterally impose its preferred outcome. This strategy brought not a placation of the anti-apartheid struggle, but its revival.

The Polarization of Politics, 1979–1986

South African political scientist Peter Vale remarks that the most positive feature of the tricameral system was its unintended effects: it led to the formation of the United Democratic Front in August 1983, established to mobilize resistance on a national scale to Coloured and Indian participation in the tricameral institutions.[16] More than anything else, the new constitution precipitated the widespread domestic and subsequent international revolt against the South African government in the mid-1980s. Opponents of the system realized that the government was prepared to adjust white minority domination but not abolish it. That realization led

[16] Interview with the author, 3 March 1991.

to a popular upsurge, or as O'Donnell, Schmitter, and Whitehead have termed similar events, the "explosion of a highly re-politicized and angry society" (1986: pt. 4, p. 49).

The revolt against Botha's reform apartheid plans can be divided into two phases.[17] The first phase is the interim period between the revival of the struggle in the late 1970s (aided by the legalization of African trade unions in 1979) and the introduction of a nationwide state of emergency in July 1986, and the second phase is the post–state of emergency period from 1986 to the advent of the de Klerk administration in early 1989.[18] The spiraling cycle of revolt and repression that accompanied reform without real change had widened the base of anti-apartheid opposition in society. Churches, white liberals, and the press were newly targeted as enemies of the state, leading to a *polarization of politics* both across the political spectrum and within both the system and the struggle.

By the early 1980s, the Black Consciousness movement had been virtually decimated by the detention of its leadership, and the ANC in exile had not been able to successfully maintain a viable internal organization (Lodge 1988a). The only organizations capable of effectively countering the power of the state internally were the emergent trade unions, although the lack of an organized political counterpart caused them to limit their activities primarily to industrial action.

The UDF was officially inaugurated in August 1983, when more than 600 delegates from 320 organizations met outside Cape Town to constitute the loose federation of anti-apartheid groups. The UDF, according to its own inaugural statement, set out to "[unite] all our people, wherever they may be in the cities and countryside, the factories and mines, schools, colleges, and universities, houses and sports fields, churches, mosques, and temples, to fight for our freedom" (Barrell 1984:12). The UDF quickly grew to become the most important legal opposition movement in the country.

Why did the UDF grow so quickly in this environment? The UDF organized itself around principles in resistance to the co-optive nature of the tricameral system, and placed itself in line as the internal successor to the ANC. It pledged allegiance to the Freedom Charter and emphasized a nonracial vision of a future South African society; it actively sought to ratchet up international pressure against the regime. The UDF was, above all, a Charterist organization.[19] The UDF appealed across generation,

---

[17] This distinction is based in part on the analysis of van zyl Slabbert (1989:75–83), although for this work the earlier period is argued to have begun in roughly 1979.

[18] A well-detailed overview of this period in the struggle is *Washington Post* reporter Steven Mufson's recent book (1990).

[19] The National Forum, representing a more exclusive Black Consciousness stance, was also founded in late 1983 as an Africanist counterpoint to the UDF.

ethnic, and class divisions, generalizing dissent over a wide range of political, economic, and social issues. At its height in 1985–86, the UDF comprised some 700 organizations. Mobilization by the UDF in 1984 focused around what would emerge as the two dominant principles of the internal struggle throughout both phases of the revolt and repression: noncollaboration and ungovernability. Both led to a surge of township resistance aimed at countering the total strategy reforms, which Friedman calls a "rising spiral of random militancy and [state] repression" (1986:20).

The critical test of the struggle's response to the tricameral plans came in August 1984, the date set for elections to the Coloured and Indian chambers of the Tricameral Parliament. The elections—which were characterized by the outbreak of revolutionary violence—were a catastrophe for the reformist plan. In an effort to squelch preelection resistance, the security forces rounded up virtually all the UDF leadership, thereby removing any potential legitimacy from the result. Despite the detentions, the boycotts of what then-UDF activist Rushdie Sears calls "dummy elections" were a resounding success.[20] In the polling for the Coloured House of Representatives, only 18 percent of the eligible voters turned out, and even fewer (16.6 percent) of the eligible Indian population voted.[21] The reform process had begun to slip from the regime's control.

On 3 September 1984, the townships once again erupted in a campaign of violent resistance that would—unlike Sharpeville and Soweto—not be quickly repressed. Nineteen-eighty-five proved to be the worst year in memory in the minds of many South Africans, black and white. As an omen of the breadth of opposition that would develop over the course of that turbulent year, riots and general civil unrest during January began to escalate in and around the Johannesburg area and in many other cities. By mid-June, the upsurge of unrest had engulfed virtually every region of the country.[22] In this revolutionary climate, the ANC held its Second Consultative Conference in Kabwe, Zambia, on 16–23 June 1985. It resolved to launch a "people's war" that would culminate in a National Democratic Revolution and the overthrow of the white minority state. The purpose of the National Democratic Revolution was clear: it aimed to provide the critical catalyst in a spontaneous revolution and to "defeat the enemy."[23]

The Kabwe conference was the ANC's affirmation of its perception of the conflict as a zero-sum game in which its aim was the total collapse of the regime and the installation of a people's government. Whether the underlying goal was to achieve an armed insurrection in classic revolu-

[20] Interview with the author, 17 April 1991.

[21] See Patel 1984 for a critical analysis of the turnout figures.

[22] For a chronology of civil unrest during the first half of 1985, see IPSA 1985:6–9.

[23] Ellis, in a cogent summary of the ANC's experiences in exile, notes that "the ANC's confidence in its military triumph . . . was misplaced" (1991:446).

tionary fashion or simply to "force Pretoria to the negotiating table," the end effect was the same.[24] Rantete and Giliomee (1992), outlining the ANC's consideration of negotiation versus revolution, suggest that both strategies sought to achieve the same goal: a "transfer of power" to the ANC as a national liberation movement in a classic decolonization model.

The result of this widespread revolt and repression, especially in 1984–86, was the polarization of politics in South Africa. A clear division developed between a regime seeking to impose a co-optive solution and the widely growing sentiment that an end to apartheid could be accomplished only through the unequivocal overthrow of the National party government. Any moderate center that might have existed at the onset of the reform program at the beginning of the decade had, following the onset of a cycle of revolt and repression, evaporated. The thrust of the political system under these circumstances was *centrifugal*.

Following the imposition of a nationwide state of emergency in mid-1986, a second period of revolt and repression set in, one in which the reform process virtually halted and the anti-apartheid forces settled in for yet another long period of sustained revolt under deeply trying conditions. For the struggle, the people's war was not likely to succeed in dislodging the largest, best-trained, and best-equipped security force in Africa, and for the system, no amount of co-optive enticement would bring it the legitimacy it needed to survive indefinitely. A stalemate ensued.

Although the Botha administration had gone ahead with some planned reforms even in the face of the violence of 1985–86, such as the abolition of influx control, by early 1987 Botha decided to seek a new mandate from the white electorate before making further moves. In the election, held 6 May 1987, the white electorate returned the National party to power, albeit with its lowest popular majority (52 percent) since the 1948 election. The Conservative party (CP), in its first nationwide test of strength in a general election, outpolled the liberal Progressive Federal party (PFP) and captured nearly 27 percent of the vote. The CP became the official opposition in the white House of Assembly; its strategy of outbidding the reformist NP had succeeded. The National party had lost its ideological rudder; Peter Gastrow, then an independent MP (later a member of the Democratic party, the successor to the PFP), said, "The Nationalists are in the ideological wilderness. After feeding the country a steady diet of apartheid for the last 40 years, they are now totally confused. They can't

[24] Lodge argues that these apparently differing strategies were not the result of factional divisions within the ANC, but were instead "a difference separating realists from romantics" (1988a:251). The ANC was not a state in exile, he argues, and any wholesale smashing of the South African state in Leninist fashion was not in the interest of the organization; its interest lay in inheriting the edifice of the South African state, not destroying it.

say where they're going, because they don't know."[25] Despite a mediocre attempt during 1988 to get a National Statutory Council off the ground—the legislation had been once again amended—no further reforms ensued until January 1989, when the succession struggle to replace an aging and ailing Botha began.

The UDF/ANC, on the other hand, though successful in preventing co-optation, was not in a position to enforce a solution on the regime. From both perspectives, a hegemonic strategy to defeat the enemy had failed to produce the desired result. The interaction of reform, revolt, and repression had yielded a political stalemate, one that imposed unacceptably high costs on the system and the struggle. It was what South African Institute of Race Relations executive director John Kane-Berman has called "a violent equilibrium" (1988:i).

The stalemate was essentially an inconclusive "struggle over state power, capacities, and resources" (James 1989:15). Oscar Dhlomo, executive chair of the Institute for Multi-party Democracy, argues that both sides of the polarized divided had reached a "cul-de-sac" in their strategies to wage the conflict: "The government had reached the realization that the policy of apartheid didn't have a future. It had reached some sort of cul-de-sac; it couldn't be taken further. The ANC . . . too had reached a cul-de-sac, of sorts. For over thirty years they had been involved in a strategy of change that didn't seem to work."[26]

The stalemate also precipitated a condition of a dual power in South Africa, roughly equal in the balance. The UDF and other ANC-allied forces held sway in most townships and possessed international credibility, whereas the government controlled the central organs of the state— including, notably, the security forces and the commanding heights of the economy. Owing to these power bases, these actors and their allies became the two main contenders for power in South Africa. Cheryl Carolus, a South African Communist party (SACP) and ANC member, outlined the power dynamic that had developed:

> One had arrived at a dual power in South Africa where . . . you had the two chief contenders for power, the National party and the ANC, and each had a broad range of supporters. . . . These two key performers occupied different aspects of political power in South Africa, exclusively so. . . . So it became impossible for the government to implement its own policies; the ANC could effectively checkmate that. Both parties realized that they occupy strategic positions, they are very powerful, but also lacked key elements of being able to seize overall political power in the country. Because of that realization, they realized that they had to enter into negotiation.[27]

[25] *Christian Science Monitor,* 24 February 1988.
[26] Interview with the author, 20 May 1991.
[27] Interview with the author, 24 April 1991.

The stalemate in South Africa created conditions under which negotiation was mutually beneficial for both sides, but it was the confluence of several precipitating factors that brought the parties to the table, many of which would have been unpredictable in 1987–88.

BREAKTHROUGH

The political stalemate that reached its nadir in early 1989 had many observers convinced that South Africa would remain involved in a "protracted social conflict" (Azar and Burton 1986) that was unlikely to be soon transformed. Comparatively, pessimism seemed warranted for South Africa. Well-respected scholars of politics in divided societies, such as Adrian Guelke, saw nothing but bleakness in South Africa's future in early 1989. "The durability of the impasse in South Africa should not be underestimated. . . . The roots of political impasse are to be found in the gulf between the political solutions prescribed by the outside world and the actual political possibilities based on the relative strength of the various protagonists inside . . . a useful if unpalatable conclusion for both analysts and policymakers" (1991:160, 161).[28] The conventional wisdom was wrong. A confluence of events in 1989 that produced a dramatic breakthrough in South Africa was a logical turn of the conflict, spurred by unpredictable precipitating events.

Prenegotiation

There are many antecedent events to the onset of negotiations that enabled de Klerk to take dramatic steps on 2 February 1990. These events form the prenegotiation, or "diagnostic," phase (Zartman 1989) of negotiation, which, following Saunders (1985), can be considered in four stages: arrival at a shared definition of the problem; commitment to a negotiated settlement when parties conclude a fair settlement is likely; arrangement of the negotiation; and commencement of negotiation. These stages are not necessarily in sequence, but each is necessary if formal negotiation is to bear fruit. In some cases, like South Africa, parties can begin negotiation without a shared definition of the problem— negotiation was initially a tactic by which they could prevail.

The first reported meetings between top government officials and jailed members of the ANC date back as early as 1987, during the height of the state of emergency and the subsequent repression. According to reporter Hennie Serfontein of the *Weekly Mail*, the first discussions involved talks between Nelson Mandela and minister of justice Kobie Coetsee, held in

---

[28] Despite the publication date of January 1991, it clear from the text that Guelke's analysis of South Africa leaves off sometime in early 1989.

July 1987 at the minister's home in Cape Town.[29] In these early talks, which took place on and off over a period of eighteen months, the government tried to persuade Mandela to abandon core tenets of ANC strategy—including the armed struggle, alignment with the South African Communist party, sanctions, disinvestment and international isolation, and mass mobilization—as a precondition to his release and to negotiation with the ANC.[30] The talks deadlocked over Mandela's refusal to abandon armed struggle, and, in order to rejuvenate the dialogue, the agenda shifted to the release from prison of older members of the ANC still in custody, particularly aging ANC leaders Govan Mbeki and Walter Sisulu.

Mandela later confirmed these early discussions, and emphasized that preconditions would not be accepted outright because the government had to "consider us discussing the future of South Africa—as equals" (as cited in Rantete and Giliomee 1992:518). These initial exploratory talks were important in terms of the earlier stages of prenegotiation—political leaders could examine the option of negotiation away from the public eye, assess the intentions of other parties and the likelihood of reciprocity, all with a low "exit cost" if talks did not ensue (Stein 1989:246).

In the light of this murky backdrop, a secret letter Nelson Mandela wrote in March 1989 to President Botha makes sense. The letter was later leaked and illegally published by the *Weekly Mail*—Mandela, after all, was a banned person and could not be quoted. It contained several key paragraphs that were critical to the onset of negotiation. Penned in his own hand, Mandela's letter said:

> At the outset, I must point out that I make this move without consultation with the ANC. I am a loyal and disciplined member of the ANC. . . . The step I am taking should, therefore, not be seen as the beginning of actual negotiations between the government and the ANC. My task is a limited one, and that is to bring the country's two major political bodies to the negotiating table. The renunciation of violence by either the government or the ANC should not be a pre-condition to but the result of negotiation.
>
> The key to the whole situation is a negotiated settlement, and a meeting between the government and the ANC will be the first major step toward lasting peace in the country. . . . Two political issues will have to be addressed at such a meeting: first, the demand for majority rule in a unitary state; secondly,

[29] *Weekly Mail,* 4–10 August 1989.

[30] Such demands by the government would certainly coincide with public statements made by Botha several times, as early as January 1985, that Mandela would be released if armed struggle was renounced. According to Rantete and Giliomee (1992), there were three specific demands: renunciation of violence, an ANC break with the SACP, and an abandonment of the majority rule principle.

the concern of white South Africa over this demand, as well as the insistence of whites on structural guarantees that majority rule will not mean domination of the white minority by blacks.

Mandela continued on the question of how a negotiation process could be established:

It may well be that this should be done at least in two stages. In the first, the organization and the government will work out together the preconditions for a proper climate for negotiations. Up to now both parties have simply been broadcasting their conditions for negotiations without putting them directly to each other. The second stage would be the actual negotiations themselves when the climate is ripe for doing so. Any other approach would contain the danger of an irresolvable stalemate.

He concluded:

The move I have taken provides you with the opportunity to overcome the current deadlock, and to normalize the country's political situation. I hope you will seize it without delay.[31]

This letter set the stage for the 5 July 1989 meeting between P. W. Botha, president, and Nelson Mandela, prisoner (which Mandela had apparently insisted on at the onset of the consultations with Coetsee and the government negotiating team).[32] The Mandela letter is absolutely critical to understanding the subsequent course of negotiations in South Africa. Prenegotiation communications serve to structure the negotiation through specifying the boundaries of discussion (i.e., defining the issues to be on the table) and defining the participants (Stein 1989:252). Thus, the earlier stages of the negotiation process have an important bearing on the outcome.

However, in between these events (and to a lesser extent, preceding them), several important sets of interactions took place beyond the direct contacts that would later serve to facilitate the dialogue between the regime and the ANC. In August 1985, Professor H. W. van der Merwe of the University of Cape Town and Afrikaans newspaper editor (*Beeld*) Piet Muller ventured to Harare, Zimbabwe, for meetings with the ANC. This

[31] *Weekly Mail*, 26 January 1990; the very last paragraph is reported as part of the same letter in the *Christian Science Monitor*, 26 January 1990, although it is not included in the *Weekly Mail*'s report. According to Rantete and Giliomee, a further demand was made in Mandela's prison writings, namely that "the political situation could not be normalized through negotiations while apartheid laws were still on the statute book" (1992:519).

[32] The letter was passed on to the ANC's mission in exile through Mandela's "own means" and was the basis for what became the ANC-backed OAU Harare Declaration (discussed below).

initial meeting was followed up in September by a group of major South African industrialists, who had flown to Lusaka, Zambia, for talks with the leaders of the exiled ANC National Executive Committee on the economy and political system in South Africa after apartheid. Following these first groundbreaking trips, a whole series of meetings—at least seventy-five over 1985–89—began to take place between white South African liberals and the ANC. The meetings were first conducted by primarily English-speaking whites, but later also Afrikaners, and began to melt down the propagandized visions of the enemy that permeated white society during the years of the total onslaught ideology.[33]

Perhaps the most important of these "second track diplomacy" meetings was the July 1987 Dakar encounter, organized by IDASA, between some fifty mostly Afrikaans-speaking whites and members of the ANC, and the July 1989 conference in Lusaka organized by the Five Freedoms Forum. The final communiqué of the Dakar conference resoundingly supported the notion that a negotiated settlement to South Africa's conflict could result only if the regime recognized the role of the ANC: it noted that "serious discussions with the ANC must form part of the search for the resolution of conflict and the transition toward a peaceful and just future."[34] These meetings helped inculcate an understanding among political elites on both vends of the political spectrum that negotiation could in fact yield a mutually beneficial outcome. In terms of prenegotiation, such track-two diplomacy served to help the parties arrive at a common definition of the problem, explore negotiations as the most attractive alternative available to the players, create a core of moderation in an environment of overwhelming polarization, and begin to lay the groundwork for public acceptance of a negotiated solution (Stein 1989). Second-track diplomacy was also important for within-group politics, bolstering moderates in both camps who believed whites and blacks could live together harmoniously in South Africa.

Yet the event that signaled the onset of the impending, far-reaching change in South Africa was an unpredictable one: in early January 1989, President P. W. Botha suffered a stroke. A peculiar situation developed within the National party when in February then–minister of national

---

[33] Price (1991:240) provides a chronology of these trips (both successful and unsuccessful) with a list of the delegations; see Louw 1989:160–67 for a more extensive list, although many meetings with the ANC and South Africans from "home" were never reported.

[34] The concluding press statement from the conference is printed in *Democracy in Action* (IDASA), August 1987. Price (1991:241) also cites the passage. The Dakar conference had a tremendous impact on a number of very influential Afrikaners, including University of Cape Town academic Hermann Giliomee, who upon returning to South Africa wrote a widely read column in the *Sunday Times* urging "The Third Way," implicitly calling for direct talks with the ANC. The editorial and the series of newspaper debates it provoked are reprinted in Giliomee and Schlemmer 1989b:10–26.

education F. W. de Klerk was elected national leader of the party.[35] In March, a bitter power struggle ensued in which the party attempted to nudge Botha from his very powerful position as state president, while the obstinate seventy-two year-old—nicknamed the Big Crocodile—clung to power. The intraparty crisis was resolved in April when Botha announced elections for September 1989, after which it was understood he would step down.

During this period, Botha remained in power as state president, although de Klerk clearly emerged as the new NP leader. When the National party held its preelection Federal Congress in June 1989, there was little indication of the wide-ranging moves de Klerk would take the following year. Indeed, in July 1989, addressing the Cape Congress of the National party, de Klerk said that he would not negotiate with the ANC if it continued to support violence as a means for change.[36]

At the 5 July Botha-Mandela meeting at the president's mansion in Cape Town, Tuynhuys, Mandela presented Botha with the thirteen-point letter he had written in March, setting out the reasons why the ANC would refuse to reject its armed struggle as a precondition to talks with the government. Botha sought once again to persuade Mandela to abandon armed struggle.[37] In a brief statement following the unusual encounter, Mandela refused to renounce violence and insisted that negotiations take place with the Mass Democratic movement itself, and not solely with him.[38] His release was not the issue, he said in a statement given to the prison authorities: "I would only like to contribute to the creation of a climate which will promote peace in South Africa."[39] When de Klerk accepted an invitation by Zambian president Kenneth Kaunda in August to meet for talks in Lusaka, it was the last straw for the Big Crocodile. Botha resigned as state president on 14 August accusing de Klerk and other cabinet ministers of initiating a breech of faith, ignoring his wishes, and falling into the hands of the ANC. Just prior to his trip to Lusaka, de Klerk became acting state president.

[35] De Klerk narrowly edged out two other candidates for the top post: Foreign Affairs minister "Pik" Botha and minister of finance Barend du Plessis. The widespread support for du Plessis, a well-known verligte, indicated the strength of the reformist faction in the caucus, in part explaining de Klerk's later lurch to the left on the intra–National party political spectrum.

[36] *Business Day*, 25 July 1989.

[37] *Star*, 10 July 1989.

[38] The term Mass Democratic movement (MDM) emerged in the mid-1980s, as defined by Price "to distinguish that segment of the opposition or liberation struggle that defined itself in terms of the nonracial Charterist tradition" (1991:280n). Known most commonly by its acronym, the MDM consists of the ANC, COSATU, and the UDF and its affiliate organizations.

[39] *Business Day*, 13 July 1989.

Two events in August 1989 furthered enriched the ground for the dramatic changes to come in early 1990. The first was the aforementioned change in leadership in the National party and the second was the adoption by the ANC on 21 August of the Harare Declaration, which set forth specific preconditions for negotiations with Pretoria. Lodge (1989:42–55) reviews the evolution of the debate within the ANC over the twin strategies of negotiation versus the "people's war"—which he refers to as an intellectual "dualism"—and points to a 1987 document in which the ANC affirmed its readiness to negotiate provided that the outcome would be a united, nonracial democracy. This debate, which in some ways mirrored the tension between the verkrampte and verligte factions within the regime, illustrates the importance of within-group decision making and cohesiveness concerning decisions to pursue negotiation.

Based on a draft forged on 10 August 1989 in Luanda under the leadership of ANC president Oliver Tambo, the Organization of African Unity's (OAU) ad hoc Committee on Southern Africa adopted the Harare Declaration on 21 August. Under a heading titled "Principles," the declaration states that "a conjuncture of circumstances exists which, if there is a demonstrable readiness on the part of the Pretoria regime to engage in negotiations genuinely and seriously, could create the possibility to end apartheid through negotiations."[40] The Harare Declaration was crucial in that it signaled within the ANC the apparent ascendancy of the idea of supporting negotiation over a revolutionary people's war. The principles of the Harare Declaration were subsequently adopted by the Non-aligned Movement in September 1989, the UN General Assembly in December 1989,[41] and the Congress for a Democratic Future, held by the MDM in the same month.

In the context of new leadership of the National party, an election was held on September 6 in which, for the first time in South Africa, whites and persons of color voted on the same day, albeit on communal voting rolls. The boycotts of the Coloured and Indian elections in September 1989 were just as effective as those in 1984. Voter turnout for the Coloured house was a meager 25 percent, and for the Indian house, no more than 15 percent; the tricameral system still lacked legitimacy in these communities. As Olivier notes, the election boycotts demonstrated to the government that "a new constitution is an undeniable urgent necessity— an absolute sine qua non for peace and stability in South Africa" (1989:1).

Nevertheless, de Klerk got his mandate—however vague it may have been—to proceed with a newly energized reform program. The National

[40] The Harare Declaration is reprinted (without the OAU preamble) in Cooper et al. 1990:641–44.

[41] UN General Assembly Resolution S-16/1, 14 December 1989.

party was returned to power by the white voters, although it had once again lost support to outbidders on the right, as well as to the left this time. The National party's percentage of the popular vote declined from 52 percent in 1987 to 48 percent, while the CP's climbed from 26 percent to 31 percent. The newly formed Democratic party (DP) on the left polled 20 percent, up from the 16 percent garnered by its predecessor, the PFP, in 1987. Once again, thanks to the distorting effects of the first-past-the-post electoral system, a minority of votes translated into a fifty-four-seat working majority in the controlling white House of Assembly. For the first time since the 1948 election, the National party did not enjoy the popular support of a majority of whites.

For de Klerk, the lessons of the 1989 election were clear: if he wanted to prevent the further erosion of support on both the right and left, he could no longer ride the horns of the reformer's dilemma, as Botha had. A clear departure from the policies of the past—one way or another—was needed.

de Klerk's Gambit

Many have pointed to the courageous leadership of F. W. de Klerk as a factor in his decision to pursue direct negotiations with the ANC. Analysts noted that de Klerk, unlike his predecessor, P. W. Botha, was the first National party leader who was not a member of that generation of NP members that erected apartheid.[42] Yet there were no indications that de Klerk was any different from his predecessor in terms of his commitment to basic apartheid-based thinking. He was perceived then as verkrampte, a cautious mover, although it was acknowledged that he brought a change in style, if not substance, to the National party. Very simply, there was nothing in de Klerk's past—he had always been a strong "own affairs" man—that would have led one to suspect that he would accept direct negotiation with the ANC.[43] In fact, there are indications that de Klerk initially was prepared not to negotiate with the ANC.[44]

[42] Coleader of the Democratic party (and a former NP ambassador to the United Kingdom), Denis Worrall, explained: "De Klerk came to parliament when apartheid was on the rack. . . . The previous generation, of which P. W. Botha was a member, actually formulated apartheid policies, internalized it, and mobilized around it. . . . It was very difficult for them to admit that they had been wrong for those forty years, but de Klerk could" (interview with the author, 5 May 1991).

[43] For a good summary of de Klerk's background and rise to the top of the National party hierarchy, see Kotzé and Geldenhuys 1990.

[44] De Klerk's brother, Willem, has written that in September 1990, just after the election, the president sent a National Intelligence Service official to persuade him (a well-known liberal) not to "give any prominence to the ANC since it could never play a role in negotiations" (as summarized in Rantete and Giliomee 1992:519).

What explains de Klerk's apparent conversion? De Klerk saw the rising costs and declining benefits of a prolonged stalemate and of an impending crisis even greater than the nearly three-year crisis of his predecessor. Indeed, Stein considers the move toward negotiation to be triggered by the need to escape a crisis or, as applicable to the South African case, to avoid an impending crisis (1989:239–40). It is possible to reconstruct the scenarios that he faced in the political, economic, and international spheres once he gained unrestricted control of the South African government in late 1989. These risk scenarios changed the relative weighting of the alternative strategies of further repression or negotiation that were undoubtedly on de Klerk's desk.

On the political front, the MDM had continued to gain strength, even with members of the tricameral parties, notably the DP, and participated in mass demonstrations in September 1989. On the economic front, real GDP growth in 1989 had been only 2.1 percent, down from 3.7 percent in 1988, and projections for 1990 were for growth at 1 percent, with some estimates of growth as low as 0.5 percent. The gold price had dropped from an average of $437 per ounce in 1988 to $362 in September 1989. The official inflation rate was nearly 15 percent, which was up from 1988 (13 percent), but down slightly from the more turbulent years of 1986–87. Price (1987) and Lewis (1990) have shown that capital flight during the 1980s was substantial. On the international front, South Africa faced the prospect of increased isolation and condemnation.

In the midst of this multifaceted crisis, de Klerk first met with Mandela in December 1989. He had received Mandela's reply to Botha's response to Mandela's earlier letters, and the ANC leader's arguments must have left an important impact on him. Having already released seven senior leaders of the ANC in October and allowed nonviolent protests to occur without intervention by the police, de Klerk met with the jailed ANC leader on Wednesday, 13 December. The meeting was reportedly initiated by Nelson Mandela, and it came just four days after the Conference for a Democratic Future—representing the internal players in the struggle—adopted the guidelines of the Harare Declaration. At this first de Klerk–Mandela meeting "ways and means to address current obstacles in the way of meaningful dialogues" were discussed, according to Justice Minister Coetsee.[45]

It is likely, in retrospect, that the meeting went very well. This encounter was critical in establishing a central function of the prenegotiation period: establishing a belief in reciprocity, that good-faith concessions would be matched. Exchanges and assurances of good faith give parties the confidence to enter negotiation and to establish a pattern of coopera-

---

[45] *Weekly Mail,* 15 December 1990.

tive interaction. Just two months later, Mandela would use his developing personal relationship with de Klerk as a justification for preliminary talks with Pretoria; "He is a man of integrity who is acutely aware of the danger of a public figure not honoring his undertaking," Mandela said on the day de Klerk released him from twenty-seven years of imprisonment.[46] The de Klerk-Mandela synergy would help to propel the negotiation process for some time to come. The ANC's new year's message for 1990, even though it continued to sound a militant tone, offered de Klerk an opening: "For our part, we are committed to seize any real opportunity that might emerge, genuinely to seek a political agreement for a speedy end to the apartheid system."[47] In this light, de Klerk's move to call for direct negotiation entailed much less risk than had been perceived by most analysts at the time.

De Klerk made the move on 2 February in a landmark speech that went beyond most public expectations, including those of the ANC. Opening the first parliamentary session at the helm of the South African government, he took the "leap of reform" that Botha would not. De Klerk announced the following measures:

- The lifting of bans on the ANC, PAC, and the SACP
- The indemnification of returning exiles unless common law crimes against them were pending
- His intention to release all political prisoners
- Suspension of executions for both political and criminal offenses
- The lifting of bans on 110 listed communists and 65 ANC members
- The lifting of restrictions on the UDF, Congress of South African Trade Unions (COSATU), and thirty other anti-apartheid organizations (and one right-wing group)
- The repeal of emergency regulations imposing press censorship on printed media
- The lifting of the state of emergency
- The unconditional release of Nelson Mandela
- The scrapping of the Separate Amenities Act and the declaration of other apartheid laws as "obstacles"
- The according of "highest priority" to negotiations[48]

The most momentous quote from the speech—the sound bite that was used in news reports around the world—summarized de Klerk's new strategy:

[46] *Washington Post,* 12 February 1990.
[47] *Business Day,* 8 January 1990.
[48] "Address by the State President, Mr. F. W. de Klerk, DMS, at the Opening of the Second Session of the Ninth Parliament of the Republic of South Africa, Cape Town, 2 February 1990" (Washington D.C., Embassy of South Africa), mimeo.

Walk through the open door, take your place at the negotiating table together with the government and other leaders who have important power bases inside and outside of parliament. . . . The time for negotiation has arrived.[49]

Exactly how was the decision taken, and what were the underlying calculations? A lengthy interview I had with one of those present at the internal cabinet deliberations, Stoffel van der Merwe (then a cabinet minister), reveals that the decision was a reasoned, calculated one based on three primary considerations: apartheid "would never work as it was intended"; in the wake of collapse of communism in Easter Europe, the time was "ripe"; and the argument of de Klerk (quoted by van der Merwe) that "if it is necessary to take the decision, let's do it now."[50] The final decision to make the announcement in February was first discussed in a secluded cabinet meeting in December but finally made only "two or three days" before the speech, according to van der Merwe.

These events are important because they show that the decision was taken after a careful consideration of many options and following de Klerk's meeting with Mandela in December. Analyst Steven Friedman assesses the essential calculation in the government's thinking: "There emerged a perception that the benefits of negotiating a transition—because negotiating a transition always means that it is a very different process than revolution; you retain a veto over the form of the new society—the prospects for that were better than the prospects of maintaining the system."[51] This suggests a more reactive reason for de Klerk's leap of reform. Indeed, de Klerk said in March 1990 that "we did not wait until the position of power dominance turned against us before we decided to negotiate a peaceful settlement" (Rantete and Giliomee 1992:518). De Klerk's choice for negotiation was thus the result of a reasoned decision and a thorough assessment of the alternatives. As Zartman (1989:10) suggests, prenegotiation involves the process of eliminating worse alternatives, whereas formal negotiation involves selection or choice of new ones.

Mandela was released less than two weeks later, on 11 February. De Klerk announced the move on the tenth, and revealed that he, constitutional affairs minister Gerrit Viljoen, and Coetsee had met again with Mandela at Victer Vorster Prison on the ninth. On the day of his release Mandela addressed a huge rally from the balcony of Cape Town City Hall, overlooking the city's Grand Parade. In a historic address broadcast live around the world, Mandela saluted the long history of the struggle and reiterated a justification of the ANC's decision to take up arms in

---

[49] Ibid.
[50] Interview with the author, 25 June 1991.
[51] Interview with the author, 15 May 1991.

1960. "We hope," he added, "that a climate conducive to a negotiated settlement would be created soon, so that there may be no longer the need for the armed struggle."[52]

On 16 February, the ANC National Executive Committee met in Lusaka, Zambia, with Mandela present, to formulate its response to de Klerk's gambit. It was decided to send a delegation to meet with de Klerk to discuss the preconditions for negotiation. The process of direct government-ANC "talks about talks" had begun. For a critical mass of actors in the center of this deeply polarized political spectrum, negotiation was perceived to possibly yield mutual gain; both major actors saw greater benefits than costs to cooperation. Even though both parties thought, at the time, that they could favorably control the process (Rantete and Giliomee 1992), accepting negotiation was a recognition that others had bargaining power and that a unilateral strategy was likely to be not only unsuccessful but self-defeating.

Why Negotiate?

In South Africa in late 1989 and early 1990, a combination of domestic and international, political, economic, and social factors converged at a critical time, allowing the conditions for the move from protracted stalemate to negotiation. The onset of a negotiation signaled a sea change from the zero-sum view of the conflict that had existed into the late 1980s to one of a potential for a positive-sum outcome. What brought the parties to the table?

For the government, apartheid had failed for practical, demographic, and economic reasons. The government faced a worsening economic scenario, and negotiation was seen as a way to arrest the economic decline. Finally, strains on the resources and performance of the security forces required the regime to change strategies. From the exogenous environment, sanctions had taken their toll on the government by creating worsening economic conditions and making vulnerable a steady supply of resources to the security establishment and for other government expenditures. Conservative Western leaders, particularly British prime minister Margaret Thatcher and U.S. president George Bush, relayed to the government that they would no longer be able to hold the line against de-

---

[52] The speech is printed verbatim in the *New York Times*, 2 February 1990. Mandela reported on his secret talks with the government, dating back to 1987 (as discussed above). He said the aim had been the normalization of the political climate in the country, but reassured his followers that he had not yet begun to discuss the "basic demands" of the struggle. Mandela said, "I wish to stress that I myself have at no time entered negotiations about the future of our country, except to insist on a meeting between the ANC and the government."

mands for further sanctions as they had in the past. And the Soviet Union no longer was perceived as a threat, allowing the NP to point to the decline in the superpower's involvement in regional conflicts in Africa as an easing of the perceived total onslaught against South Africa. Finally, a successful resolution of the Namibia conflict provided a demonstration effect for the potential resolution of the conflict in South Africa, that black enfranchisement would not necessarily lead to a winner-take-all outcome.

The onset of negotiation in South Africa reflected the fact that both the government and the ANC saw the conflict in terms of a bargaining problem. Such a problem has three important general characteristics (Pillar 1983:37). First, and most important, the de Klerk regime and the ANC saw continued unacceptable costs in the absence of an agreement, or at least in the failure to convene a process toward an agreement. Inversely, they saw mutual benefit arising from an eventual agreement with each other; a settlement could be mutually profitable. Third, neither actor could be seen as solely responsible for the initiation of the process. Viewing the onset of negotiation in terms of a bargaining problem can outline some critical questions in assessing how and when such talks can begin. The question of how they *can* begin points to the need to specify the presence or absence of certain structural conditions. The question of when they *do* begin points to the need to specify precipitating conditions.

The will to avoid a worse outcome is a necessary condition for the onset of negotiation. Actors must realize that without an agreement, mutually destructive conflict will persist. A critical step is the realization that the pursuit of a zero-sum strategy is unlikely to succeed, and that a range of possible outcomes includes some which are positive sum. It is possible, even likely, that a party could enter into negotiations not with a view of obtaining a positive-sum settlement to the conflict but with an eye toward other short-term gains (Pillar 1983:51). If negotiation is induced in this way in divided societies, it implies that the conditions for realization of the self-negating prediction have not been met: the actors pursue a hegemonic outcome, using negotiation as simply another strategy in that quest.

However, in the case of South Africa, the existence of a stalemate and the relative balance of power—and the critical economic and social interdependence relationships among racial groups—underscored to the actors that hegemonic victory was unattainable. The course of continued conflict would not have appreciably changed the outcome. Once the parties converge on a common view of the conflict as a stalemate with unacceptable costs, the conditions for positive-sum negotiations are present. At this point, actors share expectations of a mutually beneficial outcome. Conversely, as Rangarajan (1985:46) argues, dissatisfaction with the status quo becomes unbearable. In terms of reaching agreement, the essential cost/benefit calculus of the bargaining problem lies at the heart of the decision to enter talks or continue the fight. These considerations brought the parties to the table and, in the course of transition, drove them toward agreement. Conflict would go on, but negotiation was preferred in order to limit the damage of such conflict and to define and pursue mutual interests.

The simple presence of the structural conditions for talks does not necessarily mean that negotiation is inevitable. Indeed, the stalemate condition mentioned above might well have continued on indefinitely in an "impasse" were there not sufficient precipitating conditions; that is, if the conditions for a settlement, while existent, were not yet "ripe" (Zartman 1985:9). The underlying structural conditions for a positive-sum view of the settlement were indeed present in the form of a mutually hurting stalemate that reached its precipice in late 1989. When is a conflict ripe? Zartman notes that ripe moments are defined in three overlapping ways: "As mutual, painful stalemates marked by a recent or impending catastrophe; as a time when both parties' efforts at unilateral solutions or 'tracks' are blocked and bilateral solutions or 'tracks' are conceivable; and/or as a place on a long slope where the 'ins' start to slip and the 'outs' start to surge" (1985:9). The conditions of ripeness were present in South Africa in 1989, and certain precipitating events led the major actors to seize the opportunity for cooperative action through negotiation. These precipitating conditions are critical to moving beyond a situation of conflict and crisis toward a redefinition through negotiation of the rules of the political game. The precipitating conditions in the South African conflict— changes in leadership and in the exogenous environment, and changes in parties' perception of the other as a result of track-two diplomacy—all played a role in the move from stalemate and ripeness to negotiations.

Prenegotiation was an important phase of South Africa's transition. During this phase the problem was defined, vital interests were clarified, and nascent elite cooperation began—the actors *learned* (Stein 1989), both about themselves and about each other. The experience of South Africa shows that negotiation in divided societies, even in the wake of a polarized political struggle in which many died and many more suffered, can begin if the right factors converge at once. In South Africa, a mixture of the proper underlying conditions, a role for human ingenuity, and even a bit of luck came together at the right moment.

CHAPTER 3

The Uncertain Interregnum

THE ONSET of negotiation in South Africa did not lead to more peaceful politics. On the contrary, political violence increased, politics became increasingly chaotic and uncertain, and the specter of civil war loomed at times on the horizon. This chapter explores the evolution of the *preliminary phase* of negotiation in South Africa from the first formal government-ANC bilateral talks to the first multilateral pact, the National Peace Accord, reached in September 1991 in an effort to quell political violence. During this phase the "preliminaries," or preconditions to formal constitutional negotiations, topped the talks agenda. Tracing this phase of the process reveals how these negotiations involved institutionalizing the newfound commitment to negotiated change in informal rule structures through a series of pacts aimed at assuring the protection of parties' vital interests. It also highlights the importance of relationships between violence and negotiation and of mass-elite relations in the course of transition.

The road to the National Peace Accord was a process that moved toward the creation of a *nascent institution* in a democratic transition and was arrived at through pacts. Particularly, this phase of negotiations in South Africa was characterized by: increasing, rather than decreasing political violence; a start-and-stop process of bilateral government-ANC negotiations; the progressive meeting of the demands set out by the Harare Declaration by the government; moves by de Klerk to repeal apartheid laws (with the exception of the 1984 constitution); the intervention of domestic mediators—church and business groups—in June 1991 to resolve deadlocks; and intensive debate and planning over the central questions of institutional choice: what new political rules should replace the old system, both in the future and for the process through which they would be negotiated. The first five issues are the subject of this chapter. The last point, a central concern of this book, is the focus of chapters 4 and 5.

PRELIMINARY PACT MAKING: 1990

The ANC's National Executive Committee met in Harare, Zimbabwe, on 16 February 1990, when it decided to send a delegation to meet de Klerk to discuss "talks about talks" and to reestablish itself as an organized force within the country. While the basic preconditions of the Harare Declaration had not been met, the ANC believed that the release of political prisoners, the return of exiles, and the state of emergency could be the subject of preliminary talks. By March 1990, the ANC committed itself to the new situation, reopened a national headquarters in Johannesburg, and, a month later, organized regional branches around the country. However, the armed struggle would, in theory at least, continue.

In the wake of de Klerk's 2 February opening of political space, a wave of factional violence erupted in the townships among supporters of the ANC and members of the Zulu-based Inkatha. The violence was first limited to the Natal province, Inkatha's stronghold by virtue of its control of the KwaZulu homeland government, but by midyear it spread to the PWV region. Within weeks of Mandela's release in mid-February, intense fighting broke out in Natal between supporters of the ANC/UDF and Inkatha. The Natal violence, which began in late 1987, flared anew, especially in the volatile Edendale valley.[1] In fact, the months after de Klerk's dramatic speech were the bloodiest months to date in South Africa's conflict. Between January and March, close to seven hundred lost their lives in clashes in Natal, up more than 200 percent for the same period in the previous year.

Despite efforts by Mandela to arrange a personal meeting with Inkatha leader and KwaZulu chief minister Mangosuthu Buthelezi to quell the fighting between their constituents—and forge a common African negotiating position vis à vis the white minority government—outrage by ANC regional officials, particularly Natal Midlands leader Harry Gwala, prevented him from carrying it through. Nevertheless, Mandela sought to bring peace to Natal. Addressing an estimated crowd of 100,000 in Durban in late February, shortly after his release, he said: "My message to those of you involved in this battle of brother against brother is this: take your guns, knives and pangas [hatchets] and throw them into the sea. . . . If we do not bring a halt to this conflict, we will be in grave danger of corrupting the proud legacy of our struggle. We endanger the peace process in the whole of the country."[2] Mandela's calls were ignored. In March, the Edendale Valley erupted; observers described the fighting as full-scale civil war.

Despite the mounting violence and the unmet demands of the Harare Declaration, the ANC agreed to create one of the many joint committees that would serve as one of the new institutions of the negotiation process,

---

[1] The Natal violence, termed by many a civil war, had already claimed many lives. According to the South African Police, the number of deaths related to the violence in Natal between September 1987 and 31 January 1991 was 1,230 with nearly half of these deaths occurring between February 1989 and January 1990 (Cooper, et al. 1990:250).

[2] *Star*, 26 February 1990.

the Steering Committee. The committee, set up in behind-the-scenes talks in the weeks following de Klerk's speech, was charged with arranging the first round of direct parleys. In these preliminary talks, held beyond the eye of the press, the details of public talks—the agenda, location, size and composition of the delegations, security, and related procedural issues—were thrashed out. The government's top constitutional adviser, Fanie van der Merwe, and the ANC's head of intelligence, Jacob Zuma, led the discussions. Even after the first round of formal negotiation, the Steering Committee continued to serve as a mechanism for resolving deadlocks in other negotiating forums (discussed below). Zuma flew to South Africa in late February, and by early March the Steering Committee had set a date (although the venue was kept secret): 11 April.

In April, as the Steering Committee was working through the details of a first round of talks, the ANC suspended the proposed meeting with the government in protest against police action in Sebokeng (southern Transvaal) at which at least eleven people were killed when security forces opened fire on a crowd of demonstrators protesting high rents and poor living conditions in the township. Despite the fact that de Klerk had allegedly severed the role of the police from any political objectives—in January he had told a gathering of top police commanders, "We will not use you any longer as instruments to attain political goals. . . . This is the responsibility of the politicians"[3]—elements in the security forces did not comply. In a statement, the ANC said, "The ANC once again reiterates that people of South Africa have a right to assemble and demonstrate in support of their just demands. We claim this as an inalienable right, not as a favor conceded by the regime at its discretion."[4]

Following the row, de Klerk and Mandela and three senior ANC officials met directly on 5 April at Tuynhuys, the president's office in Cape Town (where Mandela and Botha had met some nine months before). De Klerk assured Mandela that the Sebokeng events would be investigated and the police would be reined in; the two agreed that the talks would go ahead on 2–4 May. In this initial period, the de Klerk-Mandela rapport, based on a personal trust between them, turned crises into breakthroughs.

The Groote Schuur Minute

The first full-scale bilateral meeting between the government and the ANC was held at the Groote Schuur mansion at the foot of Table Mountain near Cape Town. By all accounts, the talks were surprisingly cordial;

---

[3] *Sunday Times*, 28 January 1990 (as cited in Welsh 1990:7).
[4] *City Press*, 1 April 1990, as quoted in Cooper, et al. 1990:678.

participants mingled freely and socialized openly. The spirit of Groote Schuur reflected the general euphoria that had gripped South African society in early 1990, a euphoria steeped in the belief that fundamental peace would rapidly come to South Africa. The return of the exiled leadership was a historic breakthrough. When the meetings began on 2 May, the two leaders, de Klerk and Mandela, appeared together on the steps of the mansion before a crowd of two hundred local and international journalists. Both spoke confidently of their ability to reach agreement through dialogue.

Inside, when the negotiations began, the mood was formal, earnest, and businesslike. One of the delegates noted: "The remarkable thing was that nobody was posturing, and there were no opening shots. It was a very business-like meeting . . . simply a question of putting all our cards on the table at once."[5] Many present expressed sentiments of a common "South African-ness"; the recognition of a shared destiny had also featured prominently in meetings by whites with the ANC in exile. ANC director of international affairs, Thabo Mbeki, who participated in the Groote Schuur talks, said, "We were a bit surprised, I think, at how foolish all of us had been, because in a matter of minutes everybody in the room realized that nobody there had horns."[6] As Adam notes, "children of the same soil realized what they had in common" (1990:10).

After three days of intensive bargaining, the delegations again appeared before the press. Mandela summed up the talks as "a realization of a dream" for the ANC, but said "at the end not only are we, the government and the ANC, closer together, but we are all victors—South Africa is the victor."[7] A joint document, the Groote Schuur Minute, was produced. For its part, the government agreed to eventually meet the central demands of the Harare Declaration: release all political prisoners; allow the return of exiles under conditions of immunity; amend security legislation; and lift the state of emergency. While not explicitly pledging to withdraw from the armed struggle, the ANC agreed to language that effectively curtailed its ability to take up armed action while the negotiation process was in place.

The document set the framework for a mutual commitment to the process and a renunciation of violence; it begins:

> The Government and the ANC agree on a common commitment towards the resolution of the existing climate of violence and intimidation from whatever quarter as well as a commitment to stability and to a peaceful process of negotiations.

[5] *Argus* ("Men of Destiny," special supplement), 30 January 1991.
[6] Ibid.
[7] Ibid.

The government and ANC also agreed to

- establish a Working Group on Political Offenses to hammer out an operational definition of "political offenses" and the mechanisms for the release and indemnification of prisoners or those in exile convicted or accused of political crimes;
- grant temporary immunity for political offenses to key ANC officials to enable them to return to South Africa "to assist in bringing violence to an end and to take part in peaceful political negotiations";
- ensure normal and free political activities;
- lift the state of emergency and the establish "channels of communication between the Government and the ANC . . . in order to curb the violence and intimidation from whatever quarter effectively." (Cooper et al. 1990:731–32)

The Groote Schuur Minute was the first in the series of three specific agreements between the government and the ANC in the run-up to the National Peace Accord. As the first, its aims were understandably modest; it was a mostly a set of promises. In this phase, however, the institutions that would ultimately guide the transition began to evolve. With the creation of the Steering Committee and the second working group, the consultative structures that would eventually be formally ratified by the accord found their origins. The genesis of regularized rules for the transition are found here: new institutions evolved out of the need to escape a common problem. The most important result of the Groote Schuur meeting was the belief by regime and opposition alike that concessions made would be reciprocated by the opponent; it was thus a very successful initial pact from the government's point of view, one that justified tolerance of the opposition (Marks 1992:413).

Although the first talks were successful in that they were mutually beneficial, the ANC continued to publicly press its demands for the return of exiles and the release of political prisoners. Later in May, Mandela, addressing a crowd of sixty thousand, threatened to stop negotiations unless political prisoners were immediately released, political trials were ended, the state of emergency was lifted immediately, and South African Defense Force (SADF) troops were removed from the townships. Nevertheless, the Groote Schuur process netted concrete results for the ANC. Shortly following the talks, thirty-eight top ANC exiles were indemnified, including the commander of MK, Chris Hani, and Jacob Zuma. By late May, the Tricameral Parliament had passed an Indemnity Bill for political offenders (although the responsibility for defining such offenses was placed with the working group), and in June de Klerk lifted the state of emergency in all parts of the country except strife-ridden Natal.

The transformation in the rules of the political game kicked off by de

Klerk's February speech also forced a realignment of South Africa's political parties. The National party, after nearly eighty years as the voice of exclusive Afrikaner (and white) nationalism, threw open its membership doors to all races in July. The same was true in black politics. In the same month, KwaZulu leader Buthelezi announced that his movement would become a national political party, the Inkatha Freedom party (IFP). It sought to extend the constituency of the party beyond Natal and into the PWV especially to gain some white supporters. The encroachment of Inkatha into the urban turf that had been an ANC stronghold ominously brought the Inkatha/ANC rivalry out of the political backwaters of Natal and onto the center stage of the country's political life.

The first major wave of violence beyond Natal began in the troubled township of Sebokeng, near Johannesburg. On 22 July, some forty-three hundred hostel-dwelling IFP supporters—so identified by distinctive red headbands—raided a rival ANC-supporting hostel following an IFP rally at the local stadium. Yet another cycle of attacks and counterattacks left scores dead and injured.

The Pretoria Minute

In the context of the flaring political violence of mid-1990, the government and ANC met for a second round of formal talks. Delegations gathered during the first week of August at the Presidency mansion in Pretoria for a fifteen-hour marathon session. Despite more difficult negotiations than at Groote Schuur, concessions were made, and once again a joint declaration signed by both parties emerged from the closed-door discussions. At a 1:00 A.M. news conference on 7 August, a joint statement, the Pretoria Minute, was released.

The Pretoria Minute further clarified the structures of transition through which—although not for more than a year later—the conditions for actual constitutional talks would finally be satisfactorily resolved. The government gained a major concession from the ANC: it would not pursue the armed struggle as long as the negotiation process went forward. The ANC agreed officially to "suspend" armed action, although this had been done in practice since February. On the other hand, the ANC secured an agreement on the specific timetable for the release of all remaining political prisoners and further indemnification of exiles.

The Pretoria Minute codified the acceptance of a report from the Working Group on Political Offenses established at Groote Schuur that drafted an operational definition of *political offense* and *political prisoner* to effect the release of such prisoners and the indemnification of those charged with political crimes. The provisions for release and indemnification extended not only to the ANC, but to "all organizations, groupings or institutions, governmental or otherwise, who committed offenses on the assumption that a particular cause was being served or opposed."[8] This allowed the government and the ANC to make significant concessions. The government agreed to amend the Internal Security Act in order to remove threats to open activity by the ANC and its allies—such as the provision that declared furthering the aims of communism illegal—and a commitment to lift the state of emergency in Natal. This was the government's counterpoint to the ANC's armed struggle concession. To give effect to the way in which such armed action was to be "suspended," the minute set up another working group, the Armed Action Working Committee, headed by law and order minister Adrian Vlok for the government and MK chief of staff Chris Hani for the ANC.

Other provisions of the Pretoria Minute include agreements to

- mandate the Working Group on Political Offenses to draw up a plan for the release of ANC-related prisoners and the granting of indemnity to affected individuals;
- commence the process of prisoner release on 1 September 1990, with a 30 April 1991 deadline of completion;
- finalize the indemnity process for those eligible for amnesty by category (e.g., convictions for belonging to a banned organization); and
- create mechanisms of communication at the local, regional, and national level to enable the communication of public grievances to the appropriate authorities.

Paragraph eight of the Pretoria Minute also reasserts a strong commitment by the parties to the goal of negotiated change:

We are convinced that what we have agreed upon today can become a milestone on the road to true peace and prosperity for our country. In this we do not pretend to be the only parties involved in the process of shaping the new South Africa. We know there are other parties committed to peaceful progress. All of us henceforth walk that road in consultation and cooperation with each other. We call upon all those who have not yet committed themselves to peaceful negotiations to do so now.[9]

The last sentence is perhaps the most important. It was believed at the time that even if the basic preconditions for further talks on substantive matters—the new constitution—had not yet been met, they would be soon. Certainly, it was thought that the agreed-upon deadline, 30 April 1991, would be met and that constitutional negotiation could begin shortly thereafter. In order to facilitate movement on substantive issues,

---

[8] *Argus*, 7 August 1990, carried the full text of the agreement.

[9] *Argus* ("Men of Destiny," special supplement), 30 January 1991.

the concluding section of the agreement, paragraph nine, stated: "Against this backdrop, the way is now open to proceed toward negotiations on a new constitution. Exploratory talks will be held before the next meeting which will be held soon."[10] To give expression to this clause, another joint government-ANC working group was set up, the Paragraph Nine Working Committee, to discuss procedural and agenda items for an as-yet-undefined constitutional conference.

The Pretoria Minute emerged as a key agreement clearing the way for substantive negotiations. The pact signaled *not* a political alliance between the two players—indeed, at the press conference announcing the moves, Mandela and de Klerk clashed over the allegations of police collusion in the violence, with Mandela saying, "Until the government has tamed the police, we will continue to be dissatisfied"[11]—but an agreement that during the transition both the regime and the liberation movement would respect each other's role as an indispensable player in the process. The state's repressive machinery would be rolled back at the same time the ANC agreed to "suspend" the armed struggle. Thus, the "vital interests" of the government and the ANC could be met: neither would be defeated unilaterally by military force as the negotiation process went forward.

Despite the gains made in Pretoria, and some degree of euphoria by observers in August and September 1990 that the violence would be controlled given the reaffirmation of the government's and the ANC's ability to work together, clashes between IFP and ANC supporters—again allegedly exacerbated by the role of the security forces—flared again. In an ominous development, on Thursday, 26 August, hundreds of Zulus wearing distinctive red headbands stormed a Soweto train platform in a gruesome attack on innocent commuters. More than three hundred died as IFP and ANC supporters clashed in the townships over that weekend.[12] Most alarmingly, the violence had apparently taken on an ethnic dimension as well. Because of the close relationship that appeared to be developing between the NP politicians and the ANC, others who feared for the protection of their interests, such as elements in the security forces and IFP, perceived the need to foment violence in order to prevent their exclusion from negotiation. To them, the Pretoria Minute and the newly developing cooperation between the ANC and the NP meant the real possibility of being sidelined.

Following yet another apparently indiscriminate attack on a Johannesburg-bound commuter train on 13 September, in which twenty-six were killed and more than one hundred injured, de Klerk and Man-

---

10 Ibid.
11 Ibid.
12 *Newsweek*, 27 August 1990.

dela met the following day in a climate of crisis. Mandela sought to convince de Klerk that elements of the security forces were fanning the flames in an effort to thwart negotiations. De Klerk seemed persuaded, and issued a vaguely worded statement conceding that "there are forces which do not wish peaceful negotiations to succeed. . . . All those desiring peace must stand together to counter these forces."[13] At the meeting, de Klerk reportedly urged Mandela to meet with Buthelezi to address the underlying causes of the violence, but Mandela responded by placing the blame at the feet of the security forces' inability to maintain public order; he said it was useless to meet with Buthelezi "because the violence is caused by certain faceless elements."[14]

Political violence spoiled the nascent mutual trust that had developed between the ANC and the government after the two first rounds of talks in 1990. Murder and bloodshed claimed some one thousand victims between early August and early September and undercut the mutual security formally agreed to in pacts. The climate for negotiation, far from improving as a result of mutual security pacts between the ANC and the government, soured instead. The de Klerk-Mandela rapport that had worked to resolve a negotiation crisis in April was seemingly gone.

De Klerk and Mandela's meeting at the Union Buildings in Pretoria on 27 November, in the wake of vituperative public exchanges between the government and the ANC, was inconclusive. A terse joint statement released afterward simply noted a vague commitment to the process—"reaffirming commitment to peaceful negotiations"—but distinctly omitted any reference to the burning issue of the day, the violence and implementation of the August agreement on exiles and political prisoners.[15] Unlike other 1990 meetings, de Klerk and Mandela did not appear together to issue their statement.

Among many ANC supporters, the perception grew that on many issues—but particularly on the questions of violence and political prisoners—the aged Mandela was getting the runaround from a younger, wily, and politically deft de Klerk. On 8 December, de Klerk and Mandela met again to specifically discuss the issue of violence. While the joint statement contained language similar to that of the late November meeting, the relationship had clearly deteriorated. All they decided at the meeting was that the Armed Action Working Group discussing the suspension of the armed struggle would be activated.[16]

Less than a week later, at a rally in Johannesburg, a disillusioned Man-

[13] *New York Times*, 16 September 1990.

[14] Ibid.

[15] *Star*, 29 November 1990.

[16] South African Press Association, 9 December 1990, as reported in the *Foreign Broadcast Information Service* (hereafter cited as *FBIS*), 10 December 1990.

dela announced that the ANC would suspend its participation in the Working Group on Political Offenses and set unilateral deadlines for the implementation of the agreement on exiles and political prisoners. On the violence issue, Mandela pointed to conspiracies to disrupt negotiation and weaken the ANC.

> The aims of those planning and directing this scourge of destruction are very clearly to destroy the prospects of peace and derail our march to freedom. . . . The government's aim is to reform apartheid out of existence while carrying over into the future accumulated privileges and advantages of white monopoly on power. The ANC on the other hand seeks to attain the total eradication of apartheid and overcome as quickly as possible its ravages on our people. These basic distinctions account for the different directions in which we are pulling.[17]

In this volatile environment, the ANC, PAC, and AZAPO (the black consciousness party) held their first party conferences inside the country in more than three decades. The PAC, which had earlier thought to be edging toward negotiation, rejected talks with Pretoria. Negotiation could be held only on the "modalities" of an immediate transfer of power, and the PAC's armed struggle (which since the days of Poqo had existed more in rhetoric than in fact) would remain. AZAPO, at its national conference, rejected any negotiations with the de Klerk government whatsoever.

On 16 December, the ANC held its first conference inside South Africa since it had been banned in 1960. Due to readjustment difficulties, it was dubbed not a full national conference, but a "consultative conference." At the conference, deep divisions emerged within ANC ranks over whether to continue negotiation with the regime, a debate strongly fueled by the mistrust generated by violence. Differences between the older generation of recently released internal leadership and the younger and exile-based leaders emerged: many of the latter sought an immediate end to the negotiation process and a return to the armed struggle. At the end of the internal wrangling, the old guard emerged with its policies of negotiations wounded but intact. A resolution passed at the conference stated, "Our patience with the regime is running out."[18]

The conference resolved several additional issues:

- A deadline of 30 April 1991 was set whereby talks would be suspended if the agreements made concerning exiles and political prisoners were not met
- There would be no more secret meetings between the leadership of the ANC and the government (based on news reports, not denied by the government or ANC leaders, de Klerk and Mandela had met secretly in the previous weeks)

[17] SAPA, 16 December 1990, as reported in FBIS, 17 December 1990.
[18] Declaration of the 1990 ANC Consultative Conference, ANC Representative (Washington, D.C.), mimeo.

- Other aspects of resistance, such as international sanctions, the creation of parallel institutions, and "mass action," or peaceful protest, would continue
- Further efforts would be made to reestablish the organization's internal structures
- The organization would step up efforts to work with other liberation forces in a Patriotic Front, such as the PAC and AZAPO
- The MK would be used to defend ANC supporters in the townships.[19]

In his closing address to the conference, Mandela said confidential meetings would in fact continue and that ANC members who opposed them "did not understand the nature of negotiations."[20] Despite the militant tone of the conference, de Klerk, Mandela, and a number of aides met again in the days following the ANC's Consultative Conference. Observers pointed to the meeting, held so quickly after the conference, as a sign that the de Klerk-Mandela rapport still existed. But the following day, in his year-end address, de Klerk—perhaps playing to his own fearful constituency alarmed by escalating violence—sounded a hard line: "The time has come for the ANC to decide what it wants. Is it really prepared to accept its leaders' commitment at Groote Schuur and Pretoria to peaceful and negotiated solutions, or does it want to return to the confrontations and conflicts of the past?"[21]

Although 1990 began with euphoria, by year's end the new era was turning out to be the prelude of an impending storm. More than ten people per day were killed in political violence in South Africa in 1990, the highest annual average death rate since the township rebellion in 1984, and the negotiation process—which had taken great strides in May and August—began to unravel in mutual recriminations and mistrust. Racial intolerance seemed to be increasing as well; white-on-black violence—in part the result of organized ultra-right-wing attacks on blacks—reportedly rose 30 percent in 1990.[22] Reporter Patrick Laurence sums up the cause of the violence and its political fallout in 1990: "A major generator of the violence . . . appears to have been a sense that power was within the grasp of the black majority. It acted as a catalyst, bringing rivalries to the surface and the rival forces into an arena where the stakes were the highest on offer: power."[23]

[19] Ibid.

[20] *Star*, 22 December 1990.

[21] "Year End" address by State President F. W. de Klerk, as reported in *FBIS*, 19 December 1990.

[22] According to the National Institute for Crime Prevention and Rehabilitation of Offenders, *South*, 24 January 1991.

[23] *Star*, 18 December 1990.

PRELIMINARY PACT MAKING: 1991

Optimism still reigned at the beginning of 1991, despite the unprecedented violence. The ANC's message on 8 January started the new year off on a conciliatory note. Taking the initiative, the organization called for the convening of an All-Party Conference, which, if successful, would lead to a settlement on a new constitution within eighteen months. The ANC perceived that the remaining obstacle to constitutional negotiation—the full implementation of the Pretoria Minute—would be quickly resolved.[24] The All-Party Conference, it said, could address its demands for a constituent assembly and interim government—a major concession to the previously expressed ANC position for elections first, then talks on a new political order. No preconditions were set for attendance at the conference other than those earlier placed on the agenda (including the previous demand that an interim government be established first). Senior ANC officials hoped that the All-Party Conference could be held as early as May, assuming, still, that the 30 April deadline for implementation of the Pretoria Minute was met.[25]

The ANC's call for the All-Party Conference, which the government had long been urging and was in all likelihood discussed at the de Klerk-Mandela meeting in late December, committed the ANC to negotiating the rules of the transition prior to the establishment of full enfranchisement on a common voters' roll. For the ANC, this was a major concession that estranged them even further from the forces to their left, the PAC and AZAPO. It further served to legitimate the white minority government's role in forging a post apartheid South Africa. The ANC's opening 1991 volley gave new life to the negotiating process.

It is also likely that at the December summit between de Klerk and Mandela, the president once again urged the ANC leader to meet with Buthelezi to launch a joint bid to halt the violence plaguing Natal and the PWV. After quiet, behind-the-scenes preparation, Buthelezi and Mandela finally met on 29 January in Durban. Embracing each other after twenty-eight years apart (they had met years earlier when they were both ANC Youth League members), they created a scene reminiscent of de Klerk and Mandela at Groote Schuur. In spite of the deep and bitter rivalries of those they represented, the country's two most eminent black leaders stood together, bolstering hope for lasting peace.

The leaders and their delegations met in an all-day negotiation session, described by participants as a "friendly" discussion; Mandela and Buthelezi laughed and joked with one another during breaks, which were

[24] *Weekly Mail*, 11 January 1991.
[25] *Business Day*, 7 January 1991.

open to the press. At the end of the thirteen-hour talks, Mandela read a "joint declaration" and Buthelezi read a "joint statement," both worked out between the ANC and Inkatha. The declaration committed both organizations to "desist from vilification" of one another and announced the reactivation of joint mechanisms that had been set up in earlier bids to curb the violence.[26] Reinforcing the symbolism of peace, Mandela and Buthelezi closed the meeting with a second public clasping of hands. Buthelezi implicitly recognized the difficulty Mandela faced with his constituency; in his speech, he said, "We all know that the reason why we have not met with the Deputy President of the ANC, Dr. Mandela, is because some people in the ANC think this would amount to him contaminating himself with me."[27]

The 29 January agreement between the ANC and the IFP was an archetypal elite pact in which the parties' mutual security in the political arena was ostensibly secured and recognized, and in which they agreed to create new institutional structures to jointly manage the conflict.[28] From the leadership summit, the parties created a joint committee of twelve delegates from the leadership of the IFP and the ANC, replete with mechanisms for dealing with incidents of violence. There was, for the moment, emerging clarity on the interim rules of the political game. As will be seen, however the pact simply could not hold because of the still lingering perception of zero-sum conflict between Mandela's and Buthelezi's constituencies. While there may have expressions of mutual recognition at the top, there simply was not the support for an accord from below. Nevertheless, the leadership of the ANC had met Inkatha's primary demand for recognition as a legitimate political actor that would eventually take a place at the negotiating table.

Shortly after the ANC-IFP agreement, de Klerk once again had the chance to set the talks agenda with the traditional opening of parliament on 1 February. A repeat of the previous year's performance would have been virtually impossible, but de Klerk surprised observers by unveiling

[26] In an earlier peace pact in March 1989, a joint committee of the UDF/COSATU and Inkatha had been set up in Ntuzuma (near KwaMashu, north of Durban) to address the civil conflict in Natal. For details on the peace process and the violence in Natal during 1989 and early 1990, see Cooper et al. (1990:250–58). The January 1991 statement contained a series of broad agreements on the principles of "political tolerance and freedom of political activity" and acknowledged the need for "an effective peace-keeping force"; called on black schoolchildren to return to school and on authorities in educational settings not to discriminate on the basis on political affiliation; acknowledged the need for reconstruction and development programs implemented in joint cooperation by the two organizations (*Argus*, 30 January 1991; see also the "Briefing Paper" on the meeting in the *Los Angeles Times*, 29 January 1991).

[27] *New York Times*, 30 January 1991.

[28] The agreement is reproduced in Cooper et al. 1992:519–21.

more dramatic reforms than had been anticipated. De Klerk reiterated his commitment to negotiation and announced the repeal of the remaining pillars of apartheid laws. "The South African statute book will be devoid within months of the remnants of racially discriminatory legislation which have become known as the cornerstones of apartheid."[29] The most significant surprise in the speech was the planned repeal of the Population Registration Act; other key points included:

- Scrapping of the Group Areas Act and Land Acts of 1913 and 1936, and the publication of a government white paper on land redistribution
- Amendments to the Internal Security Act
- A pledge to work toward "parity" in social expenditures
- Rejection of the notion of an interim government; "however, consideration may be given to certain transitional arrangements on various legislative and executive levels to give the leaders of the negotiating parties a voice in the formulation of important policy decisions"
- Changes in statutes affecting local government, enabling some unification of racially based local government structures
- The acknowledgment of the 8 January ANC call for an All-Party conference, although noting the government's call (along with homeland leaders) for a Multiparty Conference several months prior

Why did the government decide to rush so quickly to drop the final apartheid legislation? Several reasons suggest themselves: first, it was a precondition to the lifting of some economic sanctions against South Africa, notably the U.S. Comprehensive Anti-Apartheid Act; second, the laws were inconsistent with de Klerk's nonracial New South Africa ideology; third, it served to demonstrate good faith in the negotiations process; and finally, if it had to happen—and the NP leadership recognized repeal of apartheid laws would have to happen eventually—it was better to do it early in de Klerk's term, rather than later. Most important, however, de Klerk realized that his bold moves would be rewarded with demonstrable gains at home and abroad. A new incentive structure had emerged, whereby moderation paid greater dividends than extremism, undercutting the resonance of outbidding by those opposed to negotiation on the left and right.

De Klerk's moves were in fact praised around the world, even though in many quarters at home—particularly among those in the struggle—strained efforts were launched by anti-apartheid activists to reiterate the simple fact that apartheid could not be fully dismantled until blacks in South Africa had full franchise rights on a common voters roll and its

---

[29] The speech was printed in full in the *Argus*, 1 February 1991.

legacies were redressed. Indeed, as the reporter for the *New York Times* wrote, "segregation's legal foundations are going; the economic chasm remains."[30] Concerned about the NP gaining the upper hand, Mandela announced, while on a European tour, that a "premature" lifting of sanctions would lead to mass protest in South Africa. The ANC clearly wanted to note its concern that de Klerk could control the process and reap all the benefits, without acting on the critical issue of violence.

The D. F. Malan Accord

In the joint working groups established at the Groote Schuur and Pretoria talks, the lingering question of the twenty thousand to forty thousand exiles still abroad and the three thousand political prisoners at home emerged as the central issue at that juncture.[31] On 15 February, the government and ANC held a secret meeting at the D. F. Malan Airport in Cape Town, reportedly to resolve a "bust-up" in the Armed Action Working Committee meeting the previous week that had involved ANC negotiator Pallo Jordan and then–deputy minister of constitutional development Roelf Meyer. The working group deadlocked on security issues. The government pressed the ANC on what activities it would have to forego—especially the establishment of MK "defense committees" in the townships (as had been called for in the December conference), the identification and surrender of arms caches, and demobilization of MK cadres—to give meaning to the idea of an end to the armed struggle. Once again, the mechanism of last resort—the personal relationship between de Klerk and Mandela—was brought in to break the deadlock.

No agreement was reached on the unresolved issues, either because the relationship between de Klerk and Mandela was breaking down or because the positions on these issues were too rigid. Instead, the two leaders agreed to appoint a Liaison Committee to oversee a phased process for the surrender or licensing of ANC weapons. The ANC also agreed, significantly, that it and MK would be subject to the law of the land.[32] Other points concluded at the D. F. Malan meeting were that the ANC would suspend "all violent attacks, infiltration of men and material, the creation of underground structures, statements inciting violence, threats of armed action, and training inside South Africa."[33] MK would continue to train in exile, however, would transform itself into something that was to be

[30] *New York Times*, 10 February 1991.

[31] De Klerk and Mandela, along with a team of specialists, met 29 February in talks that concerned the possible establishment of a single department of education. A separate working group was brought together to formulate proposals.

[32] *Sunday Times*, 17 February 1991.

[33] Ibid.

the nucleus for integration into the SADF, and would engage in activities befitting a conventional army. Nevertheless, some members of the ANC's armed wing still held on to hegemonic aims. From hiding, MK cadre Ronnie Kasrils, who was wanted for his role in a secret ANC plot to overthrow the government, Operation Vula, told the press, "We maintain our underground structures, intact and in place. . . . The maintenance of the existing underground structures is an insurance in case things go wrong."[34]

On the remaining obstacles to substantive talks, negotiators made limited headway. After the D. F. Malan meeting, estimates of the number of political prisoners still behind bars ranged from three thousand in some ANC circles to the nine hundred identified by the regime.[35] In the meantime, the IFP continued talks with the ANC, but also stepped up talks with the de Klerk government (which it had begun in 1989) on the future of KwaZulu and other issues, notably violence. Yet the assassination of the ANC-rallied traditional leader Mhlabunzima Maphumulo by a death squad linked to the security police in late February began to unravel what was left of the goodwill that had been apparently established in Durban a month earlier. Despite negotiation and monitoring mechanisms in place all around, violence continued to prevent the consolidation of a successful arrangement to control the fighting.

In early March, violence once again broke out along ethnic lines when a battle between Zulus and Xhosas flared at the Mzimphole worker's hostel in Soweto; twenty-four were killed. Once again, the ANC claimed the attack was launched by IFP *impis* and decried police collusion.[36] When de Klerk ventured to KwaZulu later in March to open the homeland's legislative assembly (the first time this had been done by a white head of state), he warned Inkatha that violence could derail the negotiations process: "Every leader has the responsibility to ensure that his followers honor their undertakings to refrain from the use of violence."[37]

The Ultimatum

As the Pretoria Minute's 30 April deadline approached, the ANC reacted sharply to what it perceived to be the government's abetting of township

[34] *Weekend Argus*, 2 March 1991.

[35] Of the latter figure, Justice Minister Coetsee claimed that 262 had been already released, and the indemnity applications of another 760 (as part of the process agreed to in the Pretoria Minute) were at an "advanced stage." Very few of the exiles had applied for indemnity, and so the government was unable to move on that issue, he said, but 2,092 had already been indemnified and the applications of 1,400 were in the works (*Los Angeles Times*, 16 February 1991).

[36] *Cape Times*, 5 March 1991.

[37] *New African*, 14 March 1991.

violence. In a surprise move, the organization decided that if its demands on the return of exiles, the release of political prisoners, and the control of violence were not met by 30 April, it would pull out of talks about talks on a new constitution. The ANC's April bombshell meant that the organization would refuse to participate in any other meetings of the Paragraph Nine Committee on the procedural issues related to the All-Party Conference. Other working groups, however, would continue to function. Perhaps more important than its withdrawal from the working group (which had not made much progress in any event) was the call for a two-day general strike, mass protests on 15 June (the day prior to Soweto Day), a consumer boycott, and a day of fasting in support of political prisoners on 22 May. The ultimatum also demanded

- the immediate dismissal of defense minister Magnus Malan and law and order minister Adrian Vlok, as well as action against the allegedly still functioning hit squads;
- legislative action to outlaw the carrying of cultural weapons (spears, shields, knives, etc.) used in township violence;
- the visible, public dismantling and disarming of certain units in the SADF, such as Battalion 32 (mercenaries) and Koevoet (formerly used in Namibia);
- the immediate suspension of all police who were involved in the March 1990 Sebokeng shootings and an investigation into police shootings reported in Daveyton (Benoni) on 24 March 1991;
- assurances that the SADF would use restraint in crowd control;
- the phasing out of single-sex worker hostels and their transformation into family housing;
- the establishment of an independent commission to hear complaints about security-related issues.[38]

If these demand were not met, the ANC warned, it would act on its threats beginning 9 May. Other groups, notably the PAC and COSATU, backed the ANC's move.

Feeling that it had been duped into a process by a government that was not committed to relinquishing power—all the while reeling from the continuing violence in the townships—the ANC adopted a hard line against the government. The context was clear: in continuing political violence, some four hundred had already died in 1991. The purpose of the ultimatum was "to shake the government and many of our compatriots, who have become desensitized by the violence, out of their apparent complacency," according to the ANC's Pallo Jordan.[39] The ANC's ultimatum reflected its leadership's conviction that the government's hid-

[38] For widespread coverage on the ultimatum, see *New Nation*, 12 April 1991.
[39] *Weekend Argus*, 13 April 1991.

den agenda was to negotiate with one hand and destabilize the organization with the other. *New Nation,* an alternative weekly sympathetic to the ANC, wrote: "The ultimatum is an important signal that urgent [steps] needed to be made and represents the awakening of the movement to the realities on the ground. . . . What was the ANC then supposed to do? Neglect its own constituency and continue with talks as if nothing has happened while de Klerk, on the other hand, ensured the protection of his own constituency and took advantage of what he won in the violence?"[40]

De Klerk responded laggardly to the ANC's ultimatum. Speaking in the whites-only chamber of parliament, de Klerk announced the creation of a Standing Commission of Inquiry into the violence and a multiparty summit on violence in Pretoria on 24–25 May, well after the ANC deadline. Two points are most important about de Klerk's initial reaction to the ultimatum. First, he did not address the principal cause of the ANC's concerns—the role of the police and surreptitious forces in fomenting violence—and indeed called for a stepped-up role for the police and the SADF in the townships. Second, he announced the measures unilaterally. The announcements were made with little consultation with the ANC (although de Klerk had called Mandela beforehand to "advise" him of the plans), and it is no surprise that the moves were rejected without hesitation; the ANC refused participation in either the commission or the conference.

De Klerk—while continuing to resist most of the ultimatum demands—pressed on with laid plans for the Pretoria conference. But more important (given the ANC's boycott of the meeting), de Klerk acknowledged that the lack of agreement on violence "is the single largest obstacle in the way to a peaceful future."[41] For many reasons, the most pressing issue was the question of the carrying so-called cultural or traditional weapons (spears of various kinds, axes, ceremonial clubs, and so on) by Zulus in general and IFP members in particular. The issue was important not just because of the damage that could be meted out with these primitive weapons but because they carried a symbolic value as tools of war as well. The ANC demanded that the public display of such weapons be outlawed, and the police empowered to confiscate them. IFP leader Mangosuthu Buthelezi was defensive about the criticism of Zulu military accoutrements, claiming that more died in the townships from "sophisticated weapons," AK-47s, than from traditional weapons. Buthelezi argued vociferously that cultural weapons were a part of Zulu national heritage, and refused to budge on the issue. He, too, threatened not to attend the government's peace summit.

[40] *New Nation,* 12–18 April 1991.
[41] *Argus,* 19 April 1991.

De Klerk set about trying to persuade Inkatha to accept restrictions on cultural weapons and by early May had apparently worked a deal with Buthelezi—hours before the ANC deadline—following several shuttle-diplomacy meetings and a direct meeting at Tuynhuys. The government-IFP agreement called for Zulu traditional weapons to be carried only at so-called cultural functions. However, the issue was finally resolved only after de Klerk later flew to Ulundi, the capital of KwaZulu, in mid-May to persuade the IFP leader to accept the restrictions. The cultural weapons issues would recur, as the agreement was not enforced. Other ANC demands, such as the conversion of (primarily Zulu) single-sex hostels, were also brokered in behind-the-scenes talks. Nevertheless, as the ANC ultimatum deadline approached, it was clear that the government would be unable (in part the result of a flood of indemnity applications just prior to the 30 April deadline) or unwilling to meet the deadlines set out by the ANC and the agreements included in the Pretoria Minute.

Averting a Crisis: Mediation

As the talks faltered and the violence flared in early May, a group of religious leaders—including those from the Anglican, Dutch Reformed, and Jewish faiths, led by the South African Council of Churches' Dr. Frank Chikane—stepped in in a last-ditch attempt to break the deadlock. Their well-founded fears were that if the ultimatum deadline were to lapse, violence would escalate. The church delegation first met with Mandela on 3 May and on the following day with de Klerk, after a bloody week on the Witwatersrand, where ninety-seven people had been killed in clashes. Chikane said:

> We do not pretend to be mediators. Our duty is to encourage the different parties . . . to come together and talk so that we do not land up in a tragic situation. Once the threatened deadlock is resolved, then the politicians should meet to work on the details of how to go into the future. It is not our role to determine how they should do this. We have come in because of the crisis which we feel has serious implications for the country and all South Africans.[42]

Despite Chikane's claim that the churches were not mediators, the situation demanded of them that very role.

As the church group met several times with the government and the ANC, for several days in early May it seemed as if the talks would falter. As violence continued unabated in many townships, the church leaders' mission gained a heightened sense of urgency. By the end of the first week in May, over one hundred had died in violence, eighteen on 5 May alone.

---

[42] *Weekend Argus*, 4 April 1991.

The bishops of the Methodist church of Southern Africa released a statement that day which summed up the dire mood: "[The violence] is an indictment of the government, political movements, and the churches. . . . People are not convinced that all leaders are utterly committed to ending violence. . . . People are not satisfied that political leaders or security forces are impartial."[43] Violence between ANC and IFP supporters continued nonetheless, and to make matters worse, on 6 May an Inkatha spokesman in Johannesburg, Musa Myeni, threatened that Inkatha would deploy 250,000 armed fighters from rural Natal in the townships in order to protect Zulu hostel dwellers.[44] In a frantic effort to break the impasse, the church leaders continued their shuttle diplomacy and suggested that a neutral third party convene a national peace conference. By midweek, with the deadline looming, de Klerk's cabinet and the ANC's National Executive Committee (along with a meeting with COSATU and SACP leaders) were cloistered in tense meetings trying to develop responses to the crisis.

Just in time to avert a complete breakdown in the talks, the ANC and the government met in a top-level summit on the day of the ultimatum deadline, 9 May. After a grueling six-hour session in which de Klerk and Mandela conferred on a broad range of issues, an outline agreement was reached. Although the joint statement released after the discussion made no mention of the de Klerk plan to hold a summit on violence, it was quietly understood that the ANC would boycott this conference, and attend a follow-up conference held by neutral conveners. The government agreed to act legislatively on the display of cultural weapons and to step up measures to curb violence in the townships. Most important, the parties agreed to continue talking—through the working groups—about the return of exiles and political prisoners, and about armed action. The remaining demands, especially the call for resignation of contentious cabinet ministers, were patently refused by de Klerk, despite reports that the ANC had taken a hard line in the discussions. Even though the ANC announced on 20 May that it would pull out of constitutional talks (they had, after all, not yet started), the mechanisms were still in place through which the negotiation could go forward.

As if to underscore the urgency for action, one thousand armed Zulu hostel dwellers launched an attack on mainly Xhosa residents of Swanieville squatter camp, near Kagiso, in the predawn hours of 12 May, killing twenty-seven and injuring fifty (Amnesty International 1992:50–53). According to press reports, "scores" of eyewitnesses reported that the police—rather than preventing the slaughter—escorted the *impi* back

---

[43] *Argus*, 6 May 1991.
[44] *Cape Times*, 6 May 1991.

to their hostel under armed guard.[45] Despite a direct, last-minute appeal from de Klerk to Mandela for the organization to participate in the government's summit on violence planned for later that month, the ANC stuck to its demands and threatened mass action. The ANC's National Executive Committee met 18 May and again resolved not to attend the conference. A day earlier, in a speech commemorating the dead at Kagiso, Mandela delivered the most virulent attack on the government since his release, implicitly accusing de Klerk of racism. Speaking of his summit with de Klerk, Mandela said: "I was not able to move Mr. de Klerk because like all average whites he has no regard for the black man's life."[46]

When de Klerk's peace conference convened on 24–25 May, the IFP attended but many key players were noticeably absent: the ANC, SACP, PAC, AZAPO, the Conservative party, and COSATU. Even the South African Council of Churches, which had mediated, refused to attend. Professor William Kleynhans, a member of the original church delegation, said at the conference: "It is absolutely futile to carry on without the other parties here."[47] The summit was effectively paralyzed as a vehicle for peace, and for that reason a Liaison Committee was established under the auspices of former Atomic Energy Commission head Dr. Louw Alberts, to discuss with the absentees the possibility of a national peace conference under neutral auspices.

As the turbulent month of May 1991 drew to a close, the mood between the government and ANC, and the ANC and IFP, turned from bad to worse. Mutual recriminations flew amid charges of blame for the violence and "hidden agendas." Nevertheless, the 15 June marches (some forty-eight held throughout the country) led by the ANC-SACP-COSATU alliance went off without serious incident, and 16 June, Soweto Day, was remarkably calm despite the fact the ANC, PAC, and IFP all staged major rallies. The police maintained a high profile. Behind the scenes, progress was made on some of the remaining ultimatum demands, evidenced by amendments to the Internal Security Act in late June.

A quiet meeting held 22 June by Alberts's Liaison Committee set up during de Klerk's failed summit was particularly important. A group of church and business leaders met well beyond the public eye to discuss ways to convene a national peace conference which all parties would attend. The 22 June conference resulted in the formation of the Preparatory Committee, on which three members each from the three major parties—the National party, the ANC, and the IFP—would serve together, along with selected church and business leaders. As it will be

---

[45] *Time*, 5 August 1991.
[46] *Weekly Mail*, 17–23 May 1991.
[47] *Sunday Times*, 26 May 1991.

shown, this low-profile mechanism was the beginning of a process that would result in the National Peace Accord, with the work of the Preparatory Committee dubbed the National Peace Initiative. A general rule was beginning to emerge: Unilateral action by any party to control the negotiation (e.g., the ANC's ultimatum or the government's conference on violence) would be ultimately unsuccessful.

The June 1991 ANC Conference and Inkathagate

When the planned ANC National Conference approached without its ultimatum demands met, the organization faced a critical choice: to continue with negotiation (and if so, how) or return to the armed struggle. Because it was widely believed that another national conference would not be held for at least three years—after a new constitution had been negotiated, and perhaps even implemented—the conference considered a number of important decisions, including leadership elections, organization and mobilization, sanctions, negotiation, postapartheid constitutional, economic, and social policy, and a proposed Patriotic Front with other black organizations (discussed in chapter 6). In sum, it had to deal simultaneously with the transition and the posttransition period.

The historic gathering saw the organization emerge, as one reporter noted, "younger, more unified and self-assertive."[48] In his opening address to the organization, Mandela sounded a militant but measured tone. He told the 2,220 delegates: "The point which must be clearly understood is that the struggle is not over. . . . This is a struggle we must fight on all fronts. We must engage in serious discussion on how we should manage the period of transition."[49] Nevertheless, the ANC would not hold back on negotiation, but would seek to expedite it: "We must evolve a clearer idea on the composition of [the All-Party] Congress, its agenda, manner of its functioning and the length of time it should sit." It should be convened, he said, "sooner rather than later."[50] At the conference several other events took place.

- Mandela was elected to the post of president (Oliver Tambo, the previous president, had suffered a stroke in 1989)
- Younger leaders were elected to the fifty-person National Executive Committee (NEC), nine of them women, while several old-guard incumbents were ousted
- Cyril Ramaphosa, general secretary of the mineworkers union and a seasoned negotiator, was elected secretary general

[48] *Cape Times,* 8 July 1991.
[49] *New Nation,* 5–11 July 1991.
[50] Ibid.

- Five of the top ten officials—but only two trade unionists—elected to the NEC were members of the SACP, and 50 percent of the entire NEC were SACP members
- The movement softened opposition to the lifting of economic and trade sanctions, with Mandela noting in his closing remarks that an inflexible stand would "[leave us] holding a shell and nothing else"
- The body pledged to launch a recruitment drive for MK, and for the ANC membership in general; MK would be used to set up "self-defense" units in the townships
- The organization vowed to use "mass action" to boost its power at the negotiating table (looking to the examples of Eastern Europe, the organization resolved that "negotiations do not win our freedom but represent the victories we win on the ground")[51]
- The ANC opted to stay a liberation movement, and not transform itself for the time being into a political party, although it would begin canvassing support in preparation for elections

The major effect of the Durban conference was to speed up the talks' momentum. The conference, Mandela noted in his closing remarks, "gave [the leadership] a clear mandate in favor of negotiations."[52] While violence remained the largest stumbling block to further progress, the ANC decided to throw its full weight behind the National Peace Initiative.

Barely two weeks after the conference, the ANC's new "sooner the better" tactics paid off in an unexpected way. The hard-hitting *Weekly Mail* revealed that the South African security police in Natal—with the knowledge of members of the cabinet—had provided R250,000 ($89,000) to Inkatha to help the organization pay for mass rallies. For the government, the revelations were a serious crisis, even if little money was involved. Citing a full range of evidence, including top-secret memorandums, bank receipts, and internal police communications, the *Weekly Mail* showed how the security branch of the South African Police in Natal had funneled cash from a secret slush fund for massive rallies on two separate occasions—5 November 1989 and 25 March 1990—to show the international community that Buthelezi, who opposed sanctions, "had a strong base."[53] To make matters even worse, the March 1990 rally, held near Durban, had been the spark that had led to what came to be known as the Maritzburg War. Six days after the rally, 50 people had been left dead, 150 wounded, and 6,000 homeless in fighting between backers of the IFP and the ANC.

---

[51] *Argus*, 8 July 1991.
[52] *Cape Times*, 8 July 1991.
[53] *Weekly Mail*, 19–25 July 1991.

The smoking gun of police collusion with Inkatha had been found.[54]
As the details of the fiasco spread through the press with lightning speed,
the scandal threatened to bring down de Klerk's government, much like
the scandal that had brought down the government of former prime minister Vorster. De Klerk was forced to admit that the government had in
fact siphoned money from a secret fund in the Department of Foreign
Affairs—with explicit cabinet-level approval—used to conduct an anti-
sanctions campaign, but denied that the move was "party-political."
No one bought the story. The press quickly dubbed the scandal
"Inkathagate."

Mandela and the ANC, relishing the government's crisis of credibility,
reacted calmly but firmly. Overseas, the ANC leader described Inkatha in
an address to the Jamaican parliament as "the organization that has been
most active in politically motivated violence."[55] Reverend Frank Chikane,
the leader of the church delegation that had helped save the negotiations
process in May, noted that Inkathagate "has caused ordinary South Africans to lose faith in Mr. de Klerk. . . . Those of us who had called him a
man of integrity had to swallow our words."[56]

Backed into a corner by the crisis, de Klerk summoned his cabinet on
Sunday afternoon, 29 July, to his official residence in Pretoria, Libertas.
The cabinet had just met the Friday before to devise long-term strategies
to the fallout, and many columnists has begun to write that the political
storm was about to blow over. Then the bombshell was dropped: de
Klerk announced to the stunned cabinet ministers a major reshuffle. Essentially meeting the ANC's April demands, the controversial minister of
law and order, Adrian Vlok, and hard-line defense minister Magnus
Malan were dropped from their posts. In order that de Klerk not be seen
as bowing to ANC pressure, they were left in the cabinet (Vlok as minister
of prisons; Malan, the stalwart military man, as the lowly minister of
forestry and water affairs).[57] Two initially noncontroversial replacements
were made: Hernus Kriel at law and order (whose performance later generated controversy) and seasoned negotiator Roelf Meyer at minister of
defense.

While bad for the government's position as a credible negotiating partner, Inkathagate was good, if not critical, for progress in the negotiation.

---

[54] During the unfolding scandal, the *Weekly Mail* also published a "random" list detail-
ing twenty-three claims of police collusion with Inkatha fighters in clashes with the ANC, all
reported in the press (2–8 August 1991).

[55] *Cape Times*, 26 July 1991.

[56] *Cape Times*, 3 August 1991.

[57] The cabinet reshuffle is reported thoroughly in the *Star*, 30 July 1991; the full list of
cabinet changes is found in the *Cape Times*, 30 July 1991.

The scandal and the cabinet reshuffle that followed had two important and lasting effects. First, it undercut the government's ability to continue acting, as analyst Steven Friedman wrote, as the "guardian of the transition."[58] The government's claim that it could negotiate a transition away from apartheid, while keeping its hand firmly on the tiller of the ship of state, was washed away in a tide of discredit. Having always been perceived—particularly by the international community—as the party initiating and driving the negotiation process forward while the ANC delayed and dodged, the government now saw its strategy exposed. It could not be a player in the process and a legitimate referee too (to borrow the ANC's rhetoric). An interim government framework, which the ANC had been demanding, became an imperative. Second, the scandal allowed (or forced) de Klerk ultimately to concede that for the period of transition, the police and SADF would have to become more accountable at least to the government and, ultimately, to any new transitional authority. Inkathagate, and the removal of Vlok and Malan from the cabinet, also removed major obstacles to a revival of negotiation.

The ANC's deft response to the crisis allowed it to take the initiative. Walter Sisulu, the organization's deputy president, said in a press conference that the emphasis had shifted from the removal of obstacles to negotiation to the removal of the government itself.[59] However, the obstacles to negotiation on a new constitution, outlined in the Harare Declaration and reaffirmed in the April ultimatum, were already almost cleared aside. The procedures for release and indemnification of political prisoners, though jointly negotiated by the Working Group on Political Offenses, had always been contentious. When the Bush administration in the United States lifted some sanctions against South Africa in July (just after the ANC conference), it argued that, according to the definition of political prisoners used in U.S. statutes, the South African government had complied. In South Africa, however, it was by no means so clear. The Johannesburg-based Human Rights Commission reported in mid-July that there were still some 800 prisoners jailed, 166 of them in the homeland of Bophuthatswana.[60]

The question of exiles appeared satisfactorily resolved when, in August, the government reached an agreement with the United Nations High Commissioner for Refugees (in consultation with the ANC) on the voluntary repatriation of exiles. For the first time ever, a UN agency would open an office inside South Africa to monitor the return and indemnification of those who fled apartheid; estimates of the number of returnees ranged between ten thousand and forty thousand.[61] The agreement took

[58] *Weekly Mail*, 2–8 August 1991.
[59] Ibid.
[60] *Weekly Mail*, 12–18 July 1991.
[61] *Cape Times*, 17 August 1991.

the onus for coordinating repatriation out of the hands of the government and placed it with an international agency. The ANC called on all its remaining exiles in Zambia to return home.

The National Peace Accord

With Vlok and Malan sidelined, the political-prisoners-and-exiles question nearly cleared up, and the pace of negotiations speeding up, the focus of the negotiations shifted back to the quiet, behind-the-scenes work of the Preparatory Committee of the National Peace Initiative. Negotiators decided that an inclusive peace agreement specifically designed to stabilize the turbulent transition would be adopted at a forthcoming National Peace Convention. Bilateral meetings between three main protagonists—the government, ANC, and IFP—were arranged to iron out last-minute disputes over procedure and the draft text.

Anyone who thought the impending National Peace Convention would once and for all end the killings in the townships was rudely awakened even before the words were on the page. On 8 September, less than a week before the conference, the bloodiest violence of 1991 had broken out. In Thokoza, a township on the East Rand that had long been plagued by strife, while members of the IFP-allied Hostel Dwellers Association were marching to a "peace rally" at a local stadium, they were sprayed with gunfire from three unknown assailants brandishing AK-47 automatic machine guns. Eighteen were killed, 14 wounded. Retaliatory attacks and pitched street battles spread to the nearby townships of Kathelong and Tembisa and into the Johannesburg city center. At the end of Bloody Sunday (the second day to earn such a name that year), 42 were dead and at least 50 wounded.

Bloody Sunday raised tensions surrounding the upcoming peace conference, and the week leading up to the Saturday signing ceremony was wracked with more killings. By week's end, 121 had died and some 550 were wounded in what the press called "random, senseless terror attacks."[62] In the days leading up to the conference, the ANC and IFP continued to debate the still unresolved issues of "cultural weapons" and "private armies." Inkatha was fighting a ban on the former, the ANC a ban on the latter. The Peace Initiative facilitators worked to smooth the remaining disputes. De Klerk and Mandela, it was reported, met at least twice during the run-up to the conference, although no announcements were made.[63] Final agreement on the accord was reached on the day before the signing ceremony.[64]

[62] *Weekend Argus*, 14 September 1991.
[63] *Argus*, 13 September 1991.
[64] See Cooper et al. 1992:522–56 for the text of the agreement.

The terms of the accord were quite remarkable, not only for the breadth of issues covered, but for the mechanisms for resolution of disputes to which the parties agreed. Notable, too, was its preamble and chapter 1, which specifically related the accord to the process of democratization: "The establishment of a multi-party democracy in South Africa is our common goal. Democracy is impossible in a climate of violence, intimidation and fear."[65]

The accord went on to include codes of conduct for political parties and organizations, the police and SADF, as well as clauses on dangerous weapons and self-protection units and measures for socioeconomic development and reconstruction.[66] Furthermore, it created several institutions specifically to allow major political actors to jointly manage the challenge of containing political violence, as well as mechanisms for dispute resolution and compliance: a National Peace Committee, led by a neutral chairperson and vice-chairperson drawn from the business and church facilitators to oversee implementation of the agreement and to ensure compliance; a National Peace Secretariat, a permanent, full-time body to establish regional and local dispute resolution committees (later renamed peace committees); special criminal courts to hear political violence–related cases; a revived Commission of Inquiry to fully investigate the underlying causes of violence and the steps required to prevent it; and arbitration mechanisms to ensure compliance.

The National Peace Convention was a somber and tense affair. Meeting in the five-star Carlton Hotel in downtown Johannesburg, the conference got off to a rocky start when the three hundred delegates arrived to find thousands of armed IFP supporters staging mock battles in the streets outside the venue. ANC delegates fumed at the provocation. The impis reluctantly dispersed only after a direct appeal by de Klerk to Buthelezi. Indeed, Buthelezi's uncertainty about the accord was evident throughout the day-long proceedings. The IFP objected to Nobel Prize winner Archbishop Desmond Tutu chairing the proceedings, and asserted that *assegais* (long, thin spears) were not dangerous weapons, but "traditional accoutrements" of the Zulus. Buthelezi lashed out a reporter who probed the comment, saying "Only ten percent of victims have been killed with spears. It is the AK-47 that kills people."[67] Mandela, too, had words that signaled the limitations of the accord: MK, he announced, would neither be disbanded nor considered a "private army."

[65] National Peace Accord, mimeo.

[66] These items arose out of demands made by the ANC's National Executive Committee after its 20 May decision to pull out of constitutional talks (fulfilling its April ultimatum threats). They were originally proposed by the ANC's ally, COSATU. These demands were first discussed at a de Klerk-Mandela meeting in late May.

[67] *Argus*, 16 September 1991.

After a litany of speeches in which organizations pledged themselves to peace and a testy but reserved press conference by the "big three" leaders (de Klerk, Mandela, and Buthelezi, who were palpably uncomfortable with sharing a common platform), the day ended with the accord signed. Delegations from twenty-nine political, trade union, and government organizations eventually signed the agreement. The PAC and AZAPO attended the conference but refused to sign the document, arguing that it amounted to negotiation with the "racist regime." The Conservative party and other right-wing white organizations boycotted the conference altogether.

The Violence-Negotiation Nexus

The upsurge in political violence was the dominant theme of the preliminary negotiation phase of transition in South Africa. Between 1984 and late 1991, some fourteen thousand died in political violence. Moreover, the *nature* of political violence was transformed from a primarily overt conflict between the regime and the forces of liberation to a more entangled fight among a wide variety of players with disparate motives, tactics, and objectives. In the violence, there was continuity and change. The "state terrorism" counterinsurgency efforts of the regime employed during the 1980s, which included (in addition to the normal security procedures of the state, such as capital punishment and detention without trial) the extrajudicial use of vigilantes, death squads, torture, and arson and armed attacks, were for the most part curtailed. But vigilante violence, hit squads, random bombings, and the use of agents provocateurs continued apace, even as new internecine violence erupted in the townships.

Causes of Political Violence

Understanding the causes behind the violence and its relationship to the political process may help to explain the paradox of increased violence following the onset of negotiation. Schlemmer's (1991b) analysis reveals three broad causes of political violence—background or structural factors, predisposing conditions, and triggering events. This typology is helpful in analyzing the problem. However, since I do not believe there are significant differences between predisposing and structural factors in South Africa's case, I am considering them together.

Structural and Predisposing Factors. The most visible and enduring structural cause of violence in South Africa is self-evident: for the disenfranchised black majority, life is an unending struggle for survival under conditions of absolute and relative deprivation. This is the legacy of apartheid. High levels of urbanization and unemployment (reaching 60 percent in many townships) are the alienating facts of life in most of the areas of high conflict, but particularly in the urban sprawl around Johannesburg. Shortages of resources, including land, housing, and basic sustenance, reinforce this estrangement, as does the relative wealth of white South Africans. Settlement patterns, including the housing by ethnic group of migrant workers in single-sex hostels during the heyday of apartheid, were an important factor.

In these desperately poor urban and semiurban communities, social rules eroded and alternative social structures (such as gangs and "warlords") thrived. The authority and legitimacy of the state in such an atmosphere, to say nothing of family and traditional authority, sharply declined. Common social restraints on violence and killing disappeared. When gangs and similar groups became politicized, as they invariably did in the course of the struggle against apartheid, political violence—harm inflicted primarily from political motives—was the consequence.

Another factor in the upsurge of violence was the role played by migrant hostel dwellers from rural areas, who clashed frequently with urban township groups. The social tensions between rural and urban, traditional and modern, uneducated and educated manifested themselves in the conflicts between the semipeasant hostel dwellers—fiercely loyal to traditional kinship ties—and the young, urban "comrades" schooled in the radicalism of township life. Such tensions were heightened when the conflict focused on ever-scarce resources. Schlemmer, for example, writes:

> Although perhaps not fully conscious of it, urban youth and unemployed adults, Zulu migrants, other migrants and Xhosa-speaking shack dwellers are all in heightened competition for very fixed limited opportunities. [The contracting opportunities thesis] fits perfectly: expectations and opportunities rising in 1988, followed by opportunities falling in late 1989 and 1990, faster for some than for others, and with many people arriving rapidly in a situation of increased privation with few or no alternatives. (1991b:5)

The salience of ethnicity as a predisposing factor, implicitly raised by Schlemmer but more explicitly raised by other analysts, was hotly contested. Mobilization along ethnic lines did indeed occur in part as a result of rising or declining relative group worth (Horowitz 1985:143), particularly among the Zulu speakers. It is not surprising then, as South Africa struggled in the grips of a decade-long recession and South Africans remained deeply uncertain about their social location and identity, that ethnic conflict erupted. However, while ethnic identity may have been a predisposing factor, explaining the upsurge in political violence following the onset of negotiations solely in ethnic terms misses a key fact: political violence itself was rooted in the widespread confusion of politics in the course of transition. Ethnic mobilization was an expression of a much deeper insecurity.

For this reason, the violence was often cast by the international press in terms of an intense ANC-IFP rivalry, and was referred to as "black-on-black" violence or even "tribal warfare," owing to the Zulu base of the IFP and the oft-alleged Xhosa base of the ANC. Such a simple characterization was misleading because it belied the complexity of the situation in many townships (and the presence of victims and combatants from other ethnic groups). In addition, in one arena of especially intense fighting, the Midlands of Natal, the conflict was primarily intra-Zulu. Further, because it was apartheid's premise that ethnic conflict among blacks would render a unified multicultural South Africa ungovernable, it is easy to see why those opposed to racial integration would foment violence specifically along ethnic lines.[68]

Triggering Events. Once the structural and predisposing factors for violence were present, virtually any event—political, community, or even personal—set off a fresh round of fighting. Triggering events ranged from political rallies, mass demonstrations, strikes and stayaways, and political or criminal assassinations, to unexplainable random attacks on rail commuters or personal vendettas. A chain of revenge and retaliation always seemed to follow. In South Africa, all sides to the conflict, at one time or another, triggered violence.[69]

Whatever the spark, the structural causes of violence were so ubiquitous that even small, apolitical events spawned cycles of action and reaction; the problem became self-perpetuating. Structural conditions, predisposing factors, and triggering events interacted with enormous complexity with each new incident of political violence. Although many complex causes were present, the upsurge of political violence was directly related to the much broader issue of the absence of a defined set of political rules during the course of the transition. There was, during the

[68] Africa Watch describes the clandestine distribution of an anti-Zulu pamphlet allegedly circulated by security forces as a "classic destabilization tactic" to whip up anti-ANC sentiments among Zulu speakers in the township of Sebokeng (1991:58–59).

[69] Kibbe (1991:1, 3) reviews three studies that attempt to proportionally attribute responsibility for various incidents of violence to political organizations and the security forces. The upshot of the review is that while most observers lean toward blaming the IFP for precipitating of violence, all actors have at one time or another precipitated a fresh round of fighting.

uncertain interregnum, a power vacuum. As political power for the black majority neared in the run-up to a postapartheid South Africa, the ANC, IFP, and the forces of the National party-led state were locked in a high-stakes competition for political power and ascendancy. Simon Bekker of the University of Natal accurately characterizes this interregnum as plagued by "widespread confusion over how politics [is] to be conducted" (1990:23).

Violence: A Beyond-the-Table Tool

A sharp increase in political violence occurred in South Africa just prior to, or just following, major negotiation events. For example, in the first three months of 1990, when dramatic changes were taking place, 951 died in political conflict.[70] The violence tapered off following the successful conclusion of the first ANC-government pact in May 1990, the Groote Schuur Minute. However, following the Pretoria Minute, violence soared, this time to unprecedented heights and unusual brutality. Yet again after the conclusion of an agreement between the ANC and the IFP in January 1991, the cycle of violence spiraled anew. Figure 3.1 demonstrates this point.

Explaining the violence-negotiation nexus in South Africa is complicated by three factors. First, different specific events may have had different causes. Second, different observers have proportionally attributed blame for violence on different actors, and all parties to the conflict have at times perpetrated violence. Third, the role of a "third force," based in the regime's security apparatus was widely alleged to be fomenting violence; these allegations were circumstantially proven, but a coherent presidentially directed covert plan was not definitively proven. With these complicating factors in mind, there are three possible explanations for the use of violence as a tactic by actors responding to the vicissitudes of the negotiation process:

- *Violence to halt or reverse the process.* Actors opposed to the negotiation process—either because of reactionary or revolutionary motives—may foment violence at critical turning points in order to demonstrate that the negotiations themselves are unworkable and should be abandoned for a return to a zero-sum pursuit of the conflict.
- *Violence to prevent marginalization.* Political actors who support negotiations but fear exclusion from political power in the new order may foment

[70] On political violence during this period, see the August 1991 report of the Johannesburg-based Human Rights Commission, "The New Total Strategy: Twelve Months of Community Repression, July 1990 to June 1991."

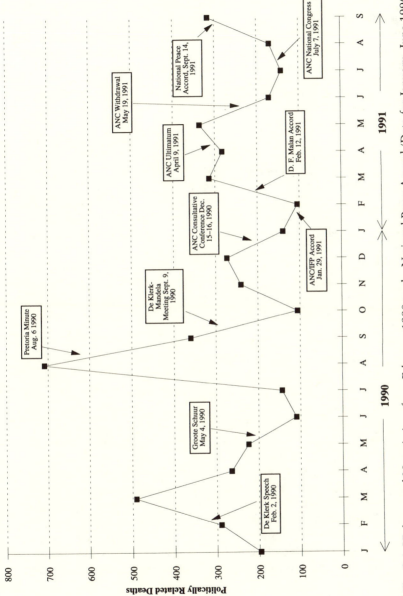

Fig. 3.1 Violence and Negotiation, from February 1990 to the National Peace Accord (Data for January–June 1990 from the *Sunday Times*, 15 September 1991. The Johannesburg-based independent Human Rights Commission began publishing data on political violence in July 1990. For July 1990–September 1991 data, see *Checkmate for Apartheid?* [Johannesburg: Human Rights Commission, July 1992].)

violence at critical turning points in the negotiations to ensure that their interests are protected in the final agreement.

- *Violence to destabilize the opponent.* Actors who fear an opponent's strength may foment violence in an effort to destabilize an opponent (or opponents), thereby enhancing their own power in an effort to strike a more favorable deal at the table. Actors seeking to strengthen the hand of weak negotiators foment political violence to demonstrate the capacity to do so.

Clearly, various political parties and organizations in South Africa had, at different times, an explicit interest in pursuing any of these tactics singularly or in concert.

Political violence was a tactic used by various actors as a "beyond-the-table" tool in pursuit of specific political aims. Schlemmer, for example, notes that: "The negotiations are, and will increasingly be, *competitive* [emphasis in original]. All major parties involved intend to negotiate to secure strategic advantages in the new system. . . . It is for this reason that so much 'position play' takes place outside of negotiations. Attempts are constantly being made to increase leverage in the negotiation by political pressures extraneous to the negotiation itself" (1991b:11).

No matter which party's members were specifically responsible for incidents of violence, the state clearly bore the onus of responsibility to protect the rights of all citizens and to expose and prosecute those responsible for violating human rights. For this reason, the focus on the state's security forces as a party to the conflict in South Africa, widely supported by evidence, emerged as a critical issue. The government's security forces sought to use violence to destabilize political opponents, especially the ANC (Africa Watch 1991; Amnesty International 1992). Some elements of the security forces, as well as right-wing paramilitary groups, used violence to thwart the negotiation process altogether. No political actor in a transition from authoritarian rule is more insecure than the old regime's security forces (O'Donnell, Schmitter, and Whitehead 1986:39). Fearful of its place in the future, uncertain of retribution that might well be meted out after so many years of repression, the military has an intrinsic interest in using violence to maintain or improve its position. In South Africa, this intrinsic interest was compounded by the fact that for the decade of the 1980s, the security network was a "state within a state." White-led security forces in South Africa encouraged black internecine violence because a divided black majority was less likely to dominate the white minority if its energies were directed at fighting among factions within the community.

Intervention in the conflict by the security forces, including the South African Police and South African Defense Force but also police in the apartheid-created homelands (e.g., the KwaZulu Police or Ciskei Defense Force), took different forms at different times. Indeed, the November 1989 revelations of the existence of death squad units within the South African Defense Force reinforced the claims that a "third force" within the security apparatus was involved in violence. The unit, called the Civil Cooperation Bureau, was allegedly responsible for the deaths of many prominent anti-apartheid activists, including Ruth First, political writer and wife of SACP secretary general Joe Slovo, David Webster, a well-known university professor, Patrick Makau, an activist, and many others. In February 1990 the SADF admitted the existence of the death-squad unit, although de Klerk said at the time he was unaware of its existence until January 1990. De Klerk immediately ordered the disbanding of the unit, and by July 1991 defense chief Magnus Malan announced that all members of the Civil Cooperation Bureau had retired or been reassigned.

Attention was specifically focused on the Department of Military Intelligence within the SADF and its alleged role in arming and training IFP hit-squads.[71] In general, the security forces were accused of a failure to protect individuals from attack, a political bias toward the IFP, an involvement in attacks on communities and residents, both alone and in concert with IFP agencies such as the KwaZulu Police, and in direct assaults, a failure to comply with legal interdicts, and the use of force to disperse township residents attempting to defend themselves from IFP attacks (Africa Watch 1991). Such actions (or inaction) were documented both in Natal and in the townships around Johannesburg.

President de Klerk repeatedly denied knowledge of rogue elements in the security forces fomenting violence. Whether de Klerk was personally involved or not, critics of the regime rightly honed in on the implicit interest of the security forces in fomenting violence as major events in negotiations occurred. According to the 19–25 July 1991 issue of the alternative weekly *New Nation:*

> We are now landed with an extensive security network, which has limitless resources, is accountable to no one and which has lost ideological coherence. Its only commitment is to show the world "that blacks are not ready to rule." And so the violence has to be kept at a peak. . . . We say that the question of national security must feature as a pre-negotiations issue that would ensure that security is removed from the incumbents and entrusted to an impartial authority. Without this, the violence will continue, and the continuation of the negotiations in the context will build not democracy but anarchy.

[71] *Weekly Mail,* 13–18 December 1991. The paper reports that the DMI used front organizations to penetrate the IFP and to provide military training to IFP cadres.

The Mass-Elite Nexus and Pact Making

The National Peace Accord was a quintessential democratization pact, the kind of accord that Dahl appropriately describes as a "mutual security agreement" (1973:13–16). But it is a document agreed to by political elites and, as such, reflects elite interests. Elite coalescence has been the hallmark of South Africa's transition. In the talks, the conflict resolution mechanism of last resort has been the de Klerk-Mandela rapport, even though the initial trust between the two has eroded in cries of mutual recrimination and bad faith and of "hidden agendas." Notwithstanding the potential for "elite-initiated conflict" (Tsebelis 1990b), the preliminary negotiation phase shows that in South Africa, the political leaders best understand the maxim that a worse outcome must be avoided. After all, it was such a realization that brought them to the table in the first place.

If the violence in South Africa was not "conspired" by political elites (an arguable premise with respect to de Klerk's relationship with the state security forces and evidence tracing some incidents of violence back to IFP leadership), where did the process break down? Why did agreements among political leaders that explicitly call for peace often result in heightened tensions? If one discounts conspiracy theories and hidden agendas, the alternative explanation is one of "slippage." Political leaders may agree on the need for peace, but at least some of their followers do not. The zero-sum perception of the conflict persisted among followers, particularly midlevel elites. Friedman correctly notes that sometimes the most mobilized and intransigent individuals are midlevel elites. He writes that "because there are weak linkages between party supporters or members and activists, what is [often] presented as a 'rank and file' view is often that of middle-level mobilized elites. . . . This is nowhere more true than [on] the violence issue."[72] For example, shortly after the ANC issued its May 1991 ultimatum, the *Weekly Mail* issued a similar call for a joint bid to end the violence: "Another face-to-face encounter between Mandela and President F. W. de Klerk, the magic formula that has ended past stand-offs, won't swing it this time," the paper wrote in a page-one story. "As long as the violence continues, the ANC will be under pressure from its township constituency, which sees the negotiations with the government as meaningless while the townships are burning, to take the kind of hard-line represented by [the] ultimatum."[73]

Thus, the mass-elite nexus is a critical phenomenon in democratic transitions. As Burton and Higley write:

[72] Correspondence with the author, 4 January 1994.
[73] *Weekly Mail*, 12–18 April 1991.

Although settlements are primarily the result of private negotiations among substantially autonomous elites, they have an important public, or nonelite, aspect. . . . Nonelite involvement presents a tricky problem for elites who would fashion a settlement. On the one hand, it is essential that compromising moderates be able to mobilize widespread, probably overwhelming, nonelite support against intransigent elite persons and groups. On the other hand, these compromisers run the risk of losing nonelite support if they are perceived as selling out their followers. (1987:301)

Elite-concluded accords do not work unless elites are able to demobilize their own constituencies. In South Africa, for example, the ANC-IFP peace agreement of January 1991 was a bilateral agreement that sought to control violence in the townships and rural areas of Natal. After the agreement was signed, thousands of copies of the accord in English and Zulu were distributed in the strife-torn areas, and flyers announcing "Leaders Make Peace" were posted throughout the Natal countryside. Within weeks, however, as violence mounted and political leaders traded insults and accusations, it was clear that the accord was a failure. Indeed, on the very day after the agreement, six people were hacked to death in Natal, and another twenty-seven were killed in ANC-IFP strife in the sprawling townships around Johannesburg.[74]

South Africa's experience shows that transitional pacts or agreements cannot be personalized; even political leaders of the stature of Mandela, de Klerk, and Buthelezi could not demobilize their constituencies. The underlying forces behind the violence were mostly beyond their control. As has been demonstrated with respect to other conflict situations, political elites can easily mobilize their constituencies to demonstrate their power in society but they are unable to demobilize them when the moment of peace arrives (Duffy and Frensley 1989:5). This inability to demobilize is especially true of midlevel elites and local party leaders, whose claims to represent grass-roots opinion are strongest (but not necessarily true).

In many ways, the National Peace Accord is a pact to acknowledge that very problem. As columnist Steven Friedman has written in the 27 September–3 October 1991 *Weekly Mail:*

The pact does not seek to end conflict but to frame binding rules for managing it—a machinery to enforce them. It has far more faith in rules and procedures

[74] *Los Angeles Times* reporter Scott Kraft has given a detailed, anecdotal account of the days and weeks immediately after the ANC/IFP peace accord, chronicling its failure. See his article, "Blood Feud," *Los Angeles Times Magazine,* 2 June 1991. This excellent, in-depth story of the violence in and around Port Shepstone, Natal, in early March 1991 goes beyond the headlines to provide a graphic, personalized picture of the human costs of violence in South Africa.

that in "goodwill" between the parties. So the Accord may reveal a strategy for peace and political tolerance which is more "cynical" but more optimistic than one which pins its hopes on a new political culture. . . . The approach behind the Accord may form the basis for a democracy in which parties don't love each other—but will stick to the rules because they can't destroy each other.

As Friedman points out, the best option elites have, if they are unable to end political violence altogether, is to jointly manage it. Joint management of violence was aimed at depoliticizing it to the extent possible so that more overtly political issues—for example, the preeminently political act of designing the new constitution—could be negotiated without the undertow of killing drowning the negotiators in conflict. Alas, as I discuss in chapter 6, the National Peace Accord was unable to fulfill this aim in the continued uncertainty of the interregnum.

As Friedman also notes, the essence of the pact is the creation of a joint set of rules to which all subscribe. Notably, the Peace Accord also included codes of conduct for political parties and the police (a code for the SADF was debated, but not included). Still other provisions of the accord reveal the strategy of jointly managing the violence problem. Regional and local peace committees set up in the pact are a clear recognition that top-down conflict management is insufficient and ineffective. The creation of permanent, full-time task forces that included local political leaders and organizers and the police and security forces, replete with standing mediators and facilitators, was an indicator of the need to address the problem from the grass roots. These substructures of the accord were an implicit recognition of the previous failure of bilateral peace agreements to solve the problems of endemic political violence.

The National Peace Accord had all of the important features of transitional pact making (di Palma 1990:86–90). It was inclusive: each signatory was guaranteed a presence at the highest level of decision making. It was fairly comprehensive: as a mutual security agreement, the rights and privileges of political parties were explicitly delineated; the police and security forces were explicitly restrained and removed from the arena of partisan political activity; it laid out in specific terms the methods for dealing with incidents of violence as well as resolution mechanisms in cases of disputes; and it bound the parties to the agreement with explicit enforcement mechanisms. Perhaps most important, the National Peace Accord focused on constructing interim rules of the new political game: it explicitly identified a democratic state as the common aim of the signatories, and it was itself a detailed set of rules for the control of violence. As a new set of political rules, the National Peace Accord represented South Africa's first postapartheid institution, albeit a nascent, transitional one.

Political violence in South Africa's transition was directly related to the talks themselves. Political actors, in a response to the reformulation of the rules of the political game at the negotiating table, resorted to violence to demonstrate their own political power, reduce the power of their adversaries, or thwart the process altogether. The violence-negotiations nexus lies in the tenuous nature of a protracted, negotiated transition: as the rules of the political game—apartheid and authoritarian white minority rule—fell away, and before the rules of the new political game were negotiated, codified, and institutionalized, both uncertainty and expectations peaked. Uncertainty peaked as political forces that once had well-defined and predictable political roles sought to redefine their roles in the new political environment. Expectations peaked as the moment of political realignment neared; parties and groups expected to gain in the new game or to lose. The uncertain interregnum is characterized by an overwhelming sense of fear and insecurity.

Political violence was a tactical response in negotiation to fear and insecurity. In transitions, political actors—especially, but by no means solely, the security forces of the incumbent regime—fear the new order because they are uncertain as to whether their vital interests will be protected: they fear marginalization or political extinction. Violence was, in part, a beyond-the-table tactic by political actors to ensure their interests were protected in the new order, to enhance their bargaining position, or simply to sabotage the process of negotiated change altogether. The fact that increased political violence tracked the negotiations process so closely in South Africa's transition to democracy reinforces the view that control of violence through pacts such as the National Peace Accord are an essential precondition to further democratization. Di Palma is correct when he writes:

> As politically open as pacts should be, they are employed first of all to introduce restraint, a sense of civility, a curb on violence and aggression. They are used to provide some orderly exit to divisive times. There exists therefore a whole range of politically motivated behaviors that, though they constitute a resource in the typical arsenals of political and state actors, need to be controlled through pacts—as nearly a prerequisite to democratization. . . . It clearly includes state violence and arbitrariness, political persecution, appeals to the military, armed rebellion, and orchestrated strife. (1990:88)

The National Peace Accord, in this respect, clearly fits the comparative pattern of a "prerequisite" pact on the path to democratization. Behind the accord lies the recognition by elites that a hegemonic pursuit of the conflict is self-defeating; the high levels of political violence indicate that this realization was not internalized by their followers. In this regard, Burton and Higley's (1987; Higley and Burton 1989) argument that elite coalescence is a precondition to democratization is convincing. South Africa's pacted transition illustrates well a gradual or incremental democratization path based on *elite settlements,* in which "warring national elite factions suddenly and deliberately reorganize their relations by negotiating compromises on their most basic disagreements" (Burton and Higley 1987:295). However, as elite agreements, temporary in scope, they did not sufficiently reduce uncertainty and beyond-the-table political posturing, particularly among lower-level functionaries. I will return to the mass-elite nexus and violence-negotiation nexus in chapter 6. South Africa's transition demonstrates that a diminution of political violence is possible but by no means assured only when the new rules of the future political order have become entrenched and the uncertainty of the interregnum wanes.

CHAPTER 4

Parties, Interests, and Institutional Choices: 1991

DURING THE preliminary negotiation phase of South Africa's transition in 1990 and 1991, most political parties and organizations articulated well-defined institutional choices for a postapartheid polity.[1] Each party based its choices on a thorough assessment of its ideological orientation and interests, its review of alternatives, and its perceived power vis à vis other parties. The differences in the models outlined by the parties were substantial, particularly considering that a significant minority—the white right wing—did not accept the basic premise that South Africans shared a common political future at all.

What were the preferences of the major political actors for the rules to govern a future state, and on what criteria were these choices based? To address this broader question, for each major party I address three questions:

- What was the party's ideological orientation?
- What interests did the party represent, and to which forces in civil society was it allied?
- What were the party's institutional choice preferences for postapartheid political structures, and how did the relative positions of the parties change over the time period leading up to formal negotiation?

In this chapter, I describe the ideological orientation and interest base of the major parties as they relate to their preferences for the institutions of a postapartheid polity, and return to an analysis of the politics of institutional choice—the power relationships—in the following chapter. I contend that an understanding of the preferences for institutions to guide the transition—whether a "constituent assembly" or "multiparty negotiating forum" would draft the new constitution, for example—requires a prior understanding of the regime model toward which each party is striving. That is, the ideologies, interests, and institutional choice preferences of the political actors must be considered prior to their preferences for the transitional institutions to guide the formal negotiation. I will pick up the chronological trail leading to formal constitutional negotiations again

---

[1] I differentiate parties and organizations because, technically, the ANC did not describe itself as a political party during 1991. However, because it intended on competing in an election, its general consideration as a party is justified.

in chapter 6 to demonstrate the linkages between the process of negotiation and its outcomes and to map the concessions that led to a democratization pact in late 1993.

THE WHITE RIGHT

An important premise differentiates the white right wing in South Africa from all other major political parties and actors. While white nationalist parties and organizations have proliferated—some working as political parties, others as social movements, other clandestinely as emergent guerrilla armies—they all have shared a single common belief: there is no South African "nation," no overarching shared destiny for the peoples that live within the territory of present-day South Africa and the homelands. Clinging to the values of Afrikaner ethnic nationalism, all of these disparate parties and organizations have strived for an ethnonationalist, exclusive state to serve the (white) Afrikaner nation. They believe fervently in the underlying principles behind grand apartheid.

The apartheid dream of an Afrikaner volkstaat (nation-state) was not only alive and well in some circles in South Africa, it became imperative as full enfranchisement approached. The National party, which had protected white and Afrikaner interests for so many years, was viewed with ultimate contempt—and branded a traitor to the *volk*. Like ethnic outbidders elsewhere, the white right claimed the collective heritage had been betrayed. I will focus here on the Conservative party, formed in 1982, because it was the flagship of the white right. (I discuss more extremist white right-wing groups as CP coalition partners in the following chapter, and in subsequent chapters outline the fragmentation that created a plethora of new right-wing groups in 1992 and 1993.)

The Conservative Party

In 1991, the Conservative party held perhaps the most "sophisticated" view of all the right-wing parties and organizations as to how to operationalize claims for an ethnic state. Because the CP has served as the official opposition in the white House of Assembly since 1987, it has been forced to respond to the Nationalist government's every move, challenging its choice for negotiation and its call for power sharing. It also vied electorally for the same constituencies among South Africa's nearly 5 million whites in the elections of 1987 and 1989. Since its founding in 1982, it outbid the National party for the support of white South Africans who held steadfast to a belief in the grand apartheid dream of Verwoerd. Nevertheless, during the 1960s, when Verwoerd's vision was running against the tide of history, particularly in Africa, the CP perceived the tide of the post—Cold War world drifting in its favor. The resurgence of ethnic nationalism in its wake seemingly bolstered arguments for Afrikaners to assert national self-determination. Just as states were created in the dust of the crumbling Soviet empire, in the rubble of postapartheid South Africa a new Afrikaner state could be constituted.

The core premises of apartheid are the heart of CP ideology. Ferdi Hartzenberg, chairman of the CP caucus in the House of Assembly during 1991 and subsequently party leader, is of the old school. In a statement that could have come from the mouth of Verwoerd himself, Hartzenberg said that "South Africa is not one nation. . . . It is thirteen different nations. That is the only way we will be free—if all nations are free. If the other people don't want to be free and sovereign, they can get together through power sharing or integration if they want someone to oppress them."[2]

The ethnonationalist CP approach of 1991 is, of course, the NP view of 1948.[3] From this basic premise, it flows that not only does the white "nation" not belong in an overarching South African nationhood, but a common national consciousness does not exist among black South Africans either. The orthodox apartheid view that separate national states are best is true for Afrikaners and for the African "nations" of southern Africa as well. These nations are fundamentally irreconcilable in a single state.

The CP's worldview thus has been one of organic nationhood for themselves and for all others. But how has CP handled the need to reconcile ethnic-versus-racial criteria for defining the nation? The "nation" is defined not solely on ascriptive terms, but in the context of "association." Hartzenberg explains: "In the CP, we see the nucleus of our nation as Afrikaners. But what is the basis for a common nationhood? A nation has the same values, same ideas, and a common past. We accept as members of our nation all of those that have the same values, and choose to associate with us."[4]

Such a statement reveals, at least on the level of rhetoric, that the CP views the nation not necessarily as a white "nation." In practice, however, the party's principle is one of white racial exclusivity in all the important spheres of life. The CP's 1989 election manifesto, for example, argues that racial segregation is essential in order to "ensure that the white's exclusive and separate community life is not . . . overwhelmed and disrupted by other communities."[5] Nevertheless, there are respected South African scholars of the CP and its allies who claim ethnic survivalism, not

[2] Interview with the author, 17 April 1991.
[3] For an in-depth treatment of this theme, see Adam and Moodley 1987.
[4] Interview with the author, 17 April 1991.
[5] "Election Manifesto of the Conservative Party," 1989.

racism, motivates the white right; they write: "We believe . . . that the label racist captures neither the fundamental nature nor the underlying intention of the rightwing movement (Grobbelar, Bekker, and Evans 1989:6)." If self-determination is based on the concept of a "people," whom has the CP represented?

CP Constituencies

Despite the claim that the nation is based on association and not race, the constituency of the party has been the downwardly mobile, poorer, and less-educated portions of the white Afrikaans-speaking community and, to a much lesser extent, similar groups of English-speaking whites.[6] There have been virtually no persons of color in the CP ranks. The intellectual discourse on the concept of nation and the right to self-determination is obscured by the simple fact that the CP has mobilized its supporters by fanning the flames of white fear.

There are two sources of such fear: one is associated with the question of relative group worth or collective esteem, and the other is a simple material concern. Downwardly mobile whites fear for their group status and identity. CP member of parliament Fanie Jacobs commented on the CP's choice for a separate Afrikaner state: "It is the interest of my people. The other side of the coin, it's the genocide of my people that will be at stake. . . . One could say . . . we are looking . . . to protect interests, and these interests in the final analysis one could only find amongst your own."[7]

A sense of ethnic belonging, however, is only half of the picture. There has been a clear class dimension to the CP's constituency base as well. Those left behind by the embourgeoisement policies of apartheid have seen their interests best protected by the CP. Afrikaner economist Sampie Terreblanche of the University of Stellenbosch, a well-known dissident, writes: "The attitudes of Afrikaners supporting the CP can be described as typical of a disgruntled and impoverishing (petit) bourgeoisie (conventional middle-class). They avail themselves of high-sounding ideological rhetoric to conceal their economic grievances."[8] In fact, the CP has stayed much closer to traditional Afrikaner constituencies—such as farmers and working class whites—than has the NP government. These include many conservative Afrikaner religious and cultural organizations, as well as tradition-oriented organizations newly formed after the split in Afri-

[6] In the 1989 election, only 5 percent of English-speaking whites voted for the CP. Data from Olivier 1989.

[7] Interview with the author, 4 June 1991.

[8] *Weekend Argus,* 14 July 1990.

kanerdom in 1982. In socioeconomic terms, the CP's primary support has come from several sources:

- *Farmers.* The backbone of the CP constituency base has been poorer white farmers who feel the pinch of increasing input costs and declining market prices, as well as the withdrawal of direct support by the NP government. Most of the seats held by the CP in parliament have been rural, with the exception of several in the PWV area. In the 1989 general election, the CP won more than half (54 percent) of the rural vote, but only 30 percent of the urban vote, in the Transvaal province. Of the areas of the Orange Free State where the CP made inroads, all were rural constituencies.
- *White laborers,* particularly those with fewer skills. The CP has had a natural support base among the lower echelons of the white labor force, particularly in state-owned corporations. The main white trade-union federation is the South African Confederation of Labor, of which the most important member is the Mine Workers' Union. Blue-collar workers would be the first to lose jobs to skilled and semiskilled black labor in the event of state-mandated affirmative action—which makes them one of the potentially most downwardly mobile groups in society. They seek to preserve the middle-class status apartheid policies created for them.
- *Some civil servants and members of the armed forces and police.* Uneasiness about the prospects of continued employment under majority rule has pushed many members of the civil service into CP ranks. But perhaps more important have been the unknown numbers of members of the SADF and the South African Police (SAP) that privately support the white right wing.

It is more revealing to underscore white constituencies that have not supported the CP. The party has enjoyed virtually no backing among two important pillars of the white community: big business and the media. The CP has garnered little support in the establishment press and even the party mouthpiece—*Die Patriot*—has had limited circulation.

Despite few resources, during 1982 to 1987 the Conservative party was the fastest growing party in South African history. After the September 1989 elections, however, it became apparent that the CP's bandwagon, if not stopped, was slowing down. While CP growth slowed in late 1988 and early 1989, it improved its parliamentary standing in the 1989 elections (thanks in part to earlier NP gerrymandering in rural areas). It netted thirty-nine seats altogether (up seventeen from 1987), increased its white popular vote from 26 percent to 31 percent, and for the first time captured seats in the Cape (two) and in the Orange Free State (six). Popular support among Afrikaans-speaking whites edged up from 38 percent in 1987 to 42 percent in 1989.[9] Thirty-nine seats was far short of the fifty

[9] Data from Olivier 1989.

to sixty seats the CP expected to win, however, and was not enough to force a hung parliament.

Following their poor showing in 1989 and the new initiatives of de Klerk, the CP reached an upper threshold of support among whites. A July 1991 Human Sciences Research Council (HSRC) poll put the support for the CP among white respondents at only 21 percent overall (Kotzé and Sisk 1991). The survey confirmed that their primary constituency was less-educated whites: nearly 34 percent of white respondents with less than a secondary school education backed the CP. Similarly, very few (4 percent) English-speaking whites backed the party. Extrapolated, these data indicate the CP could at best expect the support of only about 3 percent of the total population. The CP also has garnered support among white immigrants, including Portuguese speakers who fled to South Africa following independence in Angola and Mozambique. The CP has represented a small, resource-poor, but staunchly motivated minority of South Africa's whites.

The Politics of Partition

The CP's choice for partition consistently has raised important questions: What territory does the CP want, and how are state boundaries to be drawn? The CP's responses are vague for two reasons. First, by succinctly defining territory, the CP could possibly marginalize or alienate current or potential supporters whose landholdings are not within the defined boundaries. Second, by concealing strategy, the party could potentially maximize its outbidding of the National party for support.

The CP drew no boundaries for its volkstaat.[10] Yet, some evolution in the CP's degree of specificity occurred. While the original impetus behind the CP was to reinvigorate grand apartheid as it existed prior to the 1979 shifts in NP policy, the party subsequently realized that a Afrikaner homeland would of necessity be only a slender part of Verwoerd's white South Africa. Jacobs has said "We do not say we want to have the whole of South Africa. . . . On the boundaries we will negotiate."[11] Ambiguity within CP ranks as to exactly what a "smaller" part of South Africa

[10] This is where the CP differs most from other right-wing groups, such as the Afrikaner Volkswag (People's guard), who have not only specified their proposed homeland, but have begun a settlement campaign in the designated area. "We cannot draw boundaries," Jacobs says. "It is easy for Professor Boshoff [of the Volkswag] to draw boundaries; he does not have an electorate to which he is responsible" (interview with the author, 4 June 1991).

[11] Interview with the author, 4 June 1991. Initially, the CP advocated that the volkstaat boundaries coincide with the constituencies it won in the 1989 election; this proposal was subsequently withdrawn.

would entail persisted in the uncertainty of South Africa's transition, as did the question of if and when to negotiate, and with whom. Hard-liners such as Hartzenberg pushed for much of the old ideals, but conceded that a "land for peace" option was inevitable.

> Right now we control all of the territories outside the self-governing states and the territories of the Coloureds and Indians. This is the "white area," as it has been since 1910, and that is where will will start. If [we] experience problems—and we know there are problems—we will use land to solve problems. We must start where the large concentration of people are. . . . For example, the black areas around Port Elizabeth can be excised and put in Ciskei.[12]

The related question of what to do with highly integrated urban areas posed a similar problem. CP policy was to "couple" city-states with ethnically based national territories. The 1989 election manifesto calls for a complicated system of voting rights, for example, whereby black citizens of "white" urban areas would have the franchise only in their national states, but would gain primary responsibility over services in their urban living areas.[13]

Part of the solution is the CP's view, long a part of the Verwoerdian ideal, that after successful partition of the country, a broader confederation of southern African states could be created. Economic cooperation and integration would be coordinated in a supranational framework, as long as political independence and state sovereignty were assured. The CP refers to this solution as the European Community option: an economically integrated constellation of independent, sovereign states. Did the CP soundings on a supranational confederation mean that it might accept, in the course of negotiation, an autonomous region or similar arrangement within a unitary South Africa? Would it possibly accept consociational restraints, such as federalism or the inclusion of "group rights" in a new bill of rights? Moderates in the white right wing such as former CP parliamentarian Koos van der Merwe (he later joined the IFP) suggested autonomy without sovereignty was "potentially viable."[14] Hard-liners such as Hartzenberg were skeptical; "autonomy can be changed [at the center]. . . . We are interested in sovereignty; nothing less than that will satisfy us."[15] If these CP members were ambiguous about an autonomous region in 1991, they were of one mind on the issue of including group rights in a bill of rights as possible minority protection—they rejected it. Hartzenberg says: "We will not build our future on a bill of rights, we will build it

[12] Interview with the author, 17 April 1991.
[13] "Election Manifesto of the Conservative Party," 1989.
[14] Interview with the author, 30 May 1991.
[15] Interview with the author, 17 April 1991.

on sovereignty. . . . If you are controlled by a majority and your only protection is a bill of rights, then you are bloody stupid."[16]

SYSTEM PARTIES

During the era of reform apartheid, parties that participated in the apartheid system realized the inevitable: full enfranchisement loomed. With this realization, these parties, realizing the likelihood that they would be minority parties in a future inclusive state, began to formulate choices to ensure that minorities, however defined, would be protected against a feared tyranny of the majority. In considering the "system" parties (in the context of the apartheid system), and their interests and choices, I include the National and Democratic parties in white politics and the Inkatha Freedom party as the most relevant actors because other, smaller system parties are more likely to be coalition partners, as opposed to coalition bloc leaders or independent players, in a future party system.

The National Party

When F. W. de Klerk acquired leadership of the National party in late 1989, he brought a new ideology to the party: the New South Africa. This paradigmatic shift in ideology buried once and for all the concept of the "total onslaught" and cast grave doubt on the ultimate survivability of the Tricameral Parliament and its de jure racial representation. The National party sought to replace proscribed racial groups with a new concept: the *self-defining* group.[17] The evolution from statutory race classification to group self-definition began in the second half of the Botha term. The most important direct antecedents to the new concept can be traced to the National party's 1986 party conference, which conceded the inevitability of a common citizenship for Africans in "white" South Africa. This concession was critical, for as Dahl writes, voting rights in a democracy follow from citizenship rights and the "logic of political equality" (1989:124). Both the 1987 and 1989 election manifestos of the National party recognized the logic of a common voters' roll in a shared state. NP documents began to refer to the concept of the maintenance of "own community life," replacing the apartheid-laden notions of "white" representation.[18]

[16] Ibid.

[17] For an interesting essay on the contradictory tensions between the concepts of group and race in South Africa, see John Carlin, "The Group," *New Republic*, 27 November 1989.

[18] Lawrence Schlemmer writes that it was during this era that the National party began to think of "own community life" not simply in terms of Afrikaans cultural interests. Instead, it referred to "corporate group representation" (1988:27).

The metamorphosis of NP ideology from race group to a looser form of ascriptive group occurred in 1989 with the growing influence of the verligte faction of the National party caucus. The key feature of the 1989 Plan of Action was group rights, to be articulated within the existing distinction between "own" affairs and "general affairs."[19] Even at the time, the National party realized that its new group rights concept was troublesome. What constitutes a group, and how can groups be specifically recognized in the constitution? The 1989 Plan of Action dealt with this ideological Gordian knot through circuitous logic that illustrates well the quandary a group rights ideology produced. First, "groups" are defined and recognized through negotiation with "existing groups." This definition is tautological. Second, protection for continued, legally sanctioned, effective racial discrimination—a right to "disassociation"—is entrenched. Third, a group can be ostensibly nonascriptive, such that a person can change "groups" if accepted by the "recipient group"—again, tautological. And finally, as if to admit the nonviability of the groups rights concept at the outset, the manifesto allows for the creation of a "nongroup group." The last point is significant, for as Friedman (1991c) notes, the change implied a fundamental shift in what the NP was seeking to defend.

The call for statutory groups rights began to gradually ease from the National party platform precisely because of the terminological difficulties. By April 1990, then-minister of constitutional development Gerrit Viljoen acknowledged that the NP would no longer insist on statutory group representation: "If groups are no longer to be *essential* building blocks of the constitution, of the whole system as such, it should nevertheless remain available as one *option* for those requiring its protection."[20]

The National party made a more important shift in mid-1990 when it replaced the reactive concept of group rights with a more proactive nation-building approach. This critical shift in ideological orientation—fundamental to understanding regime strategy throughout the remainder of the transition—was predicated by a shift in expectations. Aware of the ANC's difficulty in transforming itself from a national liberation in exile to an effective, streamlined domestic political organization at home (Ottaway 1991)—and perceiving this as a sign of weakness—the National party leadership seized on the idea that it could, through alliance building across the racial divide, do well enough in an election to be a credible power-sharing partner. The NP could not win a majority in an election outright, but it could muster sufficient strength—as a multiracial political

---

[19] "Plan of Action of the National Party" (1989), election manifesto, pamphlet.

[20] "Statements of the State President and Minister of Constitutional Development on Constitutional Reform," (Pretoria: Office of the State President), mimeo.

party, not as a statutorily defined group—to ensure its interests would be protected in the long run.[21] And it would position itself to do well in subsequent elections.

The September 1990 announcement that the National party would open its doors to all races provided the first clear evidence of the ideological volte-face. In October 1990, Viljoen told the *Sunday Times* that his own views about the NP's chances in a future election "have changed dramatically" in recent weeks: "I now have a complete new vision of the future. . . . It is possible for us to be part of the majority instead of only thinking about ourselves as a minority that needs special protection."[22] The shift gave new life to the New South Africa ideology.[23] De Klerk, in his 1991 opening speech to parliament, released a "Manifesto for a New South Africa," emphasizing the theme of "nation-building."[24] The movement from race to group to nation building was complete.

Nevertheless, the continuing expectation (aspirations notwithstanding) that the NP would remain a minority party in a postapartheid election lurked behind the call for nation building. The "Manifesto for a New South Africa" included as the first (of eight) "Requirements for a New South Africa" that the "political dispensation must incorporate built-in guarantees and mechanisms which will make domination by a majority and/or a one party state impossible."[25] Despite the continued concern with structural guarantees of minority rights, the National party's ideological shift of 1991 represents a sea change from the notions that steered the party through the heyday of apartheid.

NP CONSTITUENCIES

The constituency that brought the National party to power in 1948 and maintained it for four decades no longer exists. As I mentioned earlier, the NP's solid ethnonationalist core was fragmented. This meant two important sets of changes in the party's constituency base.

Shift Class Interests. In 1948, Afrikaners were primarily still a relatively impoverished rural and traditional community; "underdevelopment" was a strong unifying force in Afrikaner nationalism. Times

---

[21] The experience of the mainstream conservative "multiracial" party in Namibia (the Democratic Turnhalle Alliance), which won enough votes to curtail a sweep in constituent assembly elections by the liberation movement SWAPO, clearly influenced NP strategizing.

[22] *Sunday Times,* 14 October 1990.

[23] The phrase "New South Africa" was first employed by de Klerk in February 1989 in his first speech to parliament as the leader of the National party.

[24] The "Manifesto for the New South Africa" was published in the *Argus,* 1 February 1991.

[25] "The NP's 8 Important Requirements for a New South Africa," National Party Federal Information Service, 1991.

changed. Dissident economist Terreblanche writes, "After being pampered, privileged and protected for the past 40 years by both the apartheid system and the political monopoly of the NP, the Afrikaners have become bourgeois in an artificial and partly undeserved manner and at a too rapid pace."[26] Since the mid-1970s, (as mentioned in chapter 2) the National party constituency has become increasingly middle class. Terreblanche colorfully comments on the new focus on class affiliation: "In sharp contrast to the NP of 1980—then still the 'shelter' of the white tribe of Africa—the new NP of 1990 has become the 'Fort Pretoria' for a typically White Bourgeoisie Society."[27] Although the white business sector (particularly Afrikaans-language business associations) had long found a conduit for its interests through the National party, the shifting class base of the party solidified these allegiances. Traditionally, Afrikaner business groups such as the Afrikaanse Handelsinstituut (Afrikaans chamber of commerce) enjoyed ready access to the levers of political power, especially through informal linkages like the Broederbond.[28]

Changing Ascriptive Characteristics. There were two important changes in the ascriptive characteristics of National party supporters that repositioned the party in society. The first change was the evolution from representation of primarily Afrikaners to a rough parity between Afrikaans- and English-speaking white supporters. The second was a subsequent broadening of the party's target constituency from whites-only to middle-class and aspiring middle-class constituencies across the color bar. Those who consider themselves potential minorities in a unitary state, such as Coloured and Indian communities in particular, gravitated to the NP fold.

As the NP's constituency changed, electoral support for the NP dropped from 85 percent of Afrikaners in 1981 to 50 percent in 1987, then to only 46 percent in 1989. At the same time, support among English-speaking whites grew from about 20 percent in 1981 to 55 percent in 1987 and at least 60 percent in 1989. With de Klerk's changes, some pundits, such as Sampie Terreblanche, estimated in 1991 that the NP would probably receive less than 40 percent of the Afrikaner vote and at least 70 percent of the non-Afrikaner vote among whites.[29] Why did English speakers shift their allegiance to the NP during the 1980s? English-speaking South Africans are a traditionally wealthy community

[26] *Argus*, 14 July 1990.

[27] Ibid.

[28] In addition to these informal networks, regular lines of influence were established through the National Manpower Commission, the President's Economic Advisory Council, and marketing boards.

[29] *Argus*, 14 July 1990.

with deeply entrenched middle-class materialistic values. They expected that the NP was the only party that could effectively protect and advance property rights in postapartheid South Africa.

The NP's shift from its position as an exclusively white party began only after the abandonment of statutorily protected group representation. Following the New South Africa manifesto, the NP sought to give expression to its new rainbow identity. The first target of the NP's ambitions was a logical one. It looked to natural allies among persons of color, the so-called Coloured representatives in the Tricameral Parliament—particularly conservative members of the Labour party who represented Coloureds in the Tricameral Parliament.[30] Having previously sought to co-opt the Labour party, it later tried to absorb it. The attempt to woo Coloureds into NP ranks was a qualified success. On 23 May, de Klerk met with twenty-one Labour party converts who switched affiliation and joined the more powerful NP. Smiling on the steps of the presidential mansion in Cape Town, de Klerk appeared with his new colleagues, saying: "I have no doubt that the National Party will eventually become the political home of all moderate South Africans who wish to ensure that the New South Africa will be a true democracy offering peace and prosperity to all its people and to every minority."[31]

The redefinition of the NP's core constituency in 1991 fueled expectations for the party's electoral chances under full enfranchisement: any minority with specific minority interests to preserve, such as religious groups (e.g., the African Zionist church, Penecostal sects, Jews) and other ascriptively based collectives, would be welcomed to the party's fold. As a collectivity of minorities, the NP sought to transform itself into a multiracial anchor of a middle-class, center-right coalition. Opinion surveys increasingly revealed the NP's attractiveness and de Klerk's personal popularity after the onset of negotiation. It is not coincidental that the NP changed its strategy when it learned, much to its surprise, that the dividends from de Klerk's dramatic moves were higher than expected. One survey showed that de Klerk as a leader had earned support among all racial groups, from as much as 22 percent of the population at large.[32]

Among whites, the NP's level of support remained steady in 1991: a June 1991 Markinor survey pegged it at 58 percent among whites.[33] The polls also confirmed the shift in support from predominantly Afrikaans

---

[30] Coloureds, sometimes referred to as "Brown Afrikaners," share a language with the Afrikaners, and as a community they are thought to be generally conservative. Moreover, most are Christian, and could relate to the "values" that the NP put forward in the manifesto. The status of coloureds has always been the Achilles heel in the apartheid system.

[31] Press statement, Office of the State President, mimeo.

[32] *Sunday Times*, 14 October 1990.

[33] *Sunday Times*, 16 June 1991.

speakers to the white community. In an HSRC survey, for example, nearly 63 percent of English-speaking whites with more than a secondary school education indicated support for the NP (Kotzé and Sisk 1991). Although the results differ widely on the level of support in the Asian and Coloured communities, the fact that there was solid backing in these communities was no longer a point of dispute. The Markinor poll reported that nearly half (49 percent) of Coloureds would back the NP in an election.[34]

Schlemmer argued that the NP's strategy for postapartheid South Africa was to anchor a "Christian Democratic Alliance." He noted that "the NP still looks to black moderates—homeland leaders, local authority councillors, church groups—as possible allies against the ANC. Now, however, this contest moves from the restrictions of the state of emergency to an open electoral battle" (1991a:6). In 1989, the National party found itself picking its way through the terminological minefield of group rights. By 1991, it fancied itself an aggressive, dynamic, expansive party with a potential—not without difficulty—for survival in the postapartheid future. Eventually, it was conceivable that it could even become part of a governing majority.

THE NP REGIME MODEL: 1991

Given this ideological orientation and its newly emerging interests, what institutional choice preferences did the National party articulate? The NP proposals, outlined in a twenty-page document circulated at the 4 September 1991 Bloemfontein conference, were titled "Participatory Democracy in a Rule-of-Law State" (Rechtstaat). Although the NP conceded the essential ANC and international community demands for a united, democratic, and nonracial state in principle, the thrust of the the plan was different: it was a prescription for power diversification and diffusion. It proposed this diversification through myriad constitutional devices to ensure that minority *parties*, not statutorily defined groups—no matter how small their support in the electorate—would have an effective veto in both legislative and executive decision making. The veto is a particularly strong mechanism that can be used on issues that affect the party's vital interests. Power diffusion was proposed through a complex federal system of nine regions and numerous local authorities, each endowed with a devolution of power and a weighted representation for minorities. As political scientist David Welsh aptly noted, the NP plan was an attempt to create "Switzerland on the veldt."[35]

---

[34] Ibid.

[35] Interview with the author, 29 May 1991. MacDonald (1992) reviews the effects of theorizing by Lijphart and Horowitz on the NP's institutional choices and highlights the socioeconomic dimensions of the choice for consociationalism.

These institutional components made up the National party regime model:

- *First tier: A unitary but federal state.* The division of South Africa into self-governing territories—the homelands—would be scrapped. The new state would comprise all South African territory and would have executive, legislative, and judicial functions. The reintegration of the TBVC states (Transkei, Bophuthatswana, Venda, Ciskei) into a common governmental framework would be negotiated.

- *Second tier: Nine regional units.* The unitary state would be divided into nine regions, each with its own "government," consisting of a legislative and an executive branch. The regions would have no ethnic or racial basis. They would have autonomy over certain affairs, plus their own tax bases.

- *Third tier: New municipal structures.* A third stratum of government would be created on the local level, with legislative, executive, and fiscal powers. Such powers would be devolved, not delegated, implying that they could not be revoked without constitutional amendment. Local neighborhood councils—a "superlocal" option—were also envisaged.

- *Bicameral legislature.* Two chambers of parliament would be created: a first house to directly reflect popular opinion and a second house to represent the interests of minorities. The first house would be elected on the basis of proportional representation by universal suffrage. The second house would be composed of representatives from the parties represented in the regional governments.

- *Executive college.* A multiparty executive college would head the state, made up of three to five members of the strongest parties in the first house of parliament, which would make decisions by consensus.

- *Proportional representation.* Elections would be required on a regular basis and conducted by secret ballot; the electoral system would be party list proportional representation.

- *Bill of rights and judicial review.* A bill of fundamental rights would be entrenched in the constitution and the courts would be empowered to enforce it.

- *Judicial Independence.* A new procedure for the appointment of judges would be developed to ensure judicial independence and impartiality. Legislation that does not conform to the constitution could be ruled invalid by ordinary courts; no special constitutional court was proposed.

The NP vision of the future was one in which minority interests would be assured, through constitutional devices that require "amicable agreement."[36] The NP's 1991 institutional choices demonstrate that it sought

---

[36] Jürg Steiner, in his study of Switzerland (1974), termed this form of collective leadership and consensus-based decision making, combined with extensive devolution of power,

as many nonascriptive "devices" for the protection of minority interests as possible. While the NP's goal clearly has been to become a majority governing party, it has continued to harbor firm expectations that it would be a minority party into the foreseeable future. By proposing a system of "amicable agreement," its institutional choices reflect that basic fact.

The Democratic Party

The Democratic party was the youngest of the major white political parties on the South African scene. The DP was launched as the united front of NP-opposed white liberals in April 1989, in time to contest the 1989 election. Three similar-thinking parties that were left of the NP—the Progressive Federal party, the Independent party, and the National Democratic movement—joined to unite white parliamentary opposition to the government. But parliamentary politics was not the sole aim of the DP when it was formed in 1989. Indeed, one of its primary goals was to bridge to the divide between the system and the struggle. To achieve this, the DP campaigned on a specific pledge to work toward direct negotiation between the ANC and the government.

The guiding ideology of the Democratic party is liberalism, an ideology that has a strong tradition in South African culture. Indeed, famous South Africans such as author Alan Paton and parliamentarian Helen Suzman are associated with this tradition. Liberalism in South Africa has been defined as "[demanding] limitations on the power of government, holding it to strict adherence to the rule of law and demanding the protection of minorities, individuals, and nongovernmental entities like the press. And to be 'democratic' is to insist unambiguously on a universal franchise, exercised in free and open elections for the country's rulers, and hence to insist on a black preponderance in government" (Butler, Elphick, and Welsh, 1987:3). This tradition in South Africa, which reaches back to the early nineteenth century in the Cape colony and flourished in the mid-1960s, has formed the backdrop for the DP ideology. It stresses the primacy of the individual, rather than organic concepts of *volk*, nation, or ethnicity. In addition to the espousing classical tenets of liberalism, outlined, for example, in its 1989 election manifesto,[37] the party has also emphasized national reconciliation and nation building. To give political expression to these ideas, the primary plank in the DP's constitutional platform is federalism. Zach de Beer explains the link between the

---

"amicable agreement." Lijphart concurs that amicable agreement "fits the consociational pattern" (1985:113).

[37] The Democratic Party, 1989, Cape Town, election manifesto, pamphlet.

DP's ideological orientation and its constitutional proposals: "The purpose of a constitution is to limit the powers of government over and above the individual. The aim is the creation of procedures with a view toward protecting the freedom of individuals. That is why we so strongly favor federalism—not just because of its administrative efficiency, but because it better protects the dignity of the individual."[38] Before turning to the DP's 1991 institutional choices, it is important to look not only at the party's ideological tenets, but at its constituency interests as well.

DP CONSTITUENCIES

The only firm test of the DP's constituency was the 1989 election. The party had hoped to capture 25 percent of the vote and reclaim the position of the official opposition in the white House of Assembly, which had been held by white liberals at one time but now belonged to the Conservative party. It captured only 20 percent of the vote, although it retained the solid support bequeathed to it by the Progressive Federal party. Nevertheless, liberal parliamentary political parties in South Africa, once the traditional home of English-speaking, well-to-do whites, could no longer rely on that base.

Indeed, the National party under de Klerk took over much of the Democratic party's issue space, a point acknowledged by the DP leadership.[39] Welsh (1991) estimated that as many as 30 percent of DP supporters swung to the National party in the wake of de Klerk's dramatic moves. The primary constituency of the DP and of the white liberal parties in the past, middle- to upper-class whites, was reflected in its strategy to create institutions that would protect middle-class Western values. This limited the party's ability to appeal to a broader base of support among other racial communities; the stronger National party seemed likelier to protect these interests in a future system.

Reorienting to the realities of transition, and given the DP's precarious position between the ANC and the National party, the party set its sights in early 1991 on obtaining 12 percent of the vote in a universal suffrage election (Welsh 1991). The DP's eventual need to choose a direction to reach out in for constituency support led to factionalism within its ranks. In 1991, three recognizable factions emerged in the DP. First, because of the realignment of South African politics in the de Klerk era, conservative DP members, such as Denis Worrall and Roger Hulley, openly urged the party to form an alliance with the National party. Second, some DP mem-

---

[38] Interview with the author, 27 March 1991.

[39] DP leader Zach de Beer is quoted in the *Weekly Mail*, 21–27 June 1991, as saying, "The government has taken over the whole of our policy."

bers, such as Jan van Eck and Jan Momberg, saw the DP's future interests best served an implicit alliance with the ANC.[40] The third faction, a small group of centrists led by party coleader Zach de Beer, perceived an independent role for the party as a facilitator between the ANC and NP in the short term. In the longer term, this faction also saw itself as a liberal opposition to an NP-ANC coalition and the core of a future black-led liberal party that would grow when the coalition failed to perform. The DP was therefore poised on the knife edge of the center of South Africa's party spectrum, a precarious position, given South Africa's polarized past.

THE DP REGIME MODEL: FEDERATION

If one single feature of the Democratic party's institutional choices stands out, it is its consistency with previous models put forward by the white parliamentary left, particularly those of the Progressive Federal party. The DP outlined its institutional choices in a September 1991 discussion paper.[41]

- *Federalism.* The DP's federation would consist of eight to twelve federal states, each with its own government. According to Worrall, the powers of the federal states would be explicitly defined in the constitution: "[The powers] must be clear, fixed, and constitutionally entrenched."[42] The TBVC states would be reintegrated into a united South African territory.
- *Bicameralism.* Based on the U.S. model, the type of federation the DP envisions calls for representatives of the various states to be disproportionately represented in the second house of a bicameral parliament.
- *Proportional representation.* A key aspect of the DP's regime model is the call for proportional representation at all levels of government.
- *A directly elected president, a parliamentarily chosen prime minister.* The DP is the only party that specifically calls for a directly elected president. The DP plan for the executive branch is very similar to the dual executive found in the French Fifth Republic, in which the president is elected directly and separately and the prime minister is chosen by the majority party in the first house of parliament.

Despite the DP's small constituency base, its institutional choices, I will argue later, are important precisely because of its position as the fulcrum of South Africa's emerging postapartheid party system.

[40] Indeed, most members of this faction subsequently defected to the ANC in 1992, giving effective representation to the organization in the Tricameral Parliament.

[41] "Constitutional Proposals," 23 August 1991, Democratic party policy discussion paper.

[42] Interview with the author, 5 May 1991.

The Inkatha Freedom Party

The Inkatha Freedom party of 1991 had an enigmatic character and a contradictory image: as a system party, it controlled the KwaZulu homeland government and earned it the label of "collaborator" with grand apartheid schemes; as an opposition party, it was in some ways the single most important obstacle to the success of apartheid. It fought running battles with the ANC in some of South Africa's most intense political conflicts at the same time it steadfastly refused to negotiate with the government until it released Nelson Mandela and legalized the ANC. It was at once a regional party with a rural, ethnic base and a national, nonracial party with a foothold in the populous PWV area and increasing appeal among white South Africans. It claimed to have the largest paid-up membership roll of any political party, yet consistently registered surprisingly low in sample surveys. For these reasons, Inkatha has been considered as "Janus-faced" (Brewer 1985).

The IFP positioned itself curiously on South Africa's political spectrum, adopting a nondoctrinaire approach to both ideology and policy. Nevertheless, behind the declared nonracial, national Inkatha Freedom party of 1991 lies a long history of Zulu-based cultural organizations and movements, and with this history a distinct set of beliefs that focuses on "liberation through culture." The key to understanding Inkatha's ambiguous ideological underpinnings is found in this past.[43] Inkatha was initially formed solely to preserve the Zulu cultural traditions—it was called a National Cultural Liberation movement. According to Leatt, Inkatha is ideologically grounded in the concept of African humanism, or Ubuntu-Botho (humanism/communalism/good citizenship), which places primary value on the person in the context of his or her cultural milieu and focuses on self-reliance and self-help (Leatt et al. 1986:130). An alternative interpretation is that Inkatha was essentially a populist ethnic movement, hence its ideological ambiguity.

This focus on cultural liberation carried over into the transition. It in part explains how Buthelezi, a Zulu traditional leader and tribal "prince," could also serve as the leader of a modern national, nonracial political party. Buthelezi's role in the KwaZulu government in the early 1970s, created by Pretoria as part of the grand apartheid scheme, reinforced the view that Inkatha was primarily a vehicle for Zulu nationalism.

---

[43] Inkatha's origins date to 1928, when a cultural organization, Inkatha yakwa Zulu, was established by Zulu king Solomon ka DinuZulu. The term *inkatha* refers to a soft pad worn on the head to balance heavy loads. For an analysis of the movement see McCaul 1988 and Schlemmer 1980.

This role fostered criticism of Inkatha's collaboration with apartheid.[44] However, when the Pretoria government offered KwaZulu independence in 1981, Buthelezi flatly refused. "If Zulus, who are the largest ethnic group in this country, had accepted independence," Buthelezi said, "apartheid would have triumphed."[45] Similarly, when in 1984 P. W. Botha tried to co-opt Buthelezi into participation in the National Statutory Council, he declined and refused to see Botha again for nearly five years. Buthelezi, a skillful politician, alternately used the promise of participation and the threat of nonparticipation to win concessions from the state, a tactic that he has carried over into the transition.

From its inception, Inkatha launched a number of initiatives aimed at broadening its role in Natal regional politics and gaining allies in the white community. The first of these was the 1980 Buthelezi Commission, which investigated alternative political options for South Africa. The commission's 1982 report recommended a consociational-type plan as South Africa's most promising political option, with a legislative assembly elected by universal adult suffrage from a number of "community of interest" areas that were not necessarily based on ethnicity.[46] This initiative fed directly the KwaNatal Indaba, a negotiating forum established in 1986 to apply the principles of the commission in a joint KwaZulu-Natal (hence the fusion KwaNatal) regional structure.[47] The KwaNatal proposals, while clearly a step away from the endorsement of either grand apartheid or a less rigid race-group federation, were quite conservative when compared with the demands of those in the struggle. The ANC rejected the plan's inclusion of guaranteed racial representation. Botha's government rejected it for insufficiently protecting white interests.

Inkatha sought to adapt to the shifting political landscape of 1990,

---

[44] Chris Hani, head of the ANC's military wing, said in 1987, "[He is] a government lackey and running dog . . . living in a fool's paradise" (*New York Times Magazine*, 17 February 1991).

[45] As quoted ibid. An analysis of Inkatha as a leading organization in the "collaborative opposition" is found in Davies, O'Meara, and Dlamini 1984. The argument that Inkatha is "the anvil on which apartheid ultimately faltered" is discussed in Maré and Ncube 1989:480–82.

[46] See the Buthelezi Commission 1982. The commission recommended a loose federal structure; a legislative assembly elected on a universal franchise; proportional representation (qualified by a minimum representation for specified minority groups); an executive coalition; a bill of rights; the minority veto; and an independent judiciary. Minority group representation was defined culturally and units of representation were defined geographically rather than on an ethnic basis. See Lijphart's critique of these proposals (1985:76–80).

[47] See IPSA 1991 on the KwaNatal Indaba.

especially the return of the ANC to the internal political scene. Its first gambit was the March 1990 Inkatha Declaration, which was a response to the ANC's Harare Declaration. It stated the movement's position favoring a negotiated settlement, although Buthelezi had already clearly said in February 1990 that he was ready to negotiate with the government, asserting that "de Klerk has reached the point of no return in his move away from apartheid."[48]

CONSTITUENCY INTERESTS

The size of Inkatha's constituency has been a large unknown in South African politics. Nevertheless, the IFP has remained, even in its own eyes, a party with a central core grounded in South Africa's largest ethnic group, the Zulus. There is much evidence that Zulu tribal chiefs—automatic members of the KwaZulu Legislative Assembly—used their coercive powers to entrench Inkatha in their territory, and a common allegation of the ANC's is that Inkatha dues have long been a form of tribal levy in many rural areas of KwaZulu. It is also alleged that in many schools in the KwaZulu area, membership in the Inkatha Youth Brigade was obligatory (McCaul 1988:150).

The politics of patronage explained the large numbers of paid-up Inkatha supporters when compared with the memberships of other political organizations in South Africa. It also pointed to a primarily rural base for the movement, although support among members of the African petit bourgeoisie, including traders, members of the business community, administrators, and teachers, also has been strong. The Zulu base of Inkatha on the political level has been reflected in its trade union arm, the United Workers' Union of South Africa (UWUSA).

The director of the Inkatha Institute, Gavin Woods, outlined the party's expectations regarding its core Zulu support base and its perceived ability to mobilize along ethnic lines:

> Inkatha accepts that its support is not 51 percent of the population. Inkatha has around 2 million members—it signs up 100,000 per year. . . . We know that each year as many members as the entire National party has [join Inkatha]. It is virtually impossible to say [how many votes Inkatha will win]. We have to wait and see. If we were to have a very intense and competitive election, then Inkatha will probably monopolize the [Zulu] ethnic vote, which is the biggest ethnic group; it will get its chunk of Sothos and whites. [The IFP] knows it has a base to rely on, a base big enough to always make it a serious and effective player.[49]

[48] *Star*, 4 April 1990.
[49] Interview with the author, 23 August 1991.

How much white support did Inkatha pick up in 1990 and 1991? Less than a year after the party opened its doors to members of all race groups, the IFP claimed more than 100,000 white members.[50] Suzanne Vos, party spokesperson, says that those whites who joined include many former Democratic party supporters, English-speaking former Nationalists, and Afrikaans-speaking students. "It's really a mixed bag," she said. "We have members ranging from housewives to company directors, sales representatives to advocates."[51] Why would white South Africans join a political party that represented primarily Zulu national interests? Inkatha's appeal among whites must be seen in terms of the context of South African politics during the uncertainty of the transition. Inkatha played on white fear of anticipated ANC rule. In a speech at the Afrikaans-speaking University of Stellenbosch, far from the heart of Zulu homeland, Inkatha Central Committee member Musa Myeni made the following membership pitch to about forty white students in mid-1991: "We are not afraid of the ANC/SACP alliance. We are their only stumbling block to power. Unless we join forces now, the next line of defense will be yourselves. Your first line of defense is Inkatha. . . . Join us now or your future will be decided by Chris Hani and [SACP secretary general] Joe Slovo."[52] At its Sixteenth National Congress in late July 1991, the party made a point of parading to the media its new white members, displaying some of the more prominent ones at a news conference, to demonstrate that Inkatha's power base extends beyond its traditional Zulu constituency into white South Africa.

Opinion surveys did not substantiate the Inkatha leadership's expectations of significant electoral support. Indeed, both Inkatha as a party and Buthelezi as a political leader showed quite poorly in opinion polls. In a 1990 survey by the Institute for Black Research, Inkatha's nationwide support was a remarkably low 1 percent, a finding that was substantiated by an HSRC poll that showed no appreciable support for Inkatha at all (IBR 1990; Kotzé and Sisk 1991). A June 1991 Markinor survey, however, yielded a support level for the party at 3 percent; confirming that many whites lean toward support of the party, the survey showed that 18 percent of whites supported Inkatha as a second choice.[53] Despite the new-look Inkatha, the evidence was strong that the Zulu nationalist backbone remained the driving force behind the party. In the black townships on the Witwatersrand, a survey by Lawrence Schlemmer showed that Inkatha's major base was the Zulu-speaking hostels; although some 15 per-

[50] *Argus*, 25 June 1991.
[51] Ibid.
[52] Remarks at the University of Stellenbosch, 25 April 1991.
[53] *Sunday Times*, 16 May 1991.

cent of the overall sample supported the IFP, among hostel dwellers, 71 percent supported the party (Schlemmer 1991c).

The party's own behavior reinforced the view that it was, above all else, a Zulu ethnonationalist entity. Buthelezi, less that a month after declaring that the IFP would be a national, nonracial political party, told a gathering of tribal chiefs in Ulundi that calls for the dissolution of the KwaZulu homeland "do not understand the depth of the commitment that we have to each other as Zulu brothers born out of Zulu warrior stock." Again, two weeks later, Buthelezi told a group of ten thousand Zulus gathered in the Natal town of Stanger that those criticizing him "know that there is something in the Zulu character which is beginning to show now as Zulus draw together and say enough is enough."[54] This enduring evidence that Inkatha was based on Zulu chauvinism cast a pall on the organization's counterclaims that its interests transcended an ethnic base.

DEVOLUTION, DOWNWARD AND OUTWARD

Inkatha's demonstrable ethnic base, despite a commonality of interest among some fearful whites, has been reflected in its choices for a future South African political system. Despite the lack of a formal policy document, its preferences, gleaned from statements and interviews, have been clear:

- *Devolution.* Inkatha's preference for federalism, hinted at by party leader Buthelezi, was more specifically outlined by Woods: "Power must be devolved down and out. There can't be powers which are granted or held by the central government; they must be constitutionally enshrined."[55]
- *Indaba-type consociational structures.* Inkatha views the structures created by the KwaNatal Indaba, such as bicameralism and proportional representation, as a point of departure. Woods noted: "It was hoped that a successful regional solution here would be replicated in other regions of the country . . . that perhaps a new South Africa would be born almost incrementally. It is now viewed as a lesson to show to other parties to say, 'Look, we can be creative together. We have gone through the experience. Let us help create a new cross-cutting interest arrangement.' Inkatha has felt that some of the lessons—the two house system, the electoral system perhaps—could be a good model for a new national system."[56]
- *Minority protection.* Part and parcel of the party's support for federalism and minority protection has been explicit protection of minority rights, and it even has gone so far as to support the concept of group rights.

---

[54] All three of these quotations are found in the *New York Times Magazine*, 17 February 1991.

[55] Interview with the author, 23 August 1991.

[56] Ibid.

More than any other political actor, except perhaps the National party government, the IFP has engaged in intense study of alternative constitutional frameworks for South Africa. These experiences clearly influenced Inkatha's institutional choices for a future South Africa, but Inkatha did not produce a clear set of constitutional guidelines during the preliminary negotiation phase. Nevertheless, the IFP played its cards strategically close to the vest. The IFP's stealth—and antagonistic relationship with others—stems from a profound expectation that the IFP would remain a junior partner among the "big three." Nevertheless, it too formulated institutional choices for the future during the preliminary negotiation phase.

THE STRUGGLE

In the wake of the 1990 removal of the ban on anti-apartheid opposition and the onset of negotiation in South Africa, there was a growing expectation that the aim of the struggle—the demise of apartheid and the introduction of majority rule—was near. With a long-hoped-for ideal soon to be realized, either through the total abdication of the white minority regime or through the process of negotiation, the actors in the struggle, too, were forced to make choices for postapartheid institutions. The broad rhetoric of the liberation struggle had to be given concrete institutional form. The ripening of the conflict itself spurred a consideration of what should replace apartheid institutions. How could the guiding principle of the struggle—one person, one vote in a democratic unitary state—be given specific form? Here I consider the following major political organizations and parties, their ideologies and interests: the ANC/SACP/COSATU alliance; the Pan-Africanist Congress; and the Azanian People's Organization.

The African National Congress

For decades, the African National Congress paid little attention to the specific form of regime model that would be created after the end of white minority rule. Such speculation was viewed as inappropriate and immature while the primary task of fighting apartheid consumed the efforts of the organization. The broad outlines of the 1955 Freedom Charter could be translated into a specific regime model only after apartheid had been eliminated. Nevertheless, the slow crumbling of the apartheid system throughout the 1980s, especially the introduction of the co-optive tricameral system, pressured the movement to flesh out its alternatives with greater specificity.

The ANC traces its constitutional policy, particularly its commitment to the principles of nonracialism and inclusive democracy, to the principles laid out in the Freedom Charter.[57] The Freedom Charter was adopted in a much different set of circumstances than prevailed in the 1980s and 1990s, so it is important to see the principles laid out in the document in this context. Reflecting the diversity of opinion of those who attended the Congress of the People and drafted the Freedom Charter, the document at once contains elements of liberalism, in its references to the protection of individual human rights; of socialism, with its call for nationalization and redistribution of wealth; and Africanism, with its observation that the people "have been robbed of their birthright." These are exactly the ideological strains, attenuated by subsequent events, that continued within the African National Congress. The Freedom Charter is a symbolic document that underpins the nonracial ideology of the ANC.

As the prospect of direct negotiations with the South African government loomed, the ANC decided at the 1985 Kabwe Conference to form a constitutional committee to consider a political system that would one day either be imposed following the victory of the National Democratic Revolution or laid on the table in a negotiation process. As a result, the ANC Constitutional Committee was organized in 1986 under the leadership of attorney Zola Skweyiya.[58] The committee produced a set of constitutional guidelines in January 1988. Consistent with the interpretation of the Freedom Charter as calling for a "free, democratic and nonracial South Africa," the guidelines were drafted to "convert [the charter] from a vision of the future into constitutional reality."[59] The guidelines called for "an independent, centralized, unitary, democratic, non-racial state with the sovereignty belonging to the people as a whole and exercised through one central legislature, executive and administration. Powers will be delegated by the central authority to subordinate administrative units for purposes of more efficient administration and democratic participation" (Skweyiya 1989).[60] They placed special emphasis on a bill of rights,

[57] The April 1991 constitutional guidelines define nonracialism as "a South Africa in which all the artificial barriers and assumptions which kept people apart and maintained domination are removed. In its negative sense, nonracial means the elimination of all color bars. In positive terms it means the affirmation of equal rights for all. It presupposes a South Africa in which every individual has an equal chance, irrespective of his or her birth or color. It recognizes the worth of each individual" ("Constitutional Principles and Structures for a Democratic South Africa," ANC Constitutional Committee, April 1991, pamphlet).

[58] The need for a statement on constitutional specifics was reinforced at the July 1987 Dakar meetings, at which IDASA asked the ANC to provide more substantive detail about its constitutional plans. Dr. Alex Boraine, president of IDASA, who was at the Dakar talks, recalls that he told the ANC, "The Freedom Charter is great, but it just doesn't answer a lot of questions." Interview with the author, 15 July 1991.

[59] The guidelines are reproduced in Liebenberg 1987, app. 1.

[60] For analysis and further information on the guidelines, see Lodge 1988 and Sachs 1989.

to be protected by an independent judiciary, guaranteeing equal treatment through the law.[61]

Above all, the guidelines stood firm on the issue of one person, one vote in a nonracial franchise. However, they did not specify an electoral system.[62] The guidelines also underscored the ANC's support for multiparty democracy in South Africa, guaranteed in a bill of rights, rather than the statutorily defined one-party state that had been typical of post-independence African regimes. Nevertheless, strong elements of the typical African paradigm were present. First, a presidential system, buttressed by a powerful central state, would serve a nation building role. Second, the constitution would contain key provisions to counter the pervasiveness of ethnicity inculcated by apartheid. Notably, the guidelines' bill of rights provision contained the following statement: "The advocacy or practice of racism, fascism, Nazism *or the incitement of ethnic or regional exclusiveness shall be outlawed*" (emphasis added).

The guidelines reflect the ANC's first-order preference, not yet mitigated by the dynamics of direct negotiations, a fact underscored by the authors of the document themselves.[63] Constitutional Committee member Albie Sachs wrote at the time: "So the debate is on. The very fact that the debate is being held already constitutes a tiny jump into a post-apartheid South Africa" (1989:60). Yet it is clear that the regime model the ANC had in mind at the time was one of unfettered majoritarianism, in which the party with the majority in the single, centralized parliament would rule unrestrained by the constitutional "devices" to limit majority rule so common in the myriad constitutional plans floated by the regime and reflected in the broad thrust of the tricameral system.

Although the August 1989 Harare Declaration outlined preconditions to direct negotiations, it also contained a brief section describing the ANC's view of a future state. The document is important in the evolution of the ANC's thinking on constitutional issues because of the subsequent adoption of this language in the UN General Assembly "consensus" resolution in December 1989, which reflected the views of two officially rec-

[61] The ANC's bill of rights proposals were being fleshed out at the same time as the overall constitutional guidelines by influential members of the Constitutional Committee, such as Albie Sachs.

[62] It was widely assumed by analysts such as Heribert Adam that the ANC would simply adopt the Westminster first-past-the-post electoral system South Africa already had at the time. Adam writes, criticizing this lack of specificity in the guidelines: "The ANC has yet to consider constitutional safeguards, for example, proportional representation, which would give meaning to legitimate claims, such as ethnicity without racism" (Adam 1988:104).

[63] Lodge writes concerning the guidelines: "If the transition takes the form of negotiation then that implies that those groups or classes who would be most favored by a revolutionary restructuring would simply be unable to impose their terms upon others unilaterally" (1988b:20).

ognized South African liberation movements, the ANC and PAC.[64] The Harare Declaration called for negotiation, albeit tempered by the view that the bottom line of such talks would be the creation of a majoritarian nonracial democracy.[65]

Even in the brief period between the 1988 guidelines and the vague 1989 Harare Declaration, the ANC's position shifted. The controversial clause on ethnic parties was amended, limited to parties that promoted racism. With the release of Mandela in February 1990, however, and the commitment to constitutional negotiation implied in the entire process of negotiation with the government, the importance of addressing white fears rose to the fore. It should be recalled that in Mandela's landmark 1989 letter to P. W. Botha, he stated the need to face head-on the problem of white fears. Mandela consistently emphasized this theme, to the consternation of many hard-liners within the radical flank of the ANC. Although Mandela made many frank and open remarks about addressing minority concerns in the constitution, perhaps none is more stark than the statements in the interview he gave to the Johannesburg-based *Star* in mid-1991:

> In the document I sent to President P. W. Botha in March 1989 I specifically raised the question of allaying the fears of the whites; this was one of the questions the ANC and the government would have to address because that fear is genuine. It is mistaken but it is genuine. . . . We are not in favor of black majority rule. We are in favor of majority rule. . . . But it may well be that we have to consider very carefully how the principle of one person, one vote should be applied in the light of our situation, especially in the first few years of a democratic government.[66]

Shortly after the ANC reemerged as a political force, it launched a new debate on constitutional issues. Whether this initiative was a matter of formulating new constitutional policies or simply of educating the constituency on the importance of constitutions in general is difficult to say.[67] This process of consultation with internal players in the struggle led to the formulation and release of a more extensive set of constitutional proposals in April 1991. But before turning to the ANC's specific institutional choices, it is important to assess more thoroughly the constituency interests and civil society forces that lined up behind the ANC.

[64] The document was drafted with UN officials and the PAC; it is considered below.

[65] "Harare Declaration of the OAU ad hoc Subcommittee on Southern Africa," 21 August 1989 (Cooper et al. 1990:641–44).

[66] *Star*, 18 July 1991.

[67] In November 1990, the ANC Constitutional Committee released two discussion documents that were widely circulated among its branches in the country; the first was titled "What is a constitution?" and the second, "A Bill of Rights for a New South Africa."

The key to understanding the ANC's institutional choices is to recognize its emphasis on populism, a remnant of the long history of the struggle. The ANC, as it defined itself, has represented the "masses of the people."

One thing has become clear about the ANC's constituency both before and after the onset of talks: the organization itself has believed it represents a majority of South Africans. In a 1991 television interview, Mandela stated very clearly the ANC's expectation that in a free and fair election, it would garner a majority of the votes: "The overriding fact is that the ANC commands the support of the majority of people in South Africa."[68] A June 1991 Markinor poll revealed that 71 percent of blacks backed the ANC, and Schlemmer's study reported that 62 percent of township blacks on the Witwatersrand backed the movement.[69] A July 1990 poll by Market Research Africa found 62 percent of the overall black community lined up behind the ANC.[70]

The ANC's most important allied organized interest group is the country's largest trade union federation, the Congress of South African Trade Unions (COSATU). The federation was formed in 1985, after nearly four years of bargaining among several "emergent" trade union federations with Charterist orientations; those with black consciousness and Africanist leanings went on to form the National Council of Trade Unions (discussed under Pan-Africanist Congress, below). Even though COSATU maintained a somewhat independent stance—leery of all political control over the labor agenda—the massive trade union federation formally adopted an alliance with the ANC and the SACP in April 1990. This agreement simply ratified a nearly decade-long cooperative working relationship among the emergent trade unions and the Charterists, through the UDF. COSATU's tight national, regional, and industry-based organization, with some 1.5 million members, was one of the ANC's most important assets.

THE SACP

The ANC's relationship with South African Communist party was equally important. While the organizations were highly integrated in terms of leadership structure, negotiating positions, and common partnership in the struggle, the marriage was thought unlikely to last after black South Africans begin to govern. This view was confirmed in the

[68] SABC-TV, 2 February 1991. Citing three recent public opinion polls, Mandela buttressed his claims with detailed empirical references.

[69] *Sunday Times* 16 June, 1991; Schlemmer (1991c:8).

[70] *Star,* 23 July 1990.

highest levels of the ANC: Mandela himself has said that "the SACP has declared their cooperation with us only up to the point of the overthrow of the apartheid state. . . . After that they will take up their own line which we will not follow. We won't follow socialism."[71] Similarly, SACP secretary general Joe Slovo said: "An alliance is not like a Catholic marriage."[72] Nevertheless, the pressures for maintaining the alliance well into the postapartheid era were equally high.

The key to the cooperative relationship between the SACP and the ANC is the "two-stage" or "dual phase" theory of revolution expounded by the party. For the SACP, alliance with black nationalist organizations has always been aimed first at eliminating the underlying conditions of "colonialism of a special type" so that the conditions necessary for the second phase of the revolution, the socialist phase, can begin. The first phase necessitated a national alliance to throw off the yoke of white colonial domination, to be followed by a class revolution in a postapartheid state.[73] The SACP foresees a South Africa after the revolution in terms of a typical bourgeois democracy, which explains its support for the ANC's constitutional proposals. The foundation of the postapartheid state would be popular, representative institutions based on one person, one vote in a universal adult franchise without qualification. The method by which the two-stage theory of revolution in South Africa was to be pursued had been, at least since 1963, an insurrectionary seizure of power in classical Leninist fashion—that is, through armed struggle.

The first change in strategy involved the need to justify the policy of negotiations with the regime, implicitly made in the 1989 party program, "The Path to Power."[74] The dramatic events of late 1989 and the unexpected moves of President de Klerk in February 1990 changed the rules of the game for the SACP, as it did for all parties. In a painful self-diagnosis of socialism's past and future, particularly the long history of the SACP's defense of Soviet policies, party leader Joe Slovo frankly admitted in an influential paper ("Has Socialism Failed?") the mistakes of Stalinism and the "distorted" implementation of socialism in Eastern Europe and the Soviet Union, but reasserted the view that the only future for South Africa was a socialist one. The central theme of the paper is that "the major

---

[71] *Star*, 18 July 1991.

[72] *Cape Times*, 20 July 1991.

[73] The party's program notes: "Within South Africa, bourgeois domination and capitalist relations of production, which emerged within the context of colonialism, have been developed and maintained since 1910 through a specific variant of bourgeois class rule— colonialism of a special type. The oppressed and the colonial majority on the other *are located within one single country*" ("The Path to Power, Programme of the South African Communist Party adopted at the 7th Congress, 1989," mimeo, p. 88, emphasis added).

[74] Ibid., p. 125.

weaknesses which have emerged in the practice of socialism are the results of distortion and misapplications. . . . They do not flow naturally from the basic concepts of Marxism, whose core is essentially humane and democratic."[75]

Even as strategies changed, the SACP's plan for a future South Africa remained that of democratic socialism; the dramatic changes in world socialism in the years 1989–91 did not dissuade the party from its guiding ideology. Slovo sought to debunk the view that the term *dictatorship of the proletariat* must necessarily be authoritarian in nature. The correct course toward democratic socialism, argued Slovo, is political pluralism. "For these historical reasons, we remain protagonists of multiparty post-apartheid democracy both in the national democratic and socialist phases."[76]

The SACP sought to translate its ideological orientation into the practical politics of democratization in South Africa. The party produced a draft Worker's Charter in 1989, published in the independent left-wing magazine *Work in Progress,* which it pressed for inclusion in a new South African constitution.[77] Key planks in the charter included a preamble setting out the goals described above, but embracing a call for broadening the class struggle to include white workers and a recognition of the need to ensure "that the immediate interests of the working people are safeguarded in the post-apartheid state."

In 1991, analysts estimated that the SACP had only about ten thousand paid members; the party did not publicly reveal its membership (Kotzé and Greyling 1991:179). Nevertheless, any estimate of the size of the SACP was clouded by the fact that many SACP leaders and rank-and-file wore "two hats," one in either the ANC or COSATU. In additional to organizational problems and an anarchic ideology, there was a limit to SACP growth. As analyst Heribert Adam pointed out, in a divided society like South Africa, solidarity within the working class is a myth, for two reasons. First, as the common struggle against apartheid winds down, the divergent interests between employed and unemployed workers emerge; "with the ranks of the unemployed swelling, the state finds ready recruits for its various police forces; local warlords organize vigilante groups from a vast pool of resentment; puritan, fundamentalist church cults vie with drug peddlers and petty criminals for the souls and pockets of the downtrodden" (Adam 1991:6). Second, while the nonracial credentials of the party's past were beyond repute, its growth clearly lay in its appeal to

[75] "Has Socialism Failed?" p. 7.

[76] "Has Socialism Failed?" For further reports on the document, see Shauna Wescott, "Slovo Gazes into the Mirror of History," *Democracy in Action* (March 1990): 10–12.

[77] *Work in Progress* 62 (November-December 1989). The document is reprinted in Cooper et al. 1990:750–52.

the unemployed in the townships (in some areas unemployment was 60 percent). This is especially true in the case of the rise of Chris Hani to the mantle of leadership. The idea that a broad alliance of workers could be forged across the color bar was at best dubious. Adam concludes, quite correctly, that "rather than joining COSATU or the ANC, the few remaining white workers flock to the neo-fascist AWB" (Adam 1991:5).

THE CIVICS, WOMEN, AND YOUTH

Less structured organizationally than COSATU or the SACP, but nevertheless an important constituency base for the ANC, are the myriad civic organizations, youth and student associations, and street and area committees that sprang up in the townships in the course of the 1980s repression and revolt. These organizations were the backbone of the UDF and were strongly allegiant to the principles and programs of the ANC. Although the UDF and many of the seven hundred groups that made it up came and went,[78] locally based advocacy organizations maintained close ties to the ANC.

The role of the youth in the ANC has long been important, as has been the ANC Women's League. They were reactivated internally after February 1990. These internal party organizations represented key ANC constituencies. The ANC Youth League had some 162 branches and more than 165,000 members in 1991, which made it the largest youth organization in the country. The generation gap between the huge numbers of ANC youth and the aging leadership was a key variable in the lack of solidarity within the party. The Women's League, with 700 branches, played an equally important role and already had considerable influence on the ANC's constitutional policy, calling for the inclusion of a Women's Charter in a future bill of rights.

Despite its strong backing in organized interests and among the broader public in sample surveys, the ANC had difficulty meeting membership goals. At its December 1990 Consultative Congress the organization set a target for recruitment of one million new members by the July 1991 National Conference. The organization fell short of the goal even after it changed its tack from recruitment—with its concomitant membership fee—to a "signatures" campaign, which required of supporters very little commitment at all. The inability of the organization to recruit paid-up, registered members is understandable, however, and did not indicate that the organization would not sweep a first postapartheid election. Many black South Africans were still concerned that overt identification with a political party, any political party, could only spell trouble from either the authorities or rival political organizations.

---

[78] The UDF was officially disbanded in August 1991.

While sample survey data showed that the ANC had the support of a majority among blacks, they also reveal the limits to the organization's ability to give substance to its credo of nonracialism. Mandela admitted, rather frankly, that the ANC was losing support to the National party among several key constituencies. In the July 1991 interview with the *Star*, he said: "[The minorities] are not certain what their position is going to be under an African government which—because of numbers—is dominated by Africans. The National Party is making a greater impact among Coloureds and Indians, and we have got to address that."[79]

As the ANC was transformed from a broad national liberation movement working mostly in exile and in underground structures to an internally based political party (whether it called itself that or not), it faced the need to clarify policy on a wide range of political, social, and economic issues (Ottaway 1991). As it did, it faced the basic fact that those constituencies it sought to represent often had very distinct interests and points of view. Splits in the ANC's ranks based on these divergent interests began to appear by 1991.

- *The generation gap.* A division emerged within the ANC between the radicalized youth—the Soweto generation—who bore the brunt of the total onslaught and the older, more moderate leadership, who spent the years of state repression behind bars.
- *The exile/internal gap.* Tension continued between those leaders who worked from exile and the more homegrown leaders of the movement who fought the system from within. The *Economist* correctly predicted the problem just after the ANC was unbanned: "In coming months the demonstrators in the townships may cheer the local men they know rather than the strange refugees with fancy university degrees."[80]
- *Ideology.* There were continued ideological tensions within the ANC, particularly between communists and noncommunists. The interests of those employed versus those unemployed, petit bourgeois businesspersons and small-scale entrepreneurs versus the wage-dependent and unskilled laborers were mirrored in the ideological debates at the top.
- *Strategy and tactics.* Finally, there were debates over strategic issues. Should the negotiation process be used as an instrument of reconciling the divisions in society—of accommodating black and white aspirations—or as another facet of the revolutionary struggle, in concert with other strategies? There was clearly a lingering faction of the ANC that continued to view the struggle in zero-sum terms.

Yet as long as the ANC mobilized as a liberation movement—around anti-apartheid symbols and not policies—it continued to enjoy party co-

[79] *Star,* 18 July 1991.
[80] *Economist,* 10 February 1990.

hesion. It remained largely a coalition of the victims of apartheid. This unifying force will remain critically important at least until a new constitution is in place and a postapartheid government is installed.

Given the ANC's rather certain expectations that it will be the majority party, supplemented by its ideological orientation of nonracialism and populism and its historical tradition as the supporter of a universal franchise and majority rule, it is no surprise that its regime model is primarily, but not entirely, one of majoritarianism. Its 1991 regime model fit an evolutionary pattern with very clear antecedents in the Freedom Charter, the 1988 constitutional guidelines, and the Harare Declaration.

The ANC's postapartheid institutional choices, outlined in an April 1991 policy document—"Constitutional Principles and Structures for a Democratic South Africa"—called for a streamlined form of centralized government that would effectively concentrate the power of the state in the hands of the party that wins a majority of the votes and incorporated the following features.

- *Presidentialism.* The ANC envisioned an elected president who would act as head of state, who would be vested with considerable powers, and who would govern concurrently with the legislature. Whether the president would be elected directly or indirectly elected by the parliament was left open.
- *Bicameralism.* The ANC proposed a bicameral system with a first house of parliament, termed the National Assembly, reflecting popular sentiment and the second house, the Senate, serving as "the guardian of the constitution." In the ANC's plan, however, these houses would be by no means equal in power. The National Assembly would be primarily responsible for the enactment of legislation, with the Senate's concurrence not necessary for the passage of a bill.
- *Proportional representation.* In its first-ever official policy statement of a preference for a postapartheid electoral system, the ANC opted for proportional representation for its all-important National Assembly.
- *Election of regional and local governments.* Within the confines of a unitary state, provision would be made for the creation of elected regional and local governments. Such governments should exercise delegated powers, "provided always that such policies do not conflict with national policies . . . [and that] boundaries of local and regional districts will be determined with due regard to economic and development considerations without regard to race, color, ethnic origin, language or creed."
- *Creation of a bill of rights, an independent judiciary, and judicial review.* The ANC's November 1990 draft bill of rights was an essential part of the ANC's institutional choices.

The Pan-Africanist Congress

The PAC has been perhaps one of the least understood of the liberation movements in South Africa, a fact that is attributable in part to its own ideological formulations and in part to the factionalism that has plagued the organization. The cornerstone of the PAC's ideological formulation has long been the rejection of the 1955 Freedom Charter, with its references to different "national groups." According to the PAC, there are no national groups as such, but rather one group—Africans. Those who are not Africans are settlers, who do not belong in a future South Africa, to be renamed Azania.[81] Does that mean that the PAC's ideology is racist, denying the rights of nonblacks in the new state? The PAC has stressed "Africanness," claiming to be neither racial nor ethnic, but cultural. Africans are not a distinguishable national group, as suggested in the Freedom Charter, but are all those who consider themselves to be Africans in terms of loyalties, cultural habits, and attitudes.

The PAC has been precariously perched between its exclusivist African ideology and racism. This was nowhere more evident than in the attempts to explain the oft-heard PAC slogan, "One settler, one bullet."[82] Patrick Laurence, reporter for the Johannesburg-based newspaper the *Star*, writes that the PAC may

> Unwittingly . . . [foster] anti-white sentiment as the binding force of black solidarity. At best the PAC is a race-conscious movement, seeking to mobilize black people against racial oppression in the land of their birth under the slogan "Africa for the Africans." In its pristine form it is pro-Black without being anti-white. . . . The dividing line between race-consciousness and racism is thin. They are separated by the thinnest of knife edge, [and] it is easy to fall into the abyss of racism.[83]

Return of the land "stolen" by colonialists and the restoration of rights to the indigenous African people is the central tenet of Africanist philosophy. The view expressed in the Freedom Charter that the land belongs to "all which work it" contrasts sharply to the view of an indigenous, traditional and common landownership as advocated by the PAC. Thus, the role of landownership and the establishment of a system of African socialism—based not on Marxian class analysis but rather on traditional

---

[81] The term is derived from the Greek *azainein*, which means "dry." In ancient times, all of the area south of present-day Ethiopia was known as Azania. Both the PAC and Black Consciousness groups use the term.

[82] The PAC's secretary general Benny Alexander explained the party's position: "The slogan is only trying to address the difference between an armed revolution and violent terror. . . . The slogan is trying to say, stop that terror and aim your bullets at the security forces instead" (*Weekly Mail*, 5–11 October 1991).

[83] *Star*, 8 November 1991.

African humanism—is a critical part of the Africanist ideology. The return of South Africa to the indigenous peoples has held a central place in the PAC's ideological platform.

THE PAC: INTERESTS, CONSTITUENCY, AND POSSIBILITIES

The PAC never had the chance to organize effectively within South Africa. Barely a year after it was formed in 1959, it was banned by the government of Prime Minister Verwoerd; by 1991, the ban had been lifted for barely over a year. During its long period in exile, the organization was wracked by endemic leadership crises, little international support—which came primarily from the People's Republic of China—and a weak and ineffective armed struggle. Given its difficult past, it is remarkable that the PAC has had the depth and breadth of support that it enjoys.

Membership figures vary widely. One team of observers (Kotzé and Greyling 1991:167) put the figure close to 25,000, while the organization itself claimed as many as 750,000 members. Both figures were difficult to confirm or dispute. Nevertheless, several basic support groups lie behind the organization, falling into three broad categories:

- *Regions.* The PAC has been strong in the Transvaal (PAC leaders alleged that the organization enjoyed the support of 65 percent of youth among the more than one million residents of Soweto)[84] and, historically, in the Western Cape. In certain areas of the Orange Free State and the Eastern Cape, the PAC has been alleged to have a "virtual monopoly."[85]
- *Trade unions.* The primary trade union base for the PAC has been the National Council of Trade Unions (NACTU), a federation whose 250,000 mainly black members divide their loyalties between Black Consciousness tendencies and Africanism. Despite NACTU's stated neutral policy toward political organizations, some observers noted that within NACTU, the PAC appeared to be gaining the upper hand. Several NACTU leaders, including the secretary general, Cunningham Ngukana, publicly supported Africanism. There were also elements of COSATU that leaned toward the PAC.
- *Youth and community organizations.* The principal youth group supporting the Africanist vision has been the Azanian Nation Youth Unity, which was reactivated in 1986. Sometimes known as the revolutionary watchdog of the PAC, the youth wing has been an important constituency for the party. The Africanist allied student organization is the Pan-Africanist Students' Organization. Given South Africa's young population, growth in the PAC would be first coordinated through the youth organizations. The PAC's women's organization is the African Organization for Women.

[84] *Natal Witness,* 8 May 1990.
[85] *Cape Times,* 2 May 1990.

Despite these core constituencies, the PAC's support base has not been very broad when measured by surveys. The 1990 IBR survey, for example, revealed a level of support for the party of only 3 percent overall, and of only 4.6 percent in the African community. Public opinion specialists dispute these results, however. Donald Simpson of Potchefstroom University and Jannie Hofmeyr of the University of Cape Town independently estimated the level of PAC support in the broader public at 10 percent.[86] Schlemmer's township study supported these higher estimates, reporting that among his sample of urban township blacks, the PAC earned the backing of 20 percent of the overall respondents (1991c:10). "We may only have 3% or 4% support, but that doesn't bother us," PAC publicity secretary Barney Desai said in April 1991.[87] While not providing a specific estimate, Desai claimed that the party had grown "very, very significantly" since the ban against it was lifted.

THE PAC'S REGIME MODEL

The PAC favored a populist, majoritarian political system. A PAC position paper released in early 1991 stated the organization's simple message: "In whose interest should state political power be wielded?" the document opens. "The PAC position is that it should be wielded primarily in the interests of the toiling masses of Africa."[88] The continuing hardline opposition to the power-sharing and devolution proposals of the National party—indeed, to any form of minority protections in a new constitution—pointed to the fact that the PAC's model was even more majoritarian than that of the ANC. The PAC positioned itself to the left of the ANC as its primary outbidder.

When the ANC crafted the 1989 Harare Declaration, which was adopted by the Organization for African Unity (OAU) and referred to the UN General Assembly for its imprimatur, the UN insisted that its resolution reflect the united views of the two organizations that it recognized as the legitimate representatives of the black majority in South Africa—the ANC and PAC. The document committed the PAC to generally defined democratic principles that reflect the common anti-apartheid, and majoritarian, principles and institutional preferences the two organizations shared.[89] The reaffirmation of these principles by PAC spokespersons indicated that the PAC remained wedded to their general thrust and, for

---

[86] *Weekly Mail,* 22–27 March 1991.

[87] Interview with the author, 8 April 1991.

[88] "PAC Position on the Constituent Assembly," mimeo.

[89] "Declaration on Apartheid and Its Destructive Consequences in South Africa," December 1989, UN General Assembly Resolution S-16/1.

example, on the issues of qualified multipartyism and the bill of rights, their detail.[90]

Beyond these very broad guidelines, however, the PAC did not describe its regime model during the preliminary negotiations phase, but nevertheless revealed its preferences in statements that reflected in part a need to respond to the more detailed proposals of others. "We reject minority or group rights and in turn guarantee the democratic principle through political and constitutional participation by all Africans," the PAC said.[91] Desai said the organization favored a unicameral legislature with proportional representation as being "the most democratic framework." The PAC was against simple majoritarian models based on the first-past-the-post electoral system. The choice for unicameralism was echoed by assistant secretary general Carter Seleka: "We are against the Pretoria regime's use of multiple chambers to divide our society; we will have a single chamber."[92] The choice of a party list proportional representation system for the constituent assembly signaled the PAC's likely choices for a future electoral system, a view noted by both Desai and Seleka in interviews with the author. This choice was made for two reasons, according to Desai. First, it allows the participation of all in the electoral system and ensures that no votes are wasted. Second, it is the best means for determining the relative strength of political parties in the electorate, of assessing exactly who has a "mandate."[93]

In conclusion, the PAC was the most viable alternative to the ANC for the black majority, especially if the talks failed. In the secrecy of the voting booth, just how many would cast their vote for the PAC was one of the most unpredictable variables in the South African transition. The PAC, in its continuing response to the shifting ground rules of transition, continually reassessed its policy decisions, particularly those on negotiation with the government and on the continuing armed struggle. The constant reassessment of core positions underscored the PAC's dilemma in the preliminary negotiations phase and beyond. If it negotiated with the government, it would lose the advantage of outbidding on the ANC's left. If it refused to participate in talks, it risked being sidelined and excluded in the post-apartheid order.

---

[90] See Barney Desai, "PAC's Ideals for Democratic SA of the Future," *Cape Times*, 2 August 1991.

[91] Interview with four PAC officials (no direct attribution), *Finance Week*, 11–17 October 1990.

[92] Interview with the author, 15 May 1991.

[93] Interview with the author, 8 April 1991.

The Azanian People's Organization

While the PAC has been perhaps the best-known Africanist movement in the liberation struggle, it has been by no means the only party espousing a black nationalist ideology. To the left of the ANC/SACP/COSATU alliance and the PAC has been the Black Consciousness movement (BCM). The movement has its origins in the black consciousness ideology as expressed by Bantu Steve Biko and the Black People's Convention, although this ideology evolved from a discrete focus on black psychological upliftment in the 1970s to more doctrinaire scientific socialism. Within South Africa of 1991, black consciousness has been primarily espoused by the Azanian People's Organization (AZAPO), founded in May 1978 in the wake of the banning orders served on most of the original black consciousness–allied organizations.

A persistent source of confusion for many analysts of the South African situation has been exactly how the philosophies of Black Consciousness (BC) differ from those of Pan-Africanism.[94] Indeed, on many points and in many ways they have been quite similar. Strini Moodley, publicity secretary for AZAPO and a member of the organization's Central Committee, explained the differences from the perspective of BC: "There are clear distinctions between Black Consciousness and Pan-Africanism. Black Consciousness goes beyond nationalism where pan-Africanism identifies the state or the nation or the continent in terms of indigenous African people. BC [says] that psychological liberation is an imperative, and therefore conscientization as a classical program of action becomes a priority in the search for liberation."[95]

For AZAPO and the BC tendency, the antidote to apartheid is, as Moodley explains, the psychological liberation through "conscientization." Black Consciousness is differentiated from these ideological strands, however, in its assertion that the principles of scientific socialism can be harnessed as an ideological tool. BC weds Africanism and scientific socialism in that it "focuses on the *material conditions* in occupied Azania . . . comprehends phenomena in their *changingness,* and studies the *struggle of opposites* as the underlying basis of . . . change."[96] This new social order would be based on, as Hirschmann writes, "the notion of African society as a man-centered system based on community-oriented activities, communal-land holdings, a closeness to the natural and spiritual, and a resistance to the dominance of technology and materialism" (1990:5–6).

[94] For commentary on the two movements, see van Staden 1990:7–10.
[95] Interview with the author, 21 May 1991.
[96] "Black Solidarity for a Socialist Azania," *Frank Talk* 2 (September 1987):1–2.

The core role of AZAPO, and BC in particular, has been that of a vanguard in the quest for black unity. It has sought to unite the "black working class" toward the aim of "land re-conquest, socialist transformation, [and] the building of a national culture in which all Azanians, irrespective of race, gender or religion, will participate" (Mosala 1991:22–23).

BC CONSTITUENCIES CONSIDERED

Despite BC's appeal in the late 1970s, the resurgence of the Charterist camp in the mid-1980s and, to a lesser extent, the growth of Africanism caused it to lose popular support. By 1991, AZAPO was a relatively small organization, although it had a significant number of followers in NACTU. In addition to this labor union support, AZAPO had a small core of ideologically devoted followers among black intellectuals and academics. In the only major 1991 survey in which AZAPO's support was reported, the IBR study, only 2 percent of the respondents overall, and only 3.4 percent of Africans, supported the party (IBR 1990).[97] The ideological complexity of the BC message, and its stilted language and approach, has limited its ability to mobilize the masses. Hirshmann notes that BC, as a reactionary type of radicalism, provided an emotive message but not a practical program. BC was "ultimately a victim of its own success. It did make a contribution to restoring to mainly young, mainly educated blacks a strong sense of self-assurance and self-reliance. However, since Black Consciousness originally conceived in the 1960s seems to have served, and therefore lost, its purpose, the notion that it was a transitional movement seems apt" (1990:12–22).

AZAPO'S AZANIA

While AZAPO refuses to reveal specific details about the types of constitutional preferences commonly associated with "bourgeois democracy," it did outline a rather clear vision of the future state it seeks to construct.[98] Such a state would be guided by the classical principles of democratic centralism as envisioned by Lenin, but with a decidedly African heritage. Moodley outlined AZAPO's institutional choices for a future political system: "AZAPO will look at models [that] base decision

---

[97] There are, however, many black youth organizations that subscribe to BC philosophy, notably the Azanian Student's Movement, the Azanian Student's Organization, and the Azanian Student's Convention. These youth movements are strong primarily in certain areas of the Witwatersrand and larger townships in the Western Cape, but are not directly linked to AZAPO structures.

[98] The most authoritative statement on the BC view of a future state was the manifesto issued by the organization and published by the *Sowetan* in February 1990. The document is reproduced in Cooper et al. 1990:694–97.

making on the creation or the participation of workers' committees and that kind of model in decision making: worker representatives from factories, community representatives from residential townships, and that kind of thing will all constitute representatives to a congress, and that congress will take the major decisions."[99]

BC may have been, as Hirschmann asserts, an ideology on the wane. Its ideas still held currency, however, among some liberation parties, such as the ANC, and in civil society groups. As the PAC grew and the ANC inched closer to real political power, the likelihood of AZAPO growth appeared quite slim. But that does not mean that it would completely disappear from the political landscape, particularly during the transitional period. Ideological coherence and complexity would prevent AZAPO from taking a role as a major political player in its own right.

[99] Interview with the author, 21 May 1991.

CHAPTER 5

The Politics of Institutional Choice: 1991

ON THE EVE of substantive constitutional negotiations, the major political parties in South Africa developed rather specific preferences for a post-apartheid political system. In this chapter, I relate these preferences to the politics of institutional choice: why the parties made the choices they made in the context of the perceived balance of power and the effects of strategic interaction. Further, I link the preferences for a future polity to preferences for the nascent institutions to guide the transition, because during this preliminary negotiations period these parties also specified clear choices for the process through which their visions of the future polity could be realized. Only with a *prior* assessment of the ideologies and interests of the various political parties on the South Africa political scene—and their preferences for rules of the postapartheid game—can their preferences over the path of transition be properly understood. Such choices are not simply tactical, because the path of the transition will necessarily effect the outcome, the rules of the new political game.

INSTITUTIONAL CHOICES FOR THE TRANSITION

Steven Friedman correctly notes that "[an] important aspect about transition is that there is no real distinction between the forum that enacts a new constitution and the nature of the new constitution."[1] In a way, Friedman explains, the distinction between the choice over rules to arrive at the new system and the nature of the new system itself is a nonissue. "If you have a constituent assembly that is elected on a universal franchise and [it] takes decisions by simple majority rule, then you have a majority rule constitution. . . . On the other hand, if you have a negotiating forum that has ten ethnic blocks, each of which has a veto over the outcome, then you have group rights. So the point . . . [is] that it is virtually impossible to negotiate the forum without negotiating the broad principles behind that forum."[2] To get from the preliminary phase of making substantive negotiation possible to the next phase of writing a postapartheid constitution, the parties had to solve the problem of how to get to the constitution-writing phase and how those rules would be legitimated and

[1] Interview with the author, 15 May 1991.
[2] Ibid.

implemented. Why is this process so critically important? In addition to the argument that the process in effect determines the outcome, the process is also critical to the ultimate viability of the new political system. If the process itself is not widely perceived as legitimate, the end product will also lack legitimacy. The question of how a new constitution will be written, as well as how the new order will be legitimated, is critical to the sustainability of the settlement. Indeed, it is critical to whether there is any settlement at all.

Interim Government versus Legal Continuity

During the course of the preliminary negotiation, particularly in the wake of the July 1991 Inkathagate scandal, the argument made by ANC and others—that the National party could not serve as "referee and player" in the process—rose to the fore. These fears were warranted, for in May 1991, before Inkathagate broke, President de Klerk had declared that the National party would "keep its hand on the tiller [of state] for the long run."[3] The necessity of choosing new institutional structures to level the playing field during the period of transition—creating interim institutions—became an imperative in the wake of Inkathagate. The process in South Africa is much different from other transitions in southern Africa, particularly Zimbabwe and Namibia, in which the international community (particularly the United Nations) played a much more assertive role. Because no existing political institution on the South African political stage was perceived as legitimate, new institutions were required.

In the preliminary phase of negotiation, there were alternative, competing scenarios for the creation of an interim government for the period of transition. In the ANC's view, a constituent assembly would be elected following the resignation of the incumbent government: it would represent the establishment of a new, sovereign body. Mandela made the demand most forcefully just following the Inkathagate scandal: "The idea of an interim government with sovereign powers over all the organs of government and not co-opting certain individuals is our demand. We are not prepared to be co-opted into the existing structures of government. We want a transfer of power from this government to an interim government."[4] The government, on the other hand, conceded the possibility of adopting "transitional measures" within the framework of the 1984 constitution, through which all significant political actors would be given a say in decision making. De Klerk was quite emphatic, however, that his

[3] *Cape Times,* 8 May 1991.
[4] *Cape Times,* 8 August 1991.

view of transitional measures prevail over the ANC's vision of an interim government. "Government by decree through an interim government in a constitutional vacuum is totally unacceptable. Transitional arrangements must be negotiated and must at all times be reconcilable with the constitution."[5]

At the heart of this debate was the question of legal continuity, which arises as a critical issue of the transition: How can a lame duck constitution be replaced with one that is both legal and legitimate? This debate was important because it required resolution as the path of transition was negotiated. I describe here the divergent views prevalent in the preliminary negotiations phase—especially the issue of the type and nature of the institution to debate, draft, and implement a new constitution—in order to later highlight the nature of subsequent convergence in the substantive phase.

System Parties: The Multiparty Negotiating Forum

The National Party. The National party proposed that its multiparty conference be transformed into a forum for the negotiation of a new constitution. The decision rule would be complete consensus. The government preferred to negotiate the constitution with the leaders of all other political parties, and then place it before the entire electorate under full enfranchisement in a yes-or-no referendum. If approved, the constitution would then be enacted by the current Tricameral Parliament in order to give it legal force. Only after the new constitution was drafted by the leaders of all parties on the basis of consensus, legitimated in a single simple majority referendum, and enacted by the present government could a founding election take place.

The National party's preference for a multiparty negotiating forum plus a referendum was complicated by President de Klerk's 1989 promise to put a new constitution to the *white* electorate in a separate referendum before it was enacted; the 1989 election, he repeatedly said, was the last white election. This promise was made in part to address Conservative party criticism that de Klerk was acting without a mandate from his core white constituency. De Klerk reiterated his promise in April 1990, although he implied that this could be done in an overall election with white votes counted separately.[6]

---

[5] *Argus,* 4 August 1991.

[6] Despite the repeal of the Population Registration Act, under the terms of the tricameral system a racially based voters' roll based on the act is still maintained. While the government claimed it was necessary for any by-elections to the race-based Tricameral Parliament, it would also facilitate a counting of white votes in a referendum that would also include those previously disenfranchised.

The Democratic Party. The DP had a similar view on the issue of an immediate elected constituent assembly, but a different view about how the transition process should proceed. DP leader Zach de Beer noted that while the party supported the eventual convening of a constituent assembly (which it called a Constitutional Conference), it did not support one based on an immediate election under universal suffrage. According to de Beer, such a plan would result in a "tyranny of the majority. . . . The ANC proposal is to elect the government before writing the constitution . . . and that is surely putting the cart before the horse, the election before the transition."[7] The DP did see the constituent assembly as a necessary step in the creation of a new constitution, however.

Inkatha Freedom Party. Inkatha, too, opposed the creation of a constituent assembly and preferred the multiparty forum plus referendum route, and for similar reasons. Mangosuthu Buthelezi laid out the IFP's position in a paper prepared for the party's 1991 National Conference:

> For the IFP, a constituent assembly contradicts the whole idea of negotiations —as compromise, give-and-take, bargaining. . . . The prime danger of a constituent assembly—with its elections before negotiations—is that it would dramatically escalate the likelihood of conflict and violence. It could even precipitate a civil war. . . . The only option we really have is of a constitution being formulated at a round-table national convention comprising all parties with a significant base of support, whose largely consensus-based decisions are subsequently ratified in a national election.[8]

Thus, as with their preferences for the future rules of the game, there was a similarity in positions among system parties regarding the interim rules to govern the transition.

Struggle Parties and the Constituent Assembly

Perhaps the most unifying demand of the major political actors of the liberation struggle was the call for an elected constituent assembly. They agreed not only on the need for the assembly itself, but also on the rule that should be used to elect it: party list proportional representation (PR). Clearly these actors were strongly influenced by the success of the transition process in Namibia, in which elections for a constituent assembly employing this electoral system provided a smooth route for the transfer of power to the forces of liberation while alleviating minority fears.

---

[7] Interview with the author, 27 March 1991.

[8] *South African Update*, June 1991. It can be inferred from the statement that a national election that "ratifies" the constitution would in fact be referendum.

The ANC.   The ANC preferred the election of a constituent assembly on a PR list basis in single national constituency, which would then negotiate and draft the constitution. It was assumed that the ANC favored as majoritarianism a decision-making rule as possible, although this was clearly an issue for negotiation. The party's primary interest was to prevent minority powers from producing deadlock in the constituent assembly. With the constituent assembly election providing the legitimacy for the new charter, the assembly itself could be transformed into a new legislature (as had been the case in Namibia) or new elections could be held. Members of the ANC's constitutional committee asserted that although firm decisions on the exact details of such a rule had not been determined in mid-1991, the planning on exactly how such an assembly should be elected was far along. Constitutional Committee member Bulelani Ngucka saw the election to a constituent assembly as a potential framework for the first parliament, and realized that it would have to include a representation threshold—a 5 percent rule, for example—in order to prevent party proliferation. The ANC rejected the NP call for a legitimating referendum if white votes were to be counted separately, which would in effect mean a racial veto over the new constitution.

The ANC's trade union ally, COSATU, also favored the principle of proportionality in the constituent assembly. Trade unionist Ebrahim Patel, the federation's principal thinker on constitutional matters, said:

> The general sense that I have is that sentiment within COSATU favors election on the proportional system, not on the constituency system, as the primary means of electing candidates. It may well be, though, that we would favor a combination of a strong list system of proportional representation combined with some mechanisms that allowed for wide constituencies—not narrow British-like constituencies. In West Germany you have a combination of proportional representation and constituency voting, where you have a region that could be a whole state or something.[9]

The PAC.   The PAC preferred the immediate election of a constituent assembly as the only way to address the conflict in South Africa. PAC assistant general secretary Carter Seleka explained the party's position and rationale: "We do not accept that whole arrangement called a multiparty conference by the regime. [It would] make us comanagers of apartheid; the [multiparty conference] is legalizing what is illegal. . . . It has been called on the terms of the regime, and we refuse to legalize something we regard as illegal in terms of the regime. We favor a constituent assembly in a united South Africa with one person, one vote on propor-

---

[9] Interview with the author, 7 June 1991.

tional basis."[10] Seleka pointed out that the PAC demand for the convening of a constituent assembly was nonnegotiable: "We are prepared to actually discuss the modalities of electing the [constituent assembly], but not the concept of it," he said.[11]

As its choice of an electoral system for selecting representatives to the constituent assembly, the PAC also preferred a party list system of proportional representation in a single national constituency. Why? The PAC, preferred the PR list because they believed it mitigated against the racially defined constituencies resulted from apartheid politics in South Africa and ensured the participation of all those in the political process in direct proportion to their strength in the electorate. Such a rule was argued to directly assess which parties had a democratic mandate. The party further spelled out the size of assembly: 265 seats allocated to political parties, along with 40 to constitutional experts appointed by the parties, proportional to their strength in the vote.[12] In the PAC's vision the constituent assembly would dissolve itself once the constitution was written, after it had decided how the process should go forward.

It is important, however, to point out the fundamental difference between the ANC and PAC on the issue of a constituent assembly. Their views are at odds on the nature of the assembly itself in terms of its relation to the interim government: for the ANC, the constituent assembly would be the preferred forum in which the transfer of power would be negotiated while an interim government performed the function of the state; for the PAC, the constituent assembly would be the *result* of a transfer of power. Seleka said: "We hope through a constituent assembly arrangement to transfer power from the oppressors to the oppressed."[13] For the PAC, the constituent assembly was the route to the interim government; for the ANC, it was the other way around. This difference reflects the parties' understanding that the path of transition has a bearing on the outcome.

AZAPO. Interestingly, AZAPO was the first liberation organization to propose a constituent assembly, having called for such a mechanism as early as 1984. AZAPO's views on the constituent assembly differed little from those of the PAC: both organizations saw a constituent assembly as resulting from all-out victory in the struggle. AZAPO's deputy president, Nchaupe Mokoape, wrote in the party magazine, *Umtapo Focus:* "The Constituent Assembly . . . is not an instrument of compromise and sur-

[10] Interview with the author, 15 May 1991.

[11] Ibid.

[12] For further details, see "On a Negotiated Political Settlement," 7 July 1990, PAC Discussion Paper, mimeo.

[13] Interview with the author, 15 May 1991.

render. It is an instrument of revolution, of victory of the masses. It is initiated and called into being by the people victorious through the democratic structures at or after the moment of victory."[14]

How did AZAPO see the election that would create the assembly? AZAPO publicity secretary Strini Moodley explained the party's position:

> The defeat of the de Klerk regime will open the way for the broad liberation movement to call in a neutral party, if it is needed, to oversee the running of the country's affairs, as well as place the existing security forces in quarantine, where they will be disarmed. In that climate, the neutral party will then oversee elections on one person, one vote, ensure that there is no intimidation or harassment, ensure that all parties are afforded equal opportunity to canvass their points of view, and consequent of the elections, each party will be accorded a pro rata number of delegates, depending on the number of votes it received.[15]

It is noteworthy, however, that the AZAPO view of a constituent assembly included a definite preference for proportionality.

POLITICAL PARTIES AND INSTITUTIONAL CHOICES

In a transition such as South Africa's, political parties undergo profound transformation in their expectations about how they may fare under the shifting rules of the political game both during the transition and in the future order. As realignment occurs, they assess their interests with a keen estimation of their power relative to that of other actors. Armed with this information, they examine the potential working properties of alternative rule structures and choose among them. As Alexander George has suggested, they exercise "analytic imagination" to forecast the consequences of alternative institutions.[16] Given such assessments, they formulate preferences for the rules for the transition and the future order, expressing choices they hope will allow them as political parties not only to survive, but to thrive and flourish. This is the politics of institutional choice. The actors had already begun to think in strategic, interactive terms of institutional choice. Why did they make the choices they made?

The White Right

As I mentioned earlier, the white right wing differs fundamentally from the other actors on the South African scene because it disavows the basic premise on which the others agree: a shared vision of the future. Nevertheless, it was widely fragmented. The Conservative party was the most organized and coherent of the white right organizations, and the only one

---

[14] *Umtapo Focus,* March 1991.
[15] Interview with the author, 21 May 1991.
[16] Correspondence with the author, 30 January 1992.

with parliamentary representation. However, other very small organizations —such as the Herstigte (purified) National party, Boerestaat (Afrikaner state) party, and the Afrikaner Volkswag—also put forth partition plans. To the very far right were the neofascist, paramilitary organizations such as the Afrikaner Weerstandsbeweging (AWB, Afrikaner Resistance movement).[17] All right-wing actors chose some form of partition as an ideal future, and rejected negotiation as a means to getting there. For the white right wing, the first preference for a political order in South Africa was the Verwoerdian dream of complete political control of all the white land (based on the Land Acts and homeland boundaries) in an exclusive white polity. Indeed, the successive splits in the National party in the years since Verwoerd were precipitated by the National party's movement away from this ideal.

Yet for most white right wingers in 1991, the cold realization set in that the original Verwoerdian vision would never be realized. The very fact that the CP and virtually all of the Afrikaner secessionist movements accepted that a new volkstaat would be only a small portion of former white South Africa was an implicit recognition of the power of the black majority. Carel Boshoff of the Afrikaner Volkswag, a movement of conservative Afrikaners seeking a small, independent Afrikaner state in the northern Cape province, summarized the rationale behind ardent Afrikaner nationalists' choice for a separate, sovereign state, one based on the reality of their minority status in South Africa: "It is reasonable and moral. White minority rule cannot be maintained. For 4.5 million Afrikaners to share power with 40 million others is self-destruction and extinction of the nation. It is not enough for us. The majority will decide. On the whole the process of Africanization cannot be checked. Reality is that the conditions for the Afrikaner to survive must be met. We feel it is not possible to survive without a part of the country."[18]

The white right wing chose partition precisely for these reasons. The CP and the white right fully expected to be a permanent minority into the indefinite future. They had little to no international support to rely on (with the exception of, for example, European neofascist groups). In 1991, they saw few coalition partners on the horizon, with the possible exception of the IFP and some conservative homeland leaders (this coalition did later congeal, as I note in chapter 6). It was once thought that the CP and the white right could ultimately rely on the backing of the security forces and police. If that was the hope, it was dashed by the August 1991 events at Ventersdorp, when white policemen opened fire on members of the reactionary AWB protesting a de Klerk speech.

[17] The neofascist AWB, formed in 1973, was the most significant paramilitary organization. See Kotzé and Greyling 1991:51ff. for an extensive list of white right-wing paramilitary groups.

[18] Interview with the author, 16 May 1991.

As Boshoff suggests above, the primary motive for the Afrikaner nationalist call for political sovereignty is that it is perceived as necessary for political, and even cultural, survival. The white right wing, a community that was relatively small, increasingly poor, and internationally and domestically scorned, sought to protect its vital interests by insulating itself from black Africa in a racially exclusive, ethnically "pure" Afrikaner homeland. When differences within the community later emerged in 1992, it was over this issue and the related question of negotiation versus unilateral secession. The fears of the white right emanated from certain expectations of being a permanent minority in an unfavorable, unbalanced power relationship.

In staking out a policy of partition, as juxtaposed against the NP's view of South Africa as a common society, the CP positioned itself to capitalize on the inevitable frustrations of South Africa's fearful white minority into the future. It is in an outbidding position on the National party's radical right. It could play on the Afrikaner's sense of pride and heroism in the face of overwhelming opposition from within South Africa and abroad. As the NP made its inevitable concessions, the CP and the wider white right could play on the fears and uncertainties of a downwardly mobile white working and agrarian class. In the run-up to majority rule, CP legislator Fanie Jacobs explained: "Partition will come after the unsuccessful story of power sharing. . . . We are waiting in the wings."[19]

The CP in 1991, playing the politics of ethnic outbidding, faced a dilemma. As the process moved toward a settlement, they faced the same participation predicament the PAC faced. If they participated, they would lose the outbidding advantage that an eschewal of negotiations provided them; if they did not, they could be forever marginalized as a political force. If the white right were to join, the critical issue would become whether they would accept some compromise—a degree of community autonomy, for example. Until the bridge was later crossed, the Conservative party, and the broader white right wing it represented, remained wedded to partition. They also remained affixed to the view that this dream would be achieved unilaterally. Thus, the Conservative party represented a small minority with few resources. It expected an unfavorable power relationship. In 1991, it chose partition for the future and unilateral secession for the transition.

The National Party

The National party's institutional choices were initially racial segregation in general and, later, its more coherent form of grand apartheid. In the

---

[19] Interview with the author, 4 June 1991.

context of 1948, these choices were grounded in the Afrikaners' history of deprivation and defeat and the ideology of Afrikaner nationalism. The bitter background of the Anglo-Boer wars and the "poor white problem" of the depression era were important historical and ideological antecedents that informed the policies of apartheid. The period of reform apartheid reflected an appreciation of the underlying nonviability of traditional Verwoerdian apartheid; the NP hoped to supplant it with the unilateral imposition of a subsequent preference choice, the tricameral system. This, too, failed because it never gained the legitimacy needed to work, and the NP was not sufficiently powerful to impose it.

As the NP has worked its way through subsequent preference choices, such as the National Statutory Council and the brief flirtation with statutory group rights, it settled on a set of choices in 1991 that, in fact, reversed some of the basic assumptions behind apartheid ideology, notably the rejection of an inextricably shared future with persons of color. What drove the litany of NP institutional choices throughout the years? Changing institutional preferences were, above all, a function of the party's expectations about the future, of the interests of its changing constituencies, and of its view of its own power relative to that of others in the complex web of strategic interaction. Though perhaps he found it difficult to admit the philosophic metamorphosis, National party general secretary Stoffel van der Merwe explained the trends:

> The National Party has shifted through several stages, as obvious from [our] original and initial preference . . . for a government of whites over the rest. But then it was changed to a government of whites for whites, and blacks for blacks, each in its separate state. That was the separate development, or apartheid, phase. Now, even then one can say one has moved through the early 1980s approach which led to the tricameral system, and where the lingering idea was that one should [have] created similarly representative bodies for black people so that you should have not a three-house parliament [but perhaps four or more]. . . . Then one has moved into a different phase now.
>
> This has not been really the product of negotiation, and even insofar, for instance, [that] the ANC has moved away from very radical positions, constitutionally and economically, it's not been really from the process of negotiation, but rather from a diffuse sort of dialogue that is taking place, but not on a negotiation basis. Everyone is trying to take a position which in its view, on the one hand, is ideologically satisfiable and perhaps, pragmatically achievable.[20]

The fundamental point that NP institutional choices were based on what is "pragmatically achievable" is echoed by minister of constitutional development and planning Gerrit Viljoen as he explained in Parliament the

[20] Interview with the author, 25 June 1991.

reasons why the NP moved away from the tricameral framework toward the "amicable agreement" model: "We are not dealing with ideals. We are also dealing with realities. The essence of the NP's adjustments and changes in policy during the past five years or more is precisely that we had to review the ideal we were striving for, which had become stranded on the hard rocks of reality, in order to adapt our ideal to reality and to what is attainable."[21] Viljoen's comment would suggest that the NP's choices were more reactive, as opposed to the more proactive logical progression of thinking outlined by van der Merwe.

If the NP's choices were based on what was "pragmatically achievable," given the "hard rocks of reality," it is important to see that the choices were based on an estimate of the power the party could muster in its interaction with other actors. Power for a political party looking toward a future democratic system is based on the size of the constituency it can draw to its policies and the resources it can count on to translate those votes into the power to affect or thwart policy change.

In 1991 South Africa, the potential NP constituency base was still a minority, but by no means an insignificant one. As discussed in the previous chapter, given the broadening middle class constituency base that lies behind de Klerk's New South Africa ideology, the NP expected to earn as much as 25 percent of the vote in a nonracial election on its own. It had, in 1991, little to fear from further erosion of its support base on the white right. Schlemmer wrote: "The evidence suggests that the NP has already lost virtually all the support it could lose to the CP. . . . More than 85% of NP supporters today in principle endorse more open, competitive policies, as long as competition and criteria for competition (i.e., standards) are protected" (1991a:7). This was, in the South African context, a medium-sized constituency, but one that wielded considerable power. The middle class—including members of the business community, landowners, civil servants (40 percent of white workers are employed in the public sector), skilled laborers, and in many cases, simply job holders—was an essential constituency for stability.

An important aspect of the NP's constituency was the power it continued to wield in the institutions of the state and the economy. An example is the party's ability to direct state resources toward political gain, even before the new system is constructed. In August 1991, the government announced a major job-creation and social-spending plan financed by the sale of strategic oil reserves. The one billion Rand ($333 million) sell-off would reportedly create 59,000 jobs and spread the benefits across a wide range of economic sectors and communities, including education, health, and welfare, and would upgrade hostels, the police, sport and community

---

[21] *Hansard Parliamentary Debate,* 16 May 1991, col. 8839.

facilities, and the infrastructure. Though few would deny that the socio-economic development funds were needed, the move was a thinly disguised attempt to demonstrate that the National party, through the state, could "deliver the goods."[22]

For the NP, state control had more than distributive effects. The military and police force were overwhelmingly white at the officer level, and those nonwhites who were members were often sympathetic to the regime. Despite some slippage to the CP among these coercive institutions of the state, the NP expected these important sectors of society to line up behind it. Through the control of the broadcast media, the NP also controlled a significant tool of communication. The situation was the same in the economy. Among South Africa's dominant economic enterprises, including the critical mining, industrial, and state-owned manufacturing sectors, the National party continued to be the primary political conduit. The state and leading sectors of the economy were critical elements of the party's perception of its power, and they were expected to remain so well into the future.[23]

State control, constituency size, and constituents' skills were only part of the power picture. The National party, despite its years of apartheid domination and repression, gained important international legitimacy in 1990 and 1991 that fed into its perception of power. Especially in the de Klerk era, the party was seen as a source of moderation in South Africa's political conflict and, to some, the defender of Western values and free market economics. These recent policies gave the National party an important set of resources among conservative Western governments, which it translated into bargaining power at the negotiating table.

With its new look as a nonracial political party, the National party also had much different alliance expectations than it had had in the past, beyond the absorption by the party of many middle-class "brown Nats" (former Coloured MPs) and their followers. The NP perceived it to be possible (but not necessarily likely) that it could be a significant player in a *majority* coalition, if not in the first postapartheid election, then in subsequent elections. The potential for NP alliance making was clear. Natural coalition partners in the new era were thought to be some of the

22 The ANC decried the move as "another top-down process of development that sees its main task as delivering a product to the people, and undermines communities rather than empowering them." It was also criticized because the funds were channeled through the discredited Black Local Authorities. The initiative is reported in the *Cape Times*, 28 August 1991; for the ANC response, see the *Cape Times*, 3 September 1991.

23 Although Schlemmer (1988:23) reports that the interest base of the National party does not come primarily from big business (he wrote instead that "there is no evidence . . . that the National Party is the handmaiden to capital"), the advent of the de Klerk administration—and the absence of the bellicose P. W. Botha—led to a much greater and direct influence of business interests in the National party.

tricameral parties, such as the Solidarity party (whose members it subsequently absorbed), the conservative African Zionist churches (despite their apolitical stance), and system-oriented homeland leaders. The possibilities of still other coalition partners also existed. The DP was considered a potential ally, and the NP's then-close relationship with the IFP was of critical importance, especially after Inkathagate. An NP-IFP alliance in many ways seemed natural: both shared a system background, free-market economic policies, an affiliation with ascriptive-based politics, and similar institutional choices. The NP could construct a broad coalition of minority interests.

The NP, however, initially decided on a policy of absorbing members of other parties, rather than of building pre-election alliances. Given its expectations of its own power base and the potential for coalition forming in the new era, the NP perceived an essentially balanced power relationship with its primary adversary, the ANC. The power stalemate that led to the onset of talks was preserved and, due to the emerging interdependence, even enlarged throughout the negotiation process itself. Yet much of its power base was rooted in the status quo. It is not surprising then that the NP's institutional choices were essentially reactive. It sought to preserve as much of the status quo into the new era as possible; it sought to first protect gains of the middle class, to prevent a downward slide in "standards" of society and standards of living. The NP did not oppose the advancement of others only because it sought to expand its support base to the broad middle class, irrespective of color or ethnicity.

The relationship between the NP's institutional proposals and its interests as a political party is clear: it sought to expand the base of participation (and therefore legitimacy) in the state while retaining as much power and influence from status quo conditions as possible. It's proposals reflect above all that it is a "rational" political actor in the Downsian (Downs 1957) sense: it seeks to get elected, to wield power, and to formulate policy in the new political era. Ultimately, the National party of 1991 was still uncertain about its power and coalition-making possibilities in two important respects. First, despite its shift to nation-building rhetoric, it had not fully resolved whether to abandon identity politics and reach widely across historic divides; Coloureds shared a common language and religion, and the moves to broaden the party to include them did not necessarily mean abandoning Afrikaner identity politics. Furthermore, it was by no means certain that it could stitch together a broad coalition of minorities sufficient to protect its interests. Party leaders realized that surveys consistently showed majority support for the ANC. The NP would then rather see ironclad guarantees written into the new constitution to ensure minority protection than risk it all by testing its new strategy in a very unpredictable first election.

The NP's aspiration to be the leader of a conservative, free-market-oriented center-right coalition was revealed in institutional choices it presented in September 1991, which are most appropriately labeled *modified consociationalism*. Although the gist of the 1991 plan is clearly consociational—resting particularly on a variety of statutory constraints to protect minority interests—these choices were modified by the process of strategic interaction that preceded them. The NP's constitutional plans contained three consociational elements.

The Minority Veto. The NP choices ensured a minority veto over a wide range of policy issues, especially through minority representation in the second house of parliament. The proposals stipulated that each region (of nine) would have an equal number of seats in the chamber and that every party which gained "a specified" level of support in regional elections would have an *equal* number of seats. The second house, which would pass all legislation before enactment, would have to pass by a "weighted majority" legislation that "amends the constitution, relates to the interests of minorities, or relates to the interests of regions." Furthermore, the house would "initiate legislation relating to circumscribed matters and which affects the specific interests of minorities and regions."[24] Given the NP's expectation of support and its geographical distribution, it was relatively certain that, depending on the electoral threshold and the level of weighted majority, it could veto legislation on issues of minority concern.

Mandated Grand Coalition. The NP proposed a mandated grand coalition in the collective executive called the *presidency*. The troika presidency would be comprised of leaders from the three largest parties in the first house of parliament, and the head of state would be a rotating position among these leaders. If the three parties together did not make a majority in the first house, more leaders could be added until such a threshold was reached. It is no coincidence that the NP in 1991, expecting to be among the three largest parties, chose such a plan.

Segmental Autonomy. The NP's superdevolution option, for example, neighborhood councils with considerable authority over local level issues, was in effect a choice to provide segmental autonomy. Given the present distribution of living areas (based on the lingering effects of the Group Areas Act), such neighborhood-based areas would be highly homogeneous in ascriptive terms. Providing local neighborhood councils

---

[24] "Constitutional Rule in a Participatory Democracy," 4 September 1991, National Party Federal Information Service, pamphlet.

with extensive powers as envisioned in the NP plan would be in effect providing them with group autonomy at the subregional level.

While these elements of consociationalism were clearly present in the NP plan, there are several important ways in which it is a modification of the consociational model. These modifications were made in the direction of majoritarianism. Perhaps the most important modification, and a shift from the NP plans of the past, was that the regional demarcation would not be based on ethnic, linguistic, or racial lines; economic criteria would be used. The idea of corporate federalism based on social segments was a major modification in the National party plan. A related modification was the absence of any referral to group rights in explicit ethnic terms. Instead, a broader standard of groups is employed, that of "communities of interests."25

How the NP sought to realize its institutional choices in the process of transition must be seen in the context of how the NP viewed other transitions and what lessons it drew from them. The cases of Zimbabwe (1980) and Namibia (1990) were most relevant. These cases were critical in terms of the NP's perception of change, because of the ways in which white settler communities in Africa were forced to adapt the inevitability of black enfranchisement.26 In the course of negotiations, the government made several key concessions in its efforts to negotiate a transition favorable to its interests. Ostensibly, by the time an interim government was agreed upon, the present government would have negotiated away its unilateral hold on state power. Nevertheless, its choice for the transition remained a consociational one in which its vital interests continued to be guaranteed: it expected to wield considerable power, to retain a hard-and-fast right to veto major change, through the multiparty conference.

The NP's institutional choice for the transition was further illustrated by what it did not want, an elected constituent assembly. The National party preferred not submit to an election for a constituency assembly because it would run counter to its basic interests and power base. An election *prior* to the formation of a constituent assembly would, it was thought, cut the ground from under its feet; although it may have been a necessary compromise down the road (and it eventually was), the NP was not willing to concede to the assembly in a way analogous to writing a blank check. Indeed, any party which perceives that it will be in a minor-

25 Ibid.

26 According to Humphries (1990), the NP learned some important lessons about the end of white minority rule; first, negotiate from a position of strength; second, do not opt for statutory minority representation (as in Zimbabwe), as that perpetuates minority status; third, try to become part of governing coalition, thus, try to build multiracial alliances (such as the Democratic Turnhalle Alliance in Namibia); and fourth, realize that the opposition will be hamstrung by world pressures in its attempts to redistribute wealth.

ity is unlikely to risk the prospects that in a constituent assembly, a single party or an alliance of parties could combine and unilaterally draft a constitution. For these reasons, the preferred rule for the transition phase was consensus. The NP's choices for the transition reflected the basic fact that, although the NP was numerically a minority, the power relationship among the parties was perceived to be effectively balanced.

The NP's choice for a referendum to legitimate a new constitution also reflects the dynamics of institutional choice. Given de Klerk's pledge to submit a new constitution to the white electorate in a referendum rather than an all-white election, there was a clear expectation of the working properties of these alternative decision rules. In the party's view, the difference is this: the NP was more certain it could get a bare majority of whites in a national referendum of white voters than an outright victory in an election under the present first-past-the-post electoral system. The National party leadership knew all too well how such an electoral system could distort an outcome. Depending on the geographic distribution of votes, and the possibility of a third party splitting NP support, it could well have lost another all-white election. It should be recalled, after all, that in 1989 it won a majority of seats with a minority (47 percent) of the white vote, just as it did in 1948. With minor shifts in key constituencies, the CP could do the same in a future all-white election. The NP knew that with the support of DP members for a "yes" vote in a white referendum, it could be confident of prevailing in a simple majority-rule white referendum. The National party, as the incumbent government, possessed significant resources. But as an expected minority party representing minority communities, it chose modified consociationalism for the future and consensus decision-making rules for the transition.

The Democratic Party

The Democratic party's institutional choices in 1991 reflected the party's singular position at the center of a historically polarized political spectrum. This uniqueness was reflected in the choices the party made for both a future democracy and the transition: it sought to pull the extremes of the political system toward the center, toward its own policies. Although the DP realized it would remain a small party, it expected that it could fit comfortably in a governing coalition with either the ANC on its left or an NP government on its right. Its repeated preference, however, was to form a coalition with them both, to be a part of a grand coalition of major political actors to stabilize a deeply divided society. It formulated a set of institutional choices that would have the effect of creating a centripetal spin to the political system.

The DP retained an identity separate from that of either the National party or the ANC, conceivably to hold the balance of power between the two following the first nonracial election. The potential for a changing constituency base was already evident. In a poll published by the Johannesburg-based *Financial Mail* in September 1991, survey results showed that the DP garnered the support of 6 percent of the white respondents and 4 percent of the blacks interviewed. Just as important, some 17 percent of whites and 10 percent of blacks responded that they would "possibly" vote for the DP in an election.[27] Given the inroads the party made in the Coloured community, and its initial efforts to recruit Africans, the DP appealed to a group of potential voters who were uncomfortable with the ANC's confrontational style but would never vote for the NP, given its legacy of apartheid.

Because of the DP's unique centrist position, historical role as a mediator, and strongly held liberal-democratic beliefs, its expectations about its role in a future system were more uncertain than those of any other political party. The opportunities were clear: it could be a coalition broker in a future system. But dangers were also present; given the factionalization of its membership—some leaned left, others leaned right—the party potentially faced absorption by the more powerful blocks on its respective flanks. The uncertainty of the DP's view of the future was critical. Exactly because of its uncertain role, it chose political institutions that favored parties of the moderate center. Its centripetal choices served such uncertainty extremely well. Moreover, the strategy was to create a convergence in the country's politics by acting as a catalyst for a broad-based grand coalition including both the NP and the ANC. It sought to consolidate what it perceived to be a balanced power relationship. How was this to be done?

Federalism. Given South Africa's history of deep divisions, federalism was argued to promote democracy by making political power accessible to as many people as possible, thereby providing stability and legitimacy to the state. The more locuses of political power, the more access people will have to it, and the less likely they will engage in violent conflict over power at the top. The DP's 1991 constitutional guidelines explain its choice, and how this choice serves the centripetal aims:

> South Africa's history is littered with examples of the use of the monopoly of centralized power to impose an oppressive philosophy on the entire country. A federal structure makes this very much more difficult, and the system also provides a variety of sites of power in which more people can exercise power, making the retention of central government power relatively less important. . . . Federalism helps to cater for [the cultural, linguistic, geographic, and

---

[27] The poll results are reported in the *New York Times*, 19 November 1991.

political] diversity by multiplying the sites of power. Moreover, by multiplying the sites of power and competition, new and transcending alliances based on regional or common interests can be forged. . . . This will certainly make the resolution of seemingly intractable problems far easier.[28]

It is important to note that the DP firmly rejected the delimitation of federal boundaries on the basis of racial or ethnic lines.

A Directly Elected Executive and Senate. The DP's plan envisioned a directly elected executive president and a prime minister chosen by parliament; these posts would be backed by a mandatory multiparty cabinet drawn from all political parties that had won at least 10 percent of the seats in the first house of parliament. The executive structures the DP envisioned have two important centripetal functions: the president, elected every seven years (by a runoff system to guarantee an absolute majority of support) with a term not coincidental with parliament, would be—if elected by a supermajority—a broad-based figure standing above party politics and day-to-day political fights. He or she would be expected to resolve deadlocks in the multiparty cabinet and to represent broad, national interests rather than narrow, communal ones.

The members of the second house of parliament proposed by the DP would also serve a seven-year term, not coincidental with that of the first house, or National Assembly. The Senate would have one hundred members, sixty-six elected in an unspecified manner by the regions (with an equal number per region), and the remaining thirty-three elected by municipal councilors acting as an electoral college.

Proportional Representation. While the party's 1991 plans offered three alternatives for an electoral system for the first house of parliament that achieved the principle of proportional representation, they were all similar in their effect. Each of the proposals sought to ensure that a candidate would have a clear incentive to advocate a position that appealed to the median voter preference; in order to be elected, the candidate would have to chase (at least) second-preference votes, or parties would have to offer lists that appealed to a wide range of voters, if a system of vote pooling were used. The DP's electoral system options demonstrated directly its choice for institutions specifically designed to induce moderation.

To summarize, the DP's 1991 made institutional choices for a form of government that encouraged moderation and consensus building among a centrist core. This aim was also reflected in the party's transition plans.

[28] "Constitutional Proposals," 23 August 1991, Democratic party policy discussion paper.

The Democratic party was at the forefront of those who proposed an interim government based on a consensus power-sharing arrangement to include all major political players in the decision-making processes of the state in virtually every sphere of public policy. It sought a transition guided by the centrist parties, and itself advocated a compromise position between the preferences of the National party and the ANC: the DP favored an multiparty conference to be followed by an elected constituent assembly. The Democratic party was poised at the center of the nascent and emerging political center, capable of making coalition partners of the parties to the right and left, or going it alone. It chose centripetalism for the future and a consensus decision rule for the transition.

The Inkatha Freedom Party

The Inkatha Freedom party had the least explicitly formulated set of institutional choices for a postapartheid democracy, despite its long history of having negotiated constitutional arrangements for the Natal province through the KwaNatal Indaba. It was widely believed, and the evidence suggests, that the party's sympathies for a postapartheid state were an outgrowth of these proposals, which includes statutory group protection, proportional representation, segmental autonomy, and a minority veto. The IFP in 1991 expressed a clear preference for devolution within a federal framework and strong protection for minorities, along with vaguely worded commitments to liberal, multiparty democracy and a free-enterprise market system. These proposals, taken together, represented a choice for consociationalism.

The lack of specificity emanating from the IFP on the aspects of a postapartheid democracy were related to institutional choice calculations. The party has a historical background that prevents it from forging alliances with the liberation movement; indeed, it puts them in direct conflict. Its populist orientation, rooted in Zulu nationalism, constrained its ability to expand its constituency base far beyond its core community and sympathetic whites. Its expectation of remaining a minority party well into the future was rather certain, and its fears of an exclusive ANC-led majority government were enormously high. It perceived an unbalanced, unfavorable power relationship with its larger, stronger foe.

Not only was its constituency small, but its resources were few; most Inkatha members are the rural poor of the Natal province and the hostel-dwelling migrant laborers in the PWV. Much of its power, however, was not in the numbers of supporters, but in their capability and willingness to wreak violence in order to ensure they would not be politically marginalized. Even though its constituency was small and its internal resources few, the party nonetheless enjoyed some support among conservative elements in the Western democracies, including direct financial support from center-right organizations in Germany, for example, as well from conservative activists in the United States.[29]

Inkatha's institutional choices remained vague throughout the preliminary negotiations phase because ambiguity served its aims in the process of transition, and these aims were rather clear. It did not want to be excluded from political power, and it believed that the key provisions in a future constitution that would protect its interests were federalism and minority group rights. The IFP sought, above all, concrete assurances of minority group protection; it wanted, at a minimum, to preserve its political power base in Natal and in the KwaZulu government. It wanted assurances—consociational-type guarantees—against an ANC hegemony. Buthelezi stated very clearly his concern about this outcome, if in somewhat coded rhetoric, in July 1991: "If we are going to avoid a very harsh black majoritarianism which would put a black party in power and leave that party the impossible task of seeking reconciliation between race groups after it has thumped its way to victory, we are going to experience enormous problems. . . . The days of dictation from whatever quarter are gone, never to return."[30] The implication is that Inkatha would likely accept any variant of a consociational system that provided such assurances.

Critical to Inkatha's calculations on institutional options was the possibility it could form a coalition with other parties.[31] While perhaps possible at one point in time, an alliance with the ANC—a common African front—was virtually inconceivable. It is clear that the party looked toward other alliance partners, particularly the National party but also the white right, as possible allies. There were consistent rumblings from both parties that a coalition between them could have been in the offing for the future. It was clear then that the NP and Inkatha had the underlying basis for a common opposition to the ANC. Their common fear of an ANC-led government, their agreement on political and economic values, and their common background as system actors reinforced these expectations.[32]

[29] Inkatha's relations with conservative elements in the Western world are long and complex. Much of Inkatha's international support stems from those who opposed the imposition of sanctions against South Africa. Inkatha was one of the few black voices to whom they could point for evidence of the claims that blacks in South Africa opposed sanctions.

[30] *South African Update* (Durban) 3 (July 1991):6.

[31] Political analyst Theodore Venter wrote about the party: "Buthelezi and the new [multiracial[Inkatha remain one of the key players in the South African power game. He is a leader with a strong regional constituency, a national profile and international support. However, the key to the political role of Inkatha in a future South Africa lies with Inkatha's ability to form effective political alliances" (*South African Foundation Review,* August 1990).

[32] The IFP, it should be noted, publicly endorsed the February 1991 "Manifesto for a New South Africa" unveiled by de Klerk. A joint government-IFP working group statement indicated "unanimous support" among IFP delegates for the manifesto (*Cape Times,* 18 February 1991).

The concern with possible exclusion from political power in the future also drove Inkatha's institutional choices over the transition. Inkatha's strategy throughout the transition process was to ensure that it remained a key player—one of the "big three"—into the new order. Its vehement rejection of a constituent assembly was clearly a reflection of the dynamics of institutional choice; Gavin Woods said of an elected assembly, "It could be the end of you politically."[33] It is not surprising, then, that the mechanism of a multiparty conference based on consensus decision making was preferred for the drafting of a new constitution, with its product to be legitimated in a national referendum. Despite nationwide aspirations, the Inkatha Freedom party remained primarily an ethnic party representing only a portion of an internally divided ethnic group. It chose consociationalism for the future and consensus decision-making rules for the transition.

The African National Congress

As the ANC's institutional choices evolved from the Freedom Charter to the 1988 Constitutional Guidelines, the Harare Declaration, and finally the April 1991 constitutional guidelines, there was considerable continuity. The basic demands of the ANC—universal franchise on a common voters' roll in a unitary state—have remained the foundation of the organization's choices. Despite the fact that these principles were never given any specific structural form, there was considerable movement in the ANC's institutional choices from the rather undiluted majoritarian proposals of the 1988 guidelines—with their ban on ethnic and racially oriented parties—to the modified majoritarian system the organization put forward in 1991. These were accompanied by important concessions related to the path of transition.

Three elements of the 1991 constitutional proposals underscore the politics of institutional choice: the dual executive, a proportional representation electoral system, and regional government structures. For the transition, the important shift was the acceptance of an all-party conference prior to the election of a constituent assembly. These proposals relate directly to the ANC's expectations regarding the power relationship. The ANC modified its proposals to reflect its concern with the principle of inclusiveness for a new political order.

Before I discuss the essentially majoritarian plan of the ANC and its modifications toward power sharing, it is important to understand the background to these choices. The ANC has historically led the liberation struggle, one it waged primarily to achieve the franchise as well as the

---

[33] Interview with the author, 23 August 1991.

political power that would be expected with the enfranchisement of the majority. This history brings with it the philosophy of nonracialism and the eschewal of ethnic or other ascriptive politics as the ANC's reaction to apartheid (Marx 1991). Its long alliance with the SACP and its more recent association with COSATU are important antecedent variables as well. Most importantly, however, the ANC expected the support of a majority of voters in the first universal franchise election. And, despite the emerging strains mentioned in the previous chapter, it further expected to remain a majority party for some time into the postapartheid era. Nevertheless, without ever having tested its expectations in an election, the ANC was uncertain, as it formulated its institutional choices in 1991, that in the long run it would always emerge as the clear majority party. Would it indeed win a clear majority, and how large would it be? Would it be able to maintain its national liberation coalition beyond the enfranchising first election?

The ANC in 1991 had not yet shifted from its position as a national liberation movement, based on symbolism, to that of a political party, based on interest. Mandela said:

> [We will not become a political party] before the new constitution is accepted. If we did transform ourselves into a political party we would be in difficulties because what unites us today is the struggle against oppression. . . . If we turn into a party then we will have to go further: we will have to decide whether we are going to be an organization that believes in the capitalist system, whether we are going to believe in Fabian socialism or whether we are going to believe in Marxist socialism. . . . That would be dangerous because it would split us from top to bottom.[34]

Nevertheless, in 1991 the ANC did act as a political party, formulating its institutional choices as if it would contest a first election. It also expected to win.

In absolute terms, the ANC of 1991 had the largest constituency of any political party in South Africa; it also had significant political power. The mobilizing capacity of the movement, combined with the strong organizational network and economic muscle that COSATU brought to the alliance, gave the ANC important resources. It enjoyed strong support in the international community and could rely to a large degree on backing for its positions from the UN General Assembly and the Organization of African Unity. Although the organization was financially strapped and its constituency relatively poor, it received considerable financial contributions from abroad. Most important, it possessed symbolic virtue, and was able to cash in, literally, on the fame and high regard of Nelson Mandela.

[34] *Star*, 18 July 1991.

Tactics employed by the ANC, such as "mass action" (demonstrations and strikes), translated these resources into political power. But because the organization did not control the institutions of the state, it was at a comparative disadvantage. As has been seen, it too could not write the rules of the new order unilaterally; despite its numerical majority, relative to the comparably high resources of the NP, the ANC was faced with a balanced-power relationship. The power parity that produced the onset of negotiation lasted into the initial stages of transition.

The ANC's institutional choices of 1991 reflected these expectations and realities. The plan presented was still a streamlined majoritarian model consistent with previous positions taken by the organization. Universal franchise, a unitary state, and no backtracking on the fundamental principle of nonracialism were enshrined. The National Assembly, or first house of parliament, would be elected by proportional representation but would take decisions by simple majority. Neither the second house nor the executive could frustrate the will of the majority party in the National Assembly. The Senate, or second house, would have the ability only to delay legislation, not to block it. Regional powers would be delegated, not devolved. Nevertheless, in three important areas a streamlined majoritarian framework was modified.

Proportional Representation. When it was formally put forward in April 1991, the ANC's choice for proportional representation was widely perceived to be a major concession to minority concerns. Surely, given South Africa's current first-past-the-post electoral framework, the ANC could have been expected to benefit from the distorting effects of this system. Its support was dispersed widely and its opposition hopelessly split on the left and right; the ANC would have been expected to achieve a majority of seats far and above its already majority proportion of support in the electorate, just like the electoral bounty the NP enjoyed for many decades. A critical question must be asked: Did the ANC ever favor a first-past-the post electoral system and, if so, why the shift to the PR system?

Even though an electoral system was not spelled out in the 1988 guidelines, most analysts assumed that the ANC would prefer a majoritarian electoral system. Steven Friedman, from the Centre for Policy Studies at the University of the Witwatersrand, said: "It was always an assumption everybody made, but it was never spelled out anywhere. It was never an issue they had specifically addressed. One theory is that they always had that [first-past-the-post] in mind and that [the choice] for PR was an inevitable recognition that compromise was going to be made."[35]

[35] Interview with the author, 15 May 1991.

The ANC's choice for party list proportional representation is explained by National Executive Committee and Constitutional Committee member Kader Asmal, who was the most important figure in arguing for its adoption by the organization. "As I say in my paper,[36] there is no ideal electoral system; electoral systems perform certain functions. . . . We present proportional representation as the fairest system—although I don't think it is in the ultimate interest of the ANC. It is extraordinary that for once it is possible to say in a society such as ours that a policy was adopted, or a position was adopted, which is considered to meet the criteria of fairness, accessibility, and legitimacy. It is a system which guarantees exact proportion of your seats to your votes."[37]

I will return to the question of the issue of the protection of interests and its relationship to fairness as a central question in institutional choice in chapter 7, but here I simply want to demonstrate the interest basis of the ANC's choice for PR. The party list proportional representation system as put forward by the ANC still served the party's interests in a future political system in several critical ways.

First is the task of constituency delimitation. The combination regional and national party list system proposed by the ANC obviates the need to delimit small, single-member constituencies, an important feature given the legacies of the Group Areas Act. John Dugard, director of the Center for Applied Legal Studies at the University of the Witwatersrand, explains the ANC's reasoning as it relates to choice for PR:

> The ANC constitutional committee adopted it largely on the views of one man, Kader Asmal, who is a very enthusiastic and effective proponent of proportional representation. I think they realize it is a fairer system. I suppose there is the fear in all quarters that the Group Areas Act has created ethnic regions. So just as the NP has no prospect of gaining support in the Soweto constituency, the ANC would have no support or constituency in the white areas. So I think there is a realization in all areas that in order to maximize their own support, they must accept PR.[38]

A second way in which proportional representation serves the interests of the ANC is in its simplicity as an electoral system. By faithfully translating the number of votes in the electorate into seats in parliament, it is easily understood. But it also lends itself to a very simple method of voting that would likely benefit the ANC in elections. A voter would cast only one vote, and that vote would go to a political party. On a single ballot, parties could be easily identified by well-known symbols. Given the high level of illiteracy (55 percent) of South Africa's potential elector-

[36] Asmal 1990.
[37] Interview with the author, 7 May 1991.
[38] Interview with the author, 13 May 1991.

ate, voting by symbol—and voting once and only for a party—could have considerable value to an organization such as the ANC. It carries the symbolic virtue of being the leader in the struggle against apartheid, obviating the need to mobilize support on the basis of too-specific policies or on the reputations of a wide range of individual candidates. For the ANC, simplicity can translate directly into support.

Yet a third way in which the party's interests in a future system are served is in a sense a negative one. If the party fully expects to achieve majority support, and it has been shown that it does, proportional representation under a system of government without checks by other institutions of the state would not frustrate the party's ability to pass legislation. With 51 percent of the overall vote, an ANC majority in the National Assembly could pass legislation—as long as it was constitutional—without difficulty. In the ANC's plan, the proposed Senate could only delay legislation, not veto it or otherwise prevent its enactment.

Most important, however, the choice for PR on the part of the ANC represents a concern with the politics of inclusion. The ANC chose it after a well-considered assessment of not only what was *desirable* but also of what was *possible,* given the preferences of others. It evolved out of the process of strategic interaction. The choice reflects the reality that minorities, potentially even right-wing white parties espousing discriminatory policies, would be included and could wield power in a postapartheid parliament. Kader Asmal, when arguing for the adoption of PR at an ANC conference on electoral systems in late 1990, quoted U.S. president Lyndon Johnson, who said, "I would rather have the son-of-a-bitch who is inside pissing out than outside pissing in."[39] The significance of the quote is this: the ANC considered it better to have opposition forces competing inside parliament rather than seeking to bring down the system from without. The ANC knows from its own experience the ability of external parties conducting guerrilla warfare to thwart a regime's ability to implement its polices. Proportional representation, it was thought, could help avert that prospect.

Regionalism and Localism.   A second important modification of the ANC's majoritarian framework was the acceptance of a role for elected regional and local governments in the new order. Despite its frequent calls for a unitary state, the ANC included the creation of quasi-independent regional and local tiers of authority. This subtle shift in ANC policy reflected not only the reality that the government and other federalist parties would demand decentralization in a new system, but also the concerns about overcentralization that bubbled up from the organization's

---

[39] Interview with the author, 7 May 1991.

own constituency. The ANC chose to support strong local and regional institutions because they gave meaning to the call for "power to the people." The unitary state concept as applied to the reincorporation of the homelands into a greater South Africa was not jeopardized, but the ANC first conceded that regional government would play a role in a future order.

Dullah Omar of the ANC Constitutional Committee outlined the organization's views on the role of regional government in 1991: "We favor regions within a unitary constitution that gives the opportunity for democracy at the regional and local level based on derived powers, not delineated. Because South Africa needs to move away from apartheid, you need a central parliament which creates uniform policies across the country; that being done, regional, and local authorities should have the flexibility and powers to deal with regional differences and problems."[40] The concessions, however, that such regional governments should be directly elected and that regional criteria be used for weighting the system of proportional representation were significant signals that on the question of "regionalism" (a euphemism for federalism), there was room for subsequent movement. Regionalism would serve the ANC's interests in some areas, such as Transkei, where it had a strong power base, but it would clearly work against its interests in, for example, the IFP stronghold of Natal.

The Dual Executive. The final modification of majoritarianism made by the ANC was the design of the executive. The ANC's preference was for a combined president and prime minister, but for an executive that would serve coincidentally with the National Assembly. The expected effect would create a greater degree of cooperation between the executive and legislative branches of government. Kader Asmal explains the thinking behind the ANC's choice:

The president's term of office should be associated with that of the National Assembly. That way, if the president's term of office is the same as the National Assembly's, she or he can't play games with the National Assembly by dissolving the National Assembly. Whereas in a directly elected presidency, if the president can't get his way with the National Assembly, he dissolves it, and there is a political crisis . . . a political crisis, not a constitutional crisis, [such as] in France. [In the ANC's constitutional proposals,] if the president wants to dissolve the National Assembly, he has to dissolve himself. That is an inducement to work with the National Assembly. So it is an inducement to work collaboratively.[41]

[40] Interview with the author, 10 April 1991.
[41] Interview with the author, 7 May 1991.

As we have seen with other parties, the institutional choices of the ANC are also intricately tied to its preferences for the transition. The ANC's 1991 call for an elected constituent assembly to draft a new constitution was in essence for a majoritarian model of transition. The ANC 8 January 1991 agreement to the all-party conference, however, was clearly a fundamental concession in the negotiation process and a modification of the essentially majoritarian process of a constituent assembly. This modification reflected the strategic interaction of the transition and indicated the ANC's acceptance of the fact that before a constituent assembly election could be held, a conference with a consensus decision rule would be required to negotiate the principles on which a new constitution would be based. The ANC knew its concessions would quicken the pace of negotiation and, it hoped, might lead to the early formation of an interim government. As long as the government controlled the military, police, and resources of the state, they could arguably be used to destabilize the ANC on the ground. The party conference was the compromise institution through which both the NP and the ANC could gain together, even if it entailed risks for the ANC of being outnumbered by the government and the litany of apartheid-spawned political players that would press to attend. The African National Congress represented a large constituency, but its resources and organizational capacity were limited. Nevertheless, it is expected to win the election that will end apartheid. Over the horizon, however, its fundamental expectations of holding on to power are ultimately *uncertain*. It perceived that the balance of power would continue to tip in its favor following the end of white minority rule, but did not know whether its parliamentary majority could be sustained given the strains of governing a postapartheid society. It chose modified majoritarianism for the future and a consensus-based party conference, to be followed by a constituent assembly, for the transition.

The PAC

The PAC favored an unqualified majoritarian system for South Africa. It strongly rejected any modifications or diminution of the majoritarian framework, with the notable exception of it choice for proportional representation (both for a future electoral system and for a constituent assembly election). How can these choices be explained? The PAC of 1991 was placed in an important position relative to the ANC, a place in which it could outbid the large nonracial party for sentiments of South Africa's disenfranchised black majority. As the ANC moderated its positions, the PAC was well placed to snare disgruntled and radicalized rank-and-file members of the ANC—it outbid the ANC for support. Despite its outbidding position, the PAC was nonetheless a small party with few internal resources and little international support. Although it was officially recognized by the United Nations as a liberation movement and had backing in the OAU, it received little support from the front-line states. Its constituency was also very exclusive, with no appreciable members from minority communities because of its Africanist philosophy. It might have hoped to form an alliance with the ANC at some later point, but its expectations of remaining a minority party were quite certain for the foreseeable future.[42] The PAC was a relatively weak party compared to the system parties and the ANC. Nevertheless, the imbalance with the NP was perceived to be short term; potentially, as a black nationalist party, the demographics were on its side.

The political battle between the ANC and the PAC was waged at the grass-roots level, among the hearts and minds of the township residents. In some areas, the PAC was ascendant even as the polls continued to show the ANC as the organization the majority of Africans supported. In areas of the Eastern Cape and the Orange Free State—as well as some townships near Cape Town on the "Cape Flats"—the PAC had a presence. Using these bases, the PAC worked quietly to build an organization at the grass-roots level. The PAC's Barney Desai said: "I wouldn't say we have a majority support in the Western Cape; that would be premature. It's well known we don't have the resources of the ANC, so we will have to depend on what we get from our own people. Our reach is limited, but we are expanding it all the time."[43]

The PAC's choice for majoritarianism was a clear indication of its outbidding position on the revolutionary left. The PAC perceived of itself as the first alternative to a faltering ANC for many Africans. The central most important economic issue for the PAC was the question of economic grievances, and chief among them, land. PAC assistant secretary general Carter Seleka stated the party's firm conviction on the urgency of land reform, and the role the issue played in the political program: "The land question is quite paramount to us. Current power is centered on an economic base. The land is therefore in focus; one cannot separate the land from the economy, especially the minerals. When we talk of power, we say we need our land back, and through that land we can exercise effective political power."[44] In order to accomplish radical economic restructuring and land redistribution in the tradition of African socialism, the PAC called for centralized, majoritarian political institutions. The party's leader, Benny Alexander, said: "There is no way negotiations can be re-

[42] Movement toward a Patriotic Front of anti-apartheid organizations was made in April 1991, following a meeting among the ANC, PAC, and other organizations in Lusaka, Zambia.

[43] *Weekly Mail,* 11 May 1990.

[44] Interview with the author, 15 May 1991.

garded as a panacea for all our social malaise. Therefore, it is bound to fail. In order to implement your economic policies you must control state political power to such an absolute degree that you are able to implement it without obstructions. The whites won't allow us to control the government, let alone the state."[45]

The PAC could capitalize on more than economic grievances in its outbidding of the ANC for support in the future. By remaining outside negotiations and insisting (in rhetoric, at least) on an outright victory for the struggle, the PAC was poised to gain from future political and economic grievances. As the ANC was forced to make compromises in the negotiation process on a new constitution, there would likely to be those within the ranks of the struggle who were unwilling to concede. If the ANC went too far in its concession making on the nature and extent of black majority rule, there would be those who felt the liberation struggle had been betrayed. The PAC's call for simple majoritarianism would be an attractive message of disagreement with the limitation of majority power that a negotiated settlement implied. Africanism, in both economic and political terms, would be a natural response to a ANC policy of nonracialism and economic compromise in the event of failed mass expectations.

The PAC's zero-sum perception was reflected in its 1991 institutional choices. The party stuck firmly to the view that a future state would be based on a streamlined majoritarian framework: As Seleka said, "We have set [our preferences for a future state] out in the UN Consensus Resolution, and the government must simply accept them."[46] The only possible point of concession in the PAC's institutional choices was its call for party proportional representation in a single national constituency, with a 4 percent threshold for representation in the constituent assembly. It rationale for this choice is interesting; the party argues (as ANC thinkers have also pointed out) that any delimitation of constituencies under the present distribution of the population at this point would be necessarily skewed by the enforced pattern of settlement imposed by the Group Areas Act. Apartheid's legacy makes any such enterprise inherently unfair. Yet it is immediately clear that as a small party, with rather certain expectations of staying small, proportional representation also serves its interests very well. If it garners only the 7–9 percent of the vote it now expects to get, it could be proportionally represented in parliament, and others (possibly the Conservative party) would be excluded. Strategically, the PAC would have the option to participate in newly negotiated institutions, even if its aim was to destroy them.

The motives behind the PAC's institutional choices for the future are

---

45 *Financial Mail*, 6 June 1990.
46 Interview with the author, 15 May 1991.

equally reflected in its choice for the transition. The PAC criticized the ANC for some time over its acceptance of participation in a party conference, and refused to sign the National Peace Accord. Both were argued to give undue legitimacy to the collapsing white minority regime. The PAC instead preferred the immediate election of a constituent assembly, agreeing only to a "preconstituent assembly" meeting to work out the procedural details of organizing an internationally monitored election but at the end leaving itself an opening to participate in party talks. Yet it is clear to see how, in the outlook of the PAC, a constituent assembly fit within its interest calculations. At first glance, it might be accurate to say that because the PAC is clearly a minority party, it would not have an interest in a constituent assembly, just as the National party did not. On the other hand, its preference for such a transition mechanism is understandable *because* it is a minority party and because its key demand is enfranchisement of the black majority. It looks forward to electoral competition under full enfranchisement, and mobilized on the constituent assembly issue. The PAC in 1991 stood at a crucial crossroads. As South African Institute of International Affairs researcher and a specialist on the PAC Gary van Staden said: "They can continue trying to outbid the ANC only until the negotiations reach the point of bargaining for power. At that point they face two choices—they can try and prevent a settlement from being implemented, but they simply don't have the muscle to achieve this, or they can enter the negotiations process and lose all the advantages of their outbidding position."[47] Despite its rejectionist rhetoric, there was a strong force pulling the PAC toward participation. In order to outbid the ANC for electoral support in the postapartheid era, it had to compete within the new institutions. Its choices, therefore, were even *more* majoritarian than those of the ANC.

The Azanian People's Organization

The PAC, too, was outbid on the left by the more doctrinaire AZAPO. By far, this black consciousness organization has been the most uncompromising of the actors in the liberation struggle, not only in its ideology, but also in its perceived role as the standard bearer of the goal of liberation in the tradition of Steve Biko and those who led the Soweto uprising in 1976. It spelled out the most revolutionary vision of change among major South African political actors.

AZAPO's institutional choices of 1991 reflected a preference for an ideologically pure—from the point of view of black consciousness and scientific socialism—form of black majority rule. The focus on the means

[47] *Weekly Mail,* 11 May 1990.

TABLE 5.1
Institutional Choices of Major Political Parties, South Africa, 1991

	CP	IFP	NP	DP	ANC	PAC	AZAPO
Historical perspective	Verwoerdian apartheid	Homeland government	Ancien régime	Facilitator	Liberation struggle: Franchise	Liberation struggle: Decolonization	Liberation struggle: Empowerment
Ideology	Afrikaner nationalism	Zulu nationalism	Technocratic, multiethnic	Liberalism	Nonracialism	Africanism	Black consciousness
Expectations	Certain	Uncertain	Uncertain	Uncertain	Certain	Certain	Certain
Expected vote share (%)	3–4	3–4	20–30	10–12	55–60	7–9	3
Estimate of power Size of constituency	Small	Small	Medium	Small	Large	Small	Small

| Resources | Few | Medium | High | Medium | Medium | Few | Few |
Coalition forming	Permanent	Possible	Possible	Possible	Permanent	Possible	Permanent
Expectation	Minority	Majority	Majority	Majority	Majority	Majority	Minority
Power relationship	Unbalanced, unfavorable	Unbalanced, unfavorable	Balanced	Balanced	Balanced	Unbalanced, favorable	Unbalanced, favorable
Transition preference	Secession	Party conference	Party conference, referendum	Party conference, constituent assembly	Party conference, constituent assembly	Constituent assembly	Constituent assembly
Institutional choice	Partition	Consociationalism	Modified consociationalism	Centripetalism	Modified majoritarianism	Majoritarianism	Majoritarianism

of production, especially land but also the commanding heights of the economy, were specifically linked to the rejection of the institutions of "bourgeois democracy." When queried about any possible consensus in South African politics about the nature of a postapartheid state, AZAPO's Strini Moodley summed up the party's view:

> There are elements in the society that are seeking to establish a kind of bourgeois democracy, a democracy which will say a lot of things on paper but which will deliver nothing in reality, with lots of high sounding rhetoric.
>
> Land and all the resources of the country cannot belong to individuals because the earth does not belong to individuals; the earth belongs to the entire human race. In Azania, we will interpret that to mean that all the land, all the natural resources, will belong to all the people. Individuals will not be allowed to own land, or to speculate with land. . . . So that would be one of the basic tenets of new constitution, it must hit directly on the land. Nobody will have the right to own land—everybody will have the right to work the land.[48]

AZAPO ruled out negotiations of any kind—"there can be no negotiations between unequals," it has said—and it did favor the election of a constituent assembly. Although principally guided by doctrinaire ideology, AZAPO was also positioned as a viable alternative to other major actors in the liberation movement. In his keynote address to AZAPO's Ninth Annual Congress in March 1990 (attended by some two hundred delegates and seven thousand observers), President Itumelang Mosala said: "The Black Consciousness Movement must provide the people of South Africa with a truly liberative alternative. Such an alternative will be grounded, first and foremost, in the economic and political aspirations of the majority of Azanians. It has to be an alternative that places squarely on the agenda of freedom the questions of land re-conquest, socialist transformation of the economy, the building of a national culture in which all Azanians, irrespective of race, gender or religion, will participate."[49]

. . .

There was clear choice for majoritarianism among all actors in the struggle up to 1991 precisely because they were competing for the same constituency base: South Africa's disenfranchised black majority. Yet these parties differed in their power and expectations, and the institutional choices reflected these differences. In terms of their political strategies, the PAC especially was positioned to the left of the ANC. If the ANC were to moderate too much for its constituency, the PAC would be wait-

---

[48] Interview with the author, 21 May 1991.

[49] The address is reprinted in *Azanian Socialist Review* 1 (21): 22–23. The Black Consciousness movement of Azanian (BCMA) encompasses AZAPO and its affiliate organizations.

ing in the wings to pick up the political fallout. In 1991, this was nowhere more evident than in these organizations' eschewal of negotiation. *Johannesburg Star* reporter Patrick Laurence wrote: "The tide appear[s] to have turned, for the present at least, against the notion of black hegemony that lies at the core of both AZAPO and PAC thinking. Observers considered that their weakness on the ground forced them to adapt a radical position in hope of further gains. In strategic terms, they were forced to rely on the assumption—or hope—that the ANC would make cardinal errors in the year[s] ahead."[50]

A side-by-side comparison of the institutional choices of the major political actors in 1991 and the variables behind these choices, as illustrated in table 5.1, reveals an important state of affairs. Even prior to the onset of formal constitutional negotiations there existed in South Africa an identifiable *core of centrist parties*—primarily the NP, DP, ANC, but also possibly the IFP—who shared, over the long term, uncertain expectations about their future role in a state. This is important when it is also seen that despite the many differences between these parties on their ideal visions of a future state, there was among them—and particularly among the NP, DP, and ANC—a considerable convergence on a postapartheid democracy, and even some agreement on the actual institutions of the new state.

[50] *South Africa Foundation Review,* January 1991.

CHAPTER 6

The Democratization Pact

BETWEEN LATE 1991 and late 1993, South Africa's main negotiating partners, led by the National party government and the African National Congress, agreed upon a set of institutions for the remainder of the transition, during which new, fully democratic institutions were to be created; these two anchored the emerging core of moderate parties that held South Africa's fragile center together. This period of transition, too, was tense and turbulent, wracked with political violence, economic decline and social malaise, and fierce competition among myriad protagonists for political power. Indeed, for a critical time during 1992, the talks were deadlocked, mired in mutual allegations of culpability in escalating political violence, and eventually suspended. South Africa teetered on the brink of civil war or, more plausibly, a slow, uncontrollable slide into anarchy.

But the talks resumed, and a settlement ultimately emerged. Why? Because the essential political dynamic that first brought the government and the ANC to the negotiating table in late 1989 and early 1990—a rough symmetry of bargaining power, combined with a realization that the pursuit of hegemony was ultimately self-defeating—kept them negotiating (and indeed brought them back to the table) despite several potentially fatal crises. The centripetal pull on the parties was greater than the centrifugal forces that normally plague divided societies.

The prevailing centripetal dynamic of South African politics during this period ultimately led to a settlement by November 1993—a democratization pact. This chapter explores the substantive talks on a new political order during the period from the Convention for a Democratic South Africa (CODESA), held in late 1991, to the democratization pact of late 1993. By tracking convergence in these negotiations, I demonstrate how the major parties' institutional choice preferences for the transition (which were an integral element of their overall institutional choices for a postapartheid polity) were reconciled. The convergence on a democratization pact illustrates that the core centrist parties committed themselves to jointly writing the rules of the new political game.

CODESA: NASCENT INSTITUTIONS IN DEMOCRATIC TRANSITIONS

In the absence of revolutions, institutions evolve through incremental change. This was South Africa's experience. Unlike decolonization, its transition was one in which the *internal* actors themselves forged a new political system, with a relatively minimal role for external actors. There was no colonial power to impose a new system, and no forceful intervention by the international community. Instead, the South African experience was more of a managed, negotiated transition in which the incumbent regime and opposition together created a set of rules for the future. In South Africa, unlike the rest of Africa, there would be no "flag-down, flag-up" experience, as van zyl Slabbert noted.[1] Given that the incumbent regime did not succumb to revolution, the South African experience is one that Rantete and Giliomee (1992) appropriately term *transition through transaction*, that is, through pact making.[2]

Convergence on CODESA

Implicitly recognizing the power of the incumbents, the ANC conceded in early 1991 to the government's demand for a constitutional conference of all political parties prior to full enfranchisement and elections to a constituent assembly. Despite the fact that substantive talks in the Pretoria Minute's Paragraph Nine Working Committee were suspended by the ANC in April 1991 over disagreement on the issue of political violence, they resumed following the signing of the National Peace Accord in September 1991; these talks ultimately led to the first round of negotiation on a postapartheid constitution—CODESA—which first met in December 1991.[3]

CODESA became a nascent institution created to structure and institutionalize negotiated change, even as the NP government remained in power. The evolution and nature of emerging institutions for negotiation like CODESA portend much for the kind of future democratic institutions that may eventually evolve. North terms this institutional continuity *path dependence:* "Path dependence means that history matters. We cannot understand today's choices . . . without tracing the incremental evolution of institutions" (1990:101).

Why did the parties converge on CODESA as an institution? Throughout 1990 the ANC had indeed resisted such a conference because all parties—irrespective of their broader support in society—would sit at such a conference, in effect, as equals. The ANC had insisted on the prior election of a constituent assembly, in which the relative strengths of parties would be tested at the ballot box. Professor John Dugard of the Uni-

[1] Interview with the author, 15 May 1991.

[2] Their term is borrowed from Share and Mainwaring's (1986) description of the Spanish experience.

[3] For an in-depth and extensive account of the CODESA process, from its beginnings in December 1991, beyond its collapse in May 1992, and into its aftermath in late 1992 and early 1993, see Friedman 1993. See also Cooper et al. 1993:473–509.

versity of the Witwatersrand explained the reason for the ANC's concession as result of the balance of power.

> Who holds power in this country? The National party holds power. . . . If there is a multiparty conference, the National party will be one of the two principal actor[s], so in a multiparty conference it will able to exercise real political influence. If a constituent assembly was set up with proportional representation, the National party would be reduced to a very small minority, with a maximum of 20 percent to 25 percent of the votes, generously estimated. So the political reality dictates the need for a multiparty conference.[4]

The ANC's concession on a conference first, elections thereafter—a two-stage transition—provided the formula for a solution to the problem of contradictory preferences for the transition. This formula was based on the experiences of South Africa during the preliminary negotiation phase, that is, on previous pact making. The prevailing balance of power determined that there would be first a founding pact creating an interim government, then a founding election leading to a sovereign constituent assembly. This reality was reflected in the announcements by the NP and the DP in October and November 1991, respectively, that (in effect) they would ultimately agree to an elected constituent assembly, the ANC's preference, as a necessary step in transition.[5]

CODESA I

To create the multiparty forum, the parties relied on a negotiating mechanism that had previously succeeded during the preliminary negotiation phase: quiet, behind-the-scenes bilateral negotiations facilitated by church and business leaders as well as influential members of the judiciary. Following the signing of the National Peace Accord in September 1991, a steering committee chaired by two senior justices was established, through which the multiparty forum's details were negotiated. This committee agreed on 25 November 1991 that the government, the ANC, and the IFP would convene a "preparatory" meeting of all parties to discuss the multiparty conference. This meeting was set for 29–30

---

[4] Interview with the author, 13 May 1991. The reality of the prevailing symmetry of power was admitted by the ANC. Advocate Dullah Omar, a member of the ANC's Constitutional Committee, said: "If we were achieving power through the revolutionary struggle, [an all-party conference] would not be necessary. . . . Taking into account the reality of negotiations, we must get all the parties together" (interview with the author, 10 April 1991).

[5] The NP first conceded on an elected constituent assembly on 31 October 1991, when minister of constitutional development Gerrit Viljoen announced in a speech that the NP would consider such a body if it were sufficiently bound by constitutional principles. On the DP's decision, see the *Saturday Star*, 16 November 1991.

November 1991, and some twenty political parties, including representatives of the homelands, attended.[6] In prior NP-ANC bilateral talks choices were made about the decision-making rules for CODESA. Most importantly, the parties arrived at a decision-making rule that would serve to structure decision making in multiparty negotiation through to the 1993 democratization pact: the principle of "sufficient consensus." Operationalized, this meant that if the major protagonists—the government and ANC (and, when possible, other parties as well)—reached agreement, sufficient consensus existed (Friedman, ed. 1993:24–25).

The sufficient consensus decision-making rule became an important aspect of the negotiation process: the parties recognized that complete consensus in a divided society such as South Africa would be unattainable. There would always be those on the extremes, outbidders, who would seek to capitalize on others' moderation. The critical question for the remainder of the transition was whether this centrist core could withstand the onslaught from the extremes. Thus, a settlement in South Africa, it was recognized, could be a narrow one, but this would not impede progress by this centrist core of those committed to negotiation and its implication—a negotiated outcome. The preparatory meeting also agreed upon CODESA's nine-point agenda: creation of a climate for free political participation; definition of general constitutional principles; agreement on a "constitution-making body/process"; creation of "transitional arrangements"; decision about the future of "independent" (TBVC) homelands; agreement on the role of the international community in negotiation; selection of a time frame; creation of mechanisms for implementation; and discussion of other issues.

The preparatory meeting was not without its detractors. Even though AZAPO and the CP predictably refused to attend (they remained outbidders), the PAC did come. Despite the PAC's October 1991 agreement to join with the ANC, some eighty trade unions, and liberation-movement-oriented civil society groups to form a unified Patriotic Front, which would confront the government (it had even agreed to draft the "Joint Approach on a Constitutional Process with Regard to Negotiations"),

[6] The twenty parties and their negotiating teams were outlined in the *Star*, 28 November 1991, and included: the PAC, the government and the NP (as separate delegations; the former as nonvoting), ANC, IFP, Labour party, Inyandza National movement (Kangwane), Transvaal and Natal Indian congresses (joint delegation), Venda government, Boputhatswana government, United People's Front (Lebowa), Solidarity, DP, Transkei government, National People's party (opposition party in the Indian House of Delegates), Ciskei government, Kikwankwetla party (Qwaqwa), Itando Yesizwe party (Kwandebele), Ximoko Progressive party (Gazankulu), and the South African Communist party. Even though COSATU had originally petitioned to attend CODESA as a separate delegation, only political parties and organizations were invited.

ANC/PAC cooperation was short-lived.[7] On the second day of the preparatory meeting, the PAC walked out of the talks, alleging a "pattern" of government-ANC collusion. Indeed, the government and ANC had already agreed on certain issues in bilateral talks, and these did not jibe with the more revolutionary PAC positions put forth at the preparatory meeting.[8] The PAC's walkout demonstrated that the centripetal dynamic in South Africa's transition was stronger than the old pattern of polarization that a common Patriotic Front implied. The emerging partnership between the government and ANC rippled on the right, as well. Mangosuthu Buthelezi, days prior to the convening of CODESA, declared his intention to boycott the meeting over the refusal of the steering committee to allow separate delegations for the IFP and the KwaZulu government, the latter to be represented by Zulu king Goodwill Zwelethini (all other nonindependent homelands were represented solely by political parties). A new pattern was emerging: the IFP began to outbid on the government's right, and behave as a potential "spoiler."

At the glittery World Trade Center near Johannesburg, 238 delegates from the nineteen remaining parties, together with nearly 1,000 international observers, gathered on 20 December for the first plenary meeting. CODESA I, as it became known, was planned as mostly ceremonial, leaving the hard bargaining to subsequent talks. The first day went according to script until de Klerk delivered his scheduled address in the late afternoon. Raising what he said was "unavoidable," de Klerk lambasted the ANC for its refusal to officially terminate its armed struggle ("suspended" by the Pretoria Minute) and reveal the location of secret arms caches. He exclaimed that "an organization which remains committed to an armed struggle cannot be fully trusted . . . when it also commits itself to peacefully negotiated solutions."[9]

Mandela, who had delivered a decidedly conciliatory address earlier in the day, grew furious. Demanding an opportunity to rebut, Mandela delivered a thirty-minute diatribe carried live on national broadcasts, personally attacking de Klerk for raising the ANC's long-dormant armed struggle. After all, delicate discussions on the issue had previously been confined to private ANC-government bilateral talks. De Klerk, the head

[7] The Patriotic Front Declaration, along with the "Joint Approach," was printed by the UN Center against Apartheid (22/91, October 1991). AZAPO was dropped from the original Patriotic Front because of a disagreement over whether the DP should be allowed to participate in the Front.

[8] PAC official Dikgang Moseneke later said: "Without exception, proposals made by the PAC were opposed by the ANC or the regime and would not be supported by the homeland or tricameral leaders. It became increasingly clear that this pattern would persist throughout the rest of the [preparatory] meeting" (*Sowetan*, 2 December 1991).

[9] De Klerk's speech is reprinted in *FBIS*, 23 December 1991.

of "an illegitimate, discredited, majority regime," Mandela said, still "[has] certain moral standards to uphold. . . . He's not fit to be a head of a government."[10] A red-faced de Klerk pounded his fists on the table, insisting he too be allowed to counter Mandela's words.

When tempers calmed after the tense encounter, reason prevailed. Mandela and de Klerk met privately later that night and agreed to address the issue quietly in a CODESA "task force." The morning of CODESA I's second day, before proceedings began, Mandela crossed the floor and shook hands with de Klerk in a public sign of reconciliation. But few, especially the hundreds of reporters covering the landmark event, noticed. So later, in his concluding address, Mandela again referred to the row, and this time with the cameras rolling, lights glaring, and the full attention of the country and world focused, crossed the floor and shook de Klerk's hand warmly and firmly.[11] This event underscored a larger dynamic in the negotiation: deep conflicts of interest remained, but the process had become resilient in the face of repeated crises.

CODESA I produced two concrete results. The first was modest: agreement on a Declaration of Intent, signed by seventeen of the nineteen parties (the IFP and Ciskei first refused, then later signed; Bophuthatwana did not sign).[12] The declaration established a set of principles and purposes to guide CODESA, eschewing apartheid and pledging support for a "united, nonracial and non-sexist state . . . multiparty democracy . . . with regular elections on the basis of universal adult suffrage on a common voters' roll," and endorsing, in principle, an electoral system based on proportional representation and a justiciable bill of rights. The declaration contained an important final paragraph, in which the government agreed, at the ANC's insistence, to clearly commit itself to be bound by the common, jointly determined rules of the new political game. The second result was to constitute CODESA as a standing nascent institution. CODESA I set up five "working groups" to negotiate broad sets of issues: the principles and structures of a new constitution; the creation of a climate conducive to peaceful political participation; the form of transitional or interim government and the future path of the transition; the constitutional future of the four homelands that had accepted nominal independence; and the implementation of agreements.

In a year that had seen continued high rates of political killings and a breakdown of direct negotiation for nearly half the year, 1991 ended on a positive note. There was a common perception that, certainly, in 1992 South Africa's turbulent transition would produce yet another milestone

---

[10] *Washington Post*, 21 December 1991.

[11] The restaged photo ran, for example, in the *New York Times*, 22 December 1991.

[12] The text of the declaration is reprinted ibid.

unthinkable a few short years ago: inauguration of an interim government and elections to a constituent assembly as an outcome of continued convergence through CODESA.

THE FRAGILITY OF NASCENT INSTITUTIONS: 1992

In fact, 1992 did begin with conciliation. Both Mandela and de Klerk, in New Year's messages, asserted that CODESA would quickly yield breakthroughs. The ANC, carrying forward the strategy forged in mid-1991 to step up the pace of talks, declared 1992 "the year of democratic elections for a constituent assembly" and called for an interim government by mid-year. On 24 January, opening 1992's session of the Tricameral Parliament, de Klerk further detailed the government's negotiating position, one that was subsequently fleshed out by cabinet ministers and party officials: CODESA would negotiate the terms of a transitional constitution as amendments to the tricameral constitution, which would ideally create a "transitional parliament"; the charter would be put before the entire new electorate for approval in a "yes-no" referendum, with white votes counted separately. If approved by the electorate at large and a majority of whites, elections to a transitional parliament would be held to draft the actual terms of a new constitution. The de Klerk plan proposed a white veto in the drafting of the new constitution.

The ANC reacted quietly to the proposals, recognizing the implicit concession toward an elected constitution-writing body but specifically rejecting the white veto. At the outset of CODESA's serious bargaining, the ANC preferred the transition to take the following path: CODESA would negotiate transitional government structures with binding authority, including control over the key areas of elections, broadcasting, budget allocation, finance, and the security forces; these proposals could indeed be approved by the Tricameral Parliament in order to give them legal force, but would not be subject to a referendum with a white veto (although a referendum would be possible). With a transitional government in place, elections for a constituent assembly would be held to draw up a new constitution; thus, elections would occur *before* any new constitution, even an interim one, had been drafted. The ANC plan also implied a compromise: with the Tricameral Parliament giving CODESA's decisions legal force, there could be legal continuity after all. The essential difference between the positions of the government and ANC—elections before or after the creation of an interim government—was believed by pundits to be fully negotiable in CODESA's behind-the-scenes working groups. A spate of news articles in early February predicted quick agreement on the path of transition.

Meeting behind closed doors, CODESA's functional working groups first met on 6 February. The IFP laid out its proposals at the first gathering of the working groups; they were more conservative than those of de Klerk and the NP, and would have left the white minority government in place until 1994 and perhaps beyond, but would require it to share power with a multiparty cabinet accountable to the Tricameral Parliament. A new constitution would be drawn up by an unelected forum created by the CODESA process. The IFP's preferences for an interim constitution reflected the institutional choice considerations outlined in chapter 5; it revealed its own understanding of being a minority, regionally based party with greater coalition-building potential with the white right—due to its ethnic orientation—than with those in the political center. The IFP also realized that even minimum majoritarianism would not favor its interests as much as an ethnic federation of some variety. Further, the IFP began to be seen not only as an outbidder on the government's right but as an insecure political foe of the ANC, thus setting itself up as a potential spoiler.

Power and Perception

Perhaps because of the relatively quick success of CODESA, those opposed to its aims reacted sharply. The uncertain outcome of the transition began to weigh heavily on the white right. De Klerk, these critics argued, was losing control of the process he had unleashed. Rising crime, township violence, falling economic output, the prospect of enforced racial integration, and a government without control all combined to create the impression that de Klerk's fate was similar to that of Mikhail Gorbachev: able to initiate the transition but unable to ensure an outcome favorable to those who benefited from the ancien régime.[13] In compromising with the ANC, de Klerk, it was widely speculated, had left his rank-and-file behind. The white right seized on the government's apparent vulnerability in late February 1992 and stepped up demonstrations against the NP. White backlash became the central issue in a 17 February by-election in the small, rural Afrikaner university town of Potchefstroom. Political analysts from across the spectrum predicted the CP would win the seat in a rout.

The Potchefstroom by-election was a much more important event than the occasion would have otherwise warranted because it was portrayed as a national barometer of white support for de Klerk's reforms. De Klerk inflated the vote's importance by personally campaigning in the constituency. The NP had only narrowly won the seat in 1989 and wanted desper-

---

[13] On the comparison, see the *Economist*, 29 February 1992, and the excellent article by Bill Keller in the *New York Times Magazine*, 31 January 1993.

ately to keep it, not because it would have affected its parliamentary majority (it would not), but for symbolic purposes. When the some seventeen thousand ballots were tallied, the NP candidate lost by more than two thousand votes, a swing of 11 percent to the CP. The winner, Andries Beyers, said: "The message to Mr. de Klerk is to resign and call a general election."[14] The ANC leader in Potchefstroom, Zacharia Malekane, said "When Mr. de Klerk crossed the bridge, he didn't cross it with the white community."[15]

The NP, having backed itself into a corner, was faced with a choice: announce a general white election, risking an uncertain result and infuriating the ANC, or call a white referendum, which he had long promised. In mid-February, de Klerk announced that a whites-only referendum would be held 17 March, and said, "If I lose . . . I will resign."[16] De Klerk's considerations are readily apparent: he knew he would win a referendum with a simple majority decision rule, but not another all-white election under the first-past-the-post electoral system, with its districts weighted toward rural areas.

The referendum was cast as a moment of truth for South African whites. CODESA negotiation was put on hold as intrawhite politics took center stage. The ANC, meanwhile, rejected the referendum as "racist," and Mandela termed the move "a serious mistake."[17] But the ANC implicitly backed a "yes" vote, refraining from mass demonstrations against the poll, and the DP urged an affirmative vote as well. The NP, seasoned at politicking among whites, waged an effective campaign: vote yes for the future, no for a return to the unhappy past; yes for negotiation, no for war. DP leader Zach de Beer astutely described the vote as "a choice between danger and disaster."[18] Clearly the threat of renewed international sanctions was also a factor.

Survey results published in the *Star* just before the election predicted a very narrow majority—55 percent—favoring a yes vote.[19] As referendum day approached, the world watched nervously as South Africa's transition teetered on the votes of several hundred thousand "undecided" whites, a

[14] *New York Times*, 20 February 1993. The NP had in fact lost all three white by-elections since 1989, each in predominantly rural, conservative Afrikaans-speaking towns (Ladybrand and Virginia, both in the Orange Free State). Potchefstroom's constituency, however, was clearly more representative of the broader white community than the constituencies in the other two districts.

[15] *Economist*, 22 February 1992.

[16] *Washington Post*, 21 February 1992. On the referendum in general, as well as for an analysis of its aftermath, see Strauss 1993.

[17] The ANC press release on the referendum is reported in the *Star*, 27 February 1992; Mandela's comment is from his op-ed article in the *Los Angeles Times*, 26 February 1992.

[18] *Christian Science Monitor*, 16 March 1992.

[19] *Washington Post*, 9 March 1992.

small minority of a minority community. The referendum campaign was tense, and this tension spilled over into the townships: during the three-week campaign, some 270 blacks lost their lives in an upsurge in political violence.[20] On voting day, de Klerk's expectations were borne out: 68.6 percent of the nearly 2.8 million voters voted yes.[21] The CP was devastated. With the NP's white outbidders effectively defeated for the time being, the way was paved—so it was thought—for a quicker tempo at the talks. The ANC lauded the victory, and urged a quick agreement at CODESA.

Most observers expected a deal on an interim government in CODESA's working groups by late April, to be ratified by a second plenary session by the end of that month. Earlier negotiation in CODESA's critical Working Group 3 (on interim government) had made considerable progress. The Working Group's rapporteur noted in mid-February, before the referendum interruption, that there was already wide agreement on basic principles for the interim government, even as a number of linked issues—especially about the process leading up to elections for a constitution-making body—had to be resolved. Following the referendum, on 23 March the government submitted a new set of transition proposals in Working Groups 2 and 3 that included some new elements. Significantly, the government suggested a set of advisory "transitional executive councils" (or multiparty cabinet committees dealing with specific issues) to level the playing field for the election and an elected bicameral transitional parliament/constitution-making body.

The new proposals envisaged a longer-term transition that preserved constitutional continuity and myriad opportunities for minority vetoes on a regional and political party basis. There was little surprise when the ANC rejected them. Differences also surfaced when the ANC countered government proposals in Working Group 2 several days later, proposing instead a 400-member constituent assembly, elected by proportional representation (with a 5 percent or less threshold for representation) and a two-thirds majority decision-making rule.[22] The critical differences that would face a second CODESA plenary were beginning to form: they centered primarily on the powers of an interim executive, the influence of minorities in the constitution-making body, and the length of time such a body would sit (the government favored several years; the ANC four months). The ANC's choice for a two-thirds decision rule in the constituent assembly, however, also demonstrated movement in the party's negotiating stance. The ANC's transitional government proposals, submitted

[20] *Washington Post*, 18 March 1992.
[21] For a regional breakdown of the referendum results, see the *Financial Times*, 19 March 1992. For further analysis, see Strauss 1993.
[22] SAPA, as reported in *FBIS*, 31 March 1992.

on 6 April, called for multiparty committees with binding power that would approve legislation passed by the Tricameral Parliament before the president could sign it.[23] In order to push the process forward, negotiators decided in early April to convene a secondary plenary, CODESA II, on 15–16 May. The hard bargaining on the path of transition would occur in the working groups, pressured by a deadline, over the intervening weeks.

CODESA II: Deadlock

On the eve of CODESA II, the ANC and its allies were clearly frustrated by an apparent toughening of the government's negotiating position following the referendum, and threatened a return to "mass action" to nudge the process forward. Less than a week before CODESA II was to convene, Mandela articulated the growing restlessness in the rank-and-file: continued high rates of political violence and government insistence on the interim government issue were quickly leading toward deadlock. Accusing the government of "clinging to the levers of power," Mandela said of CODESA II: "We have no intention of staging showdowns. We are going there with a spirit of reconciliation, wanting that something could come out of the meeting."[24]

In two days of intensive talks, negotiators reached an impasse on a critical point of disagreement arising out of Working Group 2—the number of votes in a constituent assembly required to take decisions on issues affecting regions. As noted earlier, the ANC had earlier proposed decisions be made by a two-thirds majority, or 66 percent, whereas the government had insisted on a higher threshold, 75 percent.[25] When the ANC edged up to 70 percent in the talks, the government did not budge (both sides made their proposals conditional on other issues as well, primarily the role of an upper house). Indeed, the ANC insisted on a "package deal" out of a concern that, as ANC negotiator Mohammed Valli Moosa said, "we run the risk of living with an interim constitution forever."[26]

On the evening of Friday, 15 May, Mandela and de Klerk met for an hour in an attempt to resolve the impasse, just as they had done to cool tempers at CODESA I.[27] The de Klerk-Mandela meeting did not resolve the disagreement, but it did, momentarily, rescue the talks. Mandela said

---

[23] For a good summary of the debate as it stood at the time, see "South Africa: The Gloves Come off at CODESA," *Africa Confidential*, 3 April 1992.

[24] *Financial Times*, 12 May 1992.

[25] Agreement had already been reached that the 75 percent decision rule would apply to passage of a bill of rights.

[26] *New York Times*, 24 May 1992.

[27] *Christian Science Monitor*, 18 May 1992.

after the encounter: "We have been able to save CODESA and the peace process."[28] But Mandela asserted that the government's reluctance to face majority rule resulted in the deadlock at CODESA II. The disagreements were referred to the CODESA Management Committee for further debate.

Why did CODESA II fail to achieve a settlement? Although press reports pointed to differences over entrenching regionalism, in reality the deadlock reflected a fundamental dispute over the allocation of power for both the immediate and long term and the belief that the parties had options other than compromise. The inability to horse trade over the decision-making rule on regionalism in the constituent assembly glossed over an underlying cause of its failure: the National party, fresh on the heels of an overwhelming victory in the March referendum and a number of recent breakthroughs in South Africa's international diplomacy, overplayed its hand.[29] De Klerk and his advisers overestimated their own power vis-à-vis the ANC. This was especially true of the resistance of the government to conclude a "package deal" that linked agreement on phase one of the transition (an interim government) to phase two (a constituent assembly). The government wanted an open-ended agreement on power sharing before it would commit to the uncertainty of an elected constituent assembly. Colin Eglin, a DP delegate on Working Group 2, noted that: "[the differences on decision-making majorities were] an issue but not a cause. . . . the cause was a high degree of mistrust between the ANC and NP and a high degree of tension between them. The cause, simply put, was suspicion and mistrust."[30]

CODESA II failed, in part, because the parties misperceived their power relative to that of others. A team of analysts at the Centre for Policy Studies concluded in an in-depth account that the NP still wanted a slow transition to power sharing; the ANC, through its referendum proposal, wanted quick majority rule (Friedman, ed. 1993). The NP, misreading the political climate after the whites-only referendum, perceived an asymmetrical power relationship—that it could determine the path and pace of transition—when in fact the relative balance of power remained at rough parity. The ANC, too, misperceived the situation. It thought it could pro-

[28] *New York Times*, 17 May 1993.

[29] The diplomatic breakthroughs included a return of South Africa to international sport and a highly successful trip by de Klerk to Nigeria in early April. During the Nigeria trip, the government and PAC held their first round of direct talks, which the PAC insisted take place outside South African territory. The talks were inconclusive, but did begin a process of bilateral negotiation that would eventually lead to the PAC's participation in multiparty talks in early 1993.

[30] Remarks at the Carnegie Endowment for International Peace, Washington, D.C., 4 June 1992.

duce an outcome at CODESA that would simply pave the way for an elected constituent assembly without meeting the government's demand for entrenched power sharing. Thus, as Friedman and his colleagues write, "the parties remained deadlocked over the very nature of CODESA, let alone its outcome." (Friedman, ed. 1993:28).

Frustration within the ANC/SACP/COSATU alliance over the protracted pace of negotiation, which had been evident at the party's congress in mid-1991 and throughout early 1992, reached an apex following the demise of CODESA II and drove its leadership to play one of its most important power cards in the ongoing struggle with de Klerk's regime: "mass action." At a four-day policy conference in late May the ANC shifted the conflict from the negotiating table back to the streets. Reminiscent of threats in the mid-1980s to make South Africa "ungovernable," the "rolling mass action" plan entailed coordinated strikes and street demonstrations in an attempt to force the government to agree to an interim government by the end of June. A barometer of their deteriorating negotiating relationship was Mandela's statement regarding his frequent meetings with de Klerk: "I have never attached undue importance to our relationship."[31]

The trade union federation COSATU spearheaded the mass action campaign. The federation proposed a four-phase protest action: first, local and regional strikes; second, a phase of industry-specific strikes; third, a four- to five-day general strike on 3 August; and finally, a phase purportedly culminating in the resignation of the de Klerk government. The purpose of the protest campaign was clear: the ANC aimed at a public show of power, analogous to the government's demonstration of strength in the March referendum. Although the ANC backed away from other avenues of exerting pressure on de Klerk—such as a new sports boycott that would have barred South Africa from the 1992 Olympic summer games—the call for a general strike reverberated through South Africa's business community. COSATU's threats were not idle. The federation had proven in November 1991 in a three-day strike against the government's unilateral implementation of a value-added tax that it could mount a nationwide work stoppage. The IFP, as well as the PAC and AZAPO, opposed the ANC alliance mass action campaign, and some internationally respected figures such as Anglican archbishop Desmond Tutu expressed reservations. The concern was that a "people power" protest, which had led to relatively peaceful transfers of power in Eastern Europe, could lead to a violent and bloody confrontation in South Africa.

Anxiety heightened in early June when the commission organized after the Peace Accord to investigate political violence, headed by broadly re-

[31] *New York Times*, 1 June 1992.

spected appellate judge Richard Goldstone and known as the Goldstone Commission, issued an interim report. The report confirmed long-held suspicions that the security forces were a contributing factor in ongoing political violence: "A police force and army which, for many decades, have been the instruments of oppression by successive white minority governments in maintaining a society predicated upon racial discrimination" were in part blame for the violence, Goldstone noted.[32] But he went on to add that "the primary cause of the violence . . . is the political battle between supporters of the African National Congress and the Inkatha Freedom Party."[33] By mid-June, the townships were seething with tension, strife between the ANC and the IFP was escalating, and of violent encounters within rival groups of the ANC were reported. Lloyd Vogelman, director of the Project on the Study of Violence and Reconciliation at the University of the Witwatersrand, said in mid-June: "The Vaal area could explode at any moment."[34]

Boipatong

The explosion came on 17 June 1992. On the previous day—the anniversary of the 1976 Soweto uprisings—the ANC had kicked off its mass action campaign with rallies and stayaways. Feeling the pressure from below, Mandela pleaded with thirty thousand ANC rank-and-file at a rally in Soweto not to launch guerrilla attacks in white suburbs after he had heard rumors that some MK cadres were planning them.[35] Amid such tension, on the moonlit night of 17 June some two hundred residents of the IFP-controlled KwaMadala migrant workers' hostel rampaged through the ANC stronghold of Boipatong, just south of Johannesburg. Forty-nine were killed in the macabre attack, brutally slain with primitive spears, knives, and machetes.

Mandela, witnessing the carnage in Boipatong the following day, announced the suspension of negotiation with the government. Further, he echoed earlier ANC assertions that de Klerk was personally culpable. "I can no longer explain to our people why we continue to talk to a government which is killing our people. . . . We are now convinced that his [de Klerk's] method of bringing about a solution to this country is war. We will respond to that. One thing is clear: We are back in the Sharpeville days."[36] De Klerk too had days earlier threatened to return to the polarized politics of the past, saying that the government would "not allow

[32] *New York Times*, 3 June 1992.
[33] Ibid.
[34] *Christian Science Monitor*, 15 June 1992.
[35] *New York Times*, 17 June 1992.
[36] *Washington Post*, 22 June 1992.

the country to slip into anarchy," a veiled reference to the possible rein-troduction of a state of emergency.[37]

In an apparent bid to console the victims and to gain the political high ground, the president undertook an unprecedented venture into the Boi-patong township. Angry youths mobbed de Klerk's motorcade, stoning the president's car before he could disembark. After he left, police turned their guns and fired into a crowd of three thousand, without orders and without warning, according to eyewitness journalist Allister Sparks. At least eighteen protesters died. Sparks later wrote, "De Klerk's decision to visit the scene of that atrocity is a measure of how out of touch he is with the mood of black South Africa in these dark days of frustration and fury. . . . Boipatong and its neighboring townships were boiling with rage."[38]

The ANC's leadership met in a five-hour emergency session on 23 June, at which it formulated fourteen demands for the resumption of talks and called for a UN Security Council meeting on political violence and the deployment of an international observer force.[39] However, the statement issued at the end of the session did not link the resumption of talks solely to the violence problem, but to the impasse at CODESA. "The funda-mental reason for the deadlock," the ANC said, "is whether there is to be democratic change or white-minority veto powers."[40] Throughout June 1992, South Africa was plunged into crisis. Despite these attempts to reconvene direct talks, the negotiation process was reduced to a vitupera-tive exchange of lengthy memoranda—a "war of letters"—between the government and ANC, replete with mutual recriminations and thinly veiled personal insults.[41]

In response, the international community began to step up efforts to mediate; initially led by Western diplomats in Pretoria, the mediation ef-fort broadened to include the British Commonwealth as the crisis deep-ened. In a subtle but significant policy shift, the de Klerk government began to ease its long-held position that there was no role for the interna-

[37] Ibid.

[38] *Washington Post,* 28 June 1992.

[39] The ANC initially included a reimposition of the international sports boycott in its demands, but later retracted it. In effect, this allowed a South African team to compete in the 1992 Barcelona Olympic games.

[40] *Washington Post,* 24 June 1992.

[41] The ANC sent a lengthy set of demands to de Klerk on 27 June, most important among them a reiterated call for an international force to monitor security force operations and for multiparty control over the security forces in a transitional government. The ANC communication repeated assertions that security forces fomented violence and assailed de Klerk's personal role. De Klerk responded with a nationwide address on 2 July and a thirty-one-page letter to Mandela on 3 July, calling for a resumption of bilateral talks, making some minor concessions, but at the same time asserting that the ANC had become "captive" of the more militant SACP and its revolutionary brand of "Marxism-Leninism." Mandela retorted a day later, saying de Klerk had "chosen to ignore the gravity of the demands."

tional community in South Africa's transition. The first step was the appointment of several international experts to the Goldstone Commission. The mediation efforts gathered steam in early July, when Organization of African Unity (OAU) heads of state met in Dakar, Senegal. The OAU summit was attended by UN secretary general Boutros Boutros-Ghali, who had earlier met with South African foreign minister Roelof "Pik" Botha in Nigeria. At the OAU summit, Boutros-Ghali met with Mandela, who reiterated the ANC's call for a Security Council meeting on South Africa. Boutros-Ghali also met with IFP national chairman Frank Mdalose, and said at the end of the meetings that there was consensus for a UN presence in the country and included the PAC in his references.

As the talks faltered and initial mediation efforts proved fruitless, COSATU announced a three-day general strike. The call reflected the ANC/SACP/COSATU alliance's choice for the "Leipzig option," a reference to the demonstrations in the East German city in 1989 that toppled that country's communist government. De Klerk accused the ANC and its allies of creating an "artificial crisis" in South Africa in an effort to seize power by force and boasted that the government would take "all steps necessary to prevent the country from sliding into anarchy."[42] But the violence was not the only reason for the continued deadlock; the inability of the negotiators to resolve the gap in negotiating positions and expectations of what a negotiated outcome would bring, that had led to the demise of CODESA II, was the other cause. ANC President Nelson Mandela told a Johannesburg press conference on 4 July that he had fully expected the May talks to result in agreement on an interim government. But, he said, "It became clear the regime was not prepared for that epoch-making step. . . . It is for that reason—and of course, the violence, but mainly for that reason—that we pulled out of CODESA."[43]

The United Nations as Mediator

The focus of the crisis turned to UN headquarters in New York when on 15 July the Security Council opened a two-day debate on South Africa. More than fifty speakers from South Africa and other states—among them Mandela, IFP leader Buthelezi, Foreign Minister Botha, Clarence Makwetu of the PAC, and the leaders of Transkei, Boputhatswana, and Ciskei—addressed the unprecedented meeting. Although the airing of the disagreements in the Security Council produced little movement in negotiating positions—most speeches were accusatorial—the outcome of the debate was significant. Following an opening by the government's request

[42] *Washington Post*, 3 July 1992.
[43] *New York Times*, 5 July 1992.

for "advice," and in accordance with an ANC call for the United Nations to, in Mandela's words, "intervene and end the carnage," the Security Council invited the secretary general to send a special envoy to South Africa.[44] Boutros-Ghali tapped former U.S. secretary of state Cyrus R. Vance, whose mission was to investigate the charges of security force complicity in the violence and to make recommendations on restarting the failed talks.

Vance met with an exceptionally wide range of political actors during his ten-day mission in late July, including de Klerk and Mandela, representatives from virtually all of South Africa's political parties, Judge Goldstone, and leaders of a wide range of civil-society organizations engaged in monitoring political violence. Vance's mediation efforts, though not immediately successful in restarting CODESA talks, marked an important watershed in what became a continuous international presence to monitor South Africa's transition. Out of the Vance mission, the secretary general dispatched ten UN officials to monitor the mass action campaign.[45] But Vance also concluded, in the words of the secretary general's report, that "the special desperation that apartheid brought . . . can, in the long run, only be remedied by rapid progress towards the creation of the democratic, non-racial and united South Africa that is the goal of the negotiations."[46] Vance also made an important recommendation: the UN mission should be mandated to strengthen the fragile multiparty structures of the National Peace Accord, South Africa's first broadly negotiated, and therefore legitimate, institution.

The 3 August strike was the ANC's version of the March referendum. The public display of power demonstrated that the negotiating elite had the backing of their constituencies; they had real power in society. And within the ANC alliance, it was a clear victory for COSATU. Some four million workers stayed home, according to the ANC (whether they did so out of support for the party or fear of intimidation was unknown). The strike was successful, but not without some fifty-one fatalities, although it was difficult to discern if the killings were directly related to the protest or to ongoing faction fighting in the turbulent townships and rural areas of Natal. On the third day of the strike Mandela led a group of perhaps as many as 100,000 protesters on a peaceful march through Pretoria to the Union Buildings, ending up within several hundred yards of de Klerk's office. In his remarks, Mandela reiterated the ANC's commitment to negotiation, and suggested—echoing recent conciliatory statements—that

[44] S/RES/765.

[45] The UN mission was specifically requested by Mandela in a telephone call to Boutros-Ghali. The sequence of events is reported in the secretary general's report to the Security Council, S/24389, 7 August 1992.

[46] S/24389.

the ANC, even if it were to win a majority at the polls, would include other major parties in a government of national unity.

Throughout August, the stalemate in talks and threats of renewed mass action permeated an already tense political climate. Following the mass strike, it was publicly revealed that de Klerk and Mandela had spoken on the telephone over the following weekend, fueling speculation that—now that the ANC had won its "referendum"—talks would resume. Following further revelations of security force complicity in the violence, the tide had clearly turned against the government; its self-confidence, too, had begun to dissipate. Thus, when Boutros-Ghali recommended to the Security Council that an observer mission be sent to South Africa to monitor the political violence, the government was in no position to object. In fact, the ten-member delegation had already proven that even a limited international presence could help contain violence.[47] On 17 August, the UN Security Council adopted a resolution (UNSC Resolution 772) that authorized the deployment of a fifty-member UN observer mission— the United Nations Observer Mission to South Africa and mandated its members to work in conjunction with the National Peace Accord structures.

A breakthrough in talks was reached in mid-August. The government had held a second round of direct talks with the PAC on 19 August—held for the first time within the country—that led to progress in their bilateral relationship. They reached agreement in principle on the need for an elected constituent assembly. The agreement was thought to pave the way for the PAC's inclusion in multiparty talks, which virtually all observers agreed would eventually resume. A similar development has also occurred with outbidders to the right of the political spectrum; a near split in the CP led to a change in policy indicating that when and if new talks began, the CP, too, would likely take part. Further, there were reports of behind-the-scenes negotiations between the ANC and the government—such contacts had been secretly maintained throughout the impasse—to resume direct talks.[48]

Bisho

On the heels of the successful general strike, ANC tacticians aimed at what they thought would be an easy and symbolic target—the humiliation of Ciskei's government-allied dictator, General Oupa Gqozo, by marching on the homeland's capital, Bisho. ANC officials claimed before

[47] An anecdotal example from Daveyton township in the PWV is provided in a report in the *Los Angeles Times*, 10 August 1992.
[48] *Christian Science Monitor*, 11 August 1992.

the march that the aim was to topple Gqozo's military government.[49] Knowing that a confrontation would almost certainly ensue, the National Peace Secretariat sought to intervene, organizing talks among the parties. These talks resulted in an agreement by the ANC to seek a magisterial permit for the march, with an agreed-upon route and terminus. National Peace Accord officials, UN observers, and journalists would accompany the massive protest. The weekend before the march, government ministers had sought to persuade the ANC not to proceed, fearing a violent outcome. Mandela and de Klerk exchanged letters agreeing upon the march's rules.

When the marchers left King William's Town in South African territory and paraded the short distance to Bisho, the Ciskei defense forces opened fired with automatic weapons on the vanguard of a two-mile-long column of marchers, killing twenty-eight and injuring about two hundred, according to unofficial accounts. The tragedy at Bisho occurred in a sequence of events that neither side had fully anticipated. The ANC had taken a decision two days earlier to pursue a highly provocative tactic: while the bulk of the protesters marched into a soccer stadium on the edge of town in accordance with the agreed plan, Ronnie Kasrils, a well-known SACP militant, would flank the Ciskei military and lead a breakaway group into the heart of Bisho. Kasrils's group would occupy the city center and stay there until Gqozo was forced from power. "We never thought they would open fire," Kasrils said. "We figured that with the presence of 70,000 marchers, with the ANC leadership at the head of the march, with press and peace monitors all around, they would never fire into the crowd."[50]

The initial reaction to the Bisho shootings was that South Africa's transition was in grave danger of complete collapse. Superficially, this was the logical conclusion to make. Just after the massacre, those considered hard-liners in the ANC alliance—such as SACP secretary general Chris Hani—called on the ANC to break off all communications with the government, and Mandela himself suggested that the removal of Gqozo would be an additional precondition to returning to talks.[51] But Bisho

---

[49] The ANC targeted Bisho for two important political reasons. First, Gqozo was a key ally in de Klerk's attempt to forge a "federalist" front to press for strong regional autonomy. Second, Ciskei's Xhosa-speaking residents would make fertile ground for recruiting in the run-up to South Africa's first election. Gqozo was perceived as the weak link in the chain of government allies, and his fall would lead to a domino effect in other homelands. This strategy was to be extended to KwaZulu and Boputhatswana, both ANC foes and de Klerk allies. Noting that such a strategy, especially if pursued against KwaZulu and the IFP, would inevitably lead to violence was a factor known to the ANC leadership.

[50] *Washington Post*, 9 September 1992.

[51] Hani's comments are noted in the *Christian Science Monitor*, 9 September 1992, and Mandela's in the *Financial Times*, 9 September 1992. In his remarks, Hani revealed that

did not have the effect of scuttling South Africa's talks; in fact, it pushed the parties back to the negotiating table.

Accepting a call from de Klerk for "urgent" talks, the ANC agreed, after considerable internal debate, to return. The Bisho massacre, compared to the tragedy at Boipatong, reveals an aspect of the violence-negotiation nexus. Violence tends to polarize and impede negotiation when a single party is clearly culpable, but when parties are deemed by observers—especially the international community—equally culpable, incidents of violence reinforce pressures to negotiate.[52]

De Klerk and Mandela and their delegations met on 26 September, several weeks after Bisho. Emerging from the eight-hour meeting at the World Trade Center in Johannesburg, the venue for CODESA, the leaders pledged to resume talks on the transition. In reaching an accord—termed the Record of Understanding—the government made several costly concessions to the ANC: the phased release of some five hundred prisoners convicted of murder during the armed struggle (earlier releases had excluded those accused of major terrorist crimes); the fencing of hostels; and a ban on the public display of "cultural weapons," except during certain cultural events. In turn, the ANC agreed to review its program of mass action and verbally agreed that a general amnesty would be granted by an interim government. On transitional issues, there had already been some movement in secret talks between the ANC's Ramaphosa and government constitutional minister Roelf Meyer, which had been taking place since 21 August 1992.[53] Important agreements pertaining to the creation of postapartheid institutions reached in the Record of Understanding included the following:

- An elected constituent assembly would also serve as an interim parliament
- The constituent assembly should draft the new constitution, and decisions would be taken by "special majorities"
- The constituent assembly would be bound by those principles agreed to by a reconstituted CODESA
- The constituent assembly would have "deadlock-breaking mechanisms"
- An interim government of national unity would be constituted, which would have "national and regional government" and would be empowered by an interim constitution (there would be legal continuity)[54]

---

despite the break-off of formal negotiations, Ramaphosa had been meeting directly with minister of constitutional affairs Roelf Meyer for some time.

[52] For an analysis of the effect of Bisho on the ANC's decision to return to talks, see *New York Times* reporter Bill Keller's op-ed piece, in the 13 September 1992 issue of that paper.

[53] These meetings were revealed in the Record of Understanding.

[54] Record of Understanding, 26 September 1992 (Washington, D.C.: Embassy of the Republic of South Africa), mimeo.

On the evening following the wide-ranging agreement, both de Klerk and Mandela separately appeared on nationally broadcast television. Mandela acknowledged that it was the glimpse into the abyss that brought the parties back to the table "I noticed on the face of everybody there the determination on the part of all of us to move the country away from the present crisis."[55]

He went on to emphasize a point that would later guide South Africa toward a democratization pact: through continuing negotiation, agreement would first be reached between the ANC and the government on a bilateral basis, then taken to other parties for multilateral negotiation. This approach was justified by efficacy, but also because of the parties' converging interests in a successful outcome to the negotiation process they created. Bisho had set South Africa's transition on a new track: convergence between the main two protagonists would precede a reconvening of multiparty talks. The parties implicitly agreed to avoid the messy situation at CODESA II—absence of prior bilateral agreement and too many bargaining agents.

IFP leader Buthelezi immediately rejected the Record. Clearly the agreement on fencing hostels and cultural weapons raised his ire, but perhaps most important was the convergence between the more powerful ANC and NP on the path of South Africa's transition, particularly their agreement to an elected constituent assembly. Wielding a spear and dressed in Zulu battle accoutrements at a ceremony celebrating a traditional Zulu holiday, Buthelezi decried the "connivance" between the government and ANC and broke off negotiation with de Klerk's government. In response to its perceived junior status at the center, the IFP sought coalition partners among other stakeholders in the old order. On 6 October, the IFP, other conservative homeland leaders, such as Bophuthatswanta's Lucas Mangope and Ciskei's Oupa Gqozo, and right-wing parties, such as the CP, banded together to form the Concerned South Africans Group (COSAG)—a rejectionist front on the right.

The IFP's alienation following the Record of Understanding brought into the open divisions within de Klerk's cabinet between factions supporting coalition making with the IFP and its allies against the ANC and those advocating that the government throw its lot into cooperation with the ANC. Fissures also developed within the ANC over the amnesty pledge implicit in the Record and the nature of an interim government. A Western diplomat said: "Negotiators in both the National Party and ANC are having to devote most of their energy to healing internal wounds rather than concentrating on an early return to negotiations."[56]

---

[55] SABC-TV, as reported in FBIS, 28 September 1992.
[56] Christian Science Monitor, 22 October 1992.

"A Strategic Perspective"

Resolution of the ANC's internal differences took a turn in late October when the party leadership considered a seminal document on negotiation authored by SACP chairman Joe Slovo. Writing in the party mouthpiece, *African Communist*, Slovo raised the possibility of an extended period of legally enshrined power sharing for a predetermined period of time (through "sunset clauses") to guide South Africa until the end of the century and the complete implementation of a new constitution. Slovo wrote in an article titled "Negotiation: A Strategic Perspective:"

> The conjuncture of the balance of forces (which continues to reflect current reality) provided a classical scenario which placed the possibility of negotiations on the agenda. . . . We are negotiating with the regime because an objective balance of forces makes this a feasible political strategy. . . . The immediate outcome of the negotiating process will inevitably be less than perfect when measured against our long-term liberation objectives. . . . If it is strategically acceptable then a degree of compromise will be unavoidable. And we must not fear to be up front on this reality with our mass constituency.[57]

Two other considerations entered Slovo's assessment of the acceptability of further compromise: the security forces and state bureaucracy constituted a counterrevolutionary threat. The ANC alliance should therefore consider the entire transition package in terms of the ANC's bottom lines—eventual transition to complete majority rule. Compromise in the meantime could prove mutually beneficial. The document represented more than a strategic shift in ANC thinking; it identified, in general terms, a point of possible convergence. Slovo articulated a formula for settlement framed in positive-sum terms, one that brought the institutional choices of the two major parties close to congruence.

The ANC's National Executive Committee debated Slovo's proposals at a stormy three-day meeting in late November. Key leaders of the ANC, intellectual Pallo Jordan chief among them, objected vehemently to Slovo's proposed concessions. Prior to the meeting, Jordan wrote,

> The dominant aspect of our relationship to the regime is that of opposition. To reduce this to "contradictory elements of cooperation . . . and competition," as if we were discussing a difficult marriage, is not only misleading, but dangerous. . . . The national liberation movement . . . *is explicitly about the striving for power.* . . . Negotiations . . . are not aimed at composing differences, but are aimed at liquidation of one of the antagonists as a factor in politics.

[57] The Slovo paper was reprinted in *African Communist*, Third Quarter 1992, pp. 35–40.

This crucial distinction in turn should determine the alliance's entire approach to negotiations.[58]

In the National Executive Committee debate weighing these positive-sum and zero-sum perceptions of negotiation, Slovo's argument carried the day. Exactly why the ANC agreed to the anticipated sweeping compromise on a power-sharing pact is critical to explaining the process of convergence in South Africa. According to Mac Maharaj, a senior ANC negotiator and backer of the Slovo approach, those propounding a hegemonic course of action could not offer a viable alternative to a negotiated settlement.[59]

The Slovo document produced further movement in negotiation when in December, at a secluded game lodge, twenty-member government and ANC delegations met for a three-day session of intense negotiations called, in Afrikaans, a *bosberaad* (bush meeting). Although no formal pact was reached, several understandings were concluded that would eventually find their way into the democratization pact. On the outstanding issues, bilateral working groups were to meet to iron out remaining differences, with a second round of secret bilaterals planned for early 1993.

Just as the NP government and the ANC were moving closer—and likely because of this movement—the IFP reacted with a new set of demands, illustrating once again that it was at least pursuing brinksmanship or potentially setting itself up as a spoiler. As the NP-ANC bilateral got underway, Buthelezi put forth a draft constitution for a semiautonomous Natal province—in effect, a bid for a Zulu state. The constitution stopped just short of unilateral secession. The institutional choice approach explains the IFP's move well: perceiving a diminution of power, the party moved from its consociational choice of 1991 toward partition. Frederick van zyl Slabbert explained the IFP's motive: "Buthelezi has smelled a deal between the ANC and the government, so he's staking his claim to maximum autonomy."[60]

Movement in government-ANC negotiation was further aided in late December when de Klerk, acting on irrefutable evidence from the Goldstone Commission that secret cells within the security forces—sanctioned by military intelligence—had waged a covert war against the ANC throughout the transition, retired twenty-three military officers, including the head of the SADF and its Department of Military Intelligence.

---

[58] Pallo Jordan, "Strategic Debate in the ANC," mimeo, emphasis in original. An edited version of the document was printed in *New Nation*, 19 November 1992.

[59] *Weekly Mail*, 27 November to 3 December 1992.

[60] *Christian Science Monitor*, 3 December 1992.

THE DEMOCRATIZATION PACT: 1993

When ANC president Nelson Mandela marked the organization's eighty-first anniversary on 8 January 1993, he articulated the reality that moderates in South Africa faced: "Today all South Africans realize that we need to move forward decisively and with utmost speed. Each day that passes is a day of deprivation, of hunger, of rising unemployment, of violence, increasing crime and insecurity for all." Referring to the outbidders, and in a vague reference to the IFP and its right-wing allies, he said, "There are those political formations which fear change and are totally opposed to democratic elections. Unless they are able to place the national interest above their party-political and personal agendas they will confine themselves to the role of spoilers and will be judged accordingly."[61]

Mandela's remarks set the tone for the conclusion of a democratization pact later that year. The ANC and the government—the inner core of moderate parties—had finally found each other: there would soon be agreement between them on the path of transition, and other parties could either be persuaded to go along or they would be left behind. Allister Sparks summed up the situation succinctly: "[A] hopeful prognosis grows directly out of the disasters of 1992. It took the imminent prospect of a national disaster to shock the two major parties into realizing that they had better sink their differences and work together or there would be nothing left for them to fight over."[62]

Negotiating the Democratization Pact

The stage was set for a second government-ANC bosberaad, which began at a secret venue on 20 January, and a subsequent round of talks that culminated in a Cape Town meeting on 10–12 February. During these crucial talks, the government and the ANC reached agreement on the elements of what would later evolve into a broader democratization pact. Though not written down, or at least not released, the pact entailed a series of compromises by both parties on their institutional choices for the transition. In reaching an accord, concessions were made by both sides, but its essence reflected the formula outlined in Slovo's "strategic perspective" document. The parties agreed that to the following points:

- The Tricameral Parliament would enact an interim constitution and provisional bill of rights that would be drafted by a reconstituted multiparty conference

[61] *FBIS,* 8 September 1993.
[62] *Washington Post,* 3 January 1993.

- A Transitional Executive Council, or multiparty cabinet committee, would oversee the government during the election campaign and would exercise multiparty control over broadcasting, finance, and the security forces
- An independent electoral commission would be established to organize and administer the election
- A multiparty delimitation commission on regionalism would be established to make recommendations on the powers, functions, and boundaries of the regions, and regions demarcated would be used for election of representatives to the constituent assembly
- Elections to a constituent assembly would be held under proportional representation, with half of the four hundred delegates elected on a national list, half on regional lists
- Based on the election outcome, an interim government would be constituted with all parties that received more than 5 percent of the vote guaranteed representation in the cabinet commensurate with their proportional vote share; a single president with general executive authority would be elected by the constituent assembly by simple majority rule; on specified issues, the president would be required to seek approval of at least two-thirds of the cabinet
- A two-thirds decision-making rule would prevail in the constituent assembly, which would draft and adopt the new constitution
- The bicameral constituent assembly would continue as an interim parliament after the adoption of a new constitution; the constituent assembly would accept recommendations of the commission on regionalism unless rejected by a three-fourths majority
- A five-year "sunset clause" for a "government of national unity and reconstruction" would exist after initial elections
- Elections under the new constitution would be held no later than five years after the election to a constituent assembly.

The February agreement, remarkable for its scope, represented convergence between the two major protagonists on the essential path of transition.

The government was charged with taking the "package deal" to a wary IFP, which rejected the agreement; a similar reaction came from the PAC, the CP, and AZAPO. On 17 February, the government began a crucial three-day bilateral negotiation with the IFP on the plan, seeking to persuade it that the concessions made by the ANC on regionalism—especially the decision-making rule in the constituent assembly—would be sufficient to protect IFP interests even though regional powers fell considerably short of those proposed in the IFP's "constitution." Even though the IFP failed to sign on, the February government-ANC agreement itself was a critical watershed in the South African transition;

though not a formal agreement, the government and ANC pledged to treat the understandings reached as binding, meaning that in subsequent multiparty talks to broaden and deepen support for the accord, the two would negotiate, in effect, as a bloc.

When the parties reconvened to reconstitute CODESA-style multiparty talks on 5 March, a different dynamic prevailed. Prior agreement by the NP and ANC ensured that, unlike at CODESA II, and barring the walk-out of potential rejectionists like the IFP, the talks would be a predetermined success. Scholar David Welsh refers to this government-ANC relationship as the most important "axis" in the reconstituted talks. A March planning conference was primarily symbolic, resulting in little substantive negotiation and no outcome other than the announcement of a date for future meetings. But with the participation of a broader group of parties—twenty-three in all, including the PAC, the CP, and the right-wing Volksunie (people's union, a small breakaway group split from the CP in 1992 over participation in negotiation)—symbolism was important. Following concessions by the ANC aimed at placating the IFP on the thorny issue of regionalism, the IFP agreed to participate. A place at the table was also found for some traditional leaders (but the demands of the Zulu monarch Goodwill Zwelithini for special status were not accepted). The centripetal dynamic that brought the government and ANC together was pulling other parties toward the newly consolidated political center as well. Only the neofascist AWB and Herstigte (purified) National Party and far-left AZAPO refused to participate in the new forum.

The March planning conference also showed a continuing relationship between progress in negotiation and upsurges in political violence. Even though the early months of 1993 were relatively tranquil, on the eve of the talks in early March, a massacre of six students in the violence-wracked Midlands of Natal cast a pall on the meeting, initiating a wave of violence that continued into early April. The upsurge in violence in Natal, and its failure to disrupt progress in negotiation, meant that the negotiators had reached a new understanding in the aftermath of Bisho: rather than impede negotiations, upsurges in violence would reinforce pressures to reach a settlement—even as accusations of culpability continued to fly.

The Multiparty Negotiating Process

The reconstituted multiparty conference was blandly dubbed the Multiparty Negotiating Process (MPNP) because of an inability to agree on a new name or to accept the name CODESA. The new forum was kicked off at the World Trade Center without fanfare on 1 April. Its essential tasks were to broaden acceptance and define the detail of the agreements reached in the Record of Understanding and the February government-

ANC pact; further negotiate the proposed Transitional Executive Council (TEC), independent electoral commission, and independent media commission to level the playing field in the run-up to elections; adopt an electoral act; determine the structure and decision-making rules for the constituent assembly; design the interim government of national unity; and chart the path for implementation of a new constitution. Institutionally, its structure was similar to CODESA, but without the cumbersome working groups; the arrangement of the MPNP is described in table 6.1. The central decision-making structure of the 208-member, twenty-six-party parliamentary-style assembly was the ten-person Negotiating Council, an effective decision-making body even though it still operated under the "sufficient consensus" rule that governed CODESA. An inner core of ten negotiators, the Planning Council, set the agenda. The council's work was aided by seven technical committees, made up mostly of lawyers, which were to hammer out the details and eventually draft legislation that would create the Transitional Executive Council and an interim constitution. The pattern of negotiation was to allow the details to be thrashed out by the experts in the technical committees and to leave the tough political decisions to the Negotiating Council.[63]

The MPNP picked up where CODESA and subsequent government-ANC bilateral talks left off—with agreement on the basic path of transition that lay ahead, but deep disagreement on the powers and functions of regions and the exact form of power sharing during the next phase of transition. The parties agreed to treat agreements reached at CODESA as "points of reference," but they were not to be binding. Many new issues, such as the IFP's shifting preferences for greater regional autonomy and the white right-wing demands for an Afrikaner-majority homeland, were added to the complex mix. Not all negotiation was conducted under the rubric of the MPNP. In fact, much preliminary bargaining was conducted in a series of behind-the-scenes bilateral talks throughout 1993.

The democracy talks had barely begun when on Saturday morning, 10 April, a young and virulently anticommunist immigrant from Poland, Janusz Jacub Walus, assassinated SACP party chief Chris Hani—the ANC's most popular leader after Mandela—as he stood in his driveway in the small-middle-class suburb of Boksburg, where he had lived since returning from exile. Walus was associated with the neofascist Afrikaner Weerstandsbeweging (AWB). It was later alleged that he acted as part of a

---

[63] Welsh suggests that the Constitutional Technical Committee especially "serves as a clearing house and a catalyst in spelling out the options and parameters for choices" (1993:7). Other functional areas that technical committees investigated were violence, a transitional bill of rights, the TEC, the independent media and the broadcasting commission, and an independent electoral commission. Further, a delimitation commission was constituted to work on the demarcation of regional boundaries.

TABLE 6.1
Interim Institutions: The Multiparty Negotiating Process, 1993

	Plenary
Composition	Party leaders plus nine delegates per party (at least one must be a woman) and two advisers
Function	Formal adoption of agreements
Frequency of meeting	Meets when necessary, as proposed by Negotiating Forum

	Negotiating Forum
Composition	Four delegates (at least one woman) and two advisers per party
Function	Receives and confirms reports and proposals from the Negotiating Council for submission to the Plenary
Frequency of meeting	Every two weeks
Chairpersons	A panel of six rotating chairpersons appointed by the Negotiating Council

	Negotiating Council
Composition	Two delegates (at least one must be a woman) and two advisers per party
Function	Conducts ongoing negotiations as the most important decision-making structure
Frequency of meeting	Three or four days per week
Chairpersons	A core panel of six rotating chairpersons elected from the Negotiating Council

	Planning Committee
Composition	Ten members of the Negotiating Council appointed on a rotating basis in their personal capacities, not as members of political parties
Function	To set the agenda of the Negotiating Council

	Technical Committees
Composition	Legal experts appointed by the Negotiating Council; non–South Africans excluded
Separate committees	Defense, budget, women's issues

	Administration
The Multiparty Negotiating Process is administered by the Consultative Business Movement	

Source: Adapted from *Towards Democracy* (Durban: Institute for Multiparty Democracy) (2d Quarter, 1993): 9.

broader conspiracy headed by former CP parliamentarian Clive Derby-Lewis and his wife; six conspirators were eventually arrested and convicted. Paradoxically, in the weeks before the assassination, Hani—considered a villain by many whites—had made repeated calls for peace and had denounced random attacks by the PAC's military wing on whites. Despite his militant image, Hani had been instrumental in persuading the ANC's more radical youth of the efficacy of negotiation. Hani had, in fact, been a moderate.

The tragic death of Chris Hani plunged South Africa into a perilous crisis; anger and frustration, especially among township youth, had long been building over the protracted pace of talks. Every expectation was that the townships would explode, spiraling out of control and plunging South Africa into anarchy. Mandela, as if to underscore that power was shifting slowly away from the white minority government, appeared presidential in an unprecedented national address on state television, appealing for calm and restraint. Praising a white Afrikaner woman who identified Hani's murderer, Mandela said: "Now is the time for all South Africans to stand together against those who, from any quarter, wish to destroy what Chris Hani gave his life for: the freedom of all of us."[64]

The ANC, SACP, and COSATU leadership quickly gathered to manage the crisis amid sporadic incidents of violence and deep tension. Rejecting calls from militants, the ANC leadership deftly recognized the assassination for what it was—an attempt by right-wing whites to derail talks. Affirming the post-Bisho pattern that political violence would reinforce, not undermine, negotiation, the ANC called for all parties to exercise restraint and reasserted its commitment to talks. "Hani's death," ANC leader Cyril Ramaphosa said, "should act as a catalyst, to make sure the negotiations process gathers momentum. It is what Comrade Chris would have expected us all to do."[65]

The ANC sought to channel black anger into efforts to speed up the transition and achieve an end to white minority rule. The following Wednesday was declared a day of mourning for the slain martyr; riots broke out throughout South Africa, leaving at least 8 dead and 250 wounded, including 4 killed as they were surrounded by security police in Soweto. The murder of Chris Hani demonstrated how perilously fragile South Africa's transition to democracy was, yet at the same time it reaffirmed the resilience of the leaders' commitment to a negotiated settlement. It also demonstrated an unprecedented degree of cooperation among the ANC, security forces, international observers, and the myriad regional and local peace committees established by the peace accord.

[64] *Financial Times,* 19 April 1993.
[65] *Los Angeles Times,* 12 April 1993.

The Hani assassination spurred convergence when the MPNP resumed deliberations on 26 April. The preceding weeks—which had witnessed not only the death of Hani but also CP leader Andries Treurnicht and ANC elder statesman Oliver Tambo—had dramatically changed the political climate. In the aftermath of this turbulence, new threats to moderation had emerged: heightened alienation among black youths, challenges to ANC leadership within the party by militants such as Mandela's estranged wife, Winnie, and Youth League leader Peter Mokaba, increased right-wing vigilantism, and new and emboldened hard-line leadership within the CP (Treurnicht, a long-standing proponent of nonviolence, was succeeded by the more militant Ferdi Hartzenberg).

These pressures pushed the MPNP negotiators toward the adoption on 7 May of a declaration of intent, by "sufficient consensus," to set an election date by 3 June—a signal to the restless majority that demonstrable outcomes were finally emerging from the talks. Reflecting the pattern of things to come, the parties associated with the COSAG group dissented from the resolution. David Welsh wrote about the emergence of a rejectionist "axis" at the MPNP—those on the right opposed to the government-ANC axis's formula for transition: "Essentially, COSAG represents smaller players, unsure of their ability to compete effectively in a forthcoming electoral contest. Their aim is to secure their own bailiwicks as far as they can, while the going is good—and the going is certainly better for them in a forum such as the multiparty talks than it would be in an elected constituent assembly, when elections have their inevitable winnowing effect" (1993:5).

As if to demonstrate that a moderate core had begun to congeal, outbidder parties on the left and right grew more desperate. The PAC's military wing, Azanian Peoples' Liberation Army (APLA) stepped up attacks on innocent whites and members of the security forces. The long-fragmented right-wing parties and paramilitary groups—frightened by the outpouring of militancy and reckless chants of "Kill the boer, kill the farmer" by ANC supporters at rallies—coalesced under the banner of the Afrikaner Volksfront (Afrikaner national front), headed by a committee of retired generals and security police under the leadership of former SADF chief Constand Viljoen. The Volksfront was formed just hours before the 7 May decision to set a deadline for choosing an election date. Uniting around a vague call for Afrikaner self-determination, it included virtually every significant right-wing group, among them the CP and the AWB, labor unions, and farmer associations. It quickly found common ground with the IFP and others in the COSAG group's demands for maximum devolution, sharing not only common goals but also an affinity for threats of violent resistance, or "war talk."

In spite of the left- and right-wing threats, and in the midst of virtual anarchy in many black schools and of ongoing political violence, negotiation progressed nonetheless. On 13 May, the first technical committee report on the Transitional Executive Council was put before the Negotiating Council for debate, and in the talks the government and ANC implicitly agreed that the security forces would not be subject to direct multiparty operational control in the run-up to an election (a long-standing ANC demand), but that a subcouncil of the TEC would exercise general oversight. In another significant concession, in mid-May the ANC formally agreed that a government of national unity would be created with a coalition cabinet and that entrenched regional powers would be assured in constitutional guidelines which would bind the constituent assembly. By late May, despite a surprise 25 May security force swoop of seventy-three PAC leaders by the security forces, the talks lumbered on in the technical committees after a brief but acrimonious debate on the police force action.

As the self-established 3 June deadline approached, a flurry of frantic negotiation ensued, in which the ANC conceded further on regionalism and the government (and even the IFP, for the time being at least) formally agreed that a constituent assembly would finalize a future constitution. Amid threats by ANC youth leader Peter Mokaba to make the country "ungovernable," the Negotiating Council agreed to set a "tentative" election date of 27 April 1994. Unable to bring the IFP and its COSAG allies along, the negotiators adopted the resolution by sufficient consensus but left the door open for further efforts to reach broader agreement by allowing for the date to be ratified by the full plenary of the MPNP on 25 June. Throughout June, tough bargaining revealed that the government-ANC axis and its commitment to the process set out in the September 1992 Record of Understanding was stronger than a seemingly natural alliance between the government and IFP. On the other hand, the IFP's commitment to the rejectionist coalition with COSAG grew stronger. This alignment was confirmed on 15 June, when the IFP and other COSAG parties together walked out of the talks after the government-ANC bloc rejected an IFP bid for a debate on a federal constitution. Many analysts viewed the walkout as a tactical public-relations ploy by the IFP—by leaving the talks and charging the government with collusion with the ANC, the party would win the support of alienated whites. Indeed, in the following days the IFP quietly returned to talks, whereas the CP did not.

Amid mounting violence, particularly on the East Rand near Johannesburg and in Natal, and following on the heels of intensive mediation by clergymen, a long-awaited summit between Mandela and Buthelezi was held in Johannesburg on 23 June; it was their first public bilateral summit since the failed January 1991 peace pact. Despite the glossy appearance of elite coalescence (the men exchanged kind words, were photographed shaking hands, called for a cease-fire, and agreed to joint ANC-IFP peace rallies), the underlying differences between their parties on critical constitutional issues like regionalism were unresolved. And much like early ANC-IFP peace bids, the agreements reached were short-lived.

As the MPNP negotiators at the World Trade Center were working to finalize a package deal to ratify the election date by the 25 June deadline, white right-wing rejectionists upped the ante. The most militant group, the AWB, hijacked an otherwise peaceful demonstration organized in concert with other right-wing groups to oppose a 24 June decision in the MPNF to reject an Afrikaner homeland. The demonstration was attended by fifteen hundred armed followers of all right-wing groups, including the CP and Afrikaner Volksunie. With a steel-reinforced truck, a vanguard of the AWB group smashed through the plate-glass windows of the World Trade Center. Heavily armed commandos stormed for nearly two hours through hall where negotiators had gathered, spraying graffiti, throwing punches, and insulting the negotiators; surprisingly, only minor injuries were incurred in the melee. Indeed, the most significant injury from the bizarre event was to the image of the white right wing itself—and, ostensibly, to their efforts to achieve an Afrikaner homeland. Hennie Kotzé of the University of Stellenbosch explained the growing desperation of the white right: "Until a month or two ago, the prevailing attitude was, 'Sure, let's talk to the blacks but in the end we'll come up with a ploy and stay in control.' Now, they're beginning to wake up to the fact that it's gone beyond that."[66] In any event, the negotiators had postponed the decision to ratify the election date in continued attempts to assuage IFP concerns and bring them into the moderate camp.

The parties were once again aided by a deadline, but not the self-imposed date of ratification (25 June). De Klerk and Mandela had earlier accepted an invitation to jointly receive an award presented by U.S. president Bill Clinton on 4 July in Philadelphia; they had fully expected to have reached a package agreement that would allow for Mandela to call for a lifting of international sanctions. It would have been a terrible embarrassment for the leaders to arrive for the highly publicized event without confirmed agreement on a date. Hours before back-to-back separate White House meetings for de Klerk and Mandela with Clinton on 2 July, the MPNP negotiators ratified the 27 April 1994 election date in a strongly contentious meeting over the meaning of what constitutes suffi-

[66] *Washington Post National Weekly Edition*, 31 May–6 June 1993.

cient consensus, once again without the presence of the IFP and its rejectionist partners.

The ratification of the election date set off a wave of fresh violence. In the four days following the 2 July agreement some 130 died in political violence as IFP and ANC supporters clashed amid a poor police response to the carnage; much of the fighting centered in the volatile townships of Kathelong and Thokoza, east of Johannesburg. Throughout July, some 605 died throughout the country in political violence in a period that became, according the the Johannesburg-based Human Rights Commission, the bloodiest month in South Africa since August 1990, when the Pretoria Minute was sealed. The violence was spurred by a wide variety of factors but was clearly related to the negotiation events and the realization that the final steps toward apartheid's end had officially begun.

The twenty-fifth of July marked an important turning point in South Africa's transition. At a Zulu *imbizo*, or mass meeting, in Soweto attended by some fifty thousand supporters wielding "cultural" weapons, King Goodwill Zwelithini, who commanded more influence than Buthelezi, raised the possibility that he would personally lead a war of secession.[67] Emboldened by resurgent nationalism, the IFP once again abandoned the talks on 18 July, promising to stay out until it was given a veto over a new political order. The CP also reaffirmed its rejectionist approach, claiming it would not return to the negotiating forum and warning that South Africa would be turned into "another Bosnia."

That the setting of an election date would create a backlash from the IFP and right-wing whites was expected; less expected was that violence, too, would come from the radical left. The twenty-fifth of July also witnessed the massacre of twelve and the wounding of fifty churchgoers at the multiracial St. James Anglican Church in Cape Town. This time the attack had allegedly come from the left (the PAC's military wing was blamed), but the result was the same. As the extremist parties' followers fomented new violence to derail the process, the turmoil further consolidated the center and accelerated the pace of talks. Over that chilling weekend, some forty-five had also died in strife in the townships east of Johannesburg.

The Democratization Pact

Absent the IFP and COSAG, quick progress was made toward a democratization pact. The day after the tragic weekend of late July in which so many lost their lives, a draft interim constitution was unveiled at the ne-

[67] *Southscan*, 16 July 1993.

gotiating forum. Opening the forum, MPNP chairman Pravin Gordham said that the purpose of releasing a draft of the constitution was to flesh out areas of agreement among the parties, and "then in bilaterals and multilaterals the parties can thrash out their differences before full and comprehensive debate on the constitution takes place in the negotiating council."[68] This left open the possibility that the IFP and other rejectionist concerns could be subsequently accommodated. In fact, the draft interim constitution did contain significant concessions aimed at wooing the IFP back to talks, while retaining the basic outline of the institutions agreed to in the Record of Understanding and the government-ANC February 1993 agreement. The CP, reacting to the draft, called it a "recipe for civil war."

The first draft of the interim constitution proposed the creation of a grand coalition executive for the interim period in which all parties with more than 5 percent of the vote would be assured a cabinet seat and decisions would be taken by consensus or with the agreement of 80 percent of cabinet ministers; affirmed the choice for a proportional representation electoral system and proposed a bicameral interim legislature elected on regional and national lists (which in joint sitting would comprise the constituent assembly)—a four hundred-seat National Assembly and a Senate with ten seats per region; set up a constitutional court to ensure that a final constitution would adhere to twelve constitutional principles; enumerated a fairly specific set of national, regional, and local powers, including taxation, and a permanent fiscal commission; and included an interim bill of rights. The provisions on regionalism and their fiscal implications were the most contentious, and this draft provision amounted to the creation of a hybrid unitary-federal system with concurrent and central overriding government powers. In a submission to the Negotiating Council by the commission of experts set up to demarcate regional boundaries, nine regions drawn on economic criteria were proposed. Although they preserved the integrity of KwaZulu-Natal, none would contain an Afrikaner majority.

The IFP rejected both the interim constitution and the process by which a new constitution would be adopted. Despite a last-minute three-hour meeting between de Klerk and Buthelezi, the party decided to challenge the sufficient-consensus decision-making rule in court and boycott the MPNP debate on the draft even though it had been postponed to bring the rejectionist parties back to the table. It is important to note, however, that the IFP's rejection was based not only on principle, but on expectations of losing in the electoral game. A major poll published by the *Star* in late July, for example, showed that the IFP would win only 9

[68] *Business Day*, 29 July 1993.

percent of the votes cast, barely enough to cross the threshold into representation on the interim government and not enough to, with its COSAG allies, block adoption of a constitution inimical to its perceived interest in territorial autonomy; more importantly, it showed only 30 percent of those in KwaZulu-Natal would support the IFP.[69] On the other hand, surveys also showed that the IFP was gaining popularity among whites; outbidding the NP for support among edgy whites was paying clear dividends.[70] The party perceived the incentive structure of the situation to reward extremism and to encourage outbidding parties to opt out of talks.

The rampant violence throughout July continued into August as at least thirty residents of Tembisa, an ANC stronghold, were killed by a group of some two hundred Zulus, reportedly in response to an earlier political killing of ANC loyalists by residents of an IFP-allied workers' hostel. This turmoil again pushed the government and ANC closer together as the talks progressed, with agreement emerging on the creation of a joint peacekeeping force to quell future anticipated rounds of violence throughout the ensuing election campaign; such a force would also serve as a first step toward integration of the security forces and final resolution of the long-standing disagreement over the future of the ANC military wing, MK. The peacekeeping force, it was proposed, would be under the joint control of the TEC. By 10 August, a second draft of the interim constitution was produced, outlining further the nature and extent of regional powers.

Despite the IFP's formal withdrawal from talks, it continued to negotiate bilaterally with the government and with the ANC. Although these discussions did not lead to announced breakthroughs, they revealed signs of dissension between moderates and hard-liners within the IFP as well; some soft-liners were reportedly ready to return after assurances from the ANC that regions would be allowed to adopt their own constitutions, whereas hard-liners continued to reject the constitution-writing process altogether. On 25 August, a third draft interim constitution was released at the talks, which fleshed out further detail on the executive decision-making structures of the interim government and mooted the idea of a vice- or copresidency. This would, in effect, give the NP—as the expected second largest party, according to all major surveys conducted during this period—entrenched executive power sharing for the five-year interim period.

Self-imposed deadlines once again pressured the ANC and the government to move ahead without the IFP. Legislation enabling the TEC and

[69] *Star International Edition*, 29 July–4 August 1993.
[70] The survey reported in the *Star* showed 27 percent of whites supporting the IFP.

independent electoral commission to be in place in time to organize the elections by 27 April 1994 would have to be passed by a special sitting of the Tricameral parliament, scheduled for September. Thus, the MPNP finalized—after seventeen drafts—the details of the TEC, the creation of the independent electoral commission, and the media and broadcasting commission legislation on 8 September. The TEC would be composed of one representative from each of the nineteen parties and organizations in the MPNP that agreed to it, and, once again, the door was left open to stragglers to join. The council and its seven subcouncils were empowered to peer into government decision making and operation; in effect, the changes signaled nascent, institutionalized power sharing in South Africa's transition as opposed to the less formal influence the ANC had on government policy since the onset of transition. As if to underscore the continued dangers that lay ahead, on the day following the adoption of the TEC resolution, masked gunmen opened fire on commuters at a Johannesburg taxi stand in two separate incidents, killing twenty-one and wounding twenty-five.

In a highly publicized attempt to get Buthelezi and the IFP back on board in time for the formal adoption of the TEC and related legislation by the Tricameral Parliament, de Klerk and his advisers met with Buthelezi and a full IFP delegation on 16 September. The summit provided no breakthrough, although the two parties left open bilateral channels, and the TEC bill was adopted on 24 September over the objections of the IFP (represented by two members of the Tricameral Parliament who had switched their allegiance) and amid CP cries that the National party had betrayed the Afrikaner volk. The adoption of the TEC legislation allowed Mandela, in a speech before the Special Committee on Apartheid at the United Nations on the same day, to call for the end of sanctions against South Africa. The path of transition had become clear; its sequence is outlined in figure 6.1.

Agreement on the transitional mechanisms for the election period allowed the negotiators at the World Trade Center to turn their attention to the central issue that remained before convergence in negotiation was complete—the final details of the interim constitution. However, with elements of the white right wing considering the onset of shared rule—which adoption of the TEC legislation represented—a "declaration of war," as the CP termed the measure, prudence dictated that the energies of the government and ANC be turned to wooing the rejectionists back into talks.[71] In mid-September it had been revealed that Afrikaner Volksfront leader Constand Viljoen had indeed met secretly with Mandela, and that the ANC was considering the organization's demand for some

[71] *Business Day,* 21 September 1993.

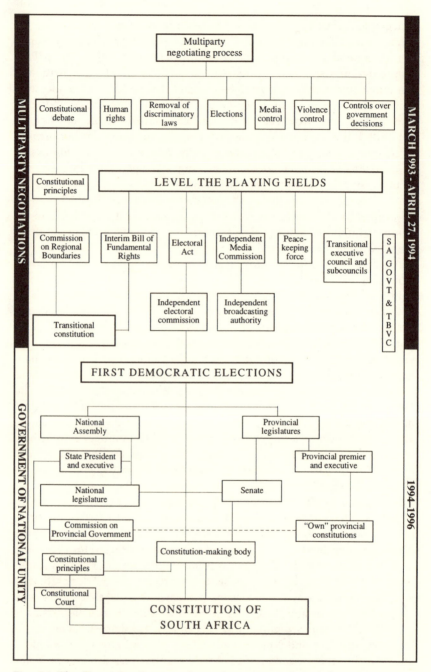

Fig. 6.1 The Transition Process, September 1993 (adapted from *People Dynamics,* September 1993)

form of Afrikaner self-rule. Amid continuing "war talk" and appeals to Zulu nationalism by Buthelezi, bilateral talks between the government and IFP also continued on the party's demand for regional autonomy. In the impending finalization of the multiparty negotiations, the tacit government-ANC partnership sought as inclusive a settlement as possible.

The impetus was on the ANC to negotiate with the Afrikaner right. Mandela, after receiving a map outlining the Volksfront's proposed volkstaat, reiterated the ANC's willingness to accommodate the white right. The demand for an Afrikaner majority area could be implicitly met, he said, but the ANC would not countenance the creation of an ethnic state—an Afrikaner homeland in classic Verwoerdian terms—to the possible detriment of non-Afrikaners living in the area. Sensing that the process was gaining steam, on 7 October the rejectionist groups and their leaders solidified their loose cooperation in COSAG into a formal negotiating coalition under the banner of the Freedom Alliance.[72] Despite its elements' disparate preferences for a postapartheid state—partition, confederalism, and federalism—the alliance pledged to negotiate as a bloc and called for a summit of all South African leaders outside the MPNP. The alliance was formed because of a coincidence of interests; each party separately was weak, but together the rejectionist front reflected a significant constituency base, possibly eclipsing the NP. The renewed threat to the transition from the right prompted de Klerk to moot a referendum as a possible way to break the impasse, a proposal that did not come to fruition because of eventual opposition from the ANC.[73]

When the MPNP talks formally resumed on 13 October, the agenda was packed with the outstanding constitutional issues in addition to "parallel track" negotiations with the Freedom Alliance. The government-ANC partnership in the talks received a boost when the Norwegian Nobel Committee awarded its 1993 Peace Prize jointly to F. W. de Klerk and Nelson Mandela. The Nobel Committee was clearly aware of the timing of its announcement, which served to renew the sagging popular credibility of the negotiators, especially de Klerk. Despite denials that a parallel track was in place, the ANC and Freedom Alliance formally met for the

[72] The alliance included the Afrikaner Volksfront, the CP, the IFP, the Afrikaner Volksunie, and the governments of Boputhatswana and Ciskei.

[73] The ANC realized, correctly so, that a successful simple majority referendum would significantly bolster de Klerk's party political interests and would not solve the problem of right-wing fears. It would also delay the April 1994 election. The ANC's alliance partner, COSATU, also sought to break the talks impasse by calling for a day-long strike on 5 November if its specific interests were not accommodated in the talks (i.e., the striking of provisions allowing employer lockouts), but this proposal also fizzled when the ANC's leadership refused to back the call.

first time at the World Trade Center on 19 October, followed by a government-ANC bilateral discussion the following day. The alliance laid on the table its core demands for amendments to the draft interim constitution as a precondition to its participation in the elections.[74] At the outset of the parallel-track talks, it was clear that there were only two possible outcomes—either the government-ANC partners would sufficiently concede to the alliance's demands for ethnic self-determination or the settlement would exclude the coalition that some analysts termed "apartheid's children."[75]

Throughout late October and into November 1993, as the formal talks at the World Trade Center went forward, the three major contenders for power—the government, the ANC, and the Freedom Alliance—were engaged in a flurry of reported and secret bilateral negotiations. Critical among these was a three-day government-ANC bosberaad that began 25 October. In these days of intensive negotiating, the government and ANC further narrowed their differences and clarified their common position vis à vis the Freedom Alliance. Most importantly, the government backed away from a formal veto in cabinet decision making, instead relying on apparent assurances from Mandela that fundamental decisions would be taken consensually. But the ANC agreed to at least two executive deputy president positions, at least one of which would be reserved for the leader of the party that polled second best in the election, presumably the NP. On the ever-present question of regional powers, the ANC agreed to give regions taxation powers and further defined the functional areas in which the regions were to have primary jurisdiction within overall "norms and standards" set by the central government. The government was charged with taking the proposals to the Freedom Alliance, and pursued talks with its leaders in the following weeks. A further critical decision was reached at the bosberaad: if the alliance could not be persuaded to go along, the government and ANC would conclude a settlement without them.

In the first two weeks of November, the final areas of contention between the government, the ANC, and other parties at the MPNP were ironed out: the nature of executive decision making, decision making in the constituent assembly, and the mechanisms for deadlock breaking; the composition of the constitutional court; the final language for the constitutional principles; national symbols; the single ballot issue; civil service tenure and pensions; the role of the police and defense forces; reincor-

---

[74] The alliance agenda included enhanced powers and functions for the regions, amendments to the deadlock-breaking mechanism in the constituent assembly, clarification of the constitutional principles, Afrikaner self-determination, and amendments to the proposed regional boundaries.

[75] *Financial Times*, 27 October 1993.

poration of the TBVC states; and regional boundaries, powers, and functions. All the while, talks ensued with the Freedom Alliance in what was then described as a last-ditch effort to get the rejectionists on board prior to settlement.

South Africa's democratization pact was sealed, in essence, at a 16 November summit meeting between de Klerk and Mandela. These last details of the overall agreement were embodied in a set of joint constitutional proposals released by the parties on 17 November. This final agreement contained six key elements that signaled convergence between these two core partners in transition:

- The government of national unity would reign for at least five years (until 1999)
- Decision making in the cabinet would not be based on predetermined majorities (as earlier drafts had sought to provide) but decisions would be made instead in a "consensus-seeking spirit," without formal restraints
- Decisions in the constituent assembly regarding the functions, boundaries, and powers of the regions would require a two-thirds majority of the senate; to break deadlocks in the assembly, a 60 percent majority in the senate would be required
- Provinces would be allowed to adopt their own constitutions, "consistent with the constitutional principles and national constitution" and certifiable by the constitutional court
- The April 1994 elections would entail a single ballot
- An elaborate deadlock-breaking mechanism was included, but one weighted more heavily toward minorities than previous proposals had been

Although it appeared that the NP had settled below its stated bottom line—the minority veto or a specific formula for cabinet decisions—the agreement was peppered with an *effective* minority veto in myriad ways. Further, a little publicized local power-sharing deal concluded on 16 November ensured a concrete minority veto in decisions that directly affected minority concerns at the local level.[76] Both the ANC and the government realized that a minority veto over decision making would occur in any event, whether or not it was actually written into the settlement. Without closing the door to subsequent negotiation with the Freedom Alliance, the agreement of 17 November finalized the process of convergence begun in CODESA and revived with the September 1992 Record of Understanding. The process of interim rule making was complete.

[76] The local government plan, included in the constitution, envisaged local government councils in which whites would be guaranteed at least 30 percent of the seats and in some cases more. Local government budgets would require at least a two-thirds majority to pass, which would in most areas give whites and other minorities an effective veto.

TABLE 6.2
Highlishts of the Interim Constitution and Electoral Act, 1993 (As Approved by the Negotiating Council, 18 November 1993)

Preamble and Formal Provisions

- The preamble cites the "need to create a new order" with common citizenship in a "democratic constitutional state in which there is equality between men and women and people of all races" in order to allow for the exercise of fundamental rights and freedoms.
- South Africa will have eleven official languages, and a Pan–South African Language Board will be established to their use and development.

Bill of Rights and Judiciary

- Chapter 3 of the constitution is a bill of "fundamental rights" that bars discrimination based on race, gender, ethnic, color, sexual orientation, and religion are also and also authorizes affirmative action and land restitution.
- Freedom of association is guaranteed, but the right may not be unfairly used to permit discrimination.
- The bill of rights includes guarantees of basic civil and political freedoms, including the right to personal privacy, freedom of religion, belief and opinion, a fair trial and administrative procedures, and prevents detention without trial.
- Trade union rights are assured, including the right to strike and to bargain collectively; however, employers may lock out strikers for the purpose of collective bargaining.
- Property rights are guaranteed, but property may be expropriated with agreed-upon or court-determined compensation, taking into account the use of the property, the history of its acquisition, its market value, and the value of investments.
- A bill children's rights is included.
- Provision is made for the "free and informed" choice of individuals to use customary law.
- A renewable twenty-one-day state of emergency can be declared under limited conditions with the consent of two-thirds of the National Assembly.
- A Constitutional Court is created that has wide original jurisdiction to determine the constitutionality of any statute, regulation, or administrative procedure.
- A broadly representative Judicial Services Commission advises on judicial appointments.

Legislative

- Parliament consists of the four hundred-member National Assembly and the ninety-member Senate.
- The four hundred representatives in the National Assembly are elected half on provincial lists and half on national party lists on a single ballot.
- The ninety members of Senate are elected by the regional legislatures (nine regions elect ten senators each).
- All South African citizens eighteen or above on voting day are eligible voters, provided they have obtained official identification or voter eligibility cards.

TABLE 6.2
(cont.)

- The general electoral principle is proportional representation. National parties not competing in specific regions and regional parties not competing nationally may pool votes
- Ordinary legislation must be passed by both houses and reconciled in a joint committee if necessary; money or appropriation bills must originate in the National Assembly and are not amendable by the Senate. Unless otherwise specified, legislation is passed by simple majority.
- A two-thirds majority of the National Assembly and the Senate in joint session can amend the interim constitution but may not detract from the essence of the constitutional principles.
- Legislation amending provincial powers must be approved by a two-thirds majority of the Senate.

The Constitutional Assembly

- The National Assembly and the Senate in joint sitting form the Constitutional Assembly, charged with the adoption of a new constitutional text in accordance with the constitutional principles.
- The new constitution requires the approval of two-thirds of the members of the Constitutional Assembly.
- The new constitution will come into effect only after the Constitutional Court, which is supreme, certifies its compliance with the thirty-two constitutional principles outlined in Schedule 4.
- Absent the necessary two-thirds majority, the consitution can be approved by an ordinary majority; the so-approved constitution must be certified by a panel of constitutional experts and ruled by the Constitutional Court as in compliance with the constitutional principles; thereafter, it must be approved in a popular referendum by 60 percent of votes cast. If the constitution fails to garner the requisite 60 percent, new elections are held and a new Constitutional Assembly must, within a year, adopt a new constitution by ordinary majority.

Executive

- A government of national unity is established, with each party receiving more than twenty seats (5 percent) in the National Assembly entitled to a proportionate number of seats in the 27-person cabinet.
- The president (head of state and military commander-in-chief) is elected from a list of candidates from the National Assembly by the Parliament by elimination until a candidate wins a simple majority.
- Every party holding a least eighty seats in the National Assembly (20 percent) is entitled to designate an executive deputy president; if no party holds eighty or more seats, the parties holding the largest and second largest number of seats are entitled to designate an executive deputy president.
- The cabinet takes decisions "in a consensus-seeking spirit."

(continued)

TABLE 6.2
(cont.)

Provincial Governments

- Nine provinces are established, each with its own provincial legislatures whose size (between thirty and one hundred seats) is based on the size of the population in that province.
- Provincial legislatures are elected by proportional representation from provincial lists; each legislature elects a provincial premier, and an executive council with representatives of each party with at least 10 percent of the seats in the legislature is constituted. The executive councils will make decisions by consensus.
- Each provincial legislature can adopt by two-thirds majority its own constitution in accordance with the national constitutional principles.
- The constitutional principles and Schedule 6 enumerate the original, concurrent, and overriding powers of the regions; regions have the capacity to generate revenue (tax) in agreement with the central government.
- The powers and functions of local governments are enumerated.
- Provision is made for establishment of traditional authorities and of provincial houses of traditional leaders, as well as of a central Council of Traditional Leaders drawn from the provincial councils.

Security

- A National Police Force is established, although provincial commissioners are created to allow for provincial differences in establishing community-based policing policies.
- A single National Defense Force is established.

Transitional Provisions

- The remaining apartheid-era laws are repealed, including those which created race-based parallel public administration, granted independence or self-governing authority to homelands, and authorized detention without trial.
- Provision is made for legal continuity in common law.

Just after midnight on 18 November, the MPNP's Negotiating Council adopted the agreement that formed the heart of South Africa's democratization pact. The draft interim constitution and companion Electoral Act—after more than two dozen drafts—were approved, culminating the negotiations over institutions for the immediate postapartheid era. The agreement's highlights are outlined in table 6.2. Justice Ismail Mohamed, chairman of the negotiating forum, hailed the agreement in a statement that reflected the mood of the weary democratizers: "The dawn has finally begun to break for a nation which has for so long so painfully and tortuously wrestled with its own soul. No force can now stop or even delay our emancipation from the pain and shame of our racist past."[77] Negotiation to broaden the agreement to include those outbidder parties on both the left (i.e., the PAC and AZAPO) and the right (i.e., the Freedom Alliance) would continue, but its essential elements would remain intact. Mandela, in a nationally televised interview from the World Trade Center, underscored that the door to participation in the new institutions remained open: "We sincerely hope that even at this late hour, wiser counsels among [the rejectionists] will prevail, and that they will join in this effort. . . . It is in their interest to join the other political organizations and be part of the process of transformation. . . . We will continue to prevail upon them, even after today, to say that the method of negotiation in peace is the most powerful weapon South Africans have to address their problems."[78]

South Africa's democratization pact was not a single agreement, but a package deal of related agreements that established the rules under which the new rules of postapartheid political institutions would be written. The democratization pact included concrete assurances for parties that their vital interests would be protected for the remainder of the transition. Its myriad guarantees for the inclusion of minority parties in decision making—particularly the structure of the interim government of national unity, the decision-making rules in the constituent assembly, and the entrenched regional provisions of the constitutional principles—ensured power sharing in the immediate future. The parties had arrived at a quasi-consociational outcome, reflecting a compromise between the NP's choice for modified consociationalism and the ANC's choice for modified majoritarianism.

The Founding Election

The violence-negotiations nexus would continue to plague the transition in South Africa until the uncertainty of the transition waned and the incentives for fomenting violence to influence negotiations subsided. Delaying the election because of the violence would, as ANC constitutional committee member Kader Asmal suggested, "hold the country hostage to violence and violent men."[79] Indeed, as figure 6.2 illustrates, the correlation between breakthroughs in negotiation and upsurges in political violence remained strong in the post–National Peace Accord era.

The challenge of controlling political violence during the election cam-

---

[77] *New York Times,* 18 November 1993.

[78] SABC-TV, 17 November 1993, as reported in *FBIS,* 18 November 1993.

[79] Interview with the author, 20 November 1992.

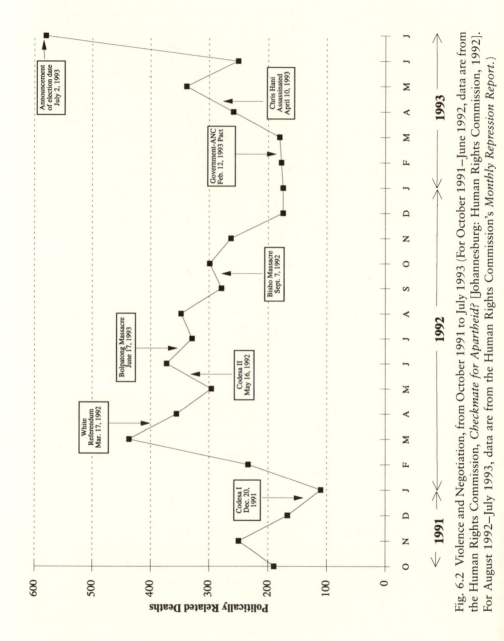

Fig. 6.2 Violence and Negotiation, from October 1991 to July 1993 (For October 1991–June 1992, data are from the Human Rights Commission, *Checkmate for Apartheid?* [Johannesburg: Human Rights Commission, 1992]. For August 1992–July 1993, data are from the Human Rights Commission's *Monthly Repression Report*.)

paign, with its inherently uncertain outcome, will be formidable. Violence will surely escalate. The challenge will not be whether an election will be held, or even whether the major parties win or lose, but whether it will be relatively peaceful. A peaceful election is a sine qua non of a "free and fair" vote, and in that regard the role of a United Nations verification mission as an external arbiter in the process—a form of mediation to ensure fairness—will be critical. So too will be the voter education, equal access by the voters to the media and information, competent and fair electoral administration, and sufficient security to prevent seemingly inevitable violence from preventing a free and fair vote. Nevertheless, the ultimate test of a successful election will be whether any major party is so dissatisfied with the outcome that it rejects playing by the rules of the new political game and chooses instead to wage the political struggle on the battlefield.

A first nonracial election will be equally important in forging stronger elite-mass relationships. South Africa's experience shows that pacts made by political leaders not backed by the constituencies they represent are unstable. A successful settlement will endure only if the constituencies too are willing to abide by the rules it establishes. The most important lesson was the 31 January 1991 Inkatha/ANC agreement described in chapter 3.[80] Pacts that fail can bring the entire process to an end, or at least further bloodshed. Steven Friedman explains the key to managing the elite-mass nexus in the course of the negotiation in South Africa. "In a society with our history of polarization, it would take a very charismatic group of leaders to persuade their followers to make compromises simply because the leaders told them to. . . . Including the doubters in negotiations could soften their resistance to compromise. Only if they are included will they gain a sense of the realities which force leaders to compromise. The road to stability lies in including as many constituencies in negotiation [as possible]."[81]

Involving as many constituencies as possible in the negotiation is a double-edged sword, as the parties learned. On the one hand, negotiated settlements may be easier to reach if they are in fact held in secret—ultimately, South African negotiators turned to secrecy before reaching success.

Nevertheless, Friedman's point—that reaching a sustainable settlement will require the participation of as many constituencies as possible—is a vital one. There was indeed an awareness by both the ANC and the National party that it was necessary to involve their supporters in the nego-

---

[80] It is recalled that when violence continued in spite of the accord reached by the leaders of these parties, with the apparent complicity of the police, the negotiation process nearly broke down altogether when the ANC issued its April 1991 ultimatum.

[81] *Weekly Mail*, 1–7 March 1991.

tiation process in some way; the March referendum and the mass-action campaign are the most accessible examples. There is no purpose in negotiating agreements if elites cannot persuade their supporters to comply with their terms and demobilize them when the moment of peace arrives. The challenge is to arrive at a proper balance. The SACP's Slovo explains the role of mass involvement in the process at large: "The achievements at the negotiating table are vitally connected with the balance of power on the ground. And there is an obvious inseparable link between negotiations and mass pressures. To pursue negotiations separate from mass pressures is obviously wrong. But to engage in mass action, ignoring considerations arising in the negotiation process, is equally wrong."[82] Ebrahim Patel, who served on the committee that drafted COSATU's constitutional principles, explained: "You reached an agreement (I suppose a bit like the peace accords) where on the ground nothing changes, while at the top there are marvelous agreements. It is a concern that we are wanting to promote a process that will bring real peace, stability and democracy. And you can only do that if you make lots of layers of people feel committed to it, and that requires some involvement."[83]

The violence in South Africa during the transition underscored for political leaders the importance of constituency participation in the negotiations process. Narrow deals made among elites are fragile if not buttressed by compliance with the new rules at the constituency level. In all likelihood, the remainder of the negotiation process in South Africa will reflect that basic fact.

The mass-elite nexus will also have an important effect on the transition's outcome. The rules of a future democratic political system will reflect the importance of constituency-based, not just elite-based, moderation and compromise. Indeed, the outcome itself may reflect the need to go beyond an elite-based pact. A critical passage in the ANC's submission to CODESA's Working Group 2 in early April 1992 provides the logic for public participation in the writing of South Africa's new rules of the political game: "Compromises openly struck, honestly agreed to for purposes of mutual advantage and frankly explained, have a much greater chance of being accepted than those negotiated in terms of secret agreements behind closed doors."[84] The first election that provides all citizens the opportunity to directly participate in the transition can vest critical legitimacy in settlements that elite-concluded pacts inherently lack. But over the longer term, more participatory politics will require government openness and a vigorous civil society.

For a successful outcome to the South African negotiations process,

---

[82] *New Nation,* 20–26 November 1992.
[83] Interview with the author, 7 June 1991.
[84] *FBIS,* 3 April 1992.

not only must the mass-elite nexus be bridged—by a deepening of moderation—the centrist core must be consolidated against the outbidding threat of extremists. Moderation must be broadened. In the run-up to a first election, there will certainly continue to be more tension between the countervailing forces of cooperation and conflict among the centrist actors and between them and the forces of reaction and revolution. To what extent these centrist players will cooperate and to what extent they will compete are determinant factors in their ability to implement a settlement. Eventually, the centrist core parties must cooperate to the degree where they preserve the basic rules of the game established in the democratization pact. The cooperation means that South Africa's future will be *codetermined* and that the state will be shared. By agreeing to a settlement and the consensus-based institutional structures it established, the core centrist parties implicitly agreed that they cannot destroy each other.

The institutional choice approach reveals why there was far more convergence on the need for appropriate rule structures for the future than on the way to create those structures. The convergence on a set of rules for a future political order is the result of the parties who perceive a balance of power and work to protect the center core from the outbidding potential of the extremists. The success of the pact does not depend on the parties' reaching consensus prior the establishment of the rules of the new political game—the precise terms of the final constitution—but just the opposite: as long as all parties stick to the rules, consensus will follow. This is also true of the political future.

The parties' willingness to follow the rules is only as strong as their realization that hegemonic pursuits are ultimately self-defeating. The more parties are interdependent and know they need each other, the more they know that unilateral defeat of the opponent is not only impossible but self-defeating, the more they are likely to follow jointly established rules. What began with the realization that the conflict could be transformed into a positive-sum game—which is why they first began to negotiate—ended with an institutionalization of an agreement to jointly manage the remainder of the transition and ultimately, to jointly craft and share power in the new institutions of the state. The logic of consensual government flowed from the process of negotiation itself. The fact that the parties may have different interpretations of the settlement agreed upon is less important than the depth of their commitment to it.

The successful implementation of an interim government in South Africa and a first election on a common voters roll will mean, finally, the end of apartheid. The democratization pact, a preelection agreement to share power by a centrist core of political parties notwithstanding the precise election outcome, mitigates the possibility of a winner-take-all conclusion to the transition. Thus, during the final phase of transition, while a constituent assembly debates, drafts, and implements a new, post-apartheid constitution, South Africa's political system will be based on power sharing. The democratization pact is an archetypal "elite settlement" (Burton and Higley 1987; Higley and Burton 1989), but one that provides for a founding election.

South's Africa ongoing transition may begin as a quasi-consociational pact—power sharing among elites representing distinct segments of society that have a prenegotiated minority veto—but this is, by agreement, a limited arrangement. What of South Africa's future? Will a power-sharing transition path yield a power-sharing constitution? I suggest that a more broadly participatory outcome is conceivable, even likely, and that is a democratic social contract in which parties eschew the guarantees of power sharing for the more uncertain and risky institutions of centripetalism, that is, institutions that stress incentives for moderation in place of entrenched minority vetoes.

CHAPTER 7

A Social Contract?

SOUTH AFRICA will continue to experience deep and enduring conflicts after apartheid. Above all, there will be conflicts over minority rights and majority prerogatives, deep class differences, ethnic and racial intolerance, and keen competition for resources under conditions of scarcity. Conflicts along these lines will be manifested at the national, regional, and local level. The critical questions, however, are whether South Africans can nonviolently channel these conflicts into legitimate, broadly inclusive, and accountable democratic political institutions, whether a companion economic compact is possible to ameliorate poverty, achieve reconstruction, development, and growth, and whether a vigorous integrated civil society will emerge to protect newly won democratic rights. Agreement on new political, economic, and social institutions in South Africa—a new social contract—would not fully resolve the many conflicts of this divided society, but it could serve to regulate them peacefully.

The first phases of South Africa's transition to democracy were based on pact making. Ultimately, the democratization pact reached in late 1993 was a compromise between the competing government and ANC preferences, respectively, for a founding pact and a founding election: when the constituent assembly is elected and convened, it will be limited by a prior agreement on constitutional principles and a considerable degree of detail. The institutions created by South Africa's democratization pact will be an experiment in power sharing. Moreover, due to the decision-making rules set forth in the democratization pact, minorities will play a significant role in drafting the final form of the constitution that emerges from the constituent assembly. If pact-based transitions of this sort lead to power-sharing outcomes, as suggested in chapter 1 and illustrated with regard to the parties' preferences for transitional institutions in chapter 5, it would follow that a future democratic system in South Africa will be based on power sharing. The power-sharing properties of the democratization pact would (under this assumption) be carried over into the long-term postapartheid future.

Yet a consociational arrangement is not the only possible democratic outcome for South Africa's long-term future. Indeed, Higley and Burton have observed a two-stage process in transitions to democracy. First, elites reorganize their relations and negotiate compromises to create a new system—an elite settlement. Elite coalescence is a precondition to democratization as it forms, they suggest, "the only indigenous [base] for changes from unstable to stable democratic (or proto-democratic) regimes" (1989:21). Further, they write that "consensually unified national elites, once formed, have everywhere perpetuated themselves." Thus, over time, in the second stage of transition, "previously unstable regimes become stable along representative lines that are conducive to the rapid or gradual spread of democratic politics." So, over the long term, an original elite settlement in South Africa could conceivably evolve into a broader and deeper commitment to democracy.

FROM PACT TO SOCIAL CONTRACT

After the agreed-upon government of national unity and the elected constituent assembly are in place, a South African democracy could form that goes beyond a transitional power sharing pact and becomes a true social contract. A social contract in South Africa would consist of a new web of political institutions for the long term that guarantees basic human rights, reconciles majority rule with minority rights, ensures nondiscrimination and equality before the law, and promotes restitution and equal economic opportunity for the long-disenfranchised black majority. But a social contract in South Africa would consist not only of a new set of basic political rules through which conflict is to be managed and rights guaranteed, but also of new economic institutions and new and invigorated civil society interest groups that transcend the racial and ethnic divisions created or exacerbated by apartheid. Although such a social contract need not be fully democratic at the outset—a period of restricted democracy may be in store in order to contain fissiparous tendencies—it could ideally evolve into a deeper participatory democracy.

The antecedents to a South African social contract began to emerge as bargaining or brokerage institutions evolved out of the institutional choice preferences of the core moderate political actors themselves during the transition from apartheid to democracy. These institutions developed on several different "tracks."

The Political Track. New political institutions were negotiated by a core of moderate centrist parties, first to structure preliminary negotiation ("talks about talks") and eventually to negotiate the rules under which the new democracy would be negotiated. Negotiation on the political track culminated in the creation of the interim government of national unity and constituent assembly but also included, for example, new ad hoc institutions to manage local government, particularly in the metropoles.

The Economic Track. New economic institutions, such as the National Economic Forum described below, were created through which economic policy-making was increasingly codetermined by business, labor, and the state. In addition, numerous negotiation forums sprouted at the local level to address core socioeconomic issues.

The Peace Track. New structures for conflict resolution were developed to cope with political violence, including the institutions of the National Peace Accord but also the multiple efforts of nongovernmental organizations.

The Civil Society Track. Although a racially and culturally integrated and autonomous civil society did not spontaneously emerge during the transition (Shubane 1991)—which was in any event not a realistic probability, given the depth of divisions—a pattern of accommodation began to emerge. In myriad local and national forums, civil society groups formerly alienated from one another during apartheid began to pursue common interests.

The 1993 democratization pact represents the convergence point of the political track. More remarkable is the fact that on every track during the transition from apartheid, a nascent commitment to intergroup moderation and bargaining was born. A social contract in South Africa would further institutionalize in a postapartheid democracy the moderation on divisive racial and ethnic themes brought about by the centrist core of political actors that arose during the transition. It would also serve to protect the new moderation from the seemingly inevitable, sometimes violent, opposition of those whose interests were better served by the old order.

A social contract could be based on commitment to adhere to the newly constructed rules of the political game, not just on an entrenched power-sharing compromise reflected in the democratization pact. The contractors to a new South African democracy—political leaders and their parties and civil society organizations—must commit themselves to the newly created rules of the game the contract establishes in exchange for the protection of rights and fair distribution of benefits a democratic state can potentially provide. A basic commitment to the negotiated rules of the new democratic game lies at the heart of a social contract, rules that institutionalize the culture of negotiation that emerged in the transition.

A social contract in South Africa would not be easily identifiable: the contract itself would not be a tablet upon which the new rules would be etched in stone; on the contrary, a social contract reflects a breathing, living commitment to the regulation of conflict through ongoing bargaining and reciprocity within the nonviolent confines of the new democratic state. It can be measured however, by the extent to which the centripetal forces of moderation on deeply divisive themes such as race and ethnicity withstand the attempt of outbidders in their communities to arouse extremism and undermine intergroup moderation. Nor would it simply be manifested in a single document like a constitution; rather, it would be a multifaceted agreement in which bargaining institutions in the political arena are reinforced by ongoing bargaining in the economic and social arenas, and vice versa.

The basis of agreement is the willingness to harness and channel the inherently centrifugal tendencies of a divided society through the brokerage institutions of the democratic state. Negotiation would not end with a new social contract in South Africa, it would just begin. Intergroup bargaining would be organized and regulated by the basic compact to peacefully arbitrate conflict through democratic institutions.

Even if new and broadly legitimate institutions emerge, there is no guarantee they can be sustained. The long-term outcome for South Africa will not inevitably be a democracy. The best that even the right kinds of political institutions—"right" in the sense that they emanate from the South Africans' own choices and reflect a consensus on a fair outcome—can do is to provide South Africans a reasonable initial chance at building a lasting democracy. The next step is for democracy to be consolidated. The successful conclusion of a social contract is a first step toward a democracy, but it by no means guarantees its success. The president of the Institute for Multiparty Democracy, Oscar Dhlomo, summed up the difficulties that lie ahead, even if a social contract emerges from subsequent negotiation in a constituent assembly:

> At some stage a multiparty democratic system makes a transition from being introduced to that of being institutionalized. Only much later, and only under the most favorable conditions, does it become engraved. The first transition is important as it marks the state of the system becoming the norm rather than the exception. The second transition, however, is much more important. It is during this phase that a multiparty democracy and the political tolerance that must inevitably underpin it become internalized and engraved on the hearts and minds of the people. . . . At this stage, and only at this stage, can the country be judged to be safe for democracy.[1]

And, as Zwelakhe Sisulu, editor-in-chief of *New Nation,* said, the vigorous defense of party-independent interests in the time of transition has important implications for the prospects of democratic consolidation: "Ultimately the democratic future of our country will be determined by that broad sector of our society known as civil society. . . . The question of democracy is not something that should be held in trust for the people by political parties. It is something that the people themselves must prac-

---

[1] *South Africa Foundation Review,* February 1991.

tice on a daily basis, not only at election time."[2] Building a nascent civil society that transcends the particularism of political organization based on identity is precisely the challenge faced in divided societies. A strong civil society is also the key to building a strong, legitimate state (Migdal 1988; du Toit 1993). There was a deep and significant debate in South Africa over the nature of civil society and its role in a postapartheid state, particularly over whether the civic associations and street committees that blossomed during the popular upsurge of the late 1980s would form the nucleus of autonomous postapartheid interest groups (see, for example, the special issue of the journal *Theoria* [vol. 79, 1992]). This debate was significant in that it helped distinguish between the romanticism of the struggle and the realities of postapartheid governance (Friedman 1991b)—a true civil society has not yet formed in South Africa.

Moreover, South Africa will continue to face the problems that plague divided societies long after apartheid: identity politics exacerbated by politicians who seek to gain by mobilizing on divisive themes, by tapping and manipulating ethnic hatred and racial bigotry. The challenge of democratization in a divided society like South Africa's is to build a social web of autonomous civil society organizations that *transcends* the narrow politics of communalism, and is indeed strong enough to withstand the challenges from the forces of racial, ethnic, religious, and communal divisiveness and to defend the new democratic institutions against their onslaught. These integrated civil society organizations interact with the new state as they press their claims that cross-cut identity cleavages in society, thereby inducing moderate behavior by ensuring the predominance of these themes on the political agenda over those based on identity. Although in the initial period, accommodation between groups that reflect underlying social conditions may be enough to arrive at a social contract, for a divided society to evolve into a pluralist democracy, civil society must transcend ascriptive social cleavages. Moreover, as Shapiro (1993:149–50) suggests, civil institutions must become internally democratic for a strong democracy to emerge. Creating such a cross-cutting civil society makes a fully democratic social contract elusive but perhaps not impossible.

CONVERGENCE AND THE SOCIAL CONTRACT

As chapter 5 illustrates, there was already considerable convergence on a set of postapartheid political institutions in the preliminary negotiation phase. The disagreements were not over whether there should be a democracy, or whether there should be minority protection, propor-

[2] Interview with the author, 13 May 1991.

tionality, or even, in effect, coalition government. The dissensus was over exactly what kinds of political institutions would produce these effects and still give expression to the most important political imperative of the democratization process in South Africa after apartheid: meaningful enfranchisement of the long-disenfranchised majority. As Hermann Giliomee correctly observed, and as I noted in chapter 5, the institutional choices of the major political actors in South Africa in 1991 were a playoff between the National party's modified consociational preference, termed "amicable agreement," versus the ANC's choice for modified majoritarianism.[3] Ultimately, for the interim, compromises were found through a convergence of the parties' institutional choices, and for a transitional period, power would be shared in the immediate postapartheid system. But in the long term, the convergence point of the institutional choices would be closer to the Democratic party's 1991 choice for centripetalism, an agreement that I suggest requires more than simple compromise—it requires commitment.

The Nature of Convergence

Before explaining the logic of a democratic social contract and its institutional form as a possible longer-term outcome to South Africa's transition, I want to stress the *nature* of convergence in negotiation. The institutional choices of the major political parties, particularly the government and the ANC, converged because, having chosen the path of negotiation, these parties increasingly shared common interests. The most important interest they shared was the transformation of the conflict itself away from self-defeating, anarchic confrontation to a more stable set of rules, or institutions, through which to peacefully regulate their underlying and deep-rooted disagreement. The political leaders of these parties realized that they had a common interest in avoiding a worse outcome, in preventing a costly and bloody stalemate, a civil war, or simply a slide into anarchy.

They also shared a common interest in protecting themselves from the ethnic and racial outbidders on their flanks who opposed negotiation and sought political gain from the major parties' moderation. Moreover, there were mutual benefits to be had: moderation, particularly for the white minority government but also for the ANC, would pay increasing dividends. This common interest created the centripetal dynamic that brought the parties to the table and kept them negotiating despite recurrent crises and continuing bloodshed. Hennie Kotzé, based on his annual survey of elite attitudes during the transition in South Africa (Kotzé

[3] See his op-ed article in the *Cape Times*, 29 August 1991.

1992a, 1993), relates pressures for further pact making in transition to the convergence of "the systematically developing value consensus on important and substantial policy matters. However, one can still not talk about a consensually unified elite," he wrote in 1992, "because there has not been much progress on the path towards the structural integration of elites" (1993:11). In pursuing their own interests, particularly their interest in intergroup moderation, elites compromised—which implied that over time they would eventually arrive at an outcome they mutually perceived as fair. And it may portend a more integrated elite when the time of power sharing arrives.

The best example of the parties' arriving at a fair outcome in pursuing their own interests is the ANC's choice for a proportional representation electoral system, a proposal that eventually found its way into the interim constitution. Kader Asmal, of the ANC's Constitutional Committee, explained the basis of the party's choice for proportional representation. His response shows that it was based on the pursuit of the ANC's own interest in forging a peaceful solution to South Africa's conflict by making elections a potentially non-zero-sum game by fostering inclusivity: "The basic assumptions [about proportional representation] are both articulated and inarticulated. The articulated one is that it provides representivity. . . . The inarticulated assumption is that there are going to be coalitions in South Africa. . . . If a person wants reconstruction and change, it is certainly not in their interest to have a coalition. But for peace in South Africa, it is not an insignificant consideration."[4]

There are two contexts in which the concept of fairness is related to the nature of convergence in the negotiation on a postapartheid future. The first can be appropriately termed the *compromise context*. Throughout the course of the negotiation on the democratization pact, the parties made often very painful compromises in order to realize their overriding common interest, conclusion of a settlement. The terms of the compromise determined the nature of the fair outcome that flowed: the democratization pact provided parties *certain* guarantees that minorities' vital interests would be protected during the period of power sharing. In this context, the discovery of what constituted a fair set of interim political institutions was based on the *compromises* of the parties away from their first-preference institutional choices through subsequent preferences until their choices ultimately converged on the institutions established by the democratization pact.

What characterizes the compromise context of fairness most is that the outcome is one that occurs under conditions of relative *certainty:* the centrist parties, the government and ANC elites, fully expected the

---

[4] Interview with the author, 7 May 1991.

power-sharing mechanisms of the democratization pact to sufficiently protect their vital interests. After all, the pact was in essence a continuation of their preexisting negotiating relationship. In negotiating the pact, parties that expected to be minorities demanded and won such guarantees. The agreement of the major parties themselves to the settlement indicates their perception that it represents a set of arrangements all parties can perceive as fair: to compromise is to work out a solution considered fair by all parties that buy into the settlement. The 1993 democratization pact reflects the politics of compromise: it is a fairness scheme that makes a nonviolent resolution of disputes possible, harnessing or domesticating conflicts into the confines of a new web of political institutions. Fairness is a necessary rational condition of cooperation; thus, the interests of all parties are protected by fairness properties the democratization pact provides.

Agreement on a set of fair interim institutions that provides certain guarantees to parties may be a necessary condition for the transition to democracy, especially in divided societies, but perhaps not a sufficient one. Over time, fair institutions based solely on compromise are not stable because the relationships and expectations change under the new rules of the democratic game—the game's consequences cannot be fully appreciated. Horowitz (1985:580–88) has pointed out the pitfalls of "grand settlements" in divided societies: party interests and situations change dramatically, and often the original agreement is not sufficiently elastic to withstand the new strains it can generate. Friedman (1993:64) notes that longer-term power-sharing arrangements in South Africa contain a number of pitfalls—the most important one being that the ANC would be unlikely to carry its constituency in an indefinite power-sharing arrangement. MacDonald (1992), too, questions the fairness of power sharing in the South African context, arguing that it reifies contrived ethnic divisions and will result in the inability to affect meaningful socioeconomic change. For the ANC, this would not be a fair outcome to the negotiation; a more fluid set of institutions is required.

The second context in which fairness is related to the bargaining process is the *uncertainty* context. As the shadow of the future extends beyond the first election, so too does the realization that parties may win at times under the new rules of the game, and may lose at other times. Indeed, the essence of democratization is to commit to the inherent *uncertainty* of electoral competition. A democracy requires what O'Donnell and Schmitter refer to as "contingent consent" (1986:59), that is, agreement to continue to play by the new rules without guaranteed representation. Thus in the longer-term, political institutions as arenas for ongoing bargaining must be flexible and must be inherently fair under conditions of uncertainty. For reasons other than compromise, in the context of uncertainty, the pursuit of interests in negotiation can yield an outcome characterized by fairness. This has important ramifications for societies seeking to democratize in general, but especially for divided societies.

Because all political actors in South Africa are ultimately uncertain of how they may fare over the long term, they have a common interest in establishing a set of fair political institutions. This pursuit of fairness is linked not only to compromise, but to the uncertainties inherent in ushering in a new democracy. John Dugard outlined in 1991 the way institutional choices were made in South Africa's transition; they were rooted in uncertainty.

> The people are meeting behind a [Rawlsian] "veil of ignorance." They don't know what degree of support that they are likely to enjoy. . . . The ANC, Mandela, and members of the Constitutional Committee have consistently expressed themselves in Rawlsian terms. They cannot predict the outcome of the first elections, so they want to be sure that the constitution is one that is favorable to them should they become the opposition. That is the principle on which they work. And I suspect that is the principle on which the government is working.[5]

Although as the first election grew closer and the ANC's uncertainty—given public opinion polls—waned, its longer-term expectations remained uncertain. Under conditions of uncertainty, it is possible that all would eschew entrenched power sharing for the more flexible and fluid coalition-making properties that centripetal institutions can potentially offer. What implications does the nature of convergence in negotiation have on the prospects for a future democratic social contract?

The Logic of a Social Contract

A democratic social contract that creates centripetal institutions is a potential outcome to further negotiation in South Africa because it would represent a set of institutions in which all of the protagonists could potentially realize mutual gain. The first election is, after all, to a constituent assembly whose purpose is to establish a set of democratic institutions—within the confines of the democratization pact—that will be more-or-less permanent. It is these institutions especially that will be chosen under conditions of uncertainty if there is no prearranged power-sharing pact. What kinds of political institutions meet the criterion of fairness, given the variables that underlie the institutional choices of the major political actors and their compromises in negotiation?

In the South African context, fair institutions are those which reconcile

---

[5] Interview with the author, 13 May 1991.

the interests of minorities with the fundamental requisite of majority rule. Bargaining to create a set of fair political institutions—that is, *mutually perceived as fair*—in the historical, social, and economic context South Africa faces is exactly what the process of negotiation is all about. For parties representing the majority, the liberation movement, consent is contingent on the concrete expression of the principle of majority rule. Minority consent will only be forthcoming for a set of political institutions in which the voters of minorities count, in which minority influence is perceived to matter. And all negotiators must feel sufficiently protected from the extremist parties within their own identity groups that seek to outbid them for support. The political institutions that meet these demands—and which arise out of the pursuit of actual party interests—are not those of entrenched power sharing but of centripetalism.

The key to the convergence on centripetal institutions for South Africa lies in the uncertainty that accompanies bargaining on the new order. Chapter 3 illustrates the way in which uncertainty was at the core of rising violence during the transition. In this respect, uncertainty is dilatory to a settlement because of the increased violence and insecurity, making compromise difficult and the underlying reconciliation elusive. The pacts reached in 1990 and 1991, I argued, were specifically designed to reduce that uncertainty-related violence and to assure actors that their vital interests would be protected in the new order; these pacts did not sufficiently perform that task because uncertainty was linked to the transition itself. The 1993 democratization pact assured all parties that subscribed to it, and who cleared the representation thresholds in the election, of their survival into the new order.

Yet the uncertainty over whether a particular political party will enjoy electoral success well into the postapartheid future—beyond the liberation election—will remain rife. Indeed, for the centrist actors in South Africa, including the ANC, there remained a constant element of uncertainty about the outcome of subsequent elections. In the context of uncertainty the parties converged on institutions whose working properties were expected to favor them whether or not they emerged as the top vote getter in a future election. Parties and party interests will change dramatically in response to the incentive structure of the new political game. To prevent party fragmentation along deeply divisive race and ethnicity line, other cleavages, such as class, must be emphasized. If intergroup power sharing is the choice of one centrist party in contrast to the majoritarian choice of the other, the convergence point is centripetalism.

Political institutions with centripetal effects for postapartheid South Africa would be based on the premise that the core centrist actors bind together to protect themselves from ethnic and racial outbidders, but do so in a way that does not directly or indirectly mandate entrenched power sharing. The nature of convergence for a democratic future reveals the trend toward a compromise between the ANC's modified majoritarianism and the NP's modified consociationalism precisely because of the uncertainty that parties will be either part of a minority or majority coalition in a balanced-power relationship. As uncertainty about winning or losing in a new political order increases, centripetal institutions become more attractive.

A new social contract would not eradicate identity politics in South Africa's long-term postapartheid future—indeed, it would recognize and protect ethnic, linguistic, and religious rights through a bill of rights—but it would not make ethnicity the basis of the national identity. A new social contract would meet to the extent possible ethnic demands through the careful distribution of regional powers, for example, but it would not make ethnic representation the basis of intergroup interaction or of the boundaries for regionalism in the new state.

ELEMENTS OF A SOCIAL CONTRACT

A central tenet of a new social contract, if it can be reached, would be the eschewal of ethnicity as the basis for representation. The will to avoid the centrifugal forces that reinforce and perpetuate division in divided societies would be codified in a set of rules that acknowledge and build upon the interdependence the parties discovered in the course of arriving at a stalemate and negotiating a mutually beneficial democratization pact. A new South African social contract would be above all a repudiation of the politics of race and ethnic nationalism and an affirmation of the new-found interest in forging nonracial and nonethnic political coalitions based on interest. Professor John Dugard, of the University of the Witwatersrand, wrote: "A post-apartheid constitution may well contain checks and balances aimed at decentralizing power, securing fair representation for minority political groups, and protecting individual liberties. But it seems clear that this will have to be achieved without any express acknowledgment of ethnicity. The memory of apartheid will ensure a new constitution is free from the taint of racism" (1990b:371).

A Bill of Rights

The ultimate instrument of convergence arising out of the institutional choices of the political parties in South Africa is the bill of rights. Every political party in South Africa that ascribed to the concept of a single nation also expressed its support for a bill of rights. Despite the adoption of the Freedom Charter in 1955 and earlier ANC calls for fundamental human rights in resistance to apartheid, a dialogue on a postapartheid bill of rights began fairly late. When in 1986 the minister of justice called upon the establishment Law Commission to conduct a study, the regime's opponents were skeptical, interpreting the concern with a bill of rights in South Africa as yet another government attempt to hold on to the reins of apartheid while giving the appearance of fundamental change. But when the ANC released its 1988 Constitutional Guidelines, it, too, began to carefully consider its conception of a bill of rights; in late 1990, the ANC published a working draft.

Although there was wide-ranging consensus on the need for a bill of rights, there was dissensus over what it should contain and what its aims should be. From the perspective of the government, the bill of rights was primarily seen as an instrument designed to protect individuals and minorities in a new order from a possible tyranny of the majority. From the perspective of the liberation struggle, the bill of rights would be a tool of empowerment and a weapon with which to eradicate the vestiges of apartheid. There were two critical debates within the overall discussion of a future bill of rights for South Africa that deserve special attention. The first is the issue of minority rights expressed as group rights, and the second is the inclusion of so-called second- and third-generation rights in a future charter. These debates revealed the differing perceptions of a bill of rights that the actors brought to the table: protection versus empowerment. (A third important arena of debate, the economic implications of the bill of rights, is discussed below.) Before honing in on the disagreements, however, I should point out that there was complete agreement among centrist parties that a bill of rights would include the common civil and political rights enumerated in the body of international human rights law.[6]

The Law Commission charged by the government to investigate the feasibility of a bill of rights was widely expected to produce a report favorable to the government's then-stated policy of explicit ethnic group protection in a bill of rights. When the commission published its report in March 1989, there was considerable disappointment in government circles. The report concluded that what the government had conceived of primarily in terms of group rights—culture, language, religion, home-language education—were justiciable only as individual rights.[7] The ANC also argued firmly that minority rights should be protected as indi-

---

[6] See Dugard 1990a and 1990b for a discussion of the application of civil and political rights to South Africa and their relationship to international norms.

[7] As Dugard pointed out, the commission found that South African law did not recognize racial or ethnic groups as personae with legal standing; thus, the commission argued that "the only way to protect cultural, religious and linguistic interests in a bill of rights is by recognizing these interests as rights, and empowering any individual to protect these interests or rights in a court proceeding" (1990b:375).

vidual, not group, rights. Although in its draft bill of rights the ANC specifically provided for minority cultural, linguistic, and religious rights, these rights belong to individuals, not groups. Indeed, in article 1 of the draft, the ANC proposed a general provision to state: "No individual or group shall receive privileges or be subjected to discrimination, or domination on the grounds of race, color, language, gender, creed, political or other opinion, birth or other status."[8] The vague reference to a group should not be interpreted to mean that the ANC would concede the group-rights issue. Kader Asmal (1991:10) wrote: "An attempt to create or instill unity is consistent with a recognition of diversity. Recognition of the basic human rights of individuals is the only way to aspire to, if not guarantee, such diversity."

Precisely because of the Law Commission's report and the ANC's rejection of the group-rights concept in a bill of rights, the debate lapsed. Minister of constitutional development Gerrit Viljoen said in late 1990 that "the NP intends on negotiating a safeguard to ensure that the Bill of Human Rights cannot be arbitrarily abolished or changed. What the bill cannot however ensure is political group rights and it is to the constitution itself that we look for these safeguards."[9]

A second area of debate concerning a new bill of rights concerns so-called second-generation rights, such as the rights to education, housing, nutrition, and employment; and third-generation rights, dealing primarily with development, peace, and a clean environment. The debate was this: the NP (and the DP), while not opposing the intent of such statements, opposed their incorporation in a bill of rights, while the ANC favored their adoption. Following the pattern elsewhere, advocates of including these rights argued that without them, the extension of political rights is of limited value. Opponents argued that they are nonjusticiable.

Perhaps the strongest proponent of the inclusion of second- and third-generation rights in a new South African bill of rights was ANC Constitutional Committee member Albie Sachs (1990, 1989). He argued that socioeconomic and developmental rights are based in the view that the limitation of a bill of rights to mere civil and political rights is archaic at best, reactionary at worst. University of Durban-Westville law professor Vinodh Jaichand reiterated the point. "The whole notion of a rights culture falls away if we don't address the basic problems of education or housing. . . . It means little or nothing at all."[10] A key element in the ANC's choice for a bill of rights would therefore be the advocacy of second- and third-generation rights.

[8] "A Bill of Rights for South Africa," 1990.
[9] 27 September 1990, Office of Constitutional Development and Planning, mimeo.
[10] Interview with the author, 22 May 1991.

An important critic of the inclusion of second- and third-generation rights in a new bill of rights was one of South Africa's foremost liberal judges, Justice J. M. Didcott. "A bill of rights is not a political manifesto, a political program. Primarily, it is a protective device. It is a shield, in other words, rather than a sword. It can state effectively and quite easily what may not be done. It cannot stipulate, with equal ease of effectiveness, what shall be done. The reason is not only that the courts, its enforcers, lack the expertise and infrastructure to get into the business of legislation or administration. It is also, and more tellingly, that they cannot raise the money."[11]

The ANC was aware that such rights would not be accorded the same status in a new constitution as civil and political rights. The ANC's 1991 constitutional policy document advocates second- and third generation rights but says only that they should be given "appropriate constitutional expression." The organization looked to the 1990 Namibian Constitution, in which constitutional negotiators agreed to append a "Directives of State Policy" provision that commits the state to the aims of second- and third-generation rights, but did not make state action, or more likely lack of it, justiciable.[12] Nonetheless, postapartheid economic issues *would* be included as provisions in a new constitution. For both the defenders of the status quo and seekers of dramatic redistribution, political economy issues were important elements of their institutional choices. Kader Asmal, of the ANC Constitutional Committee, wrote that "the effects of racial discrimination and inequality must be overcome by constitutional provisions for corrective action which guarantees a rapid and irreversible redistribution of wealth" (1991:9).

This left the debate on the bill of rights to focus on defining four basic areas: affirmative action, property rights, labor relations, and enforcement.[13] On affirmative action, a critical question for divided societies, Mandela said before a May 1991 ANC conference on the bill of rights: "Affirmative action is not a threat to either standards or individuals. It is an internationally recognized mechanism of redressing past wrongs

[11] Cited in Dugard 1990b:378.

[12] Constitution of the Republic of Namibia, chap. 11, art. 95–101. Note that such principles are not legally enforceable by the judiciary, but "shall nonetheless guide the government in making and applying laws to give effect to the fundamental objectives" (art. 101) set out in them. The Namibian Directives of State Policy follow in the tradition of the Indian constitution.

[13] The most significant means of enforcement, in the short and medium term, will be the constitutional court established in the democratization pact. Although it will take years, indeed decades, to construct an integrated judiciary and judicial system through which a bill of rights can be fully and fairly enforced, the constitutional court—starting at the top—will be a critical nucleus around which to build.

which have become part of the very structure and assumptions of our society. To reject this mechanism is to accept the status quo and to ensure that the fruits of war, colonialism, racism, sexism, and oppression continue to be nurtured in our society."[14] Policies of affirmative action would be essential in rectifying the wrongs of apartheid. Affirmative action would be an important component of a new South African bill of rights because it can lead to positive-sum outcomes: as the lesser advantaged of the population become more skilled and competent, everyone can potentially gain. Affirmative action will inevitably cause friction in the short and intermediate term. But without it, social progress is unlikely.

The convergence on the bill of rights because of its fairness properties is best illustrated by emphasizing that the actors view the purpose of a bill differently. The ANC viewed the bill of rights as a radical document that would serve to empower those whose rights have long been violated. The National party, on the other had, saw the bill of rights as a limiting document, one that would protect minority political and, above all, property rights into the future. Despite the dissensus about its purpose, the actors converged on this institution because it fits into each of their perceptions of what is ultimately fair. A bill of rights can be simultaneously a radical and restrictive institution. All sides were aware of the unhappy past from which they sought to escape. Precisely because a social contract requires individual consent, not the consent of groups per se, it is only appropriate that the most important element of the social contract is a guaranteed floor of basic political rights that apply equally for all individuals. It is therefore not surprising that a bill of rights is the most important aspect of a new South African social contract, and the aspect of a postapartheid democracy on which the widest range of parties agreed. Achieving the broadest possible individual consent for the new order is a continual challenge. As Friedman perceptively notes, "In our society, the unpalatable but real possibility is that a social contract will require and receive the support of strong, organized interests but not of unorganized individuals, whose consent will not be required as long as they cannot mobilize against the contract. That could produce a stable society but at most a limited democracy in which participation would be enjoyed by parts of the society."[15] Precisely for this reason a fully democratic social contract will remain elusive in the short-run—a deepening of it can come only over time.

[14] For a summary of the ANC's debate on a bill of rights, see "A Bill of Rights for a Democratic South Africa," May 1991, Papers and reports of a Conference Convened by the ANC Constitutional Committee. Asmal (1992) puts the ANC's bill of rights claims in the context of reparations and reconciliation.

[15] Correspondence with the author, 4 January 1994.

Majority Rule, Minority Influence

Rather than providing concrete assurances for minority protection, through, for example, a statutory minority veto, a new South African social contract would have as a primary feature a set of institutions that gives minorities influence. That is, there would be no specific guarantees for minority representation on ethnic or racial lines, but rather a set of institutions that makes the cooperation of minorities essential in effective majority rule governance. Because the National party for so many years emphasized the need for special ethnic protection, and ethnicity is perceived of by those in the liberation struggle as condoning the gist of apartheid, the counterreaction by the liberation movement works against specific minority group protection. It was the recognition of the fact that the ANC rejects such representation that led the NP to drop its insistence on constitutionally entrenched group rights.

Rather, the National party, as its institutional choices reflect, learned that constitutionally entrenched representation is neither sufficient protection for minorities nor the right kind. From the transitions from white minority rule in Zimbabwe and Namibia, the lesson has hit home to South African whites that if minority views are to be sufficiently protected, it is better to forge nonracial alliances than to insist on explicit white minority protection. Zimbabwean whites opted for statutory race-group representation; the Namibians did not. In December 1991, Mandela raised the "Zimbabwe option" as a possible compromise in South Africa.[16] But from the Zimbabwean settlement, whites learned that specifically reserved minority seats are illusory protection. In Namibia, however, whites learned that if minorities worked on an interest basis rather than on a racial or ethnic basis—that is, if they forged alliances based on common positions on specific policy issues, not on color—minorities could exert influence in postindependence politics. Interest-based coalitions —such as class alliances—offer greater security than communally based political organization. This is true despite the fact that at the local level, racial representation was effectively entrenched in the interim constitution.

If the white minority is to matter in politics in a postapartheid South Africa, they must realize that it is actually counter to their minority interest to advocate specific ascriptively based protection. The ANC's Albie Sachs has said: "The worst whites can do, from their own point of view, is continue insisting on their whiteness. . . . Even from a purely selfish, white point of view, they should think again and see that it is very much in their interests to have a political system with special guarantees that apply equally across the board, so that any attack on any point of view

---

[16] See the interview in the *Sunday Star*, 29 December 1991.

threatens everybody."[17] Further, there is a growing realization that it is incorrect to see minorities in South Africa solely in ethnic or racial terms. Schlemmer (1990:25) points out that a more appropriate concept of minorities in South Africa is that of a wide range of "political minorities" based on "needs and interests." Although the white right, the IFP, and other homeland leaders have championed minority rights in ethnic or racial terms, Schlemmer points to several examples of minority interests based not on ethnic or racial criteria but on specific economic interests: large commercial farmers who produce much of the country's food; farmworkers and subsistence farmers; owners of small businesses; professionals; and the unemployed. Minorities of many types in South Africa will matter well into the future because any postapartheid government will require their cooperation for the successful implementation of policy of national reconstruction and reconciliation. The majority and minorities are interdependent to the degree where explicitly acknowledged minority status on ethnic or racial terms could be a barrier to cooperation in divided societies such as South Africa.

The National party realized that the design of new democratic political institutions posed both a risk and an opportunity. The party's institutional choices reflected its position that perceived mandated power sharing was required, for the remainder of the transition at least, and the NP successfully persuaded the ANC to incorporate this view into a transitional government of national unity. But it also knows that it must be prepared to concede some of the more rigid aspects of its plan in deliberations over a postapartheid future. Party strategy in the transition revealed the NP's underlying belief that they are working toward a coalition arrangement in which minority protection may well be not only unnecessary but *undesirable*. As the party actively readjusted to the postapartheid realities by eschewing its racial image and recruiting among other minority communities, it revealed its underlying belief that its real interests lay in forging a significantly large coalition to make minority views count—in a potentially majority coalition. This requires greater fluidity than an entrenched minority veto allows. Steven Friedman writes that "the minority would not have the right to share in government—but it would have enough power to prevent the majority from changing the rules of the game. . . . If the majority has to rely—wholly or in part—on the minority to carry out its will, it will hesitate to take decisions that the minority finds entirely repugnant. . . . The effect could be a balance of power between the majority and the minority that would make a settlement, and progress toward a stable democracy, a strong possibility."[18]

---

[17] *New Nation,* 27 April 1990.
[18] *South Africa Foundation Review,* August 1990.

Protection of the Emergent Center

The patterns of politics in South Africa shifted greatly in the process of transition. Political parties transformed themselves to adjust to the political environment unfolding before them. As institutional choices of the political parties converged on a settlement, they developed a common interest in creating a new purpose, which is, implicitly, to create a system that pulls toward moderation rather than polarization.

The key to the protection of the moderate center is the electoral system. Choosing an electoral system for postapartheid South Africa was a critically important task for South Africa's parties, precisely because speculation on how they would possibly fare under various electoral systems was rife with uncertainty, and the outcome was unpredictable. How could the principle of "one person, one vote, one value" be appropriately manifested, given the conditions in South Africa's deeply divided society? Different electoral systems produce different effects, and electoral system choices reflect the party's preference for the kinds of effects the electoral system is expected to produce. Clearly the National party wanted a voting system that would give it sufficient representation in parliament to frustrate, even veto, policies of the anticipated ANC-led majority. The ANC wanted a system that would give meaning to the concept of majority rule. The DP, as noted in chapter 4, chose a system that was expected to produce a centripetal spin to the political system.

There are essentially three broad sets of electoral systems that were considered for voting in a future South Africa.[19] Most observers agreed that the effects the previous first-past-the-post electoral system in South Africa produced are not the kind of effects that a future system should promote. South Africans know well the potential vote/seat share distortions this system can produce: in 1948 and 1989 the National party captured a majority of the seats in parliament with minority support among the white electorate.[20] The ANC rejected first-past-the-post for several reasons, most important among them the potential problems of constituency delimitation and gerrymandering, given the racially based settlement patterns that are the legacy of apartheid's Group Areas Act.

All of the centrist political parties eventually expressed a preference that the electoral system produce proportionality in the allocation of seats from votes (the IFP briefly flirted with a constituency system). Propor-

[19] The best and most extensive scholarly research conducted on a postapartheid electoral system was done by Kotzé (1992b) and Reynolds (1993).

[20] The greatest vote/seat ratio disparity in favor of the NP was the 1981 election, in which the party won 59 percent of the white vote but received 79.5 percent of the seats in parliament. The small, extremist Herstigte Nationale party (or reconstituted National party) won nearly 15 percent of the votes in the 1981 election and received no seats at all.

tionality, it is universally argued, faithfully transfers the number of votes received in the balloting directly into seats in parliament. The advantages are that no votes are "wasted" (i.e., votes for candidates that lose), minority parties are assured of representation commensurate with their vote share, and, according to Lijphart (1990b:10), segments of a divided society can "define themselves" by representation that is not *predetermined* through statutory group recognition.

Among scholars, Lijphart (1991, 1990b; 1987) was the most consistent advocate for a form of party list PR for South Africa. Lists can be either closed, in which the enumeration of candidates on the list is fixed by the party and unalterable by the voters, or open, flexible or free, in which the voters can in some way alter the orderings of candidates (Taagepera and Shugart 1989:24–25).[21] Such systems, according to Lijphart, provide the most direct vote/seat ratio; are immune to gerrymandering; allow for delimitation of constituencies when desirable; and permit some degree of intraparty competition (through open or free lists). In this view, PR can lead to a system of mutually interdependent parties, which in turn promotes cabinet durability. Most important, the incentive structure of PR can lead to proliferation of political parties, so it is conducive to coalition forming and "consensus" government. For these reasons, Lijphart specifically argued for "list proportional representation in relatively large districts . . . to maximize proportionality" (1987:8).

Despite the overall consensus among centrist parties in South Africa on proportionality, and on "proportional representation" as such, several general problems associated with list PR were raised. The first criticism, a common one, is that a proliferation of small parties invites ethnic political leaders to mobilize around narrow themes (Sartori 1966).[22] The second problem is more directly applied to divided societies. Because PR list voting can often be a "census" of communities in conflict (its advocates consider this attribute positive), the representation of divided social segments by segmental political parties serves to consolidate and perpetu-

---

[21] In a flexible list, voters choose different parties but may alter the ordering of the list; in an open list, the voter can choose among candidates on the lists of different parties, a system that effectively allows voting for more than one party; in a free list, the party does not order its lists at all, and each voter has one vote in a multimember constituency. See the range of essays in Lijphart and Grofman (1986, esp. pts. 1 and 2) for a discussion of the varieties of PR and PR list systems.

[22] In simple party-list proportional representation, small parties tend to hold the balance of power, effectively determining when governing coalitions come and go, leading to chronic instability, not durability. South African parties have recognized the potential for party system fragmentation under PR list, and have sought to limit this with a threshold below which a small party would not be represented. The ANC and DP initially called for a 5 percent threshold, and the NP notes the need for one but does not specify a particular figure.

ate divisions in society (Tsebelis 1990b). To maximize their vote share, party leaders have incentives to appeal to narrow, segmental themes.[23]

In South Africa, those who oppose fixed party lists argue that this feature sacrifices accountability and choice. As analyst Helen Zille said, party lists amount to "jobs for the boys."[24] The strong role of political parties in a simple fixed list system of PR can effectively limit the ability of the average voter to express specific preferences on intraparty debate. A voter can choose only the party and must disregard the differing stances individuals on the party list take. Nevertheless, other forms of list representation—flexible, open, and free lists—require not only a great deal of voter discretion but also voter sophistication; they are more complex systems, not very conducive to South African conditions of underdevelopment, poverty, and illiteracy. This criticism of nonfixed party lists was also waged against the third broad set of electoral systems considered for South Africa, subsequent preference voting.[25]

The two major types of subsequent preference voting procedures are the single transferable vote (STV) and the alternative vote (AV). While the former is generally classified as a proportional system and the latter as a majoritarian system (as opposed to a plurality system), they were generally grouped together for analysis in the South African context because a primary objection to them (but by no means the only objection) by many political actors was based on the complexity inherent in voter specification of subsequent preferences.[26] Specifying subsequent preferences is argued to be a concept impossibly complicated for a highly illiterate electorate, and the transferability of votes such systems require is thought to be nearly impossible to explain.

Horowitz (1991:163–203) laid out a lengthy argument for alternative voting (AV) for South Africa, which is in stark contrast to the Lijphart prescription for PR list and parliamentary government mentioned above. Horowitz favors preference voting, and AV in particular, because of the incentives such a system is argued to provide for political leaders as they woo the second or third (or more) preference votes of those beyond their communal group. He argues that the "incentive to compromise" (1991:171) in AV has greater conflict-reducing effects than the propensity

[23] These two arguments are briefly considered in Bertus de Villiers, n.d. "An Electoral System for the New South Africa," mimeo.

[24] Interview with the author, 3 April 1991.

[25] A 1986 survey by the Human Sciences Research Council found that 55 percent of Africans over age twenty were illiterate (using a Standard 3 criteria), while the proportions of illiteracy for Coloureds, Indians, and whites were 32 percent, 20 percent, and 3 percent, respectively (Cooper et al. 1990:850).

[26] Other objections include the problems of constituency delimitation, tactical voting, and less direct proportionality in the vote/seat ratio.

to coalesce inherent in PR. The latter coalitions (based on seat pooling) are simply convenient, whereas the former (based on vote pooling) are argued to reflect coalitions of commitment (Horowitz 1985:365–95).[27] AV is suggested as the best alternative for South Africa precisely because it combines majoritarianism with proportionality effects.

Several objections were raised to subsequent preference voting systems (both AV and STV) by scholars and South African political actors, but by far the most common one is the degree of complication in voting and in tabulation.[28] Legal scholar John Dugard said: "The alternative [preference] systems are very complicated, and I think we have to accept that we have a very backward constituency, and I am not referring to the black constituency only, but the whole nation. The party list system is much easier to explain."[29] Neither AV nor STV prevailed as the consensus choice of centrist South African political parties for the first election. A complex voting system, given South Africa's lack of experience with democracy, particularly for the liberation movements, had too great a potential for unpredicatable consequences.

Formal theorists have shown that no electoral system can be judged to be ultimately "fair," if by fair it is meant that the preferences of the voters are unfailingly translated into consistent electoral outcomes (Arrow 1963). Thus, electoral systems are chosen on the basis of the effects they are expected to produce. As van zyl Slabbert and Welsh (1979:148) noted more than a decade ago, the key to the safeguard of minority interests in South Africa is to allow for not just minority representation, but for minority influence: require politicians, in order to get elected, to appeal to the interests of those minorities across ethnic and racial divides within the framework of their majority platforms. This is a tall order, indeed. In the democratization pact, the centrist political parties in South Africa converged on the principle of proportionality in an electoral system, and the

[27] Interestingly, Horowitz argues for AV, a majoritarian system with some proportionality effects, over the single transferable vote (STV), a form of PR in which voters choose individual candidates in rank order according to their preferences. Horowitz does indeed like the preference voting nature of STV—although he argues that AV is better—but writes "if the choice for a divided society is between list-system PR and the single transferable vote, STV is a far better choice than list-system PR" (1991:173–74).

[27] The most penetrating scholarly critique is Lijphart's (1991), who argues that Horowitz's call for AV runs counter to the "scholarly consensus." Lijphart criticizes several aspects of AV as proposed by Horowitz, specifically: the incentive to compromise is really an incentive toward unstable "coalitions of convenience"; AV is not qualitatively different than first-past-the-post elections or majority runoffs, and can even be worse under certain conditions; AV cannot produce sufficient party proliferation for proportionality; AV's disproportionality is especially dangerous in multimember districts; and that "unlike PR, AV makes it difficult for a minority to be represented by members of its own group."

[29] Interview with the author, 13 May 1993.

system chosen included representation from regional as well as national lists.

What were the effects such a system was expected to produce? The ANC's Kader Asmal (1990:5) wrote: "An electoral system for South Africa should develop national thinking, instill the practice of anti-racist behavior and the acquisition of genuinely shared patriotic consciousness. To encourage these basic values, an electoral system must encourage cohesiveness rather than parochialism, [centripetal] rather than fissiparous tendencies, unity over narrowness in behavior." The most informative test of South Africa's electoral system choice will be South Africa's first nonracial elections, when this system will be put to the test. Will it induce moderation?

The heterogeneous distribution of the South African population means that regions delineated on economic development lines, not on imprecise ethnic boundaries, will inevitably contain significant minorities. Because of the link to heterogeneous constituencies (and combined with a representation threshold), proportionality can be attained because there may also be an incentive for parties to put up lists that appeal broadly to voters in majority and minority groups. For a party competing in a constituency that is highly heterogeneous, its electoral interests suggest that it proffer a party list that generally reflects the array of interests in the constituency. Broad-based, moderate appeals become a response to the incentive structure of the electoral system that arises out of the institutional choices of the centrist parties themselves. DP coleader Zach de Beer sums up the incentive calculation that politicians would have under the application of this electoral system in South Africa: "I would be proud in a new South Africa to be part of a ticket which had to have a Xhosa, a Mohammedan, an Indian and a Cape Coloured."[30] Thus, a PR system like the one adopted for the constituent assembly could in fact result in interethnic vote pooling of the type Horowitz advocated for South Africa (1991:163). And, if parties take advantage of the provision in the Electoral Act that allows for interparty pacts (known as *appartement*), further vote pooling could occur.

The convergence on combined national/regional list PR was predicated on the assumption that subsequent preference schemes such as those advocated by Horowitz are simply too complicated, and that PR systems can achieve a similar effect. Yet complexity is not the only argument that has been levied against alternative voting in the South African context. The ANC opposed it, for example, because it would not serve its interests in terms of institutional choice; alternative preference voting was per-

---

[30] Interview with the author, 27 March 1991.

ceived, in practice, as potentially unfair. Asmal (1990:6) wrote: "I fear that the real reason this system is being proposed for South Africa is that it will encourage anti-ANC parties by ensuring that the transfer of votes between anti-ANC alliances will outweigh the initial and major first preferences for the ANC."

Following up on these written remarks, Asmal said in an interview:

In the South African situation, in the alternative vote you are supposed to have a contest within the party, [but] . . . we would see constituencies [and] parties being torn apart. Within parties, sectarianism of a political, religious, and cultural nature [would occur]. That is the nature of the beast. With the list system, you can have internal coalitions and representation of certain convivialities, so the ANC—if it has sense—could have an Afrikaner white high up on the list, have an English-speaking white high on the list, a Muslim Indian high on the list, a Hindu Indian high on the list, women very high on the list; that allows for representation by people who are representing particular groups in a party. So you don't have a party of your own representing a social, cultural, or ethnic group.[31]

The convergence on PR in the South African setting is an outcome that can provide the same general effects Horowitz prescribes—namely, creating a centripetal pull to the political system—albeit not with the electoral system he proposes. Parties respond to the incentives of the electoral system by offering party lists that appeal across racial and ethnic cleavages. Proportionality is achieved across the party spectrum and down the list. List system PR evolved out of the choices of the actors themselves, who opted to create a system with centripetal effects. The problem with PR is, of course, the potential for fragmentation of the party system. South African constitutional designers realize that no electoral system can meet all desiderata simultaneously. With a higher threshold for representation in subsequent elections—as high as 7 percent—PR's tendency to fragment the party system could be mitigated.

While the electoral system is an important aspect of convergence arising out of institutional choices, the entire political system as a whole establishes a set of rules that will provide incentives for the minorities' views to make a difference in the context of majority rule. Indeed, in postwar Germany, it was not an "electoral miracle" that led to moderate politics, but as Kaase writes, "it was the unique interaction of factors, including the electoral law, that can be held responsible for the outcome of a stable three-party system without grave socio-political antagonisms" (1986:164).

[31] Interview with the author, 7 May 1991.

Nonethnic Federalism

No issue divided the political parties in the course of negotiation more than the degree of powers, if any, to be devolved to local and regional governments. It was not an arcane debate: grand apartheid had created a host of political fiefdoms from which power will continue to be pursued in the postapartheid era. The centralization/decentralization debate took place in the context of the litany of failed structures of successive apartheid governments: the homeland system, regional services councils, and the immensely discredited black local authorities. It also took place against the backdrop of the highly centralized political structures that evolved out of the government's need for repressive control, particularly during the reform apartheid era. The demands for ethnic territorial autonomy from power holders in the system, such as the right wing and the homeland governments, generated a strong centrifugal undercurrent in the debate over the unity of the state versus regional and local autonomy.

The central question at the heart of the centralization/decentralization debate in South Africa was whether regional and local government powers should be delegated and revocable by the central government but not entrenched in the constitution-making process, or whether they should be irrevocably devolved; that is, whether there should be original powers, the hallmark of a federal state. Those in the liberation movement initially argued for a highly centralized state. Dullah Omar of the ANC Constitutional Committee sums up the reasoning for the organization's long-held preference for centralization of power: "For economic and social transformation to take place—for education, housing, and the important question of land—there will have to be central policies from a central parliament which has authority and power. . . . We cannot have a weak and toothless central parliament."[32]

The objection to federalism in a future state entailed the rejection of the racially and ethnically based administrative boundaries of grand apartheid. The independent and nonindependent homelands, which were based on contrived perceptions of ethnic homogeneity, were rejected as the potential boundaries for a future federation—a long-held tenet of the liberation struggle. The potential for the homelands to form the building blocks of a federation was also severely limited by their underdeveloped condition and lack of economic integrity. Despite the years of development aid, poverty and human suffering became synonymous with life in the homelands. Given the failure of grand apartheid, the issue of whether the independent homelands (the TBVC states) and the self-governing states would be eventually reincorporated was not in dispute among the major parties, although homeland despots predictably clung to power.

[32] Interview with the author, 10 April 1991.

The IFP's fear of an ANC-dominated strong central authority was a primary motive behind its choice for "devolution, downward and outward." System parties favored federalism as a vehicle that protects regionalized interests by checking the power of the central state.

Some independent analysts, such as Gerhard Erasmus of the University of Stellenbosch, have favored a federal solution as a conflict-regulating device.[33] Erasmus's argument is representative of a mainstream view among constitutional specialists on the centralization/decentralization issue. He predicated his preference for federalism on two conditions: first, that the geographic contours of such a federation be drawn anew; and second, that the legitimately elected central government would not be hampered in its ability to effectively govern. But given these conditions, proponents of federalism argue that it diffuses conflicts, particularly those which find their origins in communal disputes. As long as it would not hamper the twin goals of economic reconstruction and nation building, the federal alternative might be beneficial because it could assuage minority concerns by decentralizing decision making, thus possibly reducing conflict. Ethnic and racial minorities could exercise some power in lower tiers of government as long as these centrifugal forces did not overwhelm the overall centripetal pull of the larger South African society. Regions could be gerrymandered to ensure ethnic or racial minority influence when these forces have the power to win it, but boundaries would not be demarcated in efforts to achieve ethnic homogeneity. Ethnic homogeneity would in effect give credence to claims for group territorial self-determination, which was, after all, a central tenet of grand apartheid.

In a divided society such as South Africa, the possible centralization or decentralization of power in a new state immediately brings forth central questions: Will the creation of a system in which there is a territorial division of power assist in conflict regulation, or will it exacerbate conflict by encouraging centrifugal tendencies? Will concession to those demanding territorial autonomy inevitably result in secessionist tendencies? Can a system of elected regional and local governments effectively reconcile the goals of unity and the recognition of diversity? The most important yardstick of a federal system is whether the constitution itself defines a fixed pattern of shared powers among various tiers of government. How explicit would be the new rules of the political game in determining the horizontal distribution of power? What powers would be overriding, concurrent, or original?

These questions boil down to the question of whether the institutional choice preferences of system actors for decentralized power and the struggle actors' preferences for a centralized state were reconcilable. The

[33] Interview with the author, 6 March 1991.

principal ethnic and racial minorities, the IFP and white right wing, had the power to effectively win substantial original powers for the territory in which they were associated, and the ANC—pursuing the politics of moderation and inclusion in pursuit of its basic interests in peace—relented. Despite sharply different aims and different preferences for the degree of centralization and decentralization in a new state, the institutional choices of the major political actors converged on regionalism (as defined in the terms of the constitutional principles of the 1993 democratization pact) as one of the most entrenched features of the new order. Federalism was a natural compromise position between the choice for a unitary state by the ANC and for the confederal system by some homeland and right-wing leaders. Both independence and interdependence characterize relationships between central and regional governments in a federal system (Bogdanor 1987:229), a fact that could allow for conflict management in South Africa, but that equally could be a source of new tensions in the postapartheid era. Thus the structure of devolution in postapartheid institutions will be critical: it must ensure that the leeway afforded to regional governments does not provide incentives for secession or allow for residual "pockets of apartheid."

In the wake of the polarized politics of apartheid, a common interest in deracializing the state emerged, which avoided the politics of ethnicity and reinforced the small core of moderation that arose in this deeply divided society. Beginning with the democratization pact, and perhaps fully realized by a new set of political institutions, the politics of extremism could be delinked from the state through a set of institutions chosen precisely because they had the effect of promoting a political system that rewards moderation. In the wake of an exclusive, unilaterally dictated political system, the parties converged on a system that is fundamentally inclusive and incorporates codetermined decision making. Most important, this was achieved on the basis of consent grounded in the interests of the moderates parties, who began to discover, in pursuit of their goals, what constitutes fairness in their own milieu.

An Economic Compact

While the political institutions of a postapartheid social contract would reflect the common aim of consolidating and protecting an emergent moderate center, a social contract would also regularize interaction between new political institutions and civil society as a whole, particularly those civil society actors organized around specific economic interests. Political institutions, I argued in chapter 1, have specific distribution effects; political power is distributed, but so, too, are public goods. An agreement over political institutions and an overall accord on the generation and appropriate distribution of wealth are intricately intertwined. A postapartheid South Africa will face conditions of scarcity, as development demands overtake the ability of the economy and state to improve the quality of life. New institutions are critical because, as Rothchild and Curry write, they "[enable] the elite to manage the strains emanating from the environment . . . by [fostering] opportunities for public choice" (1978:38).

Much as the political parties did in the course of South Africa's transition, both the largest employer federation, the South African Chamber of Business (SACOB), and the major trade union federation, COSATU, put forth detailed proposals related to a future South African constitution prior to the onset of formal negotiation. Distinct from the platforms of the political parties, these manifestos demonstrated the political economy considerations of institutional choice. These civil society actors realized that their interests could well be bypassed by political parties pursuing political power aims, and so they sought to tie their interests to the political bargain by formulating their own institutional choices. The vast differences over economic policy that existed between business and labor, which were also reflected in the economic policies of the NP, ANC, and other political parties, were nowhere more evident than in the debate over the role of the constitution in shaping the postapartheid economy.

Both SACOB and COSATU sought to entrench in a new constitution broad guidelines of future economic policy and measures to regulate or enable the redistribution of wealth. Frederick van zyl Slabbert explains why the NP, with its close links to business, was adamant on the issue of private property rights: "The government will seek as far as possible to entrench key economic issues in a new constitution, for example, market-related compensation for property confiscation. The government will concede the principle that the state has the right to confiscate property, for example, for building roads, but compensation must be market related. This is one of the main concerns amongst whites."[34] The NP expected that a market-related compensation requirement in the constitution would make redistributive policies more difficult to implement. Conversely, the aim of the ANC was to ensure that policies it believed necessary for socioeconomic transformation—such as land reform—would *not* be encumbered by entrenched provisions like those of the bill of rights. Critics of government policy generally saw the emphasis on private property as an attempt to retain vestiges of racial domination. Helen Zille said: "Whites are trying to protect their interests. . . . [These

---

[34] Interview with the author, 15 May 1991.

provisions] are associated with race. In South Africa, this is a fraught concept. Bills of rights are usually to protect the weak and dispossessed, and not the powerful and wealthy."[35]

The ANC did indeed see the underlying economic ramifications of the bill of rights, particularly the critical issue of private property. The ANC recognized that the inclusion of the right to "acquire, hold, and dispose" of private property and the right to contract, if enshrined in a bill of rights, would effectively guarantee an essentially free-market economy. Business knew this as well. Although the ANC draft bill of rights guaranteed the right to "acquire, own, or dispose" of personal private property, it did specify that "the state may by legislation take steps to overcome the effects of past statutory discrimination in relation to enjoyment of property rights"; although it spelled out compensation in general, it did not relate it to the market value of the property.[36] Instead, the draft bill of rights stated that an independent tribunal and, if necessary, the courts should adjudicate disputes over compensation. By protecting only personal private property from confiscation, the ANC policies gave business owners no comfort that corporate holdings would not be seized by the state.

Capitalists dislike uncertainty, and the vague ANC guidelines caused those in the business community concern about how the new political order would affect their interests. The SACOB guidelines noted that "industry and commerce have a vital stake in the shape of a future constitution for South Africa, as it would like to see the right combination of stability and change."[37] The business community, not surprisingly, sought a set of political institutions that would ensure stable change (socioeconomic upliftment was cited as a goal held in common with labor interests) and a free-market economy. The primary vehicle for achieving this goal was the bill of rights. SACOB's position was spelled out clearly: "While an economic system or policy as such cannot be entrenched in a constitution, certain concepts fundamental to the market economy and to business confidence need to be safeguarded. These include: the law of persons; the law of property; the law of contract."[38] There were other institutional choices that SACOB made in pursuit of protecting the interests of business. In a bid to curb "excessive inflation and high taxation," the business community called for an independent reserve bank and the

---

[35] Interview with the author, 3 April 1991.

[36] "Principles and Structures of a Democratic Constitution for South Africa," ANC Constitutional Committee, pamphlet.

[37] "The Economic Aspects of a New Constitution for South Africa: A South African Chamber of Business View," 12 June 1991, SACOB, pamphlet.

[38] Ibid. Significantly, SACOB includes in its charter of rights the right to trade union organization.

possible entrenchment of limits on the government's ability to tax. It also sought extensive checks and balances among political institutions and endorsed a "maximum devolution of power." Given a decentralized, limited government and a political system that would ensure a bill of rights through the rule of law, business interests were perceived to be protected in a future settlement. SACOB's institutional choices were aimed at constitutionally limiting the capacity of the state to intervene in the economy.

COSATU criticized the attempt of business groups to constitutionally limit state intervention, but also recognized the limited capacity of the state to direct economic activity. Trade unionist Ebrahim Patel, who worked on the committee that drew up COSATU's 1991 guidelines, said: "The question of state intervention is really a question of not constructing the constitution so that an employer, or an individual for that matter, can seek to interdict those legitimate activities that the state would need to ensure economic growth and reasonable redistribution. But you can't in your constitution say: 'The state shall take the following steps.' . . . We hope we can put in there the value of the state intervening in the economy in the interests of the people at large."[39]

To guarantee its ability to participate in the determination of economic policy, COSATU sought to include the following trade union rights in the new constitution, either in the bill of rights or in, preferably, a separate Workers' Charter: to strike and picket; to organize; and to prevent interference in trade union organization. Further, it called for a separate labor court and for clauses that would allow unions to press demands for collective ownership and worker control of the means of production. It is especially interesting to note that rather than focus on specific short- and intermediate-term trade union aims, COSATU's proposals honed in on the rule-making structures of the constitution. Rather than calling for specific demands in the constitution, the trade union federation wanted the power to organize and work for the demand. In a report of the committees that drafted the trade union federation's demands for the Workers' Charter, the choice for rules over specific rights is explained: "The approach that should be adopted in respect of enshrining rights in the constitution and in the law should be procedural rather than substantive. We should seek those rights that empower the organizations of the working class to fight for the daily demands of workers. For example, rather than assert the demand for the living wage, we need to empower trade unions through centralized bargaining and the right to strike so that they take up the fight for the living wage."[40]

[39] Interview with the author, 7 June 1991.
[40] "The Joint Report of the COSATU Workers' Charter/LRA [Labor Relations Act] Committees on the Workers Charter," n.d., n.p.

In the business/trade union debate over the economic provisions of a new constitution, both sets of civil society actors made implicit concessions to one another much the same way the political parties did. SACOB recognized the need for socioeconomic upliftment and affirmative action, and COSATU recognized the need from trade unions to begin taking responsibility for economic growth through codetermination of macroeconomic policy. Business knew implicitly that it faced an uphill battle protecting corporate property rights in a new constitution. As John Dugard said: "The best one can do in a bill of rights is to protect vested personal property rights, not necessarily vested corporate property rights."[41] But COSATU knew equally well that constitutionally mandated full employment or a minimum wage standard would not be possible, given the balance of forces and the lack of state capacity. Further, both recognized that the postapartheid economic demands would exceed the capacity of the state and the economy to provide them, given conditions of scarcity. They would have to compromise. While realizing neither capitalism nor socialism would be written into the constitution, both business and labor sought to ensure that the political institutions established by a new constitution would address specifically their interests and concerns.

The SACOB/COSATU debate reflects an important fact about the search for postapartheid institutions in South Africa. As all sides of the debate—not just business and labor, but also the National party as it represented the minority middle class and the ANC as it spoke on behalf of the dispossessed—sought to advance political *and* economic interests as they constructed new rules for a postapartheid policy. The linkage between institutional rule making and postapartheid economic policy underscores that an economic compact coincidental with a political agreement is an essential ingredient of a new South African social contract. In the critical areas of redistribution, affirmative action, wage, income, and social service distribution, land reform, and public finance there will be many inevitable trade-offs in postapartheid economic policy making, as many economists have already warned (Nattrass and Roux 1991; Hugo 1992). The debate is summarized by International Monetary Fund economists, who wrote that "redistribution policies will need to be firmly supported by growth-oriented policies if the social spending gap is to be effectively bridged" (Lachman and Bercuson 1992:2).

Political institutions and their distribution effects must be complementary, so that the need to secure structures for the joint determination of politics is paralleled by the need to ensure that economic policy is also jointly determined. For a new set of political rules to be perceived as fair,

---

[41] Interview with the author, 13 May 1991.

their distributive effects must also be perceived as fair. Lodge has perceptively written: "Political democratization without economic redistribution will merely redefine the likes of social fission in South Africa, not eliminate them. Perhaps, though, that is the best one can hope for. Socioeconomic inequalities as profound as those that exist in South Africa are unlikely to be eliminated through constitutional bargaining, diplomatic maneuvering, and political finesse" (1991:149). Consensus on a political settlement will be of little value if an accompanying accord on the economy is not concluded because of the expectations on all sides of the role that future political institutions will play in the determination of economic policy. The state's role in stimulating growth and employment will be critical to managing "a revolution of rising expectations" among those long dispossessed by apartheid and to absolving white fears of widespread expropriation of property in a quest for redistribution of wealth.

The challenges of economic reconstruction, growth, and redistribution are enormous. As I discussed in chapter 2, apartheid fundamentally misallocated economic resources, and these distortions will leave a lingering legacy long after the end of white minority rule. Since 1970, and particularly since 1985, South Africa has experienced what World Bank economists have described as "dismal growth performance," stemming from internal and external factors alike, and exacerbated by shocks emanating from political volatility and the price volatility of gold, a critical primary export earner (Kahn, Senhadji, and Walton 1992).

Among the economic maladies that will plague any postapartheid government are: the maldistribution of income (see the Introduction) and social spending; a high fiscal deficit that will place restraints on future spending; inward-oriented manufacturing resulting from import substitution policies; an oligopoly-dominated private sector and large, inefficient public enterprises; massive public expenditure differentials among race groups; and the scarcity of capital due to financial sanctions (Bethlehem 1992). Further, as table 7.1 illustrates, the uncertainty of the transition and its ramifications, such as persistent political violence, plunged South Africa into a deep recession that resulted in declining incomes, growing unemployment (43 percent overall in the formal sector), declines in state revenue, and weak investor confidence.

Even though apartheid makes South Africa's seemingly dire economic predicament sui generis, its situation is not unlike that of other states at similar stages of development, such as Mexico or Brazil (Knight 1988; Kahn, Senhadji, and Walton 1992). Furthermore, the long-standing confrontation between capitalist and socialist ideologies in South Africa has waned and been replaced by a focus on the hard reality of pragmatic choices: How can a middle income, relatively industrialized oil-importing country become more prosperous while it reduces inequality and im-

TABLE 7.1
Macroeconomic Indicators, 1990–1992

					Ratios to GDP (%)			
	Growth Rates (% per annum)				Total Fixed Investment	Gross Domestic Savings	Inflation	Fiscal Deficit
	GDP	Investment	Exports	Imports				
1990	−0.08	−1.7	3.4	−3.1	20.2	21.4	14.0	−2.8
1991	−0.03	−8.4	1.9	2.5	18.2	18.8	15.3	−4.3
1992	−2.0	−8.1	1.3	8.6	21.7	—	8.0	—

Source: For 1990–91, Kahn, Senhadji, and Walton 1992:5. For 1992 data available, Economist Intelligence Unit Country Report no. 1, 1993.

proves the basic quality of life for its citizens? To meet the challenges of nearly 60 percent unemployment in some townships and a population growth rate of nearly 3 percent, South Africa will require at least a 6 percent sustained real growth in its gross domestic product for the foreseeable future in order to realize an improving standard of living for its citizens.

Indeed, the background for such a direct process of negotiation on economic issues is found in the consultative process that led to the adoption of a new Labor Relations Act, enacted in January 1991 after extensive bargaining among COSATU, NACTU, the South African Consultative Committee on Labor Affairs (SACCOLA) (the largest employers' federation) and, eventually, the government.[42] The experiences of the Labor Relations Act amendments led to increased effort to establish appropriate institutions through which organized business and labor could reach agreement on how to jointly manage the economy and determine the appropriate role for the state. The institution through which the amendments were negotiated, the National Manpower Commission, suffered a blow when the government acted unilaterally in September 1991 to implement a new sales tax (a value-added tax, replacing a general sales tax) without sufficient consultation with COSATU and the ANC. In the row over union representation on the commission, COSATU pulled out of the body and called instead for the creation of a new national forum of employers, the government, and the trade unions to negotiate all macroeconomic issues for the period of transition.

Negotiations resumed in earnest in late October 1992 with the creation of the National Economic Forum (NEF), which was convened just after

[42] The final amendments were based on the SACCOLA-COSATU-NACTU agreement of 7 May 1990. For a chronology of the two-year negotiations process that led up to the act, see *Indicator SA* 8 (2) (Autumn 1991): 93.

the government-ANC talks resumed after Bisho.[43] By late 1993, a host of broadly representative negotiation forums—new rule structures for ongoing bargaining—had been created, through which civil society organizations could negotiate among themselves and with the state. These included the National Economic Forum, but also forums on education, housing, youth and women's issues, drought, electrification, and local government; myriad local-level institutions—mirroring the bargaining patterns at the national level—were also created. These institutions will be critical to the consolidation of democracy because they represent the avenues through which civil society organizations can press their interests and interact with the state. These bargaining institutions can serve to broaden and deepen the social contract as partnerships develop among organizations with an underlying common cause: socioeconomic reconstruction and development.

If South Africa is to meet the challenges of creating a prosperous post-apartheid democracy, more than political partnership across ethnic and racial cleavages will be required; social compacts on a variety of levels with multiple partners will be required if development institutions, business, labor, and communities, working together in a spirit of codetermination, are to make any appreciable difference in the quality of life for the disadvantaged majority in South Africa. Institutions for negotiation of economic policy, like the NEF, are important not just for the opportunity they provide South Africa to create a stable industrial relations system, but for the clear rules of the game they set for regulating economic conflict.

Much like a political social contract, an economic compact will be elusive, but over the long term it is a potentially achievable goal. Organized interests in society will find it difficult to sufficiently bind their followers to agreements—civil society actors such as COSATU and SACOB may be unable to resolve their own elite-mass nexus. Achieving growth with redistribution will be painful. Compromises struck at the economic bargaining table may be even more difficult to implement than political compromises, not just because of the inevitable costs of trade-offs but because many interests in South African society are not organized. Friedman (1991a) argues that many interests are "marginalized," unrepresented by any major political force of civil society organization. "A social contract is not a magic formula; it is a way of including interests which are too strong to be ignored in decisions which they have the power to frustrate" (1991a:19). The challenge of broadening social contracts nego-

---

[43] The NEF was organized into short- and long-term working groups that, in effect, began to codetermine South Africa's macroeconomic, industrial, and centralized bargaining policies.

tiated by organized interests is to coordinate and include as many unorganized interests as possible.

Much as it is feasible to predict the results of the political debate, it is possible to assess the likely outcome of a separate economic accord. A sobering presentation on the state of the economy by finance minister Derek Keys and South African Reserve Bank governor Chris Stals helped produce the democratization pact; economic interdependence spurred convergence.[44] As the competing visions of a postapartheid economy and the role of the state converged, the institutional features began to approach the form of a social democracy. In addition to guaranteeing a fundamental level of political rights, a social contract could provide—through coordinated development as well as the welfare state—a basic floor of economic prosperity for the most disadvantaged of its citizens.

As has been shown, the whole range of choices over political institutions were based on the expected working properties of the rules they created. This was true not only of the distribution of political power, but of economic power. If a final political settlement involves a compromise between majoritarianism and consociationalism (which is manifested as centripetalism), then the analogous economic compromise would be a social democracy. Pieter Le Roux, director of the Institute for Social Development at the University of the Western Cape, writes (1990a, 1990b) about the logic of a social democracy in South Africa: "Those in power today would rather see a siege economy than accept a more radical socialist system: the oppressed would rather continue their struggle than settle for an economic system which does not alter the pattern of domination. A social democracy would thus constitute a compromise between right-wing fears and left-wing aspirations" (1990a:13–14). In the South African context, the creation of a social democracy will require first and foremost what Coetzee (1992:136) refers to as a "comprehensive, multidimensional and integrated" antipoverty strategy. This will mean an extension of the social safety net to the impoverished majority, a tremendous policy challenge but one on which South Africa's best economists have already begun to concentrate (Moll, Nattrass, and Loots 1991; Hugo 1992). Pragmatism and patience will be critical.

With a social democratic economic accord—a codetermination agreement—buttressing a political agreement, the possibility of a broadly inclusive social contract comes into focus. Socioeconomic transformation will be an indispensable element of a new social contract in South Africa, even if it is more elusive than a political settlement and may take many years to evolve as pact making occurs on a sector-specific basis. Over time, economic codetermination will be necessary for the country to alle-

[44] *Financial Times*, 17 February 1993.

viate poverty. The notion that economic negotiation, too, can be a positive-sum game is summarized by Bethlehem: "the strengthening of blacks economically should not require a concomitant weakening of whites; any such suggestion would reflect a mercantilist view of power, that is, that what is fained by one must necessarily be taken from another" (1992:80).

Schlemmer sums up the essential linkage between economic growth and the potential for democratization: "A generalized fear and concern has emerged among political observers and decision-makers that South Africa's transition to inclusive rule and a unified political system will be undermined, if not usurped, by reactions to poverty and inequality" (1991d:3). Vincent Maphai reiterates the point: "Even if a settlement were to attract massive capital injection, an economic miracle remains unlikely. It can be safely assumed that material expectations of the oppressed majority are simply not going to be met in the foreseeable future. What cannot be predicted is the likely response" (1993:234). Thus, a prolonged period of slowly rising growth and employment, guided by codetermined policy making, may be the best hope for managing unmet expectations.

Overcoming material inequality—apartheid's legacy—is an important determinant in what is perceived as a fair solution in terms of distributive justice. This makes democracy elusive in South Africa, and its actual realization more likely in the future than the short-term, but it also makes it possible. As Przeworski suggests, "Democracy continues to be rare and unstable: rare because it requires a class compromise, unstable because it is based on one" (1988:80).

CHAPTER 8

South Africa and the Politics of Divided Societies

NEGOTIATION IN South Africa entailed redefining the new rules of the political game for both the transition and the new political order. Driving negotiation forward to a settlement was the central lesson of conflict in deeply divided South Africa as it entered the postapartheid era: no single actor could unilaterally impose its rule preferences on others, given the balance of power. As a result, the institutional choices converged through strategic interaction among the major parties. Institutional choices were formulated and reformulated with an acute appreciation for what was possible, given the preferences and bargaining power of others. Clearly the dramatic transformation of politics in South Africa from the centrifugal impasse of 1984–89 to the centripetal pull of 1993 deserves careful inspection for its implications for the potential management of conflict in other deeply divided societies. Above all, this experience shows how the politics of discord in a deeply divided society can conceivably evolve toward conflict-regulating institutions through negotiation.

FROM ZERO SUM TO POSITIVE SUM

Although transition in South Africa was and will remain very turbulent, the prospects for a postapartheid democracy are far beyond the expectations of even the most optimistic observers just a few years ago. The underlying social conditions for conflict clearly remain; the patterns of conflict will be managed, but not eliminated. The reorientation of the conflict away from legally sanctioned and enforced racial segregation toward a multiethnic, democratic outcome occurred because a critical mass of centrist actors' interests were best served so. Rustow writes that "decision means choice, and while the choice of democracy does not arise until the background and preparatory conditions are in hand, it is a genuine choice and does not flow automatically from these two conditions" (1970:356). Democratic institutions will in all likelihood emerge out of the South African transition; the unresolved issue is whether they can be sustained and whether a truly participatory democracy will evolve.

South Africa's transition raises the important question of how democratic institutions can emerge in a deeply divided society even as the conditions for democratic development are not thought to be favorable. This is important not only for South Africa, but for the many communally divided states around the globe in which attempts to democratize may follow a period of polarized strife. The South African case shows how the interests of political parties can converge on democratic institutions through negotiation as they pursue their common interest in escaping stalemate in an intractable social conflict. If this is true of South Africa, it may also be true of other divided societies. How can a settlement that creates democratic institutions result even when the underlying conditions for sustaining democracy—tolerance, civil and political liberties, a culture of human rights—are absent?

Democratization proceeded in terms of redefining the rules of the political game. As the old order suffered its demise, the realization set in among the major actors who perceived themselves to be in the condition of a mutually hurting stalemate that the benefits of a positive-sum outcome to the conflict—the creation of a jointly determined set of institutions to govern a future, common society—were greater than the costs of continued confrontation in an environment ungoverned by common rules. Once this realization was made, convergence on exactly what kinds of rules should replace the old order evolved as a result of the interaction among political parties that sought a negotiated settlement. This evolution was guided by institutional choice: actors' choices converged, and will likely further converge, on institutions that are perceived as fair, given each actor's unique history, ideology, interests and power, and the effects of strategic interaction.

In divided societies, a recognition of a shared or common destiny is a recognition of interdependence. The interdependence relationship is heightened when there is a perceived balance of power among actors. Interdependence in an unbalanced power relationship leads actors either to believe that they can subdue their opponents (if they perceive the imbalance to be in their favor) or to fear their opponents will subdue them (if they perceive the imbalance to be unfavorable). In both instances, an unbalanced power relationship leads to a zero-sum view of the conflict: dominate or be dominated, submit or withdraw from the common society. The South African conflict moved from a zero-sum to positive-sum perception when the balance of power between the dominant white minority and the increasingly empowered black majority reached a level of approximate parity.[1]

These important determinants of change in South Africa—interdependence and a changing balance of power—which laid the underlying conditions for the onset of negotiation toward democratization, may not be present in other divided societies. Where an incumbent regime perceives that it can maintain its dominant power position or where an insurgency

---

[1] See Rothchild 1973 for a remarkably similar conclusion on the transition from racial oligarchy to independence in Kenya.

believes that it can prevail through armed force, negotiated democratization is an inherently limited possibility. Where interdependence is absent or unacknowledged, where the balance of power is perceived to be (either favorably or unfavorably) unbalanced, negotiation is likely to be a fruitless enterprise. But when a balance of power and interdependence do exist, the possibility of moving beyond deep-seated conflict to a positive-sum alternative is present.

A stalemate can be perpetuated in a deeply divided society even when the conditions of interdependence and a balanced power relationship are present. Indeed, intractable stalemate is the norm rather than the exception. Protracted social conflicts can go on being protracted ad infinitum. What is required to begin negotiation is a set of precipitating events that gives reluctant actors an "opportunity" to seize the moment. Mandela's March 1989 memorandum to P. W. Botha was predicated not on external events but on his own conclusions that the only viable route to peace in South Africa was a settlement that reconciled the fears of those in the system with the legitimate demands of the liberation struggle.

Negotiation, according to Zartman, occurs when there is "mutual movement" (1976:8) in the actors' negotiating positions. Mutual movement means making concessions from initial bargaining positions, from first-order institutional choice preferences. In South Africa, mutual movement did not begin until late 1989 and early 1990; while the NP had been "moving away" from strict Verwoerdian apartheid since at least 1979 (and perhaps even earlier), the ANC's movement from unbridled majoritarianism did not begin until the latter period. Negotiations are the recognition, prima facie, of at least one common goal, reaching an agreement (Zartman 1976:9).

When negotiation does begin, so does a period of intense uncertainty.[2] The relationship of uncertainty to the process of democratization is absolutely critical; "If a peaceful transition to democracy is to be possible, the first problem to be solved is how to institutionalize uncertainty without threatening the interests of those who can still reverse this process. . . . The solutions to the democratic compromise consist of institutions" (Przeworski 1986:58). The onset of transition means the impending adoption of a new set of rules, rules that are unpredictable, uncertain, and untested. Expectations, either of demise or aggrandizement, flourish. So, too, do aspirations for a better future. During this initial period of transition from authoritarianism toward a new, negotiated democracy, mobilization occurs as open political activity is first tolerated or resurrected. Political

[2] On the importance of uncertainty, see Schelling 1980. On the relationship between uncertainty and the perceptions of negotiators, both personal and "institutional" (e.g., the perceptions of political parties), see Rangarajan 1985:54–61. Rangarajan links perceptions of uncertainty and its reduction to predictability and the creation of order.

parties and actors mobilize in order to demonstrate their power in anticipation of the creation of the new rules of the political game. What makes democratic transitions so difficult is that this mobilization occurs during a period in which there is a vacuum of well-defined rules of the political game, a time of intense uncertainty. Simon Bekker, of the Centre for Social and Development Studies at the University of Natal, has written about this initial period of transition in South Africa, noting that the onset of transition resulted in "widespread confusion over how politics were to be conducted" (1990:23). The uncertainty of transition can yield the fear of political extinction, a fear strong enough to cause some to turn to violence for their own survival.

Pacts in a transition process can attempt to lower the level of uncertainty; the National Peace Accord, which culminated the process of the preliminary phase of negotiation in South Africa, is a telling example of a "prerequisite pact" in democratization. As long as the rules are followed, parties can continue playing the game without the fear that one side can use the time of flux to eliminate an opponent, through violence, altogether. A mutual security pact, such as South Africa's National Peace Accord, can potentially provide sufficient assurances to parties that their political future is secure. It can eliminate the immediate source of uncertainty over whether the new game will result in permanent political exclusion. But the Peace Accord did not immediately succeed because the uncertainty of transition continued to reign.

Whereas uncertainty over a political party's vital interests, over political survival, can potentially prevent a settlement (and it nearly did in South Africa), uncertainty over how a political party may fare under the future rules is a different matter. Uncertainty in the initial phase of transition is the fear of losing a zero-sum game. Uncertainty following a successful mutual security pact is the hope of winning the game, if not all of the time, at least some of the time. As Vanberg and Buchanan write, "The more general rules are and the longer the period over which they are expected to be in effect, the less certain people can be about the particular ways in which alternative rules will affect them. They will therefore be induced to adopt a more impartial perspective and, consequently, they will be more likely to reach an agreement" (1989:54). In a divided society, such uncertainty is absolutely critical. For any political party to continue to play by the new rules, it must expect that at least some of the time, on some occasions, the opportunity to win is likely. Within the context of a floor of basic human rights, alternation in winning and losing coalitions must be a distinct *possibility*, given the expected working properties of the new rules. Minority parties will continue playing the game within the new institutions if they can win on some issues by their ability to prevail over the will of the majority. They must not always win elections, but they must be able to win on some critical issues some of the time. When political parties anticipate the possibility of winning in the political game, they continue playing, and the essential "contingent consent" (O'Donnell and Schmitter 1986:59) necessary for democracy begins to emerge. When they continue playing, political conflict is reoriented from an anarchic, violent arena to the political institutions of the state.

But not all political players will be willing to reach agreement. It is more reasonable for them to sit on the sidelines and await (and, if possible, bring about) the failure of moderation and negotiation. Those who perceive the situation in zero-sum terms outbid those who moderate for the support of the communal bases on which political parties in divided societies in conflict ultimately rely. The outbidders in the South African conflict, ethnic nationalists and the black radical left, demonstrate this point directly. The challenge of transition is to create sufficient incentives to make participation more beneficial than self-imposed exclusion.

Moderation gives centrist actors a common incentive to cooperate in fighting the forces of outbidding and to *eschew identity politics*. An incentive to cooperate is also an incentive to converge on a new set of democratic political rules, a result that protects against the extremists and marginalizes appeals to ascriptive solidarity. As Trudeau urged, "the 'nation' in ethnic terms ceases to be the basis of the state." Uncertainty over what the future holds, combined with a common interest in fighting the force of the extremes, can lead parties to arrive at a set of political institutions that provides a gravitational pull toward the political center. For centrist parties, such a centripetal pull is ultimately fair because it is the best common position all of them can ultimately accept. Fair political institutions—a social contract—makes democracy in divided societies attractive even to, as Horowitz perceptively notes, parties who would otherwise pursue hegemonic aims: they pursue democracy "in spite of themselves" (1991:276). The democratization pact culminates the initial step toward creating a democracy, with all its uncertainties. The conclusion of such a pact is already a step in the direction of democratic consolidation. Rustow writes about such initial efforts to create democracy as "a joint learning experience. The first grand compromise that establishes democracy, if it proves at all viable, is itself a proof of the efficacy of the principle of conciliation and accommodation. The first success, therefore, may encourage contending political forces and their leaders to submit other major questions to resolution by democratic procedures" (1970:358).

INSTITUTIONAL CHOICE IN DIVIDED SOCIETIES

As illustrated in table 5.1, the politics of institutional choice in a divided society could converge on centripetal institutions as the fulcrum of compromise between consociationalism and majoritarianism because of the heightened uncertainty experienced during the transition. Institutional choice as a theoretical perspective explains the linkages between the transition and the range of potential outcomes by focusing on the choices of the actors engaged in negotiation. Consociationalism, centripetalism, and majoritarianism are distinct institutional choices of political parties in response to the new incentives of structured negotiation. Depending on the institutional choices of the major political actors and the balance of power among them, these types of institutions may also be outcomes.

Centrist political actors in divided societies are locked in a mutually dependent power relationship; this was especially true of the newly emerging center in South African politics. An unbalanced power relationship (either favorable or unfavorable) implies that an actor in a dominant position can conceivably win the conflict outright by destroying an opponent, as noted above. When the power relationship is balanced, collusive decision making becomes an enterprise in the interests of the parties themselves. As du Toit writes, "Power sharing is necessary not only because the antagonistic groups see each other as potential enemies, but because they are in fact each other's only potential *allies*" (1989b:423, 426 emphasis added). Centripetal institutions are potentially viable for conflict-regulating democratic institutions in divided societies, and can evolve out of a stalemate if mutual dependence is sufficiently strong. This leads to another important conclusion: Institutional choices in divided societies can converge on a social contract which eschews ethnic politics if there exists a centrist core of political parties with sufficient uncertainty about their potential to win outright in the new game, and if there is a roughly balanced, mutually dependent power relationship among them. These conditions will facilitate finding a formula that serves to protect the center against the outbidding extremes; they indicate a contract zone of mutual interests. Zartman writes: "Conflict resolution involves finding a formula for agreement, conceived as a common definition of the problem and a principle of justice or terms of trade that can frame a solution" (1991:13).[3] Once a process of negotiation begins, convergence flows from the parties' mutual interest in arriving at a mutually beneficial settlement. Once a zero-sum perception of the conflict has been overcome, the full implications of positive sum are a set of institutions that meets the criteria of fairness to everyone.

A negotiated transition may begin as a grim struggle for ascendancy—negotiation can be a tactical choice through which to subdue the enemy. But it can also create new pressures and incentives on the participating parties to continue negotiating toward a fair and just settlement. These

---

[3] For a definition of the concept of a formula, see Zartman and Berman 1982 and Zartman 1978.

choices involve an interplay of power and interests, but also the process of finding the right solution to a commonly recognized problem of conflict. Given sufficient consensus, a just political system can evolve out of a situation rife with ethnic or racial conflict when political parties, pursuing their own self-interest in the course of transition, derive a set of fair principles of justice that command the consent of all those committed to living by them. The substantive principles of justice are those which emanate from the choices of the political actors themselves pursuing their own interests. "Negotiations . . . become not a transition but a way of life, with a continuing role for power and justice" (Zartman 1976:3). In such negotiations, there must be agreement on both what is "just" in substantive terms, in procedural terms (i.e., an impartially enforced bill of rights), and in distributive terms.

In divided societies, democratization settlements need to be exceptionally broad and inclusive. Complete consensus is not only unobtainable given empirical conditions, it may not be desirable. The objection to consensus government is a deeper one that arises from the structure of it as a decision-making rule itself. A universal right of consent, as Rae (1975) has argued, is tantamount to "pure autocracy" if every individual has the right to veto every government policy. Therefore the need arises to arrive at nonconsensual rule that allows for a broad enough base of support that allows the new rules to survive. How inclusive should it be? A consolidated moderate center, choosing centripetal institutions to protect its own interests as it perceives them, can survive over time under conditions of democracy if it can use the very institutions of inclusive democracy to marginalize extremist opponents through the ballot box rather than through the coercive forces of the state. At first, severely limited democracy—hegemonic exchange—may be all that is possible; after all, the democratization pact was a settlement among elites. In order to govern a still-divided society, moderate elites may need to initially establish an inclusive hegemony. Friedman writes that "it is possible to envision a prolonged period of limited democracy, partial stability, and contradictory interaction between the parties. In this phase, conflict that seemed to hasten disintegration would be mixed with cooperation whenever the abyss really yawned. Given the way the parties have interacted so far . . . this may be the most realistic projection" (1993:67). For this reason, Friedman correctly refers to a long transition before the final outcome of the democratization process in South African is fully known. Over time, however, opposing moderate elites will find each other as allies rather than as enemies; fear of exclusion from the new political game can be supplanted with an expectation of winning, at least some of the time on some of the issues.

In divided societies, both cooperation and conflict will continue in the new order. A social contract in a divided society is essentially an agreement to institutionalize and maximize cooperation among the moderate center in order to avoid violent conflict. The social contractarian school of modern participatory democracy has long emphasized the basic idea that moving beyond an anarchic arena of conflict into a common polity is based on, as Kendall writes, "political equality and active participation by the citizens in the political process as an indispensable condition for 'government by consent'" (1968:376). Giving expression to the ideal of a social contract is a matter of choosing political institutions that meet the aims of establishing political equality and participation; that is, they meet the aims of fairness and justice. Rawls writes concerning the notion of justice as fairness as the elimination of arbitrary discrimination or distinctions:

> When applied to an institution (or a system of institutions), justice requires the elimination of arbitrary distinctions and the establishment within its structure of a proper balance or equilibrium among competing claims. The principles of justice specify when the balance or share is proper and which distinctions are arbitrary. . . . The concept of justice . . . applies to political institutions, that is, publicly recognized systems of rules which are generally acted upon and which, by defining offices and duties, privileges and penalties, give social activity its form and structure. (1974:99)

In divided societies emerging from an authoritarian past, the emphasis on what constitutes arbitrary distinctions is critical. In the South African case, race is the arbitrary distinction that led to unjust distribution of benefits emanating from the system of apartheid. The just alternative is a social contract in which the arbitrary distinction of race is replaced by a democracy that regulates "a proper balance or equilibrium" between the competing claims of the diverse elements of South Africa's divided society. The criterion for fairness is the possibility of mutual acceptance of the competing claims, or in Rawlsian terms, "justice as reciprocity" (Rawls 1958:661). A recognition of the need for reciprocity lies at the heart of the contractualist conception of a just alternative for divided societies. Vanberg and Buchanan sum up this perspective succinctly: "Cooperation can replace conflict only if the differing interests, held with varying intensities by persons, can be traded-off or compromised, actually or symbolically, in a *social contract*" (1989:61, emphasis in original).

A social contract is possible in a divided society like South Africa despite the persistence of deep conflicts of interest. Above all, a shared sense of common destiny and the realization that hegemonic aims are self-defeating are required. But with these perceptions, there is an alternative to strictly defined guarantees for minority community rights, one that may offer better hope for longer-term conflict management. This alternative is an approach in which the views of majorities and minorities are reconciled through the recognition of the mutual dependence and its institutionalization in democratic political institutions. Political actors in a divided society must *themselves* choose to eschew destructive communal politics in favor of an overarching state that fairly regulates divergent interests. A limited but inclusive hegemony, a less-than-democratic social contract restricted to elites, is a possible outcome, but even that would be preferable to the unregulated conflict that normally prevails in a divided society. Indeed, a democratic social contract may *not* emerge in South Africa, but it is conceivable and—as long as the pattern of politics remains centripetal and the incentives for ongoing bargaining prevail— likely.

Epilogue

"This is, for all South Africans, an unforgettable occasion," ANC president Nelson Mandela said as he cast his ballot on 27 April in the election that ended apartheid and inaugurated democracy. "We have moved from an era of pessimism, division, turmoil and conflict. We are starting a new era of hope, reconciliation and nation-building."[1] The 1994 election and the subsequent inauguration of Mandela as president of the national unity government on 10 May marked the end of the four-year transition, four decades of apartheid, and three-and-a-half centuries of white minority rule. Many onlookers remarked that the relative peacefulness of the election was a miracle. However, the holding of the election according to the terms of the democratization pact of November 1993 and its widely inclusive nature (with the IFP and the white right wing taking part) were in fact not a miracle but rather the result of the parties pursuing their own interests. The onset of negotiation in 1990 brought a new set of incentives and disincentives, which drove the parties to a settlement and produced the election.

The path to an inclusive election in South Africa was not an easy one. Following the Multiparty Negotiating Forum agreement on an interim constitution in November 1993, marathon "last-minute" negotiations were held between the NP-ANC bloc and the rejectionist Freedom Alliance before the pact's adoption by the Tricameral Parliament. The talks continued to concern issues of the devolution of powers to the regions, self-determination for ethnic groups such as Afrikaners and Zulus, and the single ballot. Underlying the debate was the critical difference between those favoring the new constitution and those opposed: Should the new South African state specifically recognize ethnic-group representation on a territorial basis? The Freedom Front, dubbed the "children of apartheid," demanded such recognition and threatened to spoil the election; they clearly had the capability to do so. Final touches were put on the interim constitution in early December and the Transitional Executive Council convened 7 December, beginning de facto multiparty rule during the election campaign and event. By mid-December, the interim constitution was adopted without the concurrence of the Freedom Alliance opponents, despite intensive talks among the parties and rumors of splits among the rejectionist ranks. It appeared then that the settlement would

---

[1] *Washington Post,* 28 April 1994.

not be inclusive and that the election—if it could be held at all—would be wracked by violence.

As the year of liberation dawned in South Africa and the campaign began to gather steam, many analysts predicted that the country would suffer one of the more common results of democratization: ethnic challenges to the new order. In January, the Conservative party moved to set up a "shadow government" for Afrikaners, and the Inkatha Freedom party began to mute the prospect of a unilateral declaration of independence and the establishment of a sovereign Zulu state. IFP leader Buthelezi warned his followers to prepare for the "politics of resistance." "Last-minute" negotiations continued in late January, when the deadline for de Klerk's proclamation of the election loomed. The Freedom Alliance sought its delay. However, cracks in the Freedom Alliance began to show when Ciskei headman Oupa Gqozo broke ranks and joined the TEC. As the campaign intensified, so too did the virulent rhetoric, leading some to speculate that the election would produce a civil war.

In a critical set of concessions, the NP and ANC agreed in early February to amend the interim constitution and Electoral Act to allow for a double ballot (one for the central parliament, one for regional assemblies) and to grant greater powers, including original taxing powers, to the regions. In continuing efforts to broaden participation in the election, the parties also agreed to extend the registration deadline. Further, an additional constitutional principle was included that acknowledged the right to self-determination, and a provision was added to set up a postelection commission on Afrikaner claims for a volkstaat. The name of the Natal region was changed to KwaZulu/Natal. The election, however, would not be delayed. "This is our sign of good faith," Mandela said.[2]

In an effort to break the impasse, Mandela and Buthelezi met for a summit on 2 March. In order to avoid a perception of failure, they made further concessions in the seven-hour talks. The ANC agreed to submit the differences over regionalism to international mediation, and the IFP "provisionally" registered for the election. Yet the underlying differences remained, with Buthelezi continuing to argue for postponement of the election and a complete revision of the interim constitution.

With the election six short weeks away—and with it the demise of the homelands, according to the constitution—a crisis developed in Boputhatswana. Homeland leader Lucas Mangope announced a boycott of the poll and refused to allow campaign rallies or voter education in the territory. Boputhatswana civil servants, fearful for their salaries and pensions, launched a strike. In a direct challenge, the TEC passed a resolution de-

[2] *Christian Science Monitor*, 18 February 1994.

manding that the homeland be opened for the vote. As rioting in the capital, Mmbatho, ensued, the beleaguered Mangope regime appealed to right-wing whites to intervene. In response, the TEC dispatched the South African Defense Force. In a melee on the streets of Mmbatho, pitched battles between the homeland army and armed white right wingers occurred; in the fighting, two members of the far-right paramilitary AWB were shot in cold blood before a television crew. The images were broadcast around the world. The Mangope regime fell, and the TEC took control of the homeland. The event was important because it served as a clear demonstration to Buthelezi of the potential costs of spoiling the election and of the relative impotence of the white right wing. Within the extremist white groups, the balance of power shifted demonstrably away from the violence-prone radicals to General Constand Viljoen's Freedom Front, which had registered for the election minutes before the extended deadline of 4 March. With the white right wing split and humiliated, Buthelezi and the IFP were left wholly isolated.

The IFP's election boycott moved onto the country's central stage in late March, when a rally by tens of thousands of Zulu royalists in support of King Goodwill Zwelithini's call earlier in the month for a sovereign monarchy in KwaZulu/Natal turned violent. The march to the ANC headquarters in the Johannesburg city center drew gunfire from ANC security guards, and at least 53 were killed as rioting erupted. The violence quickly spread to the townships, where up to 250 died in related factional fighting, and to Natal, which had already witnessed an upsurge in violence throughout the early months of 1994—breaking earlier records of political fatalities in the province. A state of emergency was declared by de Klerk in KwaZulu/Natal following an announcement in early April that the prospects for a free and fair election in the province were impossible; the announcement heightened tensions and the belief that South Africa's first step toward democracy would be a bloody one. Buthelezi's rhetoric grew more incendiary.

The escalating violence and the prospects for even wider carnage in Natal during the election produced an unprecedented four-way summit on 8 April, featuring de Klerk, Mandela, Buthelezi, and King Zwelithini. Armed with a concession that the status of the Zulu monarch would be protected in postapartheid South Africa, Mandela had sought to split the Zulu leaders or at least minimize their obstruction of the election. This summit, too, ended in impasse, with the Zulu king and Buthelezi holding out for a postponement of the vote. After the failed bid, attention turned to the arrival of international mediators, led by former U.S. secretary of state Henry Kissinger and Britain's Lord Carrington, both of whom had been instrumental in Zimbabwe's independence talks. But the effort failed even before it began when the parties could not agree on the mediators' terms of reference. The mediators left South Africa barely a day after they arrived.

As the eleventh hour waned and South Africa's election loomed less than a week away, Buthelezi and the IFP reversed course in a surprise move on 19 April and agreed to participate in the poll. One member of the international team, Kenyan professor Washington Okumu, had stayed behind to mount a behind-the-scenes mediation effort that led to the IFP leader's decision to contest the election. A close friend of Buthelezi's for some twenty years, Okumu was also close to Mandela and de Klerk and brought a perspective that Kissinger and Carrington could not: that of a fellow African. "Okumu read him the African future," one participant in the talks said. "He told him, you're staring into the abyss."[3] In reaching an accord with Buthelezi and the Zulu king, the NP and ANC agreed in a trilateral Memorandum of Understanding that in exchange for the IFP's participation in the election, the Zulu monarch would be given a constitutionally enshrined role in KwaZulu/Natal. Although the same package deal could have been obtained by Buthelezi and the monarch weeks or months earlier, Okumu's mediation provided a face-saving exit from the corner into which the IFP had painted itself. Election officials made quick arrangements for an IFP sticker to be added at the bottom of the nearly ninety million printed ballots; Buthelezi mounted an intensive five-day election campaign.

With the IFP's inclusion, the prospect of a peaceful election heightened, and optimism replaced pessimism as South Africa faced its moment of truth. In the days before the election, however, a series of powerful car bombs erupted near sites related to the voting. In downtown Johannesburg, a blast between the ANC national and regional headquarters killed nine and injured scores more on 24 April, two days before the scheduled three days of balloting. The bombing campaign, believed to be the work of white right wingers (thirty-one right wingers were later charged in the plot), did not dampen the determination to proceed with the polling. As voting began on 26 April (the first day was reserved for the hospitalized and infirm), a sense of calm settled on South Africa and little election-related violence was reported.

South Africa's April 1994 election was a cathartic experience. Millions of South Africans, the vast majority voting for the first time in their lives, formed lines that in many instances snaked for miles. At over ten thousand polling stations nationwide, voters channeled through lines to present their identity cards, dip their hands in indelible ink, mark their ballots, and deposit them in a sealed box. Polling sites were secured by the

[3] *Financial Times*, 20 April 1994.

police and security forces and monitored by a legion of domestic and international observers. The United Nations observer mission fielded some eighteen hundred monitors. Anglican archbishop Desmond Tutu summed up the mood of the day: "It's an incredible experience, like falling in love."[4]

With the eyes of the world watching—international media gave the event widespread and often live coverage—black and white lined up together to inaugurate a new democracy. The mood was festive; the act of voting was a liberation from the chains of oppression for black South Africans and began to lift the mantle of guilt for whites. The atmosphere was electrifying, exciting, full of expectation, hope, and, among some, fear. However, the voting was plagued by administrative problems and logistical snafus, some related to the late entry of the IFP but others from the sheer difficulty of managing an election in a country where so few had ever voted before. Amid numerous complaints of fraud, ballot stuffing, and other irregularities, the balloting was extended for a fourth day. At one angry moment, Mandela alleged widespread fraud in Natal.

When the voting ended on 29 April, South Africans and the world alike were astounded by the sense of tolerance and cooperation that the vote reflected. The election was equally cathartic for the international community. Some commentators drew parallels with the fall of the Berlin Wall in 1989; others noted the demise of the last form of settler rule in Africa. The historical significance of the election was lost on no one.

For nearly a week after the vote, the level of anxiety was high as the vote counting proceeded at a snail's pace. The Independent Electoral Commission, which organized and ran the election, came under widespread criticism for allowing irregularities. With barely half the votes counted, de Klerk conceded victory to Mandela on 2 May and pledged to work with him as deputy president in the national unity government. In a moving speech echoing the words of civil rights leader Martin Luther King, Jr., Mandela proclaimed black South Africans "free at last." Both speeches were overwhelming in their appeals for reconciliation and the mutual accolades for both men's roles in the transition. The well-timed speeches served their purpose: although the tallies had not yet been completed, the outcome of the transition was already known. Both men easily slipped from the often fiery rhetoric of the campaign into appeals for national reconciliation.

Final results were not released until 6 May, when the Independent Electoral Commission declared the election "substantially free and fair" and all parties agreed to the results. When announcing the results, commission chairman Johann Kriegler admitted the process had been flawed, but

---

[4] *Washington Post*, 28 April 1994.

TABLE E.1
South Africa's April 1994 Election: Official Results

Party	Votes		National Assembly Seats	Cabinet Seats
	N	Percentage		
African National Congress	12,237,655	62.6	252	18
National party	3,983,690	20.4	82	6
Inkatha Freedom party	2,058,294	10.5	43	3
Freedom Front	424,555	2.2	9	0
Democratic party	338,426	1.7	7	0
Pan-Africanist Congress	243,478	1.3	5	0
African Christian Democratic party	88,104	0.5	2	0

Source: *Washington Post*, 7 May 1994.

"that was peripheral. . . . The heart of the matter is that we were able to establish the will of the people."[5] In fact, the precise results were the outcome of negotiation. Kriegler admitted that the parties "are in a power game with each other, and if they want to settle [vote fraud claims], there's nothing wrong with it ethically or legally."[6] The results of the national election are presented in table E.1.

The parties' agreement on the outcome was especially important in Natal, which had experienced the most widespread and serious vote tampering and logistical problems. In that province, amid ANC claims of fraud by IFP officials, the parties agreed that the IFP won with 50.3 percent of the vote—the ANC conceded the barest of majorities—to the ANC's 32.2 percent; the NP came in third with 11.2 percent. The ANC won all of the other regions with the exception of the Western Cape, which was won by the NP. With the official results certified, South Africa's first postapartheid parliament met on 9 May and duly elected Nelson Mandela president of the new South Africa.

The events between the adoption of the democratization pact in late 1993 and the highly successful founding election in April 1994 reinforce the essential themes that emerged during the transition. First, the centripetal force of the political system was reaffirmed as one after another of the rejectionist parties responded to the incentives of inclusion and participation and the disincentives of spoiling. The IFP chose brinksmanship over spoiling and jumped aboard the train at the latest of moments. Second, political violence—an endemic feature of the transition—would not dis-

[5] *Washington Post*, 7 May 1994.
[6] *Newsweek*, 16 May 1994.

rupt the process. As the election neared, tensions soared and many lives were lost as uncertainty and anxiety gripped the country. Yet heightened political violence reinforced the determination of the moderate parties to proceed with the transition. Third, the transition was based on pact making. For example, bringing in the IFP entailed a pact that assured its vital interests—perpetuation of the traditional and tribal authority structures —would be protected in the new order. Finally, the institutions chosen by the parties themselves proved to have conflict-mitigating effects. The election, fought under proportional representation, generally met the parties' expectations of how the electoral system would perform and allowed each of the major protagonists to gain a share of power in the new order, both at the national and regional level. Their expectations of how they would fare were also met.

The successful conclusion of South Africa's transition does not mean that underlying conflicts have been resolved. Real conflicts of interest remain. Indeed, the campaign itself reflected the fact that the society remains deeply divided. The ANC earned very few white votes, and the NP won very few African votes (although it carried a majority of Coloured and Indian votes); the IFP mobilized on ethnic chauvinism. The building of truly integrated political parties, and of civil society, must await the era of nation building. And racial and ethnic outbidding will remain a constant danger, especially if strong economic performance is not forthcoming. Yet with a successful founding election, South Africa's negotiated transition—and the institutions created in the course of those negotiations—are imbued with legitimacy. The challenge ahead will be to use that legitimacy to create a set of permanent postapartheid institutions that perpetuate the moderation, borne of necessity, that arose during South Africa's transition from apartheid to democracy.

South Africa in Transition, 1989–1993: A Negotiation Chronology

March 1989	Nelson Mandela sends thirteen-point memorandum suggesting ANC-government talks to president P. W. Botha.
5 July 1989	Botha, president, meets Mandela, prisoner.
14 August 1989	Botha resigns and is succeeded by F. W. de Klerk.
21 August 1989	Harare Declaration is adopted.
13 December 1989	De Klerk confers with Nelson Mandela to discuss preconditions for negotiation.
2 February 1990	President F. W. de Klerk lifts bans on the ANC, PAC, and SACP, announces release of Mandela, and calls for negotiation.
9 February 1990	De Klerk again meets with Mandela.
11 February 1990	Nelson Mandela is released after twenty-seven years in prison.
16 February 1990	The ANC agrees to direct talks with de Klerk's government.
April 1990	ANC, SACP, and COSATU announce a formal alliance.
2–4 May 1990	ANC and government conclude the first pact, the Groote Schuur Minute.
July 1990	The National party and Inkatha separately declare membership in their parties open to all races; violence in the townships and Natal soars.
6–7 August 1990	A second round of formal ANC-government talks results in the Pretoria Minute.
September 1990	Conflict between IFP and ANC supporters further spreads from Natal to townships near Johannesburg.
8 January 1991	ANC calls for an All-Party Congress.

31 January 1991	Joint ANC-IFP delegations meet in Durban; IFP leader Buthelezi and Mandela meet for the first time in twenty-eight years.
15 February 1991	The government and ANC conclude the D. F. Malan Minute.
March 1991	ANC releases "Constitutional Principles and Structures for a Democratic South Africa."
6 April 1991	ANC "ultimatum" links talks to diminution of violence.
30 April 1991	Pretoria Minute deadline lapses.
18 May 1991	ANC withdraws from negotiation.
17 June 1991	Population Registration Act repealed.
22 June 1991	Church and business leaders plan national peace conference.
2–7 July 1991	The ANC's Forty-eighth National Conference is held.
19 July 1991	The *Weekly Mail* publishes reports detailing police funding of IFP rallies.
8 September 1991	Just prior to the National Peace Convention, 18 are killed and 14 wounded in violence near Johannesburg; by week's end, some 121 die and 550 are wounded in factional violence.
14 September 1991	National Peace Accord signed.
27 October 1991	The ANC, PAC, and seventy other parties form short-lived Patriotic Front.
20 December 1991	CODESA, the first formal constitutional negotiation, is convened.
17 February 1992	NP loses a key by-election.
17 March 1992	Whites vote overwhelmingly (67.8 percent) to back de Klerk's reforms, amid widespread violence in the townships.
April 1992	Working Groups set up by CODESA negotiate transition path.
15–16 May 1992	CODESA II results in deadlock.
17 June 1992	Boipatong massacre leaves forty-nine dead; ANC withdraws from negotiation.

15 July 1992	UN Security Council debate on South Africa.
23 July 1992	Mandela relates talks withdrawal to CODESA II deadlock.
August 1992	Following secret talks with the government, the PAC agrees to attend relaunched multiparty talks; following a split, the CP too agrees to talks.
3 August 1992	COSATU spearheads a three-day general strike.
7 September 1992	ANC protestors march on Ciskei's capital, Bisho; twenty-eight are killed by Ciskei security forces, after which "urgent" government-ANC bilaterals resume.
26 September 1992	Government, ANC agree to the Record of Understanding, which charts the basic path of further transition.
October 1992	SACP leader Joe Slovo publishes "Negotiation: A Strategic Perspective," proposing power sharing.
6 October 1992	Buthelezi, some homeland leaders, and white right-wing groups form a rejectionist front, the Concerned South Africans Group (COSAG).
12 February 1993	The government and ANC conclude a wide-ranging agreement that reflects the formula outlined in "Negotiation: A Strategic Perspective."
17 February 1993	Government-IFP negotiation fails to win IFP backing of power-sharing deal.
5 March 1993	Multiparty Negotiating Process (MPNP) planned.
1 April 1993	MPNP's first plenary session launched at the World Trade Center in Johannesburg.
10 April 1993	Chris Hani, SACP leader, assassinated.
3 June 1993	MPNP Negotiating Council "tentatively" agrees on 27 April 1994 election date; the IFP and its COSAG allies object.
25 June 1993	Armed right wingers invade the MPNP forum.
2 July 1993	Nineteen of twenty-six parties at the MPNP affirm the 27 April 1994 election date; over July, some six hundred die in political violence.
18 July 1993	The IFP withdraws from the MPNP over election date.

25 July 1993	Five gunmen attack churchgoers in Cape Town, killing 12 and wounding 147.
26 July 1993	MPNP negotiators present first draft of an interim constitution.
8 September 1993	Negotiating Council agrees on transitional structures.
16 September 1993	Government negotiators fail to woo the IFP back to talks.
24 September 1993	Parliament adopts the transitional executive council legislation, and Mandela calls for the lifting of most remaining sanctions.
7 October 1993	Black and white right-wing rejectionist groups form the Freedom Alliance.
15 October 1993	De Klerk and Mandela win the Nobel Peace Prize.
16 November 1993	De Klerk and Mandela conclude final power-sharing agreements.
18 November 1993	Interim constitution adopted by the Negotiating Council of the Multiparty Negotiating Process.

Interviews

(Titles are those held by the respondents at the time of the interview.)

Laurie Ackerman Professor of Human Rights Law University of Stellenbosch	19 April 1991	Stellenbosch
Rowley Israel Arenstein Attorney	21 May 1991	Durban
Kader Asmal Member, Constitutional Committee African National Congress	7 May 1991 20 November 1992 27 November 1992	Belleville Belleville Port Elizabeth
Z. J. de Beer Coleader and Parliamentary Leader Democratic Party	27 March 1991 18 November 1992	Cape Town Johannesburg
Hercules Booysen Professor of Public Law University of South Africa	17 May 1991	Pretoria
Alex L. Boraine Executive Director Institute for a Democratic Alterna- tive for South Africa	15 July 1991	Cape Town
Carel W. H. Boshoff Leader Afrikaner Volkswag	16 May 1991	Pretoria
Sheila Camerer Member of Parliament National Party	11 March 1991	Cape Town
Cheryl Carolus Member, Interim Leadership Committee South African Communist Party	24 April 1991	Belleville
Fanie Cloete Head, Department of Development Studies Rand Afrikaanse University	14 May 1991	Johannesburg
Brian N. Currin Director Lawyers for Human Rights	17 May 1991 16 November 1992	Pretoria Pretoria

Barney Desai Publicity Secretary Pan-Africanist Congress	8 April 1991	Cape Town
Oscar Dhlomo Executive Director Institute for Multiparty Democracy	20 May 1991	Durban
John Dugard Director, Center for Applied Legal Studies University of the Witwatersrand	13 May 1991	Johannesburg
M. G. Erasmus Professor of Law University of Stellenbosch	6 March 1991	Stellenbosch
H. P. Fourie Executive Director Department of Constitutional Services	30 April 1991	Cape Town
Steven Friedman Director Centre for Policy Studies	15 May 1991 17 November 1992	Johannesburg Johannesburg
Peter Gastrow National Peace Secretariat and Member of Parliament Democratic Party	19 November 1992	Durban
Ferdi Hartzenberg Chairman of the Caucus Conservative Party	17 April 1991	Cape Town
Johnny Issel Western Cape Regional Organizer African National Congress	24 April 1991	Langa
Fanie Jacobs Member of Parliament Conservative Party	4 June 1991	Cape Town
Vinodh Jaichand Senior Lecturer in Law University of Durban, Westville	22 May 1991	Durban
Frances Kendall Author	15 May 1991	Johannesburg
Gavin Lewis Director South Africa Foundation	13 May 1991	Johannesburg

Fatima Meer Director, Institute for Black Research University of Natal	21 May 1991	Durban
H. W. van der Merwe Director Centre for Inter-Group Studies	2 April 1991	Cape Town
Koos van der Merwe Member of Parliament Conservative Party	30 May 1991	Cape Town
S. S. van der Merwe Director General Department of Constitutional Services	18 June 1991	Cape Town
Stoffel van der Merwe Minister of Education and Training National Party	25 June 1991	Cape Town
Roelf P. Meyer Deputy Minister, Constitutional Development National Party	20 June 1991	Cape Town
Strini Moodley Publicity Secretary Azanian People's Organization	21 May 1991	Durban
Bulelani Ngcuka Member, Constitutional Committee African National Congress	30 April 1991	Belleville
Dullah Omar Member, Constitutional Committee African National Congress	10 April 1991	Belleville
Ebrahim Patel Member, Constitutional Committee Congress of South African Trade Unions	7 June 1991	Cape Town
Hennie Potgieter Director, Bill of Rights Project South African Law Commission	17 May 1991	Pretoria
Mamphele Ramphele Professor of Social Anthropology University of Cape Town	18 June 1991	Cape Town

I. G. Rautenbach Professor of Law Rand Afrikaanse University	14 May 1991	Johannesburg
J. N. Reddy Leader Solidarity Party	5 May 1991	Cape Town
Rushdie Sears Director, Center for Development Studies University of the Western Cape	17 April 1991	Belleville
Carter Seleka Assistant General Secretary Pan-Africanist Congress	15 May 1991	Johannesburg
James Selfe Member, President's Council Democratic Party	3 April 1991	Cape Town
Zwelakhe Sisulu Editor-in-Chief *New Nation*	13 May 1991	Johannesburg
Frederick van zyl Slabbert Director, Institute for a Democratic Alternative for South Africa	13 May 1991	Johannesburg
Franklin Sonn President Penninsula Technikon	22 April 1991	Belleville
Sampie Terreblanche Professor of Economics University of Stellenbosch	4 June 1991	Stellenbosch
Peter Vale Professor of Political Science University of the Western Cape	13 March 1991	Belleville
Bertus de Villiers Director, Centre for Constitutional Analysis Human Sciences Research Council	16 May 1991	Pretoria
Geert de Wet Head, Department of Economics University of Pretoria	16 May 1991	Pretoria
David Welsh Professor of Political Science University of Cape Town	29 May 1991	Cape Town

Gavin Woods	23 August 1991	Durban
Director	19 November 1992	Durban
Inkatha Institute for South Africa		
Dennis Worrall	5 May 1991	Cape Town
Co-Leader		
Democratic Party		
Dawid van Wyk	17 May 1991	Pretoria
Professor of Public Law		
University of South Africa		
Helen Zille	3 April 1991	Cape Town
Member, National Executive		
Black Sash		

Bibliography

Adam, Heribert. 1991. "Eastern Europe and South African Socialism: Engaging Joe Slovo." IDASA Occasional Paper no. 29. Cape Town: Institute for a Democratic Alternative.

———. 1990. "Getting Together." *London Review of Books* (14 June):10–11.

———. 1988. "Exile and Resistance: The African National Congress, the South African Communist Party, and the Pan-Africanist Congress." In *A Future South Africa: Visions, Strategies, and Realities,* Peter L. Berger and Bobby Godsell, eds. Cape Town: Human and Rousseau Tafelberg.

———. 1984. "Racist Capitalism versus Capitalist Nonracialism in South Africa." *Ethnic and Racial Studies* 7:269–82.

———. 1983. "Outside Influence on South Africa: Afrikanerdom in Disarray." *Journal of Modern African Studies* 21 (2):235–51.

———. 1978. "Survival Politics: Afrikanerdom in Search of a New Ideology." *Journal of Modern African Studies* 16 (4):657–69.

Adam, Heribert, and Hermann Giliomee, eds. 1979a. *Ethnic Power Mobilized: Can South Africa Change?* New Haven: Yale University Press.

———. 1979b. *The Rise and Crisis of Afrikaner Power.* Cape Town: David Philip.

Adam, Heribert, and Kogila Moodley. 1989. "Negotiations about What in South Africa?" *Journal of Modern African Studies* 27 (3):367–81.

———. 1987. "The Ultraright in South Africa and Ethnic Nationalism." *Canadian Review of Studies in Nationalism* 4 (1) (Spring):83–92.

———. 1986. *South Africa without Apartheid: Dismantling Racial Domination.* Berkeley and Los Angeles: University of California Press.

Africa Watch. 1991. *The Killings in South Africa: The Role of the Security Forces and the Response of the State.* New York: Africa Watch.

Aitschison, John. 1989. "The Civil War in Natal." In *South African Review 5,* Glenn Moss and Ingrid Obery, eds. Johannesburg: Ravan Press.

Alexander, Neville (No Sizwe). 1979. *One Azania, One Nation: The National Question in South Africa.* London: Zed Press.

Amnesty International. 1992. *South Africa: State of Fear.* New York: Amnesty International USA.

Arrow, Kenneth J. 1963. *Social Choice and Individual Values.* New Haven: Yale University Press.

Asmal, Kader. 1992. "Victims, Survivors and Citizens—Human Rights, Reparations and Reconciliation." Inaugural lecture. Publications of the University of the Western Cape, series A, no. 64.

———. 1991. "Democracy and Human Rights: Developing a South African Human Rights Culture." Paper prepared for conference, Constitution-Making in South Africa. University of the Western Cape, 24–26 March.

———. 1990. "Electoral Systems: A Critical Survey." Occasional Paper. University of the Western Cape, Centre for Development Studies.

Axelrod, Robert. 1984. *The Evolution of Cooperation*. New York: Basic Books.

Azar, Edward, and John W. Burton. 1986. *International Conflict Resolution: Theory and Practice*. Boulder, Colo.: Lynne Rienner Publisher.

Bacharach, S. B., and E. J. Lawler. 1981. *Bargaining: Power, Tactics and Outcomes*. San Francisco: Jossey-Bass.

Baker, Pauline H. 1990. "A Turbulent Transition." *Journal of Democracy* 1 (4):7–24.

———. 1988. "The Myth of Middle Class Moderation: African Lessons for South Africa." *Issue* 26 (2):45–48.

———. 1987–88. "The Afrikaner Angst." *Foreign Policy* 69:61–79.

Banton, Michael. 1980. "Ethnic Groups and the Theory of Rational Choice." In *Sociological Theories: Race and Colonialism*. Paris: UNESCO.

———. 1983. *Racial and Ethnic Competition*. Cambridge: Cambridge University Press.

Barrell, Howard. 1984. "The United Democratic Front and National Forum: Their Emergence, Composition and Trends." In *South African Review* 2, Glenn Moss and Ingrid Obery, eds. Johannesburg: Ravan Press.

Barry, Brian. 1975. "Review Article: Political Accommodation and Consociational Democracy." *British Journal of Political Science* 5 (October):477–505.

Bates, Robert H. 1992. *Beyond the Miracle of the Market: The Political Economy of Agricultural Development in Kenya*. Cambridge: Cambridge University Press.

———. 1988. "Contra Contractarianism: Some Reflections on the New Institutionalism." *Politics and Society* 16:387–401.

———. 1981. *Markets and States in Tropical Africa: The Political Basis of Agricultural Policies*. Berkeley and Los Angeles: University of California Press.

Becker, Charles M. 1988. "The Impact of Sanctions on South Africa and Its Periphery." *African Studies Review* 31:61–88.

Bekker, Simon. 1990. "Transition Politics: Playing by the New Rules." *Indicator SA* 7 (3):22–24.

Bekker, Simon, and Janis Grobbelaar. 1989. "Has the Conservative Party Bandwagon Slowed Down?" *Indicator SA* 6 (1–2):9–11.

Bennett, Mark, and Deborah Quin. 1988. "Kamikaze Politics: Assessing Non-Collaboration Tactics." In *Overview of Political Conflict in South Africa: Data Trends, 1984–1988*. Indicator Project South Africa. Durban: University of Natal.

Berger, Peter, and Bobby Godsell, eds. 1988. *A Future South Africa: Visions, Strategies and Realities*. Cape Town: Human and Rousseau Tafelberg.

Bethlehem, Ronald W. 1992. "Economic Development in South Africa." In *Towards a Post-Apartheid Future: Political and Economic Relations in Southern Africa*, Gavin Maasdorp and Alan Whiteside, eds. New York: St. Martin's Press.

———. 1988. *Economics in a Revolutionary Society: Sanctions and the Transformation of South Africa*. Johannesburg: A. D. Donker.

Blalock, Hubert M. 1989. *Power and Conflict: Toward a General Theory*. Newbury Park, Calif.: Sage Publications.

Bogdanor, Vernon, ed. 1987. *The Blackwell Encyclopedia of Political Institutions*. New York: Basil Blackwell.

Booth, Douglas. 1990. "South Africa: Reform, Resistance and Negotiations." *Politics* 25:22–36.

Boulle, Lawrence J. 1984. *Constitutional Reform and the Apartheid State: Legitimacy, Consociationalism, and Control in South Africa*. New York: St. Martin's Press.

Brady, David, and Jongryn Mo. 1992. "Electoral Systems and Institutional Choice: A Case Study of the 1988 Korean Elections." *Comparative Political Studies* 24 (2):405–29.

Brams, Steven J. 1990. *Negotiation Games*. New York: Routledge.

——. 1985. *Rational Politics*. Washington, D.C.: Congressional Quarterly Press.

Brams, Steven J., and Ann E. Doherty. 1992. "Intransigence in Negotiations: The Dynamics of Disagreement." Paper presented at the Annual Meeting of the American Political Science Association, Chicago.

Brass, Paul, ed. 1985. *Ethnic Groups and the State*. Totowa, N.J.: Barnes and Noble Books.

Brewer, John D., ed. 1989. *Can South Africa Survive?* London: Macmillan Press.

Brewer, John D. 1985. "The Membership of Inkatha in KwaMashu." *African Affairs* 84 (334):111–35.

Buchanan, James M. 1988. "Justifications of the Compound Republic: The *Calculus* in Retrospect." In *Public Choice and Constitutional Economics*, James D. Gwartney and Richard E. Wagner, eds. Greenwich, Conn.: JAI Press.

Buchanan, James M., and Victor Vanberg. 1989. "A Theory of Leadership and Deference in Constitutional Construction." *Public Choice* 61:15–27.

Burton, Michael G, and John Higley. 1987. "Elite Settlements." *American Sociological Review* 52:295–307.

Buthelezi Commission. 1982. *The Buthelezi Commission: The Requirements for Stability and Development in KwaZulu and Natal*. Vols. 1 and 2. Durban: H & H Publications.

Butler, Jeffrey, Richard Elphick, and David Welsh, eds. 1987. *Democratic Liberalism in South Africa: Its History and Prospect*. Cape Town: David Philip.

Carter, Gwendolyn. 1958. *The Politics of Inequality*. London: Thames and Hudson.

Cawthra, Gavin. 1990. "The Security Forces in Transition." IDASA Occasional Paper no. 38. Cape Town: Institute for a Democratic Alternative.

Cell, John W. 1982. *The Highest Stage of White Supremacy*. Cambridge: Cambridge University Press.

Chapman, John W. 1974. "Justice and Fairness." In *Justice, Nomos VI*, Carl J. Friedrich and John W. Chapman, eds. New York: Lieber Atherton.

Chazan, Naomi. 1982. "The New Politics of Participation in Tropical Africa." *Comparative Politics* 14 (2):169–89.

Cock, Jacklyn. 1989. "A Map of Political Violence in Contemporary South Africa." IDASA Occasional Paper no. 17. Cape Town: Institute for a Democratic Alternative.

Coetzee, Stef. 1992. "Towards an Anti-Poverty Strategy for South Africa." In *Redistribution and Affirmative Action: Working on the South African Political Economy,* Pierre Hugo, ed. Cape Town: Southern Book Publishers.

Coker, Christopher. 1989. "Changes and Limits of a Siege Economy." In *RSA 2000* 11 (1) (Pretoria, Human Sciences Research Council):50–57.

Cooper, Carole, Robin Hamilton, Harry Mashabela, Shaun Mackay, Elizabeth Sidiropolous, Claire Gordon-Brown, Stuart Murphy, and Colleen Markham. 1993. *Race Relations Survey 1992/1993.* Johannesburg: South African Institute of Race Relations.

Cooper, Carole, Robin Hamilton, Harry Mashabela, Shaun Mackay, Joe Kelly, Elizabeth Sidiropolous, Claire Gordon-Brown, and John Gary Moonsamy. 1992. *Race Relations Survey 1991/1992.* Johannesburg: South African Institute of Race Relations.

Cooper, Carole, Colleen McCaul, Robin Hamilton, Isabelle Delvare, John Gary Moonsamy, and Kristine Mueller. 1990. *Race Relations Survey 1989/1990.* Johannesburg: South African Institute of Race Relations.

Daalder, Hans. 1974. "The Consociational Democracy Theme." *World Politics* 26 (July):604–21.

———. 1971. "On Building Consociatonal Nations: The Cases of the Netherlands and Switzerland." *Legislative Studies Quarterly* 3 (February):11–25.

Dahl, Robert A. 1989. *Democracy and Its Critics.* New Haven: Yale University Press.

———. 1973. "Introduction." In *Regimes and Oppositions,* Robert Dahl, ed. New Haven: Yale University Press.

———. 1971. *Polyarchy: Participation and Opposition.* New Haven: Yale University Press.

Davies, Rob, Dan O'Meara, and Sipho Dlamini. 1984. *The Struggle for South Africa: A Reference Guide to Movements, Organizations and Institutions.* Vol. 2. London: Zed Books.

Diamond, Larry. 1992. "Economic Development and Democracy Reconsidered." *American Behavioral Scientist* 35 (4–5):450–99.

———. 1990. "Three Paradoxes of Democracy." *Journal of Democracy* 1 (3):48–60.

Diamond, Larry, Seymour Martin Lipset, and Juan Linz. 1987. "Building and Sustaining Democratic Government in Developing Countries: Some Tentative Findings." *World Affairs* 150 (1):5–20.

di Palma, Guiseppe. 1990. *To Craft Democracies: An Essay on Democratic Transitions.* Berkeley and Los Angeles: University of California Press.

Dostal, E. 1990. *Business Futures 1991.* Stellenbosch: Institute for Futures Research.

Downs, Anthony. 1957. *An Economic Theory of Democracy.* New York: Harper and Row.

Duchacek, Ivo. 1973. *Power Maps: Comparative Politics of Constitutions.* Santa Barbara, Calif.: ABC-Clio Press.

Duffy, Gavin, and Natalie Frensley. 1989. "Community Conflict Processes: Mobilization and Demobilization in Northern Ireland." Program on the Analysis and Resolution of Conflicts, Working Paper no. 13. Syracuse, N.Y.: Maxwell School of Citizenship and Public Affairs.

Dugard, John. 1990a. "A Bill of Rights for South Africa?" *Cornell International Law Journal* 23:441–66.

———. 1990b. "Towards a Democratic Legal Order for South Africa." *Revue Africaine de Droit International et Comparé* 2:361–83.

du Toit, Pierre. 1993. "Civil Society, Democracy and State-Building in South Africa." Research Report no. 1 of 1993. Stellenbosch: Centre for International and Comparative Politics.

———. 1989a. "Bargaining about Bargaining: Inducing the Self-Negating Prediction in Deeply Divided Societies: The Case of South Africa." *Journal of Conflict Resolution* 33:210–33.

———. 1989b. "Consociational Democracy and Bargaining Power." *Comparative Politics* 17:419–30.

du Toit, Pierre, and Willie Esterhuyse, eds. 1990. *The Myth Makers: The Elusive Search for South Africa's Bargain*. Johannesburg: Southern Book Publishers.

Ellis, Stephen. 1991. "The ANC in Exile." *African Affairs* 90:439–47.

———. 1992. *Comrades against Apartheid: The ANC and the South African Communist Party in Exile, 1960–1990*. Bloomington: Indiana University Press.

Esman, Milton J. 1987. "Ethnic Politics and Economic Power." *Comparative Politics* 19 (4):395–418.

Evans, Rob. 1988. "Participation versus Boycott Scenarios: Assessing BLA Election Data." In *Overview of Political Conflict in South Africa: Data Trends, 1984–1988*, Indicator Project South Africa. Durban: University of Natal.

Frankel, Philip. 1988. "Beyond Apartheid: Pathways for Transition." In *State, Resistance and Change in South Africa*, Philip Frankel, Noam Pines, and Mark Swilling, eds. London: Croom Helm.

———. 1987. *Pretoria's Praetorians: Civil-Military Relations in South Africa*. Cambridge: Cambridge University Press.

Frankel, Philip, Noam Pines, and Mark Swilling, eds. 1988. *State, Resistance and Change in South Africa*. London: Croom Helm.

Frederickson, George. 1988. *White Supremacy: A Comparative Perspective*. New York: Oxford University Press.

Friedman, Steven. 1993. "South Africa's Reluctant Transition." *Journal of Democracy* 4 (2):56–69.

———. 1991a. "Another Elephant? Prospects for a South African Social Contract." *Policy Issues and Actors* 4 (1) (May).

———. 1991b. "An Unlikely Utopia: State and Civil Society in South African." *Politikon* 19 (1):5–19.

———. 1991c. "The National Party and the South African Transition." In *Transitions to Democracy: Policy Perspectives, 1991*, Robin Lee and Lawrence Schlemmer, eds. Cape Town: Oxford University Press.

———. 1987. *Building Tomorrow Today: African Workers in Trade Unions, 1970–1984*. Johannesburg: Ravan Press.

———. 1986. "Black Politics at the Crossroads." South African Institute of Race Relations Occasional Paper. Johannesburg.

————, ed. 1993. *The Long Journey: South Africa's Quest for a Negotiated Settlement*. Johannesburg: Ravan Press.

Geddes, Barbara. 1990. "Democratic Institutions as a Bargain Among Self-Interested Politicians." Paper presented at the Annual Meeting of the American Political Science Association, San Francisco.

Geertz, Clifford. 1963. "The Integrative Revolution: Primordial Sentiments and Civil Politics in the New States." In *Old Societies and New States: The Quest for Modernity in Asia and Africa*, Clifford Geertz, ed. New York: Free Press of Glencoe.

Giliomee, Hermann. 1992. "*Broedertwis*: Intra-Afrikaner Conflicts in the Transition from Apartheid, 1969–1991." *African Affaris* 91:339–64.

————. 1989. "The Ideology of Apartheid." in *SA Perspectives*, Pierre Hugo, ed. Cape Town: Die Suid Afrikaan.

————. 1988. "The Freedom Charter and the Future." In *The Freedom Charter and the Future*, James A. Polley, ed. Cape Town: Institute for a Democratic Alternative.

————. 1982. *The Parting of the Ways: South African Politics, 1976–1982*. Cape Town: David Philip.

————. 1979. "The Afrikaner Economic Advance." In *The Rise and Crisis of Afrikaner Power*, Heribert Adam and Hermann Gilioimee, eds. Cape Town: David Philip.

Giliomee, Hermann, and Jannie Gagiano, eds. 1990. *The Elusive Search for Peace: South Africa, Israel, Northern Ireland*. Cape Town: Oxford University Press.

Giliomee, Hermann, and Lawrence Schlemmer. 1989a. *From Apartheid to Nation-Building*. Cape Town: Oxford University Press.

————, eds. 1989b. *Negotiating South Africa's Future*. Johannesburg: Southern Book Publishers.

Goodin, Robert E. 1976. *The Politics of Rational Man*. New York: John Wiley & Sons.

Gould, Julius. 1964. "Ideology." In *A Dictionary of the Social Sciences*, Julius Gould and William L. Colb, eds. New York: Free Press.

Greenberg, Stanley B. 1987a. *Legitimizing the Illegitimate: State, Markets and Resistance in South Africa*. Berkeley and Los Angeles: University of California Press.

————. 1987b. "Ideological Struggles within the South African State." In *The Politics of Race, Class and Nationalism in Twentieth Century South Africa*, Shula Marks and Stanley Trapido, eds. London: Longman.

————. 1980. *Race and State in Capitalist Development*. New Haven: Yale University Press.

Grobbelaar, Janis, Simon Bekker, and Robert Evans. 1989. *Vir Volk and Vaderland: A Guide to the White Right*. Durban: University of Natal, Indicator Project South Africa.

Grundy, Kenneth. 1987. *The Militarization of South African Politics*. New York: Oxford University Press.

Guelke, Adrian, 1991. "The Political Impasse in South Africa and Northern Ireland." *Comparative Politics* 23 (2):143–62.

Guyer, Melvin J. 1980. *Social Traps*. Ann Arbor: University of Michigan Press.

Hagopian, Frances. 1990. "Democracy by Undemocratic Means? Elites, Political Pacts, and Regime Transition in Brazil." *Comparative Political Studies* 23 (2):147–170.

Haines, Richard, and Gina Buijs. 1985. *The Struggle for Social and Economic Space: Urbanization in Twentieth Century South Africa*. Durban: University of Durban-Westville, Institute for Social and Economic Research.

Higley, John, and Michael G. Burton. 1989. "The Elite Variable in Democratic Transitions and Breakdowns." *American Sociological Review* 54:17–32.

Hirschmann, David. 1990. "The Black Consciousness Movement in South Africa." *Journal of Modern African Studies* 28 (1):1–22.

Horowitz, Donald. 1993. "Democracy in Divided Societies." *Journal of Democracy* 4 (4):18–38.

———. 1991. *A Democratic South Africa? Constitutonal Engineering in a Divided Society*. Berkeley and Los Angeles: University of California Press.

———. 1990. "Making Moderation Pay." In *Conflict and Peacemaking in Multiethnic Societies*, Joseph Montville, ed. Lexington, Mass.: Lexington Books.

———. 1985. *Ethnic Groups in Conflict*. Berkeley and Los Angeles: University of California Press.

Houghton, D. Hobart. 1976. *The South African Economy*. 4th ed. Cape Town: Oxford University Press.

Howe, Graham. 1985. "Deadlock in Emergent States, 1960/61 & 1984/85." *Indicator SA* 3 (2):1–5.

Hugo, Pierre, ed. 1992. *Redistribution and Affirmative Action: Working on the South African Political Economy*. Johannesburg: Southern Book Publishers.

Humphries, Richard. 1990. "It's Not Inside, It's on Top." *Indicator SA* 8 (1) (Summer):7–10.

Huntington, Samuel P. 1984. "Will More Countries Become Democratic?" *Political Science Quarterly* 99:193–218.

———. 1981. "Reform and Stability in a Modernizing, Multi-Ethnic Society." *Politikon* 8 (2):8–26.

———. 1972. "Foreword." In "Conflict Resolution in Divided Societies," by Eric Nordlinger. Occasional Papers in International Affairs no. 29. Cambridge: Harvard University, Center for International Affairs.

Hyslop, Johnathan. 1989. "Introduction." In *South African Review 5*, Glenn Moss and Ingrid Obery, eds. Johannesburg: Ravan Press.

IBR (Institute for Black Research). 1990. "The People Speak: Negotiations and Change." Durban: University of Natal, Institute for Black Research. Pamphlet.

IPSA (Indicator Project South Africa). 1991. "Natal/KwaZulu: Negotiating the Future." Durban: University of Natal, IPSA Issue Focus.

———. 1989. "An Overview of Political Conflict in South Africa: Data Trends, 1984–1988." Durban: University of Natal, IPSA Issue Focus.

———. 1985. "Countdown to State of Emergency: A Chronology of Township Revolt." *Indicator SA* 3 (2):6–9.

IRRC (Investor Responsibility Research Center). 1990. *The Impact of Sanctions on South Africa, Part I*. Washington, D.C.: IRRC.

James, Wilmot G. 1989. "Beyond Diversity: Notes on the Political Economy of

Stalemate." Paper delivered at conference, Ending Apartheid and Reaching a Settlement in South Africa, Gustav-Streseman Institute, Bonn.

Jenkins, Carolyn. 1990. "Sanctions, Economic Growth and Change." In *The Political Economy of South Africa,* Nicoli Nattrass and Elisabeth Ardington, eds. Cape Town: Oxford University Press.

Kaase, Max. 1986. "Personalized Proportional Representation: The 'Model' of the West German Electoral System." In *Choosing an Electoral System: Issues and Alternatives.* Arend Lijphart and Bernard Grofman, eds. New York: Praeger.

Kahn, Brian, Abdel Senhadji, and Michael Walton. 1992. "South Africa: Macroeconomic Issues for the Transition." Informal Discussion Papers on Aspects of the Economy of South Africa. Washington, D.C.: World Bank.

Kane-Berman, John. 1990. "The Apartheid Legacy." In *Critical Choices for South Africa: An Agenda for the 1990s,* Robert Schrire, ed. Cape Town: Oxford University Press.

―――. 1988. "Preface." *The Prisoners of Tradition and the Politics of Nation-Building.* Charles Simkins, ed. Johannesburg: South African Institute of Race Relations.

―――. 1978. *Soweto: Black Revolt, White Reaction.* Johannesburg: Ravan Press.

Karis, Thomas G. 1986–87. "South African Liberation—The Communist Factor." *Foreign Affairs* 65 (2):267–87.

Karis, Thomas G., and Gwendolyn M. Carter, eds. 1972. *From Protest to Challenge: A Documentary History of African Politics in South Africa.* 3 vols. Stanford, Calif.: Hoover Institution Press.

Karl, Terry Lynn. 1990. "Dilemmas of Democratization in Latin America." *Comparative Politics* 23 (1):1–21.

Kendall, Willmoore. 1968. "Social Contract." *International Encyclopedia of the Social Sciences.* London: Macmillan.

Knight, J. B. 1988. "A Comparative Analysis of South Africa as a Semi-Industrialized Developing Country." *Journal of Modern African Studies* 26 (3):473–94.

Kotzé, Hennie. 1993. "Attitudes towards an Elite Settlement." *Indicator SA* 10:5–11.

―――. 1992a. "Transitional Politics in South Africa: An Attitude Survey of Opinion-Leaders." Research Report no. 3 of 1992. Stellenbosch: University of Stellenbosch, Centre for International and Comparative Studies.

―――. 1992b. "Let All Votes Count in South Africa: Choosing an Electoral System for a Deeply Divided Society." Research Report no. 2 of 1992. University of Stellenbosch, Centre for International and Comparative Politics.

Kotzé, Hennie, and Deon Geldenhuys. 1990. "Damascus Road." *Leadership* 6:12–28.

Kotzé, Hennie, and Anneke Greyling. 1991. *South African Politics A to Z.* Cape Town: Tafelberg.

Kotzé, Hennie, and Timothy Sisk. 1991. "Parties and Politics: Run-up to the Multiparty Conference." *Information Update* (Human Science Research Council) 1 (4):3–8.

Kriek, D. J. 1976. "Politieke Alternatiewe vir Suid Afrika: Op Soek na 'n Paradigma" (Political alternatives for South Africa: The search for a paradigm). *Politikon* 3 (1):64–67.

Lachman, Desmond and Kenneth Bercuson, eds. 1992. "Economic Policies for a New South Africa." Occasional Paper no. 91. Washington, D.C.: International Monetary Fund.

Laurence, Patrick. 1991. "Key Developments in Black Politics." *South Africa Foundation Review* 17 (1):3.

Leatt, James, et al., eds. 1986. *Contending Ideologies in South Africa*. Cape Town: David Philip.

Leggasick, M. 1974. "Legislation, Ideology and Economy in Post-1948 South Africa." *Journal of Southern African Studies* 1 (1).

Lembruch, Gerhard. 1979. "Consociational Democracy, Class Conflict, and the New Corporatism." In *Trends Toward Corporate Intermediation*, Phillipe C. Schmitter and Gerhard Lembruch, eds. Beverly Hill, Calif.: Sage.

Lemon, Anthony. 1987. *Apartheid in Transition*. Aldershot and Hants: Gower.

———. 1976. *Apartheid: A Geography of Segregation*. Westmead: Saxon House.

Le Roux, Pieter. 1990a. "Social Democracy: The Art of Compromise." *Indicator SA* 7 (2):13–16.

———. 1990b. "The Case for a Social Democratic Compromise." In *The Political Economy of South Africa*, Nicoli Nattrass and Elisabeth Ardington, eds. Cape Town: Oxford University Press.

Levi, Margaret, and Michael Hechter. 1985. "A Rational Choice Approach to the Rise and Decline of Ethnoregional Political Parties." In *New Nationalisms of the Developed West*, R. Tiryakian and Ronald Rogowski, eds. Boston: Allen and Unwin.

Lewis, Stephen R., Jr. 1990. *The Economics of Apartheid*. New York: Council on Foreign Relations Press.

Liebenberg, Ian. 1987. "Responses to the ANC's Constitutional Guidelines," IDASA Occasional Paper no. 25. Cape Town: Institute for a Democratic South Africa.

Lijphart, Arend. 1992. "Constitutional Choices in Poland, Hungary and Czechoslovakia, 1989–1991." *Journal of Theoretical Politics* 4 (2):207–24.

———. 1991. "The Alternative Vote: A Realistic Alternative for South Africa?" *Politikon* 18 (2):91–101.

———. 1990a. "The Political Consequences of Electoral Laws, 1945–1985." *American Political Science Review* 84:481–96.

———. 1990b. "Electoral Systems, Party Systems and Conflict Management in Segmented Societies." In *Critical Choices for South Africa: An Agenda for the 1990s,* Robert Schrire, ed. Cape Town: Oxford University Press.

———. 1989. "The Ethnic Factor and Democratic Constitution-Making in South Africa." In *South Africa in Southern Africa*, Edmond J. Keller and Louis A. Picard, eds. Boulder, Colo.: Lynne Rienner Publishers.

———. 1987. "Choosing an Electoral System for Democratic Elections in South Africa: An Evaluation of the Principal Options." Critical Choices for South African Society, Occasional Paper. Cape Town: University of Cape Town, Institute for the Study of Public Policy.

———. 1985, *Power-Sharing in South Africa*. Policy Papers in International Affairs no. 24. Berkeley: University of California, Berkeley, Institute of International Studies.

——. 1977a. *Democracy in Plural Societies*. New Haven: Yale University Press.

——. 1977b. "Majority Rule versus Consociationalism in Deeply Divided Societies." *Politikon* 4 (December):113–26.

——. 1969. "Consociational Democracy." *World Politics* 4 (January): 207–25.

——. 1968. *The Politics of Accommodation: Pluralism and Democracy in the Netherlands*. Berkeley and Los Angeles: University of California Press.

Lijphart, Arend, and Bernard Grofman, eds. 1986. *Choosing an Electoral System: Issues and Alternatives*. New York: Praeger.

Linz, Juan J. 1990. "The Perils of Presidentialism." *Journal of Democracy* 1 (1):72–84.

Lipset, Seymour Martin. 1990. "The Centrality of Political Culture." *Journal of Democracy* 1 (4):80–83.

Lipton, Merle. 1988. Sanctions and South Africa: The Dynamics of Economic Isolation. Special Report, no. 1119. London: Economist Intelligence Unit.

——. 1985. *Capitalism and Apartheid*. London: Gower.

Lodge, Tom. 1991. "Perspectives on Conflict Resolution in South Africa." In *Conflict Resolution in Africa*, I. William Zartman and Francis Deng, eds. Washington, D.C.: Brookings Institution.

——. 1989. "People's War or Negotiation? African National Congress Strategies in the 1980s." In *South African Review 5*, Glenn Moss and Ingrid Obery, eds. Johannesberg: Ravan Press.

——. 1988a. "State of Exile: The African National Congress of South Africa, 1976–86." In *State, Resistance and Change in South Africa*, Philip Frankel, Noam Pines, and Mark Swilling, eds. London: Croom Helm.

——. 1988b. "The ANC's Constitutional Guidelines." *Leadership* 17.

——. 1987. "The African National Congress after the Kabwe Conference." In *South African Review 4*, Glenn Moss and Ingrid Obery, eds. Johannesberg: Ravan Press.

——. 1986a. "'Mayihlome!—Let Us Go to War!': From Nkomati to Kabwe, the African National Congress, January 1984–June 1985." In *South African Review 3*, Glenn Moss and Ingrid Obery, eds. Johannesburg: Ravan Press.

——. 1986b. "The Poqo Insurrection." In *Resistance and Ideology in Settler Societies*, Tom Lodge, ed. Johannesburg: Ravan Press.

——. 1983. *Black Politics in South Africa since 1945*. London: Longman.

Lodge, Tom, Bill Nasson, Steven Mufson, Khela Shubane, and Nokwanda Sithole. 1991. *All, Here, and How: Black Politics in South Africa in the 1980s*. New York: Ford Foundation and Foreign Policy Association.

Louw, Raymond ed. 1989. *Four Days in Lusaka: Whites in a Changing Society* Excom, South Africa: Five Freedoms Forum.

Love, Janice. 1988. "The Potential Impact of Economic Sanctions against South Africa." *Journal of Modern African Studies* 26 (1):91–112.

Lustick, Ian. 1980. *Arabs in the Jewish State: Israel's Control of a National Minority*. Austin: University of Texas Press.

——. 1979. "Stability in Deeply Divided Societies: Consociationalism versus Control." *World Politics* 31:325–44.

MacDonald, Michael. 1992. "The Siren's Song: The Political Logic of Power-Sharing in South Africa." *Journal of Southern African Studies* 18 (4):709–21.

Magubane, Bernard Makhosezwe. 1979. *The Political Economy of Race and Class in South Africa.* New York: Monthly Review Press.

Maphai, Vincent. 1993. "Prospects for a Democratic South Africa." *International Affairs* 69 (2):223–37.

March, James G., and Charles A. Lave. 1975. *An Introduction to Models in the Social Sciences.* New York: Harper and Row.

March, James G., and Johan P. Olsen. 1989. *Rediscovering Institutions: The Organizational Basis of Politics.* New York: Free Press.

———. 1984. "The New Institutionalism: Organizational Factors in Political Life." *American Political Science Review* 78:734–49.

Maré, Gerhard, and Muntu Ncube. 1989. "Inkatha: Marching from Natal to Pretoria." In *South African Review 5,* Glenn Moss and Ingrid Obery, eds. Johannesburg: Ravan Press.

Marks, Gary. 1992. "Rational Sources of Chaos in Democratic Transition." *American Behavioral Scientist* 35 (4–5):397–421.

Marks, Shula, and Stanley Trapido, eds. 1987. *The Politics of Race, Class, and Nationalism in Twentieth Century South Africa.* London: Longman.

Marx, Anthony W. 1992. *Lessons of Struggle: South African Internal Opposition, 1960–1990.* Oxford: Oxford University Press.

———. 1991. "Race, Nation, and Class Based Ideologies of Recent Opposition in South Africa." *Comparative Politics* 23 (3):313–26.

McCaul, Colleen. 1988. "The Wild Card: Inkatha and Contemporary Black Politics." In *State, Resistance and Change in South Africa,* Philip Frankel, Noam Pines, and Mark Swilling, eds. London: Croom Helm.

McClintock, Cynthia. 1989. "The Prospects for Democratic Consolidation in a 'Least Likely' Case: Peru." *Comparative Politics* 21 (2):127–48.

McGrath, Michael. 1990. "Income Redistribution: The Challenge of the 1990s." In *Critical Choices for South Africa: An Agenda for the 1990s,* Robert Schrire, ed. Cape Town: Oxford University Press.

———. 1985. "Economic Growth and the Distribution of Racial Incomes in the South African Economy." *South Africa International* 15:223–32.

Meadwell, Hudson. 1991. "A Rational Choice Approach to Political Regionalism." *Comparative Politics* 23 (4):401–22.

———. 1989. "Ethnic Nationalism and Collective Choice Theory." *Comparative Political Studies* 22 (2):139–54.

Meli, Francis. 1988. *South Africa Belongs to Us: A History of the ANC.* Bloomington: Indiana University Press.

Migdal, Joel. 1988. *Strong Societies and Weak States: State-Society Relations and State Capabilities in the Third World.* Princeton: Princeton University Press.

Mill, John Stuart. [1861] 1958. *Considerations on Representative Government.* New York: Liberal Arts Press.

Miller, Nicholas R. 1983. "Pluralism and Social Choice." *American Political Science Review* 77:734–47.

Mlambo, Johnson. 1988. "The Future Democratic Azania: The Pan-Africanist Congress View." *Parliamentarian* 69 (1) (April):76–80.

Moll, Peter, Nicoli Nattrass, and Lieb Loots, eds. 1991. *Redistribution: How Can It Work in South Africa?* Cape Town: David Philip.

Moll, Terence. 1990. "From Booster to Brake? Apartheid and Economic Growth in Comparative Perspective." In *The Political Economy of South Africa,* Nicoli Nattrass and Elisabeth Ardington, eds. Cape Town: Oxford University Press.

Moodie, T. Dunbar. 1980. *The Rise of Afrikanerdom: Power, Apartheid, and the Afrikaner Civil Religion.* Berkeley and Los Angeles: University of California Press.

Moodley, Kogila. 1986. "The Legitimation Crisis of the South African State." *Journal of Modern African Studies* 24 (2):187–201.

Mosala, Itumeleng. 1991. "Opening Address." *Azanian Socials Review* 1 (1):22–23.

Moss, Glenn, and Ingrid Obery, eds. 1987. *South African Review 4.* Johannesburg: Ravan Press.

Mozaffar, Shaheen. 1992. "A New Institutionalism Perspective on Regime Change in Contemporary Africa." Paper presented at the 1992 Annual Meeting of the American Political Science Association, Chicago.

Mufson, Steven. 1990–91. "South Africa 1990." *Foreign Affairs* 70 (1):120–41.

———. 1990. *Fighting Years: Black Resistance and the Struggle for a New South Africa.* Boston: Beacon Press.

Nattrass, Jill. 1988. *The South African Economy: Its Growth and Change.* 2d ed. Cape Town: Oxford University Press.

Nattrass, Nicoli, and Elisabeth Ardington, eds. 1990. *The Political Economy of South Africa.* Cape Town: Oxford University Press.

Nattrass, Nicoli, and André Roux. 1991. "Making Social Spending Work." In *Redistribution: How Can it Work in South Africa?* Peter Moll, Nicoli Nattrass, and Lieb Loots, eds. Cape Town: David Philip.

Neame, L. E. 1962. *The History of Apartheid: The Story of the Color Bar in South Africa.* London: Pall Mall.

Nordlinger, Eric A. 1972. *Conflict Regulation in Divided Societies.* Cambridge: Harvard University, Center for International Affairs.

North, Douglass C. 1990. *Institutions, Institutional Change and Economic Performance.* Cambridge: Cambridge University Press.

———. 1986. "A Neoclassical Theory of the State." In *Rational Choice,* Jon Elster, ed. New York: New York University Press.

O'Donnell, Guillermo, and Phillipe C. Schmitter. 1986. "Tentative Conclusions about Uncertain Democracies," in *Transitions from Authoritarian Rule: Prospects for Democracy,* pt. 4, Guillermo O'Donnell, Philippe C. Schmitter, and Laurence Whitehead, eds. Baltimore and London: Johns Hopkins University Press.

O'Donnell, Guillermo, Phillippe C. Schmitter, and Laurence Whitehead, eds. 1986. Part 4 of *Transitions from Authoritarian Rule: Prospects for Democracy.* Baltimore and London: Johns Hopkins University Press.

Olivier, N. J. J. 1989. "The General Election of 1989 in Perspective." Mimeo.

O'Meara, Dan. 1983. *Volkskapitalisme: Class, Capital, and Ideology in the Development of Afrikaner Nationalism, 1934–1948.* London: Cambridge University Press.

Ostrom, Elinor. 1991. "Rational Choice Theory and Institutional Analysis: Toward Complementarity." *American Political Science Review* 85 (1) (March 1991):237–43.

———. 1990. *Governing the Commons: The Evolution of Institutions for Collective Action.* Cambridge: Cambridge University Press.

Ottaway, Marina. 1993. *South Africa: The Struggle for a New Order.* Washington: Brookings Institution.

———. 1991. "Liberation Movements and Transition to Democracy: The Case of the A.N.C." *Journal of Modern African Studies* 29 (1):61–82.

Ozgür, Ozdemir. 1982. *Apartheid, the United Nations and Peaceful Change.* Dobbs Ferry, N.Y.: Transnational Publishers.

Pappalardo, Adriano. 1981. "The Conditions for Consociatonal Democracy: A Logical and Empirical Critique." *European Journal of Political Research* 8 (December):365–90.

Patel, Ebrahim. 1984. "Legitimacy and Statistics: A Critical Analysis of the First Tricameral Parliamentary Elections." Southern Africa Labour and Development Research Unit Working Paper no. 61. Cape Town: University of Cape Town.

Pillar, Paul, R. 1983. *Negotiating Peace: War Termination as a Bargaining Process.* Princeton: Princeton University Press.

Popkin, Samuel. 1988. "Political Entrepreneurs and Peasant Movements in Vietnam." In *Rationality and Revolution,* Michael Taylor, ed. Cambridge: Cambridge University Press.

———. 1979. *The Rational Peasant.* Berkeley and Los Angeles: University of California Press.

President's Council. 1992. "Report of the Committee for Constitutional Affairs on a Proportional Polling System for South Africa in a New Constitutional Dispensation." PC 2/1992. Cape Town: Government Printer.

Price, Robert M. 1991. *The Apartheid State in Crisis: Political Transformation in South Africa, 1975–1990.* New York: Oxford University Press.

———. 1987. "Security versus Growth: The International Factor in South African Policy." *Annals of the American Society of Political and Social Science* 489:103–22.

Przeworski, Adam. 1991. *Democracy and the Market.* Cambridge: Cambridge University Press.

———. 1988. "Democracy as a Contingent Outcome of Conflicts." In *Constitutionalism and Democracy,* Jon Elster and Rune Slagstad, eds. Cambridge: Cambridge University Press.

———. 1986. "Some Problems in the Study of the Transition to Democracy." In *Transitions from Authoritarian Rule: Prospects for Democracy,* Guillermo O'Donnell, Phillippe C. Schmitter, and Laurence Whitehead, eds., pt. 4. Baltimore and London: Johns Hopkins University Press.

Rabushka, Alvin, and Kenneth A. Shepsle. 1972. *Politics in Plural Societies: A Theory of Democratic Instability.* Columbus, Ohio: Charles E. Merrill.

Rae, Douglas W. 1975. "The Limits of Consensual Decision." *American Political Science Review* 69:1270–94.

———. 1969. "Decision-Rules and Individual Values in Constitutional Choice." *American Political Science Review* 63:40–56.

Rae, Douglas W., and Michael Taylor. 1970. *The Analysis of Political Cleavages*. New Haven: Yale University Press.

Rangarajan, L. N. 1985. *The Limitation of Conflict: A Theory of Bargaining and Negotiation*. New York: St. Martin's Press.

Rantete, Johannes, and Hermann Giliomee. 1992. "Transition to Democracy through Transaction: Bilateral Negotiations between the ANC and NP in South Africa." *African Affairs* 91:515–42.

Rawls, John. 1974. "Constitutional Liberty and the Concept of Justice." In *Justice, Nomos VI*, Carl J. Friedrich and John W. Chapman, eds. New York: Lieber Atherton.

———. 1971. *A Theory of Justice*. Cambridge: Harvard University Press.

———. 1958. "Justice as Fairness." *Philosophical Review* 67:164–94.

"Report on the ANC Consultative Conference on Local Government." 1990. Occasional Paper. Johannesburg: University of the Western Cape, Center for Development Studies.

Reynolds, Andrew. 1993. *Voting for a New South Africa*. Cape Town: Maskew Miller Longman Publishers.

Riker, William H. 1962. *The Theory of Political Coalitions*. New Haven: Yale University Press.

Riker, William H., and Peter C. Ordeshook. 1973. *An Introduction to Positive Political Theory*. Englewood Cliffs, N.J.: Prentice-Hall.

Rogowski, Ronald. 1985. "Causes and Varieties of Ethnic Nationalism: A Rationalist Account." In *New Nationalisms of the Developed West*, R. Tiryakian and Ronald Rogowski, eds. Boston: Allen and Unwin.

Rothchild, Donald. 1991. "An Interactive Model for State-Ethnic Relations." In *Conflict Resolution in Africa*, Francis M. Deng and I. William Zartman, eds. Washington, D.C.: Brookings Institution.

———. 1989. "From Exhortation to Incentive Strategies: Mediation Efforts in South Africa in the Mid-1980s." In *South Africa in Southern Africa*, Edmond J. Keller and Loius A. Picard, eds. Boulder, Colo.: Lynne Rienner Publishers.

———. 1986. "Hegemonial Exchange: An Alternative Model for Managing Conflict in Middle Africa." In *Ethnicity, Politics and Development*, Dennis L. Thompson and Dov Ronen, eds. Boulder: Lynne Rienner Publishers.

———. 1973. *Racial Bargaining in Independent Kenya: A Study of Minorities and Deconoloniation*. New York: Oxford University Press.

Rothchild, Donald, and Robert L. Curry, Jr. 1978. *Scarcity, Choice and Public Policy in Middle Africa*. Berkeley and Los Angeles: University of California Press.

Rothchild, Donald, and Michael W. Foley. 1988. "African States and the Politics of Inclusive Coalitions," in *The Precarious Balance: State and Society in Africa*, Donald Rothchild and Naomi Chazan, eds. Boulder, Colo.: Westview Press.

Rustow, Dankwart A. 1970. "Transitions to Democracy: Toward a Dynamic Model." *Comparative Politics* 2 (3):337–63.

Sachs, Albie, 1990. *Protecting Human Rights in a New South Africa*. Cape Town: Oxford University Press.

———. 1989. "Post-Apartheid South Africa: A Constitutional Framework." *World Policy Journal* 6 (3):503–29.

SAIRR (South African Institute of Race Relations). 1978. *Laws Affecting Race Relations in South Africa, 1948–1976.* Johannesburg: South African Institute of Race Relations.

Sait, Edward M. 1938. *Political Institutions: A Preface.* New York: Appleton Century.

Sartori, Giovanni. 1968. "Political Development and Political Engineering." In *Public Policy,* vol. 17, John D. Montgomery and Alfred O. Hirschmann, eds. Cambridge: Harvard University Press.

———. 1966. "European Political Parties: The Case of Polarized Pluralism." In *Political Parties and Political Development,* Joseph La Palombara and Myron Weiner, eds. Princeton: Princeton University Press.

Saul, John S., and Stephen Gelb. 1986. *The Crisis in South Africa: Class Revolt, Class Defense.* Rev. ed. London: Zed Books.

Saunders, Harold. 1985. "We Need a Larger Theory of Negotiation: The Importance of Pre-negotiating Phases." *Journal of Conflict Resolution* 1 (3):249–62.

Schelling, Thomas. 1980. *The Strategy of Conflict.* Cambridge: Harvard University Press.

Schlemmer, Lawrence. 1991a. "Christian Democratic Alliance." *Barometer* (August 1991):6–7.

———. 1991b. "Dimensions of Turmoil: Position Paper on Current Violence in South Africa." *Policy Issues and Actors* (University of the Witwatersrand, Centre for Policy Studies) 4 (2) (22 May 1991).

———. 1991c. "Township Residents amidst Protests, Negotiation and Violence: An Empirical Study." Johannesburg: Centre for Policy Studies. Research brief.

———. 1991d. "A South African Social Market Economy? Review and Discussion of a German-South African Dialgoue." Workshop Proceeding no. 5. Johannesburg: Centre for Policy Studies.

———. 1990. "Minority Rights and Political Justice." *Indicator SA* 7(3):25–28.

———. 1988. "South Africa's National Party Government." In *A Future South Africa: Visions, Strategies and Realities,* Peter Berger and Bobby Godsell, eds. Cape Town: Human and Rousseau Tafelberg.

———. 1980. "The Stirring Giant: Observations on Inkatha and Other Black Political Movements in South Africa." In *The Apartheid Regime: Political Power and Racial Domination,* Robert Price and Carl Rosberg, eds. Cape Town: David Philip.

Schmitter, Phillippe, and Gerhard Lembruch, eds. 1970. *Trends toward Corporatist Intermediation.* London: Sage.

Sened, Itai. 1991. "Contemporary Theory of Institutions in Perspective." *Journal of Theoretical Politics* 3 (4):379–402.

Shapiro, Ian. 1993. "Democratic Innovation: South Africa in Comparative Context." *World Politics* 46:121–50.

Share, Donald. 1986. *The Making of Spanish Democracy.* New York: Praeger.

Share, Donald, and Scott Mainwaring. 1986. "Transitions through Transaction: Democratization in Brazil and Spain." In *Political Liberalization in Brazil: Dynamics, Dilemmas and Future Prospects,* Wayne Selcher, ed. Boulder, Colo.: Westview Press.

Shils, Edward. 1968. "Ideology." *International Encyclopedia of the Social Sciences*. London: Macmillan.

Shubane, Khehla. 1991. "Civil Society in South Africa." *Journal of Democracy* 2 (3):53–55.

Simeon, Richard, and Michael Banting eds. 1985. *The Politics of Constitutional Change in Industrialized Nations: Redesigning the State*. London: Macmillan Press.

Simons, R. E., and H. J. Simons. 1969. *Class and Colour in South Africa, 1850–1950*. Baltimore: Penguin.

Sklar, Richard. 1987. "Developmental Democracy." *Comparative Studies in Society and History* 29:688–714.

Skweyiye, Zola. 1989. "A Vital Contribution to the Struggle against Apartheid." *Sechaba* (June):2, 4–10.

Smith, M. G. 1965. *The Plural Society in the British West Indies*. Berkeley and Los Angeles: University of California Press.

Southall, Roger. 1988. "Apartheid and the Case for Sanctions." *Journal of Commonwealth and Comparative Politics* 26 (1):104–24.

Stadler, Alfred William. 1987. *The Political Economy of Modern South Africa*. Cape Town: David Phillip.

Stedman, Stephen John. 1991. *Peacemaking in Civil War: International Mediation in Zimbabwe, 1974–1980*. Boulder, Colo.: Lynne Rienner Publishers.

Stein, Janice Gross. 1989. "Getting to the Table: The Triggers, Stages, Functions and Consequences of Prenegotiation." In *Getting to the Table: The Processes of International Prenegotiation*, Janice Gross Stein, ed. Baltimore: Johns Hopkins University Press.

Steiner, Jürg. 1981a. "The Consociational Theory and Beyond." *Comparative Politics* 13 (April):348–51.

———. 1981b. "Research Strategies beyond Consociational Theory." *Journal of Politics* (November):1241–50.

———. 1974. *Amicable Agreement versus Majority Rule: Conflict Resolution in Switzerland*. Chapel Hill: University of North Carolina Press.

Strauss, Annette. 1993. "The 1992 Referendum in South Africa." *Journal of Modern African Studies* 32 (2):339–60.

Stultz, Newell M. 1987. "The Apartheid Issue at the General Assembly: Stalemate or Gathering Storm?" *African Affairs* 86 (342):25–45.

Swilling, Mark. 1988a. "Introduction: The Politics of Stalemate." In *State, Resistance and Change in South Africa*, Phillip Frankel, Noam Pines, and Mark Swilling, eds. London: Croom Helm.

———. 1988b. "The Extra-Parliamentary Movement: Strategies and Prospects." In *Negotiating South Africa's Future*, Hermann Giliomee and Lawrence Schlemmer eds. Johannesburg: Southern Book Publishers.

Taagepera, Rein, and Matthew Soberg Shugart. 1989. *Seats and Votes: The Effects and Determinants of Electoral Systems*. New Haven: Yale University Press.

Taylor, Michael. 1988. "Rationality and Revolutionary Collective Action" In *Rationality and Revolution*, Michael Taylor, ed. Cambridge and New York: Cambridge University Press.

Thompson, Leonard. 1990. *A History of South Africa*. New Haven: Yale University Press.

―――. 1985. *The Political Mythology of Apartheid*. New Haven: Yale University Press.

Touval, Saadia, and I. William Zartman, eds. 1985. *International Mediation in Theory and Practice*. Boulder, Colo.: Westview Press, 1985.

Tsebelis, George. 1990a. *Nested Games: Rational Choice in Comparative Politics*. Berkeley and Los Angeles: University of California Press.

―――. 1990b. "Elite Interaction and Constitution Building in Consociatonal Democracies." *Journal of Theoretical Politics* 2 (1):5–29.

Vanberg, Viktor, and James Buchanan. 1989. "Interests and Theories in Constitutional Choice." *Journal of Theoretical Politics* 1:49–62.

van Staden, Gary. 1990. "Outside the MDM: An A to Z of Azanian Politics." *Indicator SA* 7 (3) (Winter):7–10.

van zyl Slabbert, Frederick. 1990. "From Domination to Democracy." *Leadership* 9 (4):66–76.

―――. 1989. *The System and the Struggle: Reform, Revolt and Reaction in South Africa*. Johannesburg: Johnathan Ball.

―――. 1987. "The Dynamic of Reform and Revolt in South Africa." IDASA Occasional Paper nos. 7–9 (3 Lectures). Cape Town: Institute for a Democratic Alternative in South Africa.

―――. 1985. *The Last White Parliament*. Johannesburg: Johnathan Ball.

van zyl Slabbert, Frederick, and Jeff Opland, eds. 1980. *South Africa: Dilemmas of Evolutionary Change*. Grahamstown: Rhodes University, Institute of Social and Economic Research.

van zyl Slabbert, Frederick, and David Welsh. 1979. *South Africa's Options: Strategies for Sharing Power*. New York: St. Martin's Press.

Venter, Theodore. 1990. "The New Inkatha: Responding to the Challenge," *South Africa Foundation Review* 16 (8) (August):4.

Welsh, David. 1993. "Holding the Centre." *Towards Democracy* (Second quarter):2–12.

―――. 1991. "The Democratic Party." *South African Foundation Review* 17 (2) (February):7–8.

―――. 1990. "F. W. de Klerk and Constitutional Change." *Issue* 18 (2):3–5.

Wilson, Francis, and Mamphele Ramphele. 1989. *Uprooting Poverty: The South African Challenge. Report of the Second Carnegie Enquiry into Poverty and Development in Southern Africa*. New York: W. W. Norton and Company.

Wolpe, Howard. 1972. "Capitalism and Cheap Labor Power in South Africa, from Segregation to Apartheid." *Economy and Society* 1:425–58.

Woods, Dwayne. 1992. "Civil Society in Europe and Africa: Limiting State Power through a Public Sphere." *African Studies Review* 35 (2):77–100.

World Bank. 1989. *Sub-Saharan Africa: From Crisis to Sustainable Growth*. Washington, D.C.: World Bank.

Wright, Stephen G., and William H. Riker. 1989. "Plurality and Runoff Systems and Numbers of Candidates." *Public Choice* 60:155–75.

Zartman, I. William. 1991. "Conflict and Resolution: Contest, Cost and

Change." *Annals of the American Society of Political and Social Science* 518 (November):11–22.

———. 1989. "Prenegotiation: Phases and Functions." In *Getting to the Table: The Processes of International Prenegotiation,* Janice Gross Stein, ed. Baltimore: Johns Hopkins University Press.

———. 1985. *Ripe for Resolution: Conflict and Intervention in Africa.* New York: Oxford University Press.

———. 1983. "The Strategy of Preventive Diplomacy in Third World Conflicts." In *Managing U.S.-Soviet Rivalry,* Alexander George, ed. Boulder, Colo.: Westview Press.

———. 1976. "Introduction." In *The 50% Solution,* I. William Zartman, ed. New York: Doubleday, Anchor Press.

———, ed. 1978. *The Negotiation Process.* Beverly Hills, Calif.: Sage.

Zartman, I. William, and Maureen Berman. 1982. *The Practical Negotiator.* New Haven: Yale University Press.

Index